THE COMPARATIVE APPROACH
TO AMERICAN HISTORY

THE COMPARATIVE APPROACH TO AMERICAN HISTORY

EDITED BY

C. Vann Woodward

NEW YORK   OXFORD

Oxford University Press

1997

Oxford University Press

Oxford   New York

Athens   Aukland   Bangkok   Bogota   Bombay   Buenos Aires
Calcutta   Cape Town   Dar es Salaam   Delhi   Florence   Hong Kong
Istanbul   Karachi   Kuala Lampur   Madrea   Madrid   Melbourne
Mexico City   Nairobi   Paris   Singapore   Taipei   Tokyo   Toronto   Warsaw

and associated companies
Berlin   Ibadan

Copyright © 1968, 1997 by C. Vann Woodward

Originally published by Basic Books in 1968

Published by Oxford University Press
198 Madison Avenue, New York, New York 10016

Oxford is a registered trademark of Oxford University Press

Library of Congress Cataloging-in-Publication Data
The comparative approach to American history / edited by C. Vann Woodward.
p.   cm.
"Originally published by Basic Books in 1968"—T.p. verso.
Based on a series of lectures prepared for the Voice of America
with a new introduction for this ed.
Includes bibliographical references and index.
ISBN 0–19–511260–1
1. United States—History.   I. Woodward, C. Vann (Comer Vann),
1908–   .   II. Voice of America (Organization)
E178.6.C66   1997
973—dc21   97–24202

1 3 5 7 9 8 6 4 2
Printed in the United States of America
on acid-free paper

Contents

The Contributors

RAY ALLEN BILLINGTON (1903–1981) taught history at several universities before settling at the Henry E. Huntington Library as research associate his last fifteen years. Historian of frontiers, he wrote, for example, *The Westward Movement in the United States* (1959), *America's Frontier Heritage* (1966), and a biography of his mentor, *Frederick Jackson Turner: Historian, Scholar, and Teacher* (1973).

JOHN MORTON BLUM (1921–   ) is Professor of History Emeritus at Yale. His field is American political history in the twentieth century, and among his many books are *The Republican Roosevelt* (1954), *The Progressive Presidents* (1980), and *Year of Discord* (1991).

ALFRED D. CHANDLER, JR. (1918–   ) is Professor of Business History Emeritus at Harvard Business School. Among his books in this field are *Giant Enterprise* (1964), *The Visible Hand* (1978), and *The Coming of Managerial Capitalism* (1985).

THOMAS C. COCHRAN (1902–   ) was long Professor of History at the University of Pennsylvania and a specialist in industrial history. His books include *The American Business System: A Historical Perspective* (1957), *Business in American Life: A History* (1972), and *200 Years of American Business* (1977).

DAVID BRION DAVIS (1927–   ) is Professor of History at Yale. He has devoted his career largely to multivolumed studies of slavery on a broad scale. Among them are *The Problem of Slavery in Western Culture* (1966), *The Problem of Slavery in the Age of Revolution, 1770–1823* (1975), and *Slavery and Human Progress* (1986).

JOHN HOPE FRANKLIN (1915–   ) is Professor of Legal History Emeritus at Duke Law School. His books include *The Free Negro in North Carolina* (1943), *The Militant South* (1956), and *From Slavery to Freedom: A History of African Americans* (7th edition, 1994).

PETER GAY (1923–   ) is Professor of Comparative European History Emeritus at Yale. Prominent among his many books *The Enlightenment: An Interpretation* (1966, 1969), *Freud: A Life for Our Time* (1988), and *The Bourgeois Experience, Victoria to Freud* (5 volumes, 1984–1997).

JOHN HIGHAM (1920–   ) is Professor of History Emeritus at Johns Hopkins. His books include *Strangers in the Land: Patterns of American Nativism, 1860–1925* (1955), *Writing American History: Essays on Modern Scholarship* (1970), and *Send These to Me: Jews and Other Immigrants in Urban America* (1975).

RICHARD HOFSTADTER (1916–1970) taught at Columbia as Professor of History at the time of his death. Among his many books are *The American Political Tradition and the Men Who Made It* (1948), *The Age of Reform: From Bryan to F.D.R.* (1962), and *The Progressive Historians: Turner, Beard, Parrington* (1968)

MERRILL JENSEN (1905–1980) was Professor of History at the University of Wisconsin until his retirement in 1976. His books include *The New Nation: A History of the United States During the Confederation, 1781–1789* (1950), *The Making of the American Constitution* (1964), and *The Founding of a Nation: A History of the American Revolution* (1968).

WILLIAM E. LEUCHTENBURG (1922–   ) is Professor of History Emeritus at the University of North Carolina at Chapel Hill. Among his books are *Franklin D. Roosevelt and the New Deal, 1932–1940* (1963), *New Deal and Global War* (1964), and *In the Shadow of FDR: From Harry Truman to Ronald Reagan* (1983).

SEYMOUR MARTIN LIPSET (1922–), is Professor of Political Science and Sociology at Stanford and Senior Fellow at the Hoover Institute. His books of most interest here are *Revolution and Counter Revolution* (1968), *The Divided Academy* (1975), and *American Exceptionalism: A Double-Edged Sword* (1996).

ERNEST R. MAY (1928–) is Professor of History at Harvard. Among his works are *The World War and American Isolation* (1959), *"Lessons" of the Past: The Use and Misuse of History in American Foreign Policy* (1973), and *A Proud Nation* (1983).

ARNO J. MAYER (1926–) is Professor of History at Princeton. A comparative theme runs through his books on diplomatic history: *Political Origins of the New Diplomacy* (1959), *Politics and Diplomacy in Peace Making* (1967), and *The Persistence of the Old Regime* (1981).

ERIC L. McKITRICK (1919–) is Professor of History Emeritus at Columbia; he works in two periods. He is the author of *Andrew Johnson and Reconstruction* (1960), *Andrew Johnson: A Profile* (1960), and (with Stanley Elkins) *The Age of Federalism* (1993).

GEORGE E. MOWRY (1909–1984) served last as Professor of History at the University of North Carolina at Chapel Hill. His writings include *The Era of Theodore Roosevelt, 1900–1912* (1958), *The Federal Union* (1964), and *The Urban Nation, 1920–1960* (1965).

R. R. PALMER (1909–) is Professor of History Emeritus at Yale. Among his works are *Catholics and Unbelievers in Eighteenth Century France* (1939), *The Age of Democratic Revolution* (1959, 1964), and *The Two Tocquevilles: Father and Son on the Coming of the French Revolution* (1987).

GEORGE W. PIERSON (1904–1993) was Professor of History at Yale and author of *Tocqueville and Beaumont in America* (1938), *Yale College: An Educational History* (1952), and *The Moving American* (1973).

DAVID M. POTTER (1910–1971) was Professor of History at Stanford the last ten years of his life. Among his books are

Lincoln and His Party in the Secession Crisis (1942), *People of Plenty: Economic Abundance and the American Character* (1954), and *The Impending Crisis, 1848–1861* (1976).

DAVID A. SHANNON (1920–   ) is Professor of History at the University of Virginia. He wrote *The Socialist Party of America: A History* (1955), *The Decline of American Communism: A History of the Communist Party of the United States Since 1945* (1959), and *Twentieth Century America* (1963).

Introduction to the New Edition

It has now been thirty years since this book was first published, and it has been out of print for over a decade. A new edition after so long a time calls for some account of its original reception, its subsequent influence, and what it is that is thought to justify a new edition.

It was to be expected that critics should take exception to some views on comparative history expressed by one or another of the twenty-three contributors, no matter how distinguished they were in their own special fields. Nevertheless, reviewers did express praise and support strong enough to encourage hopes for the influence and the future of the book.

For example, in an essay review Carl N. Degler said, "There are enough suggestions here of what comparative history has to offer the historians of the United States to provide an impetus to such studies." Michael Kammen's predictions were even stronger. "Professor Woodward's book is a major publishing event. It will make an exciting teaching device and stimulate scholarship in many fields."

Measured by the comparative history work produced in the years immediately following, however, these expectations now seem misguided. In 1970 John Higham deplored the fact that comparative studies "should have been so long delayed," and were "still sparce and scattered." In 1980 George M. Fredrickson was impressed "not [by] how much has been done but rather how little." And in 1985 Raymond Grew found historians in agreement that "comparative approaches have not taken root in American historiography."

Several explanations have been suggested. Historians have pointed out that doing comparative history usually demands a broader range of interest and competence than what has been required in the training of historians of late. For one thing academic stress on early publication in a specialized field has not encouraged wide-ranging interests. Others contend that recent emphases upon social history, local history, and neglected aspects of race, class, ethnic, and minority history share the blame. As Raymond Grew viewed the consequences, "Comparisons must begin from what the scholar knows best, but to compare one hillock to another is likely to prove inconsequential."

I have suggested elsewhere that some attitudes toward comparisons may arise from the peculiar historical experiences of the country, apart from the South. These include a remarkable absence of military threats on any of its borders, a freedom from hostile invasion, and until recent years enough "free security" and military victories to encourage the myth of invincibility. This along with numerous other peculiarities, fostered and to some degree justified the doctrine of American Exceptionalism. Those who mistakenly thought comparative work limited to "hunting out resemblances" instead of what Marc Bloch regarded as its "primary interest," which he held to be "the observation of differences," tended to be indifferent or impatient toward comparative history. Why compare the incomparable, exceptionalists would ask, and if the purpose of comparison were the search for similarities, where might suitable comparative partners be found?

Whether or not these or other explanations account for the delay of comparative American history, there has undoubtedly occurred a recent explosion of excellent, sometimes brilliant work of this kind. To name only a few of the more outstanding examples, the volumes by David Brian Davis on slavery the world around immediately come to mind. And with them the studies of race relations, ideology, and segregation in the United States and South Africa by George M. Fredrickson. One by Carl Degler compares race relations in Brazil and the United States, and a study comparing Brazil, the United States, and South Africa in these respects by Anthony W. Marx is forthcoming. A most illuminating study by Peter Kolchin compares American slavery and Russian serfdom, and the author plans another comparing the abolition of both systems of "unfree labor."

These and numerous other recent works combine to make this one of the most exciting periods of American historical scholarship for a century. It is not surprising to find George Fredrickson, who was quoted above as deploring the lack of comparative work twenty-five years earlier, saying in 1995 that "the prospects for the development of comparative history seem brighter than in 1980—indeed than ever before."

As for any part the book here republished might have had in stimulating this outpouring I should like to quote a statement I published a few years ago: "I would not for a moment think of crediting that book with the outburst of comparative activity that took place among American historians in the following years." Nevertheless, I confess taking pleasure in an essay by Carl J. Guarneri in the September 1995 issue of *Reviews in American History*, "Reconsidering" the old book in the light of recent developments. "In this changed environment," he writes, "Woodward's anthology, bypassed the first time around, has recovered its relevance." Acknowledging oversights and omissions more apparent now after the passage of so many years, he nevertheless believes that the book represents "an idea whose time has returned," that it may "have a greater impact this time around," and that "we ought to profit from its example."

New Haven   C. VANN WOODWARD
February 1996

THE COMPARATIVE APPROACH
TO AMERICAN HISTORY

1

The Comparability of American History

C. VANN WOODWARD

To limit the subject of historical study within national boundaries is always to invite the charge of narrow perspective and historical nationalism. Historians of all nations have in some measure incurred that risk, but Americans have been accused of more than the normal share of this type of parochialism. They are said to lay excessive claims to distinctiveness and uniqueness in their national experience, to plead immunity from the influence of historical forces that have swept most other nations, to shun or deprecate comparisons between their history and that of other people, and to seek within their own borders all the significant forces that have shaped their history. These charges assume more sharpness and urgency as America approaches total involvement in world history. The striking paradox of a nation that professes historical parochialism and practices cosmopolitan involvement calls for attention from professional historians.

There is no denying a certain justification for such charges. It will appear on further analysis, however, that they have had more validity in some periods than in others, that there have always been exceptions among historians, and that of late a significant countercurrent has asserted itself in American historical thought.

I

From the start of settlement certain aspects of the American experience undoubtedly encouraged among the transplanted Europeans, and to some degree justified, an emphasis on distinctiveness and an aversion to comparison. This was for the settlers in many ways a *new* world. Both the uniqueness and the influence of free land and the fabled frontier that advanced steadily across the continent for three centuries have probably been exaggerated, but they were impressive evidence of distinctiveness for those involved in the drama. Americans were slower to grasp the distinctive significance of their having skipped the feudal phase of history that was common to all the older nations and not wholly avoided by some of the newer ones. They thought they understood what Alexis de Tocqueville meant, however, when he wrote that they were "born equal." Whatever equality meant, the American brand was assumed at the time to be something distinctive.

Still another historic circumstance that Americans enjoyed for a long and crucial period without fully comprehending it was the blessing of military security that was not only effective but relatively free. It came as a bounty of nature and benign circumstance—the presence of vast oceans and the absence of powerful neighbors. It was free in the sense that it took the place of costly fortifications and even more costly armies and navies that burdened less fortunate people with crushing taxes and harsh discipline. Between the world wars of the eighteenth century and those of the twentieth the only major military burdens Americans bore were due not to foreign attack but to domestic quarrels—the first two of them to establish independence from the mother country, the third to deny independence to the southern states. In the century from 1815 to 1914 the United States enjoyed a security from invasion so complete and so free as to enable the government virtually to dispense with an army and for the greater part of the period with an effective navy as well. Americans came to regard free security much as they did free land and equality, as a natural right. Since they neither possessed the instruments of power nor incurred the guilt of using them, they fostered the myth (ignoring certain adventures in Mexico and the Caribbean area) that they were an innocent nation in a wicked world and resented comparisons with nations that had to seek with the sword what Americans enjoyed freely and, they believed, without guilt.

The very absence of powerful and rival nations on the borders of the United States or, indeed, within its entire hemisphere was not only another circumstance that set the American experience apart as unique. It also removed a powerful incentive and stimulus for international comparison. Britain, America's nine-teenth-century foreign standard of comparison, cultural irritant, and model, was across the wide Atlantic. Nearly all other nations lived constantly with the physical proximity of strong national rivals for territory, influence, prestige, markets, or priority in science, the arts, and technology. While rivalries foster stereo-types, the comparative frame of reference is an ingrained habit of mind and sometimes a condition of survival among rival nations. For America alone among the major nations, this in-centive for comparative analysis and reflection was long absent or physically remote.

As "the first new nation," the first to break from colonial status as well as the one to inaugurate the age of democratic revolution, America found no suitable models among her eighteenth-century contemporaries and few precedents for her experiments. Founding fathers often cited models of antiquity and theories of John Locke, but the patriot was impressed with the originality of their statecraft, and insistence on the unique-ness of national institutions became part of conventional pa-triotism.

Emphasis on uniqueness and distinctiveness, not only of national institutions but of national character, became an im-portant means of asserting and defining national identity. The new nation suffered from an understandable insecurity of identity. Older nations were secure on this score in their common ethnic, or religious, or linguistic, or political heritage. Some nations could lay claim to unity in several of these important sources of identity and a few in all of them. The American nation could claim unity in none of them. With the exception of the aborigines the Americans were immigrants or the descendants of immigrants from all parts of Europe, many parts of Africa, and some parts of Asia. Lacking a common racial, religious, linguistic, or political heritage, they had to look elsewhere for the bases of nationality. Their anxiety over this quest for national identity helps explain what David M. Potter has described as "a somewhat compulsive preoccupation with the question of their Americanism." This preoccupation has found expression in innumerable, often confusing and contradictory efforts to define the national character. Such attempts have naturally emphasized what was assumed to be unique or peculiar to America. The effect of such inquiries was to minimize comparability or to use comparison only to stress distinctiveness.

There were obvious reasons why a young and relatively undeveloped country might well shun comparisons between its history and that of old and mature nations, rich and glamorous with famous names, celebrated achievements, and venerable monuments. The risks of such comparisons were illustrated by Henry James, who undertook in the 1870's to "enumerate the items of high civilization, as it exists in other countries, which are absent from the texture of American life." His inventory of missing items was not calculated to flatter the pride of patriots, though good Jacksonian democrats might shrug them off:

No State, in the European sense of the word, and indeed barely a specific national name. No sovereign, no court, no personal loyalty, no aristocracy, no church, no clergy, no army, no diplomatic service, no country gentlemen, no palaces, no castles, nor manors, nor old country houses, nor parsonages, nor thatched cottages, nor ivied ruins; no cathedrals, nor abbeys, nor little Norman churches; no great universities nor public schools—no Oxford, nor Eton, nor Harrow . . . no Epsom nor Ascot!

To invite comparison was to risk an exposure of pretensions, a withering of national pride or native complacency. The wide currency of the old chestnut that "comparisons are odious" was understandable under the circumstances. Americans have been notoriously eager throughout their history for praise of their institutions from foreign visitors, but they have also been sensitive to condescension and fearful of being patronized.

II

If there were forces at work in American history to discourage the comparative view, there were also certain circumstances that had a contrary effect. The very fact that America was a nation composed of the people of many nations meant that nearly all Americans were the heirs of more than one historical heritage—the American as well as that of the country or countries from which they or their forebears emigrated. The whole experience of emigration and immigration was charged with tensions of comparison. The decision to leave the Old World for the New often involved agonizing comparisons based on limited information and conjecture. Life for the first-generation immigrants was a daily round of comparisons, rueful or gratifying; and the second generation never ceased to hear "how it was in the Old Country." Well into the twentieth century, first-generation immigrants in vast numbers continued to repeat this exercise and to pass on to succeeding generations their comparative frame of reference. Some of the boldest recent experiments in American comparative history have been the works of historians who come of recent immigrant backgrounds.

Consciousness of the Old Country heritage and habituation to the comparative frame of reference tended to diminish in proportion to the remoteness of arrival in the New World and to decline more markedly after the first-generation immigrants. Identification with the country of origin tended also to be diffused and blurred as various nationalities interbred. Hecter St. John de Crèvecoeur knew an American family in 1782 "whose grandfather was an Englishman, whose wife was Dutch, whose son married a French woman, and whose present four sons have now four wives of different nations." Most of the later generations rather arbitrarily settled upon one country (however many might actually have been involved) as the traditional place of family origin and spoke of themselves as being of "English stock," or

"Italian background," or "Scandinavian extraction." Negro Americans, most of them descended from eighteenth-century arrivals whose African culture was largely obliterated by the slavery experience, were the only ethnic exceptions to the American norm of multiple historical heritage, and interbreeding with whites mitigated the effect of this exception. Diffused, diminished, or conventionalized, the "Old Country" referent remained a part of the mental furniture of many Americans to some degree down through the generations. However cautious and reluctant the professional historian may be about comparisons, the layman has blandly indulged in them as a matter of course.

Among the historians themselves, broadly speaking, there has been over the centuries, until recent years, a declining consciousness of the European origins, context, and connections of American history. In general, and in particular the professionals among them, historians have tended to regard the fragment as the whole, to neglect the larger world for the offshoot, and to restrict their search for the compelling forces and dynamics of American history to their native soil. This has not always been true. Historians in the colonial period, when America was part of a thriving empire and they were closer to their European roots, were as acutely aware of the oppressions and conditions they had fled as they were of new problems they faced, of what they had brought with them as of what they had found on this side of the Atlantic. They knew they were a frontier, but they had not forgotten what they were a frontier of. In some ways the colonials were more cosmopolitan in outlook than their more sophisticated and worldly descendants.

Historians during the early years of the Republic, nationalistic and patriotic though they were, supported their exalted claims for American achievements in freedom, justice, and equality with comparative reference to the Old World, where they found these blessings less prevalent. The romantic school of historians in the middle and later nineteenth century may have been simple in outlook and untutored in method, but their books speak eloquently of broader and more cosmopolitan horizons than those their academic successors normally explored. Francis Parkman's great work, *France and England in North America,* is full of dramatic contrasts and comparisons and is profoundly conscious of European origins and influences. William Prescott's romantic narrative of Spanish conquests in the New World offers a comparison of frontier influences that contrast strikingly with frontier influences just north of the Rio Grande.

The first generation of professional academic historians in America, who flourished in the last quarter of the nineteenth century, learned from their German masters a peculiarly Teutonic brand of comparative history. They were taught to look back to the German forests for the origins of "Anglo-Saxon" institutions and national character. The findings of this school fostered national pride and carried overtones of racial superiority. The methods of the Teutonic or "scientific" historians were not truly comparative, however, for what they were seeking were congenial similarities or flattering analogies and continuities. They closed their eyes to the contrasts and differences that are an essential part of comparative analysis. As a consequence they were betrayed into advancing sterile hypotheses and indefensible generalizations.

III

A devastating attack on the sterility and absurdities of the teachers of the germ theory was mounted by their own students. Their attack demolished the Teutonic hypothesis so thoroughly that it had few defenders after the turn of the century. This was a valuable service rendered by the new Progressive historians. But in throwing out the discredited and teleological uses of the comparative method made by the scientific school they discredited the valid uses as well and ended by virtually abandoning them. In effect they turned their backs on the larger world to concentrate on the fragment, to look inward subjectively for the answers to historical problems. They were given to dwelling on the newness of the New World and on what they were prone to suggest was the *in*comparable in American experience.

Frederick Jackson Turner, the famous exponent of the Frontier Thesis, took part in the attack on the Teutonic hypothesis and gave to the new school many of its distinguishing traits. Announcing that "the germ theory of politics has been sufficiently emphasized," he turned to his native West for the key to American development. It was not only the influence of Europe he deprecated, but that of the American East as well. "The true point of view in the history of this nation is not the Atlantic Coast," he wrote; "it is the Great West." Turner was predominantly an environmentalist and had little time for ideologies and theories. "American democracy was born of no theorist's dreams," he declared. It was not something imported from Europe. "It came out of the American forest . . ." Comparisons with what came out of the forests to the north and to the south of the American borders were left to others. "Neither the French nor the Spanish frontier is within the scope of the volume," he announced. Turner was more interested in what America did to Europeans than in what Europeans did to America. "The wilderness masters the colonist," he said. The enchanted wood was the great Americanizer, the generator of national identity. "Thus the advance of the frontier has meant a steady movement away from the influence of Europe, a steady growth of independence on American lines." It was clear that the historian rejoiced in this "steady movement" and believed that it indicated the proper direction of historical interpretation as well.

In this respect it would appear anomalous to bracket Charles A. Beard, another dominant figure of the Progressive school, with Turner. Beard had a rather more cosmopolitan style of thought and life. He enjoyed several years of study and work abroad, in England as a youth and in Japan in later life. Moreover, he studied and wrote European as well as American history. While both men employed economic interpretations, Turner's emphasis was on geographic environment and Beard's on class and interest conflicts, phenomena that lent themselves more readily to generalization and comparison. In writing of such conflicts in American history, Beard was aware in an abstract way of parallels in other lands. But in locating the dynamics of national history and what he deemed the essential forces that shaped American institutions and the development of democracy, Beard like Turner looked steadily within. The Beardean determinants were domestic conflicts between economic interests—agrarians and industrialists, holders of personal and real property, debtor and creditor, labor and capital, radicals and conservatives. He did not turn back to consider the inherited postulates, the given consensus of doctrine within which these domestic conflicts took place, and lacked therefore a comparative measure of the relatively narrow margins of difference between the opposing sides.

The work of Turner and Beard and that of Vernon Louis Parrington, the intellectual historian who belonged to the same school, has been subjected to searching criticism in the last thirty years. None of the critics has so far attained an influence comparable with that exercised by the masters of the old school, however, and none has so far put forward a comprehensive reconstruction of American history to replace those attacked. While many of the findings and methods of the Progressive school have been rejected, the underlying assumptions of the inward determinants and the subjective nature of American historical analysis have been more rarely challenged and still have numerous adherents.

The recent vogue of American studies, encouraging national boundaries to the study of culture, has probably had the effect of enhancing the subjective and inward tendency. The establishment of this discipline in a number of foreign universities in Europe and Asia has so far done little to alter the tendency, since foreign scholars have largely followed the lead of American interpretations. Europeans are increasingly willing to study American history but little inclined so far to subject it to comparative analysis.[1] "To teach American history in isolation," complains Geoffrey Barraclough, "as a separate branch of study parallel to European history, is to commit the very errors of which our teaching of European history has been guilty."

IV

The end of American isolation and the explosive involvement of the United States in world politics and power struggles that came as a consequence of World War II have not left historians

[1] One notable exception is J. R. Pole, *Political Representation in England and the Origins of the American Republic* (London and New York, 1966).

untouched. Government programs recruited teachers from American universities for foreign lectureships in universities around the globe, and hundreds of refugee scholars from abroad joined the American intellectual community. The intellectual capital of the country became host to the United Nations, and the political capital became a forum for debate of world problems.

One response of historians to the end of isolation has been a significant increase in the comparative approach to national history. This movement has not resulted in anything that could be called a "school." Nor have the comparative historians agreed upon any common method, fixed upon any typical subject of study, or arrived at any overriding hypothesis such as the Teutonic germ theory. The comparative studies that have been made have been highly individual, the methods experimental and diverse, the subjects of study scattered over many periods and fields, the findings broadly pluralistic and sometimes contradictory. If these historians have any common disposition, it might be an interest in the methods and studies of the social sciences, but some of them disavow and resist such interests and stick to traditional methods. And in spite of the expected and indeed predominant effect of turning historical thought outward, some of the comparative studies have had the tendency of enhancing the emphasis on uniqueness formerly associated with the subjective and inward analysis.

Daniel J. Boorstin is one practitioner of comparative history. To be sure, his study of American history is informed by wide acquaintance with European history and life and characterized by constant comparison and contrast. But the result is to stress the uniqueness of the American experience, to deny the importance or persistence of European influence and ideas, and to turn inward again for the keys to American history. He pictures an American historical landscape littered with the wreckage of European plans, blueprints, theories, and grand designs, a graveyard of European categories, social distinctions, and sociological "laws." Americans owe nothing to "garret-spawned European illuminati" and have little gift for theorizing or interest in theory. Their political "genius" lay in inspired improvisation, free-wheeling pragmatism, versatile adaptation to brute fact, compelling circumstances, and practical problems, He echoes the Turnerian refrain "that American values spring from the circumstances of the New World, that these are the secret of the 'American Way of Life.' "

Louis Hartz, who makes comparative history the basis of his critique, believes that "the American historian at practically every stage has functioned quite inside the nation: he has tended to be an erudite reflection of the limited social perspective of the average American himself." Like Boorstin, he finds confirmation of "our national uniqueness" in comparison. "How can we know the uniqueness of anything," he asks, "except by contrasting it with what is not unique?" The failure of the Progressive historians lay in the fact that "they did not attempt the European correlations." Had they done so, he thinks, they would have seen that all the domestic social conflict between "radicals" and "conservatives" which they described took place within a Lockean consensus. Since "America was grounded in escape from the European past" and succeeded in skipping the feudal stage, it had no *ancien régime* and therefore no real radicals to overthrow it and no reactionaries to restore it. Conservatives could, paradoxically, only conserve John Locke. Only by viewing America from the "outside," as did Tocqueville, does its true distinctiveness appear. From this perspective Hartz and his collaborators have produced a comparative study of the "fragmentation" of European culture and the development of new societies in Latin America, South Africa, Canada, and Australia, as well as the United States.

Another outlet for the comparative impulse has been to give a transatlantic dimension to historical experiences common to both America and Europe. One of the finest achievements of recent years in this field is Robert R. Palmer's *Age of Democratic Revolution*, which has the subtitle *A Political History of Europe and America, 1760–1800*. Reversing the conventional pattern of Europe transmitting and America receiving influences and ideas, Palmer stresses the American origins of an age of revolution and traces the profound impact the first of the democratic revolutions had upon the numerous European revolutions that followed. Also reflecting the transatlantic tendency of historiography are Alan Simpson's *Puritanism in Old and New England* (1955), Boyd Shafer's *Nationalism* (1955), and Felix Gilbert's *To the Farewell Address* (1964). Barrington Moore, Jr., has added transpacific to transatlantic comparisons in his *Social Origins of Dictatorship and Democracy* (1966) to give modern world history a whole new conceptual framework.[2]

V

The comparative history so far mentioned has been done with traditional methods and, with the exception of Mr. Moore, by guild historians. Social scientists have increasingly invaded this field of late, and one of them, Seymour Martin Lipset, in *The First New Nation* (1963), pursues a bold line of wide-ranging comparison and analogy. Using concepts and methods developed by such social scientists as Karl Deutsch and Talcott Parsons, Lipset undertakes "to elucidate through comparative analysis some of the problems and some of the developmental processes that are common to all new nations." As was the case in the Age of Democratic Revolution, America as the "first new nation" is seen as teacher and initiator rather than pupil and follower, giving to latter-day new nations "clues as to how revolutionary equalitarian and populist values may eventually become incorporated into a stable nonauthoritarian polity."

The subject of slavery, long caught in the grip of sectional recrimination, has recently been lifted to an international and intercontinental plane by comparative studies. The discussion of slavery has quickened in response to the sudden relevance of the contrasting cultural determinants, legal traditions, and religious practices of three continents and a hundred islands. Much credit for the stimulation of this discussion is due to Stanley M. Elkins,

[2] It should be noted in passing that a far larger proportion of historians in America work on the history of other nations than do historians in European countries, though this does not necessarily result in more comparative history.

who in his *Slavery* (1959) not only made provocative comparisons between the institution under Latin-Catholic auspices and under Anglo-Saxon-Protestant control, but initiated a reconsideration of the impact of slavery upon Negro personality with daring psychological analogies, and spotlighted peculiarities of American abolitionists by a comparison with the British abolitionists. The comparative analysis has been broadened by anthropological contributions and refined by detailed studies of slavery in Brazil, Africa, and islands of the West Indies with various national heritages. More recently David B. Davis' *The Problem of Slavery in Western Culture* (1966), a work of elegant scholarship and wide learning, has extended the range of comparative analysis of both slavery and thought about slavery back to the Greeks.

Secession, Civil War, and Reconstruction, usually considered culture-bound subjects of exclusively national negotiability, have profited from hints, suggestions, and limited experiments of a comparative nature. The stimulus of comparative analysis, they prove, need not be limited to the kind derived from formal and detailed comparisons. Overextended comparisons can in fact be self-defeating. If not pushed too far or elaborated too much, comparative reference can illuminate a discussion after the manner of an imaginative and disciplined use of simile, metaphor, or analogy. As in literary usage, the spirit of play is not without relevance in such exercises. In various essays David M. Potter has enriched our comprehension of the American sectional crisis by invoking suggestive comparisons with other separatist and unification movements and other conflicts between men's loyalties. Roy F. Nichols has rendered comparable service in an essay setting the American Civil War in the full context of numerous internal struggles over the location of power within the Anglo-American community going back to the Wars of the Roses. And Eric L. McKitrick has invaded the jealous parochial sovereignty of the Reconstruction field with reference to peace-making processes in Germany and Japan after World War II. These are but samples of the numerous experiments with comparative analysis in American historiography, and there are many others. Not all of them have been fully successful or entirely convincing, but the same may be said of more conventional types of history.

Once the stream of American history descends to the plains of industrial, mass society in the late nineteenth century the opportunities, temptations, and the available data for comparative experiments multiply rapidly. National variations with the classic experiences of industrialization, migration, urbanization, race problems, and labor relations are numerous. These subjects lend themselves to quantified study and are more amenable to the methods of the social sciences. An affinity between comparative history and social science will naturally encourage additional experiments of comparison among historians of these fields. As for historians who cope with the period after America moves out of isolation into involvement in world politics and world wars, they are likely to regard comparative exercises as more of a necessity than a diversion.

There is a tradition in the historical guild and an instinctive aversion among its votaries against the abstract. In every true historian there is still a humanist with a profound respect for the varied particularity of human experience and a jealous regard for the precise integrity of time and place in the remembrance of things past. These instincts inevitably create tension between the historian and the social scientist, who deals freely with categories, prototypes, and statistical variables that override limits of space and time and lend themselves to comparisons. When the historian combines the instincts of his guild with a conviction about the distinctiveness and uniqueness of the national experience he studies, he is likely to be skeptical about experiments with comparative analysis.

Marc Bloch, the brilliant French comparative historian, observed, "It is too often supposed that the method has no other purpose than hunting out resemblances." But, he pointed out, "correctly understood, the primary interest of the comparative method is, on the contrary, the observation of differences." With all his devotion to the unique and the particular, Marc Bloch could boast with impunity, "I have used a powerful magic wand, namely, the comparative method." If the sorcerer's apprentices use the wand with the master's regard for particularity and uniqueness, the consequences need not be disastrous and the magic may continue to work.

BIBLIOGRAPHY

Two classic pronouncements on the comparative method in history by European historians are one by Marc Bloch, "Toward a Comparative History of European Societies" (1928), in Frederic C. Lane and J. C. Riemersma, eds., *Enterprise and Secular Change* (Homewood, Ill., 1953), pp. 494–521; and the other by Henri Pirenne, "What Historians Are Trying to Do," in Stuart A. Rice (ed.), *Methods in Social Science* (Chicago, 1931), pp. 444–59. A periodical that is especially hospitable to comparative history is one edited by Sylvia L. Thrupp, *Comparative Studies in Society and History* (1958–   ). In this journal (Vol. V, pp. 365–77) Louis Hartz, in "American Historiography and Comparative Analysis," examines the comparative theme in the writing of American history. Older traditions and recent trends in the United States are analyzed in John Higham *et al., History* (Englewood Cliffs, N.J., 1965); and by John Herman Randall, Jr., and George Haines, IV, in *Theory and Practice in Historical Study*, Bulletin 54, Social Science Research Council (New York, 1946), pp. 17–52. The case for comparative history is considered in Geoffrey Barraclough, *History in a Changing World* (Norman, Okla., 1956); and in Louis Gottschalk (ed.), *Generalization in the Writing of History* (Chicago, 1963).

2

The Colonial Phase

MERRILL JENSEN

For nearly three centuries the New World was a part of the colonial empires of western European nations, most notably Spain, Portugal, France, and England. It was not until nearly three centuries after Columbus' first voyage in 1492 that the first of the European colonies began the movement that was to free most of the New World from European domination by the 1820's. In 1776 thirteen of England's thirty American colonies declared their independence as the United States of America. It has been only 190 years since the founding of the United States in 1776, as contrasted with the 284 years of colonial history which preceded it. Thus the colonial history of the New World is far longer than its history as a group of independent nations. Furthermore, the colonial history is longer than that of the European colonies in Asia and Africa which have won their independence in the twentieth century, with the sole exception of the Philippines, where in 1565 Spain created a colonial government modeled on that of Mexico, a government that lasted until 1898.

During the first century of the colonial era Spain and Portugal dominated the New World, for France and England were too weak and too divided by internal disputes to do more than send out exploring expeditions which established claims to lands they were to colonize during the seventeenth century. Portugal governed what was to become the nation of Brazil. Spain ruled over the rest of South America, Central America, certain islands in the West Indies, and southern and western parts of what was to become the United States.

These were the lands which Europeans believed to be the most valuable parts of the New World, for they were tropical or semitropical and could produce fruits and other crops, such as sugar, which could not be grown in Europe. Far more important, however, was the fact that Spain found great mines of gold and silver within her empire. The treasure which soon began flowing from America to Europe had an impact which no one at the time foresaw. In an age in which national power was equated with the possession of precious metals, Spain was looked upon as a great power, and was feared and hated by other European nations. The myth of Spanish power lasted far longer than its reality. Spain became accustomed to living on the wealth from New World mines and did not develop commerce and industry as did other European nations. As a result, Spain went into a political and economic decline from which she recovered only briefly in the last half of the eighteenth century.

American treasure, however, found its way from Spain to other parts of Europe, and its impact was far different from that in Spain. Trade and industry had expanded during the fourteenth and fifteenth centuries but the supply of money had not kept up with economic growth and hence prices had tended to decline or remain static. The Spanish mines in Peru and Mexico solved the problem of money supply, and by 1600 the quantity of precious metals in Europe was perhaps three times greater than it had been when Columbus discovered the New World in 1492.

But while American treasure solved one problem, it created even greater problems, for it helped bring about a "price revolution" in western Europe. Prices went up and up and their rise had a drastic effect on a society in which most of the people lived on land and most of the land, in turn, was owned by a relatively small number of people. Europe's agrarian society had been stable for decades, and rents and other income from land tended to remain fixed over long periods of time, even from generation to generation. Hence the income of the landed aristocracies of Europe did not rise with other prices during a long period of inflation, and these aristocracies seemed doomed to relative poverty as compared with the rising class of ever-richer merchants and manufacturers. At the other end of the social scale, small landowners, tenant farmers, and farm laborers had an even smaller share in the benefits of economic expansion than the large landowners—and they suffered far more. As a result there was widespread discontent and, in some countries, increasing unemployment.

All these facts were to play an important part in the history of colonization, and particularly in the history of the English colonies during the seventeenth century. Many of the English landed gentry turned to colonizing ventures in order to restore or increase their fortunes, whereas the English government looked upon America as a place where it could dispose of the hordes of vagrants and unemployed which seemed to threaten the very foundations of English society. And the poor in turn, both of England and of other European nations, came to look upon the English colonies as a place where they might achieve a better life.

Those who gained the most from the economic boom during the sixteenth century were the merchants and the manufacturers. They were the men who helped transform Europe from a relatively static agrarian society, whose politics and economic life had been dominated by a landowning aristocracy, into a society which was dominated—economically at least—by the ideals and practices of commerce and industry. The merchants, most notably those of England, channeled their profits into more and more overseas trading ventures, all the way from Asia to America, and at the beginning of the seventeenth century they were the leaders in the planting of the first English colonies in the New World.

The discovery of the New World had an impact on the relations between Europe and Asia, as well as upon Europe itself. For centuries Europeans had traded with Asia for luxuries such as silk and spices, and the discovery of America was an accidental by-product of the search for an easier and cheaper route by which to carry on the trade with Asia. Many a European looked upon America as an obstacle to that trade, and for generations after its discovery men continued to search for a sea route to Asia through or around the New World.

But in the end America made possible a greater European trade with Asia than ever before. Asians demanded gold and silver for their products, not the relatively primitive manufactured goods of western Europe, and the mines of Spanish America provided the precious metals needed to expand trade between Europe and Asia. During the last half of the sixteenth century perhaps half a million pounds sterling worth of gold and silver, most of it from America, was shipped to the Orient each year, and during the first half of the seventeenth century the amount sent was worth perhaps a million pounds sterling a year. And the profits from the trade between Europe and Asia were enormous. During the seventeenth century the English East India Company paid dividends of about 100 per cent a year on the capital invested in the company.

In 1776, at the end of the colonial era of American history, Adam Smith published *The Wealth of Nations*. As he looked back on what had happened during the past three centuries, he declared that "the discovery of America and that of a passage to the East Indies by way of the Cape of Good Hope are the two greatest and most important events recorded in the history of mankind."

I

Adam Smith was looking back at a world that had undergone a great revolution; but in the same year in which he published his book, thirteen of England's American colonies looked ahead to quite another "new world" when they adopted the Declaration of Independence and proclaimed themselves the United

States of America. In their Declaration of Independence they attacked the very foundations of Old World society by asserting that "all men are created equal" and endowed with "certain unalienable rights," among which are "life, liberty, and the pursuit of happiness"; that governments deriving their powers from "the consent of the governed" are established to secure those rights, and that when a government becomes destructive of those rights it is "the right of the people to alter or abolish it, and to institute new government. . . ."

The Americans thus based their right to revolt on the principles of democracy in a world dominated by monarchical and aristocratic governments; and they won their revolt, the first time in history that colonies had ever done so. The American example was not lost on discontented people in Europe, nor was it lost on the discontented inhabitants of the Spanish colonies in America. One by one those colonies revolted and established their independence—and modeled their political institutions on those of the United States.

II

The histories of the independent nations in the New World have many differences, differences rooted in the colonial past which did much to shape their institutions, ideas, and political practices. It is a past which influences them even now. It is true that as colonies, wherever they might be, they had certain things in common. All European nations tried to govern their colonies without consulting the wishes of the colonists. The economic development of the colonies was expected to conform to the interests of the colonizing nations, and not to the needs and interests of the colonies. Even socially, the inhabitants of the colonies, although they might be pure Spanish or English in origin, were looked upon as subject peoples, if not as an inferior breed of men.

Yet the differences among the American colonies were more important than their similarities. Those differences were due in part to varying geographic and climatic conditions, and to the wide range of natural resources to be found in the New World.

But most importantly, their different histories as colonies, and later as independent nations, were the result of the different social and political institutions of the European nations which colonized America, and of the different colonial policies they adopted. The Spanish, French, and Portuguese colonies were remarkably alike, but they were quite unlike the English colonies. The contrast can be best illustrated by the histories of the Spanish and English colonies in America.

III

Spain was governed by an absolute monarchy which tried to transplant a cross-section of Spanish society to the New World and to impose Spanish rule upon a great Indian population. Spanish adventurers soon conquered and destroyed two of the most remarkable civilizations in the history of the world. The first to fall was the Aztec empire in Mexico, which had a population of about fifteen million. Shortly thereafter the Inca empire of Peru, with perhaps six million people, was brought down. Within decades these Indian people were almost wiped out, not by Spanish arms, but by European diseases. Mexico City and Lima, Peru, the capitals of the two great Indian empires, became the centers of Spanish power in America.

The Spanish government rigidly controlled emigration to America. Aside from Negro slaves, who were brought in to supply labor, only Spanish people were allowed in the Spanish colonies, and even they had to have a license to leave Spain. Noblemen, clergymen, tradesmen, and farmers were sent to the New World in numbers roughly equivalent to their proportion of the population of Spain.

The Catholic Church was as firmly established in the colonies as in the mother country, and there was no trace of the religious freedom that became so common in the English colonies.

The land was parceled out among great landlords, and the mass of the population—both Indians and Negro slaves—was forced to work upon the land and in the mines.

Spanish policies were so successful that long before the first English colony was founded in Virginia in 1607, the Spanish empire in America had taken the form it was to retain until it was destroyed in the nineteenth century. Before the first English colony was founded, nearly two hundred thousand Spaniards had settled in America, more than two hundred chartered towns had been established, and the two oldest universities in the New World, one in Mexico City and one in Lima, Peru, had been created in 1553.

IV

Throughout the colonial period, Spanish-born officials and other natives of Spain outranked the growing number of Spaniards born in the colonies and the multitude of people of mixed races. The Spanish government rigidly controlled the political and economic life of the colonies from the beginning. Eventually Spanish America was divided up into four great viceregal kingdoms, each ruled absolutely by a viceroy who was the direct representative of the Spanish monarch. Thus the people of the Spanish colonies, when they did revolt and create independent nations, did not have the experience with self-government that the people of the English colonies had before they revolted. Hence, although the new Spanish American nations adopted constitutions modeled after those of the United States, they were more accustomed to arbitrary and dictatorial government—and down to the present day the history of many Spanish American nations, despite the outward forms of constitutional government, is a history of revolution and dictatorship.

V

The English government, unlike that of Spain, played almost no role in founding colonies. The monarch of England, like Spain's, claimed ownership by right of discovery, but he refused to give any financial support. All the monarch did was to grant charters to groups and individuals willing to pay the expense of colonization themselves. However, the royal charters gave the colonizers wide control over the political and economic life of the colonies they founded. It was only after the first English colonies became successful and permanent societies that England began to develop a colonial policy which attempted to limit the political and economic independence granted to the founders of colonies in their charters. The policies were never completely effective; and in the end, when England tried to enforce her policies with military power, the result was the American Revolution and the independence of the United States.

England made no attempt to control the migration of people to her colonies, as Spain did. The government looked upon the colonies as places to send undesirables, the unemployed and the convicts, and tens of thousands of both kinds were sent to America. Nor did the English government oppose the great migration of non-English peoples during the eighteenth century, and it positively encouraged the trade in Negro slaves from Africa to the colonies.

The result was that the English colonies contained a mixture of nationalities and peoples to be found in no other colonies, a fact which was to give the future United States a unique quality among nations, and the tradition of being a refuge for the poor and oppressed of the world, despite the evil heritage resulting from Negro slavery.

VI

When the English began colonization, they were forced to settle in what were thought to be the less desirable areas of the New World, except for the smaller islands in the West Indies which Spain had not occupied. Throughout the colonial era England looked upon her West Indian colonies as the most valuable because they produced sugar and other tropical crops. Nevertheless, the most populous, wealthy, and powerful English colonies were those that grew up on the North American mainland.

At first this did not seem likely, nor did Englishmen foresee the kinds of colonies that would develop, in fact had to develop, if they were to succeed. The merchants who established the first English colony in Virginia in 1607 looked upon it as a trading post. The settlers were ordered to find gold, or some other quick payment for the money invested in the colony, or at least to find a sea route to Asia. The result was a disaster; and the English soon learned that if the mainland colonies were to succeed, they must become self-supporting agricultural settlements. Fortunately for Virginia, the early discovery that tobacco could be grown there transformed it from a failure into a success. As other colonies were founded, they too became agricultural colonies, although the settlers also turned to fishing, lumbering, and the fur trade. Nevertheless, to the end of the colonial era, and far into the nineteenth century, the English colonies, and the later United States, remained a predominantly agricultural society. In 1776 at least 90 per cent of the people lived on farms; and most farmers were small farmers, not great landlords, although such men were to be found in every colony.

The founders of colonies had various motives, but most of them wanted to make fortunes or to increase the fortunes they possessed. Even the religious dissenters who founded Massachusetts and Pennsylvania as places where they could practice their religious beliefs as they pleased were not exempt from the hope of bettering themselves economically. The men who founded colonies realized that if they were to make money, they must bring laborers and farmers from England and Europe to work upon the vast areas of unsettled wilderness. Therefore the founders advertised their colonies as regions of opportunity where land was either free or cheap, and where any man, no matter how poor, could hope to better himself.

During the seventeenth century the colonizers appealed to the landless and the unemployed of England and helped to transport them to America. Men without money to pay their passage across the ocean could sign contracts to work as indentured servants in order to pay for their passage. At the end of their contracts, which usually ran for from four to seven years, they were promised tools and clothing, and in some colonies a tract of land as well. These indentured servants were the principal source of labor in English America during the seventeenth century, although by the end of the century Negro slaves were taking the place of servants, particularly in the southern mainland and the West Indian colonies. Nevertheless, many of the non-English migrants of the eighteenth century also came as indentured servants. It has been estimated that from one half to two thirds of all the people who came to the English colonies during the colonial era were indentured servants who labored for years before they became free men.

During the eighteenth century most of the immigrants were non-English. Among them were Germans, Scotch-Irish from northern Ireland, Irish from southern Ireland, Swiss, Jews, and Highland Scots. Some were artisans and mechanics of various sorts but most were farmers, tenants, and farm laborers who were attracted by the promise of cheap or free land.

They were also attracted to the English colonies because most of the founders of colonies, whatever their own religious beliefs, offered religious freedom to all who would come. In an age in which all were required to belong to state churches, and in an age when the host of dissenting sects spawned by the Protestant Reformation were persecuted by governments and state churches alike, the promise of religious freedom in English America was as powerful a magnet as the promise of land.

There was an opportunity for social, religious, and political experimentation in America which was impossible any place else in the world. Thus Roger Williams could establish religious freedom and political democracy in seventeenth-century Rhode Island. Such ideas were to be found in Europe, but European governments suppressed them ruthlessly whenever they appeared. America therefore attracted an ever-growing number of religious and political groups from the continent of Europe, some of which established communistic societies modeled upon those of the first Christians. The English colonies were so far from the social and political controls of England that almost any experiment was possible. Not all the experiments succeeded, but the important fact was that the English colonies were places where they could be attempted.

Those colonies, therefore, represented a unique opportunity. The migrants from Europe came from societies in which most of them were destined to remain in the class in which they had been born. Tenants and farm laborers who could never hope to own a square foot of Europe's soil, no matter how long and hard they worked, and the laborers in the towns who were doomed to remain laborers all their lives, were given an opportunity to achieve a new status. The New World soon evolved a class structure, but its lines were not hard and fast. It mattered not what position one had occupied in the Old World, or what ancestry one had; the acquisition of wealth in any form in America was enough to give a man a new place in society.

By no means all the immigrants succeeded, but an astonishing number became independent landowners and artisans, and some became men of wealth and influence. Enough people achieved a new position, a new independence, to create in them, and in the society of which they were a part, an optimism, an aggressive spirit, and a sense of individual dignity, which marked them off from the ordinary people in Europe.

The mixture of many nationalities and religions, the opportunity for a man of ability to get ahead, no matter what his Old World background, helped to shape the character and the feelings of the Americans. And Americans they became, as the Frenchman, Hector St. John de Crèvecoeur, and many another man in the eighteenth century realized. Perhaps Crèvecoeur painted too glowing a picture in his *Letters from an American Farmer*, but he did sum up better than most writers what happened to the people who migrated from the Old World to the New. "The American is a new man, who acts upon new principles; he must therefore entertain new ideas, and form new opinions. From involuntary idleness, servile dependence, penury, and useless labor, he has passed to toils of a very different nature, rewarded by ample subsistence. This is an American." As Crèvecoeur and many another observer realized, the "common man" in the English colonies was a "new man," who had no counterpart either in Europe or in other European colonies.

The uniqueness of the English colonies, as compared with those of other European nations, in terms of economic opportunity, religious freedom, and the mixture of nationalities, was at least matched by the political institutions that grew up in them.

The very first colonists began with certain constitutional guarantees of their rights. Although the charters gave the founders of colonies the right to govern and make laws, they were required to make their laws conform to the laws of England. More important was the guarantee in every charter that the people who migrated to the colonies, and their children born in them, should have all the rights and privileges of Englishmen, as if they had remained in England.

Such guarantees might have been meaningless if the colonies had not developed elected legislatures in which the colonists could voice their feelings and exert their growing power. The precedent was set in the first colony, Virginia, and it was not set by the King or Parliament in England but by the Virginia Company of London, which had no intention of establishing a legislature in America. Trading company charters provided for an organization which was essentially democratic. That is, all the stockholders meeting together elected all officers and enacted all the rules for the regulation of the company. The Virginia Company was such a company. In order to attract settlers, it promised that each person who went to Virginia would become a stockholder in the company, just as if he had bought stock and remained in England.

At first the colony was governed by a council and then by governors who were given absolute power. In order to appease the discontent of the colonists, the company decided in 1618 that the "stockholders" in Virginia should meet together to make rules for their own government, subject to the veto of the company in London. However, when the delegates from the various settlements in the colony met as the House of Burgesses in 1619, they at once began acting like a legislature and consciously modeled their rules and procedures upon those of the House of Commons in England. When the King of England took over the colony as a royal colony in 1624, he sent out governors as the company had done; but within a few years, the idea of a representative legislature was accepted as an integral part of the government of the colony.

Once the precedent was established, it was followed by other colonies as they were founded. The Puritans who settled Massachusetts Bay brought their trading company charter with them, and the stockholders automatically became the legislature of the colony. The proprietor of the colony of Maryland was given virtually dictatorial powers by his charter, but he was required to assemble the inhabitants to approve his laws. The inhabitants at once insisted that they had a right to disapprove the proprietor's laws and to make laws for themselves. They thus began a battle that was to last for nearly a century and which was to end in a victory for the elected legislature of Maryland.

Step by step, as the colonies grew, their legislatures gained more power over the governors sent out from England. The principal weapon of the colonial legislatures was their power to tax; and like Parliament in its struggle with the Crown in England, they insisted that they had the sole right to levy taxes, and the sole right to direct the spending of the money raised by taxes. As a result, it was recognized in both England and America by the middle of the eighteenth century that the colonies were virtually self-governing in their internal affairs. Thus the English colonists became accustomed to governing themselves by voting rather than by turning to armed force, although they did so in order to win their independence. But having won it, they returned to settling their affairs by political action.

The English colonies were political societies in which more men could vote than in any other place in the world; for the ownership of fifty acres of land gave men the right to vote in most colonies, and land was easy to acquire. However, the colonial governments which achieved virtual self-government as opposed to England did not always respond to the wishes of the voters. During the rapid territorial expansion of the eighteenth century, the colonial legislatures, controlled by the old settlements along the seacoast, were slow to extend representation to newly settled areas on the frontiers, and all too often were indifferent to their needs. On occasion, therefore, the inhabitants of the new areas either revolted or threatened to revolt in order to achieve their demands. But on the whole the colonists preferred to settle their problems by political means, by the mechanism of representative government.

Thus when the English colonies declared their independence in 1776, they had behind them a century and a half of political experience in which they had developed representative legislatures, had become accustomed to having a widespread voting population, and on the whole had accepted the idea that they must abide by the will of the majority of voters and of the majority of the men elected to the legislatures, even when they bitterly objected to the results. They had become accustomed, in fact, to campaigning for a change at the next election, rather than turning to armed revolt against the decisions of the majority of those who voted.

By 1776 some men were also insisting that every man should have the right to vote because he was a man, not because he owned a certain amount of property. The proclamation in the Declaration of Independence that all men are created equal was taken seriously by many Americans in the years after 1776 and used as a weapon to reform what they considered to be evils of American society. However good that society might be, many believed that it could be improved, and in time might even become perfect.

And although some Americans were horrified by the idea of democracy, an old idea in America by 1776, more and more Americans subscribed to the proposition that democratic government was the most workable and best kind of government that mankind could hope for. Some were idealists who thought such government could be achieved in their own lifetimes. Others believed that it was an ideal that might never be achieved but nevertheless was worth striving for.

VII

The English colonies that became the United States in 1776 thus possessed a unique heritage of ideas and institutions as compared with other colonies in the New World, and with colonies in other parts of the world that have become independent nations in the twentieth century. Elements of that heritage can be found in the history of other European colonies, but not in the combination or in the quality and quantity that existed in the English colonies. Most of the new nations created from colonies during the nineteenth and twentieth centuries have lacked the relative stability that the United States was able to achieve almost at once. They have lacked it because they did not acquire, as colonies, the institutions, the experience, and the ideas, which the United States acquired over a century and a half before it ever became an independent nation.

VIII

The foregoing sketch of the New World colonies is based upon the proposition that if we are to understand the evolution of nations that once were colonies, especially during their early years of independence, we must understand their history as colonies. This is as true of the nations that have won their independence in the twentieth century as it is of those that won their independence in the eighteenth and nineteenth centuries.

In studying those histories one may emphasize their differences, as I have done, or one may emphasize their similarities. But whatever approach we may take, we have much to gain, not only in our knowledge of the past, but also in our ability to understand the present, and—hopefully—in our capacity to anticipate what may happen in the future.

BIBLIOGRAPHY

Tens of thousands of books, articles, and documents have been printed to illustrate the colonial history of the Americas. The following books therefore will serve as only the slightest of introductions to that history, but most of them contain bibliographies so that the interested student may work his way ever deeper into the literature of the subject.

Very little has been done as yet in the comparative history of colonization. A pioneer venture was that of Albert G. Keller, *Colonization: A Study of the Founding of New Societies* (New York, 1908). In 1950, Robert L. Reynolds and Merrill Jensen published "European Colonial Experience. A Plea for Comparative Studies," in *Studi in Onore Di Gino Luzzato* (4 vols.; Milan, Italy, 1950), Vol. IV, pp. 75–90, in which they pointed to some of the common experiences of European nations as colonizing agencies over the centuries from the Middle Ages down to the twentieth century. A few years later, as a part of a projected history of the Americas, Max Savelle published an "outline" for such a comparative history of the colonies in America, including excellent bibliographies, in *United States: Colonial Period* (Mexico City, 1953).

More recently, J. H. Parry, in *The Age of Reconnaissance* (Cleveland and London, 1963), discusses European colonization to about the middle of the seventeenth century, but he pays little attention to the English and French colonies. D. K. Fieldhouse, *The Colonial Empires* (New York and London, 1966) is a compact survey of the history of colonies in the nineteenth century as well as of earlier colonies.

However, it is still necessary to turn to the history of the colonies of particular nations, and a number of books are excellent introductions. They are J. H. Parry, *The Spanish Seaborne Empire* (London, 1966); C. R. Boxer, *The Dutch Seaborne Empire: 1600–1800* (New York, 1965); Clarence Ver Steeg, *The Formative Years, 1607–1763* (English mainland colonies) (New York, 1964); and Herbert I. Priestly, *France Overseas* (New York, 1938). The best introduction to the history of the West Indies, which played so crucial a role in the history of all the American colonies, is A. P. Newton, *The European Nations in the West Indies* (London, 1933).

 3

The
Enlightenment

PETER GAY

I

To compare the American with the European Enlightenment is a risky business, not because they have nothing in common— they have in fact a great deal in common—but because they are not of the same logical order. The Enlightenment was a great revolution in man's style of thinking that came to dominate the Western world in the eighteenth century. It was composed of the interplay among ideas and events, inventions and expectations; its raw materials were the triumph of Newtonian science, striking improvements in industrial and agricultural techniques, a widespread loss of religious fervor and a corresponding rise of "reasonable" religion, an ever bolder play of the critical spirit among the old mysteries of church and state which had for centuries escaped criticism, a new sense of confidence in man's power over his worldly destiny. The *philosophes* in many areas, including the British colonies in America, articulated and organized these developments into a coherent philosophy and made it into a set of demands, a full-fledged political program. In this enterprise, each area had its part to play; each was at once unique and tied to the others as a member of a family. The American Enlightenment was one such member, prominent though not of the first rank, in the family of the Western Enlightenment; it can be properly compared only with other individuals in that family—the Scottish, say, or the Genevan Enlightenment.

Yet the traditional procedure of comparing the American with the whole European Enlightenment has persisted in both major schools of thought among American historians, both among those who regard the American Enlightenment as a pernicious myth and those who regard it as a glorious reality. It has persisted because these two schools of historians, for all their differences, share an almost unqualified admiration for what, in short, I want to call the American *philosophes*—the politician-intellectuals who led the revolution and rationalized it, drafted the Constitution and governed the young country. The first school sees Franklin, Jefferson, and their fellows as statesmen so practical that they did not need theories, or even ideas, and steered clear, with unspoiled instinct, of the treacherous rocks of European ideologies. The second school sees Franklin, Jefferson, and their fellows as thinkers indeed, but as tough-minded realistic thinkers who managed to discard the fantasies of European theoreticians.

Both these interpretations misstate the relation of theory to practice, ideas to experience, and, worse, the relation of America to Europe; both are a direct consequence of compressing the variety of the European experience into a specious unity. Each local enlightenment, whether American or French or Lombard, generated, transformed, and echoed certain ideas, and each modified its ideas through its particular experience. The commitment to practicality, on which Americans have often thought they hold a monopoly, is after all itself an idea, an idea in fact with a long and honored history. Precisely like the *philosophes* in France or England and following their lead, the American *philosophes* acquired their respect for practicality from a close reading of the Roman classics. Cicero especially was for all *philosophes* everywhere a model of the thoughtful statesman; he was the philosopher in politics. In addition, the Americans learned to value practicality by studying the attacks on metaphysics and what was derisively called "system-making" launched by Locke and Newton, justified by Hume and Condillac, and popularized by Voltaire and d'Alembert. Like the other *philosophes,* the Americans got some of their respect for practicality from being practical men, much of it from being readers. What made the American *philosophes* distinctive was not that they were realists while their English and French brethren were dreamers, but rather that their particular experience taught them lessons different from the lessons that experience taught the *philosophes* in Scotland or France or Milan. Fortunately for the Americans, the American experience included the winning of a revolution which gave them a captive audience for their ideas. Franklin was no more of an empiricist than, say, Voltaire; Turgot was as tough-minded a political thinker as, say, Jefferson—indeed, considering Jefferson's visionary and embarrassing revolutionary pronouncements, more tough-minded. John Adams, as caustic a critic of Utopian optimism as the American Enlightenment produced, acknowledged Turgot, along with Price and Mably, to be a man with "experience in public affairs, and ample information respecting the nature of man, the necessities of society, and the science of government." The relations of *philosophes* to their state and their society differed in country after country; but the difference was not one of varying degrees of practicality, it was one of power. Whereas in the European countries vested interests managed to defeat, absorb, or partially to honor the demands of the *philosophes,* in America the *philosophes* became the vested interest; they were compelled to be practical: their good fortune forced them to test their ideas in sober reality.

It should therefore surprise no one that the American *philosophes* sounded in most respects precisely like their European brethren. If anyone has had the reputation of a Utopian in Europe, it was Condorcet. In his *Essay on the Progress of the Human Mind,* written in hiding from the Jacobins in 1793–1794, Condorcet forecast a future in which the further improvement of the natural sciences and the establishment of the social sciences would bring to all men an enviable existence, with substantial equality, high standards of living, and a life indefinitely prolonged and freed from anxiety and disease. Among the Americans, it became fashionable to ridicule Condorcet's naïve hopes, though Jefferson for one professed to agree with Condorcet's trust in human perfectibility. But Benjamin Franklin, who has become a byword for realism, accepted and in fact anticipated Condorcet's brilliant picture of the future. "The rapid Progress *true* Science now makes," he wrote to Priestley in 1780, "occasions my regretting sometimes that I was born so soon. It is impossible to imagine the Height to which may be carried, in a thousand years, the Power of Man over Matter. We may perhaps learn to deprive large Masses of their Gravity, and give them absolute Levity, for the sake of easy Transport. Agriculture may diminish its Labour and double its Produce; all Diseases may by sure means be prevented or cured, not excepted even that of Old Age, and our Lives lengthened at pleasure even beyond the antediluvian Standards." To be sure, there was one area in which man showed as yet little progress: "O that moral Science were in as fair a way of Improvement, that Men would cease to be Wolves to one another, and the human Beings would at length learn what they now improperly call Humanity!" But this wistful qualification, this distinction between material and moral progress, was a commonplace among the Scottish, French, and German *philosophes,* and in fact deeply troubled Condorcet himself: the French Utopian was not so naïve, the American Realist not so skeptical, it seems, as has often been supposed. To say, as Adrienne Koch has said, that "the French Enlightenment, in all its brilliant achievements and rich profusion of doctrines and dogmas, did not cast up the kind of sagacious and flexible leadership that came to the highest places of power in the American Revolution and in the ensuing years of Confederation and Constitutional Republic" is to underestimate both what *philosophes* all over the Western world had in common and the opportunities which the American *philosophes* had for displaying their sagacity.

II

Since the unique dimension of the American Enlightenment was its preparation for revolution, the Revolution, and what it did with the Revolution, the special claim of the American Enlightenment to historical distinction must lie in the decades of the 1760's, 1770's, and 1780's. Properly enough, Koch dates the

American Enlightenment from 1765 to 1815. But by 1765, *philosophes* from Edinburgh to Milan, London to Berlin, had completed the structure of scientific, aesthetic, social, religious, and political ideas that constitute the Enlightenment. In the making of these ideas, for all of Franklin's reputation as a scientist, the American colonists had no part. The period before 1765 was the prehistory of the American Enlightenment; in this period the Americans were consumers, depending heavily, almost exclusively, on borrowings from overseas. To be sure, not all was dependence; like the others, the American *philosophes* developed their particular intellectual style by listening to domestic developments in Boston or Philadelphia or Richmond or the frontier that lay just beyond. But just as the American Puritans had shaped their ideas by following the course of events and the evolution of thinking among English Dissenters, so the American *philosophes,* most of them still young men before 1765, went to school to a handful of European thinkers.

This dependence of America on Europe is easy to document in detail, for the Americans never thought of concealing it. Benjamin Franklin formed his style on Addison's *Spectator,* found his way into deism by reading English religious controversy, perfected his scientific knowledge by studying English Newtonians. He attributed his turn toward humanitarianism to a reading of Cotton Mather's *Essays to Do Good,* but he minimizes this single concession to local pride almost as soon as he has made it by mentioning, in the same breath, Defoe's *Essay on Projects.* John Adams, though contemptuous of the "naïve optimism" of Helvétius and Rousseau, developed his theory of lawful revolution by close study of the legal writings of Grotius, Pufendorf, Barbeyrac, and other European lawyers, shaped his political outlook by close study of Harrington, Locke, Montesquieu, and other European political theorists, and sought for an adequate theory of human nature by close study of Hutcheson, Ferguson, Bolingbroke, and other European philosophers. Adams made much— and much has been made since—of his disagreements with European "dreamers," but then Adams liked developing his own thought in opposition; and besides, even if he rejected some European *philosophes,* he rejected them in the name, and with the aid, of other European *philosophes.* Jefferson was notoriously dependent on Europe. Adams' comment, malicious in intent, that Jefferson "drank freely of the French philosophy, in religion, in science, in politics," is not so much inaccurate as it is incomplete; Jefferson was open to his Virginian experience and drank as freely from English as he did from French thought, and more freely from English than from French literary models. It is well known that he called Bacon, Newton, and Locke his "trinity of the three greatest men the world had ever seen"—a trinity, we should note, not merely *of* Europeans, but worshiped by Europeans; it was precisely the trinity adored by Voltaire, d'Alembert, Hume, Lichtenberg, and Kant. Jefferson was, like the British *philosophes,* a Francophile; and he was, like the French and German *philosophes,* an Anglomaniac. Madison's political thought, in turn, is inexplicable without reference to the Scottish Enlightenment and Montesquieu's political ideas. Madison was, much like Franklin, a disciple of Addison, and echoed Voltaire's Anglomania in Voltaire's very words. Alexander Hamilton stands a little isolated from this group, with his admiration of monarchy and—if we may believe Jefferson—for Julius Caesar; but he made it perfectly plain that he had drawn his political principles from such unimpeachable European sources as Grotius, Pufendorf, Locke, and Montesquieu, and that he claimed to abhor—in good European fashion—that most impeachable of European theorists, Hobbes. Hamilton's rhetoric, and I think his political program, was that of the European Enlightenment; tender words like "reason" and "humanity" punctuate his most tough-minded pronouncements, and not as flourishes alone.

What holds true of these giants holds true of the less celebrated figures. As Bernard Bailyn has shown, the American radicals who from the early 1760's on began to wonder out loud whether the colonies could continue to live under the tyranny of a corrupt British homeland drew their arguments almost exclusively from Europe. Jonathan Mayhew, James Otis, John Dickinson, and the others larded their pamphlets with ideas—and sometimes plagiarized long passages—from Scottish and English, French and Milanese *philosophes,* from English common lawyers, and above all from English republicans of the seventeenth and eighteenth centuries: Milton, Harrington, Sidney,

Trenchard, Gordon, and that much maligned, much underestimated Latitudinarian prelate, Bishop Hoadly. Indeed, it was this last group, with their cohorts, who represented to the American rebels the sum of modern political wisdom. England, it was clear, had the best constitution man had ever devised—the mixed constitution—and if it became necessary to rebel it was only because England was now departing from this glorious invention; England, it seemed, must be rescued from herself. In sum, there can be no doubt: in the formation of the American Enlightenment, European thinkers played a decisive part, and American *philosophes* were apt and candid disciples.

Disciples often apply their lessons a generation late, and their finest productions may bear the character of an anachronism. So it was in the American Enlightenment: the Declaration of Independence, which must always remain the most celebrated production of the American Enlightenment, is, from the philosophical point of view, a reminder of arguments that were losing their respectable status. At a time when European thinkers were turning to Utilitarianism, the declaration persisted in employing the logic of natural law: as everyone knows, it justified separation by appealing to "the laws of nature," and to "nature's God," and to "self-evident" truths. But by 1776, Hume, Helvétius, Beccaria, and Bentham had thrown serious doubts on the possibility of discovering moral laws of nature; had discarded God, even nature's God; and had denied self-evident truths outside of mathematics. Natural law and natural rights remained good battle cries: Tom Paine and Condorcet used them to the end, and so did the authors of the French Declaration of the Rights of Man. Locke's political ideas—at least as simplified by his hasty readers —retained their usefulness long after they had been riddled by criticism. The Declaration of Independence, a disciple's production, exhibits that usefulness by disregarding these criticisms.

III

I insist on this point here not to patronize the Declaration of Independence, but to characterize the relation of American to English, Scottish, and French thought. After all, the declaration was a political rather than a philosophical document, and it was, on its own terms, supremely successful. It was clear, circumstantial, dignified, and persuasive. And it was more than that; the Declaration of Independence is a symbol of the shift of the American Enlightenment from consumer to producer, from importer to exporter, a shift that became manifest in the 1770's. Now what the American Enlightenment exported was, of course, first of all itself. America became the model for Europeans of good hope—living, heartening proof that men had a capacity for growth, that reason and humanity could become governing rather than merely critical principles. America was, to be sure, a model that pointed in two opposite directions at once; admirers of primitive simplicity could call on it just as much as could admirers of refined civilization. And this duality was the secret of Benjamin Franklin's enormous success as a missionary of the American cause: he seemed to embody both the virtues of nature and the triumphs of civility; he was—or rather, in his shrewdness, enormously enjoyed playing—the savage as philosopher. David Hume, no primitivist and not given to excesses of flattery, was enchanted with this commodity exported by the American Enlightenment. "America has sent us many good things," he wrote to Franklin, "gold, silver, sugar, tobacco, indigo, etc., but you are the first philosopher, and indeed the first great man of letters, for whom we are beholden to her." John Adams, who did not much like Franklin, was half amused, half irritated, to discover in Paris in 1779 that Franklin was widely considered a universal genius, "another Voltaire and Hume," and the "great Philosopher and the great Legislator of America," as well as a great wit. These were claims that Adams felt constrained to dispute, but the tribute paid to Franklin by Europe was more than a personal tribute: it was expression of the great hope that the ideas of the Enlightenment might become reality. And later, as the American colonies gained their independence, survived the tests of the first years, and succeeded in transcending parochialism in that magnificent compromise, the Constitution of the United States, the myth that Franklin represented appeared to have, after all, a good deal of substance.

The American *philosophes* were not slow to celebrate their

political sagacity. Madison especially, looking back, was fond of describing the American "experiment" as an "example of a free system," and he was confident that that system would be "more of a Pilot to a good Port, than a Beacon warning from a bad one." America had constructed a "great Political Machine," and as a result, the whole "Civilized World" had discovered the blessings of "Representative Government." Unquestionably, he insisted, the United States was the "workshop of liberty," and the people of the United States "enjoy the great merit of having established a system of Government on the basis of human rights, and of giving to it a form without example"—America was new, it had no model but was a model to others. And even John Adams, who had little trust in human nature and whose political thought increasingly turned away from equality and freedom to devices for social control, felt constrained to admit that America had been splendid: "The last twenty-five years of the last century," he wrote in 1815, "and the first fifteen years of this, may be called the age of revolutions and constitutions. We began the dance . . ."

We can understand the reasons for this self-congratulation without wholly sharing it; if America began the dance, it was Scots and Englishmen and Frenchmen who had designed the figures for it. Yet there is some reality in these claims; the historical role of the young United States seemed to be to act as a laboratory for Enlightenment ideas. Now it is precisely at this point that the task of comparative history becomes exceedingly complicated; we need much further work to understand just how much the political ideals of the young republic owed to the ideas of the Enlightenment, how much to the improvisation of the moment, how much to ideas of sound administration that any sensible man in the eighteenth century would have applied, Enlightenment or no Enlightenment. It is certain that the colonies were good soil for the ideas of the European Enlightenment; a relatively long period of peace, and new conditions for work, had brought the colonists experiences in self-government, peaceful cooperation, and class mobility that were unavailable back in Europe. "Most of the legislation," Felix Gilbert has said, "which the *philosophes* in Europe advocated, had become a reality in America," and so there were some fights the American *philosophes* did not need to fight, or could fight with good prospects of success. This holds true even if we are constrained to admit, with skeptics like Leonard Levy, that under the pressure of events, from sheer intellectual confusion and the kind of helplessness that believing in one's own cant always produces, the Americans often behaved less creditably as statesmen than they had sounded as *philosophes*.

But in what, precisely, does the Enlightened quality of the American experiment consist? It lies, I think, in what I should like to call its "pragmatic rationalism." This quality has been, paradoxically enough, obscured by the ranting of articulate Americans against the French Revolution, and, later, by historians wrongly associating Americans with Burke. The leading American *philosophes* in fact rejected the cardinal principle of Burke's conservatism: that a constitution cannot be made, but must grow. John Adams, early and late, thought politics a "divine science," and was confident that men could discover "principles of political architecture." He cautioned, to be sure, that this architecture was "an art or mystery very difficult to learn, and still harder to practice," but after all, the Americans had learned and practiced it, so it was not on principle impossible. The authors of the *Federalist Papers*—and it is this document rather than the Declaration of Independence that strikes me as the most characteristic product of the American Enlightenment—distinguished between Utopian political blueprints and sensible political machines, but they never doubted that the state could be made into a successful mechanism promoting freedom while repressing the anarchy of passion. Madison's favorite phrase, "political experiment," deserves to be given its full weight: just as men learned from history—which was, as it were, a record book of both unsuccessful and successful experiments—so men could learn from present experience, as a physicist learns in the laboratory. The prevalence of bad machines, and the difficulty of devising good machines, did not deter the American *philosophes* from striving to become Newtonians of statesmanship—precisely the thing that Burke denounced as supreme, impious folly. It was this hardheaded confidence in the cooperation of reason with experience—a confidence which Madison and Adams shared with Voltaire and Kant—that produced the hardheaded optimism of the American *philosophes* which, once again, they shared with their brethren in Europe. It was an optimism that survives, indeed incorporates, a relatively low estimate of human nature. Much—too much, I think—has been made of the Calvinist, or Hobbesian, pessimism of the founding fathers. Like most of the *philosophes* in Europe, the founding fathers believed that passion is ruthless and undirected, and that the lower orders, guided by passion, lack the political wisdom to make the political machine work. Institutions, therefore, are the public superego, designed to restrain the passionate will and guide it into productive paths. The science of freedom required repression—for the sake of freedom. The mixing of constitutional elements, the balancing of political forces—ideas taken from classical political theory, modern political sociology, and Newtonian imagery— was, the founding fathers expected, the method that would provide the salutary mixture of freedom and control. If there was optimism, then, it rested on the conviction that America was essentially an experiment—pragmatic rationalism and ultimate optimism are two sides of the same principle. Writing to Count Sarsfield in 1786, John Adams expressed this conjunction with particular felicity: "It has ever been my hobby-horse," he wrote, "to see rising in America an empire of liberty, and a prospect of two or three hundred millions of freemen, without one noble or one king among them. You say it is impossible. If I should agree with you in this"—and it is obvious that he does not—"I would still say, let us try the experiment." This temper— realistic yet hopeful, scientific but humanist, respectful but secular, trusting in institutions yet treating them as provisional, and looking to the day when all men are autonomous—is the link that ties the American Enlightenment to its colleagues in Scotland and England and France and Prussia; for it is the authentic, the characteristic temper of the Western Enlightenment as a whole.

BIBLIOGRAPHY

The definition of Enlightenment that underlies this essay has been worked out in detail in my *The Enlightenment: An Interpretation,* Vol. I, *The Rise of Modern Paganism* (New York, 1966); the book also suggests the basis on which valid comparisons may be made. Adrienne Koch's anthology, *The American Enlightenment: The Shaping of the American Experiment and a Free Society* (New York, 1965), offers judicious selections from Franklin, Adams, Jefferson, Madison, and Hamilton. Koch's essays, collected under the title *Power, Morals and the Founding Fathers* (Ithaca, N.Y., 1961), are, if not profound, lucid and helpful. I must confess that I have found the various writings of Daniel J. Boorstin, such as his *The Genius of American Politics* (Chicago, 1953) and *The Americans: The Colonial Experience* (New York, 1958), stimulating mainly through the opposition their conscious anti-intellectualism aroused in me. The best work on comparing the American and European experiences has been done by Bernard Bailyn: see his splendid article, "Political Experience and Enlightenment Ideas in Eighteenth-Century America," *American Historical Review,* LXVII, No. 2 (January 1962), 339–351, which, however, sees the question of "practicality" rather differently from the way I see it in this essay. Bailyn's General Introduction to Bailyn (ed.), *Pamphlets of the American Revolution, 1750–1776,* Vol. I, *1750–1765* (Cambridge, Mass., 1965), offers a brilliant and persuasive conspectus of American political ideas in a time of ferment; it may be profitably read in conjunction with Caroline Robbins, *The Eighteenth-Century Commonwealthman* (Cambridge, Mass., 1959), which, though on England, is supremely relevant to America.

For the decisive period before the Revolution—a subject that has been much explored—see the judicious survey by Edmund S. Morgan, *The Birth of the Republic, 1763–1789* (Chicago, 1956), and Edmund S. and Helen M. Morgan, *The Stamp Act Crisis: Prologue to Revolution* (2nd ed.; New York, 1963). Max Savelle, *Seeds of Liberty* (New York, 1948), and Clinton Rossiter, *Seedtime of the Republic* (New York, 1953), are both (as their titles imply) rather favorable to the American myth, but both are informative. Robert E. Brown, *Middle-Class Democracy and the Revolution in Massachusetts, 1691–1780* (Ithaca, N.Y., 1955), is belligerently revisionist but remains stimulating.

Another revisionist book of importance is Leonard Levy's *Jefferson and Civil Liberties: The Darker Side* (Cambridge, Mass., 1963); it reports, with an advocate's fervor, on the failings of an American hero.

There is room here for only one biography on each of the major American *philosophes*. See Carl Van Doren, *Benjamin Franklin* (New York, 1938); Gilbert Chinard, *Honest John Adams* (Boston, 1933); Dumas Malone, *Jefferson and His Time*, 3 vols.: *Jefferson the Virginian* (Boston, 1948), *Jefferson and the Rights of Man* (Boston, 1951), *Jefferson and the Ordeal of Liberty* (Boston, 1962); Irving Brant, *James Madison*, 6 vols. (New York, 1941–1961); John C. Miller, *Alexander Hamilton: Portrait in Paradox* (New York, 1959).

On the growth of religious to enlightened America, see my study, *A Loss of Mastery: Puritan Historians in Colonial America* (Berkeley and Los Angeles, 1966), which contains a full bibliographical essay.

 4

The

Revolution

R. R. PALMER

The United States of America, as a political organization, was undoubtedly created by a revolution, which found its expression in the Declaration of Independence of 1776. The experience of revolution is therefore one which Americans share with others. In a book devoted to comparative history it is important to try to see the American Revolution in a comparative light, assessing both resemblances and differences between it and other revolutions, and the effects it may have had on revolutionary developments in other parts of the world.

The task is not easy. Nor is it new, for Americans have been concerned with their special relationship to the rest of the world from the time of the Revolution itself, and indeed since the first settlement of the country. Europeans, and others also, have found much in the American experience to illuminate their own. But though old, the question has its relevancy today, when some see the United States as the great conservative power opposed to twentieth-century revolutions, while others, such as Senator Robert Kennedy of New York, believed that the American revolutionary example should be carried to Latin America and elsewhere. It may be added that what is called the "Negro revolution" in the United States today—that is, the struggle for equality for American citizens of whatever race—may be seen as a contemporary manifestation of principles deriving from the American Revolution.

There are many possible views. Some have thought that there was really no revolution in America at all, in any modern sense of the word, but only a successful war of independence, which removed British control but left the country internally much the same. Closely related is the idea that the American revolt was really a conservative movement, to protect old liberties against novel demands by Great Britain, somewhat like the revolt of the Belgian estates in 1789 against the attempted reforms of the Emperor Joseph II. This idea, which later found favor in conservative circles in the United States, appeared in Europe as early as the 1790's, when Friedrich Gentz, for example, praised the conservatism of the American Revolution in order to attack the French. Other European conservatives of the time, however, for example the Abbé Barruel, insisted that the French Revolution had been anticipated in America. It was in America, said Barruel, that a "sect" of secret revolutionaries had first announced "its code of equality, liberty, and sovereignty of the people." Though no one now agrees with Barruel's conspiratorial theory of the Revolution, he nevertheless shared in a third view, indeed the classic view, common to persons of both conservative and liberal inclination, that the American Revolution was the first episode in a long revolutionary period extending from about 1770 through the European revolutions of 1848, and principally marked by the great French Revolution of 1789. Within this view many nuances exist, depending on how much one wishes to stress similarities or national differences. George Lefebvre, the eminent French historian, thought that the American Revolution had more in common with the English revolution of the seventeenth century than with the French, believing that the Anglo-Saxon revolutions, as he called them, were primarily concerned with liberty, while the French Revolution aimed most especially at equality. While the idea of equality took on a far wider range of meanings in the French Revolution, it seems certain that Lefebvre greatly underestimated its importance in America. For Alexis de Tocqueville, writing his *Democracy in*

America in the 1830's, the United States offered the world's leading example of "equality," though it is true that Tocqueville
did not relate his observation to the American Revolution.

The various revolutions up to 1848, including the American,
and that of England in the seventeenth century, have sometimes
been put together as the "bourgeois revolution," a view congenial
to Marxists but not limited to them, and one in which everything depends on what is meant by the "bourgeoisie." Since, in
brief, the English revolution was an affair of fairly aristocratic
landowners, the American of small farmers, planters, and country
lawyers, and the French of a large composite urban middle class
reinforced by peasants and workers, with occasional nobles and
priests, the conception of a bourgeoisie must for this purpose become excessively generalized, and signify hardly more than persons who possessed or aspired to possess private property, in land
or in goods, in amounts either very large or very small. Indeed,
strong emphasis on the concept of a "bourgeois revolution" is
likely to imply a future stage of development in which the
bourgeoisie is to be succeeded by a new dominant group, with
private property in income-producing goods abolished. Such
came to be the message of revolutionary or Marxist socialism
in Europe after the mid-nineteenth century. In the rise of this
movement, the American Revolution was of little significance.
There has been little affinity between the American Revolution
and the Russian Revolution as it developed after 1917, or the
Chinese Revolution as it developed after World War II.

There is another category of revolutions, those aiming at
national independence, in which the American Revolution is
seen as a precedent, since, whatever else it may also have been, it
was clearly a struggle for independence against Great Britain.
In general, such revolutionary movements ran their course in
Latin America through the nineteenth century, and in Europe
through the close of World War I, producing such newly independent states as Czechoslovakia and Ireland. They have been
in progress since that time in Africa and Asia, in the form of
resistance to the European colonial rule. The leaders of such
movements of national independence have often looked to the
American Revolution as an example to follow, and have characteristically been befriended by the government of the United

States. The situation becomes confused when movements of national independence take on a strong social character, and are directed against foreign capitalism, foreign economic control, or foreign ideas, influence, or privileges, as in the Mexican Revolution after 1910, the Cuban Revolution since 1959, and indeed in the Russian and Chinese revolutions also. The extreme of aggressive xenophobia, with doctrinaire rejection of Western civilization, individual liberty, representative government, and even of reason itself, as in the National Socialist movement in Germany, has nothing in common with the American or any other eighteenth-century revolution.

Let us consider at greater length only two matters suggested by the preceding survey: first, the relationship of the American Revolution to the French and European revolutions of almost two hundred years ago; and second, the relationship of the American Revolution, whether in resemblance or by contrast, to the anticolonialist revolutionary disturbances in the Asian-African-Latin American world in recent times.

As for the first, the view taken here is a form of what has already been called the "classical" interpretation. There was one great revolutionary period from about 1770 to 1848; this was *the* European revolution or revolution of Western civilization. The American Revolution was part of this process, was indeed the opening movements of this general European or "Atlantic" phenomenon. On the other hand, the American Revolution was directed *against* Europe—Europe as a whole, and not merely Great Britain. Hence it has a positive significance for anticolonialist revolutionaries today, who are fundamentally anti-European, and can with some justice see the American Revolution as the opening movement of *their* revolution also. But in both cases we run into difficulties and paradoxes. The American Revolution of 1776 was different from the French Revolution of 1789, if only because Americans were not Europeans. But it is different also from later anti-colonial and anti-European movements because the Americans are, after all, a species of Europeans—the "colony of all Europe" as Thomas Paine said in 1776, the "daughter of Europe," as General Charles de Gaulle remarked in 1965.

Similarities between the revolutions in America and in Europe in the eighteenth century are impossible to deny. It is idle to pretend that the uprising in America was not truly revolutionary, or to see it as primarily a conservative protest. The Americans rebelled against the legal authority of the British crown and Parliament, they passed from more moderate to more radical stages, reaching the point of armed conflict and a secession from the British empire which many Americans were unwilling to accept, so that the war of independence was at the same time a civil or revolutionary struggle between native Americans, in the course of which, as a few years later in France, there was a good deal of intimidation, if not actual "terror," emigration of tens of thousands who remained loyal to Britain, and confiscation of the property of these political émigrés. Victorious after a long struggle, thanks to the intervention of France, the revolutionary Americans set up new governments according to new principles, and to a large extent operated by new men, of a kind who could not have achieved prominence had the colonies remained British. This is true not only of such notables as George Washington or John Adams. A study has recently been made of men who sat in legislatures of the colonies just before independence, and of the corresponding states just after, according to the classifications of "wealthy," "well-to-do," and "moderate." In New York, New Jersey, and New Hampshire, between 1770 and 1784, the proportion called "moderate"—i.e., in wealth, not opinion—rose from 17 to 62 per cent, with corresponding loss of the "wealthy" and "well-to-do." Even in the South the "wealthy" lost their predominance in the legislatures. When classified by occupation, the proportion of merchants and lawyers greatly declined, whereas the proportion of farmers doubled. In short, the revolt in America meets the external criteria of a true revolution, and of a revolution in a democratic direction, since it was a former upper or "aristocratic" class that was displaced.

It is in principles, purposes, and ideas, or what may be called "ideology," that the resemblance between the American and the French or European revolutions is most evident. On the plane of actual politics, the modern doctrines of liberty and equality, or natural rights and the sovereignty of the people, were first proclaimed by the American Revolution. The Declaration of Independence, as is well known, announced that "all men are created equal," with an equal right to "life, liberty, and the pursuit of happiness." There has been much discussion of what Jefferson meant by inserting "happiness" into this document; the Americans had not really been "unhappy" under British rule, and "happiness" makes a vague political program; but all students of the eighteenth century will recognize that "happiness," *le bonheur, la félicité publique,* was a common idea of the European Enlightenment. It was the revolutionary belief that men may take action to improve their conditions of life, even against the established authorities of law, state, church, or society—as St.-Just remarked a few years later, at the height of the French Revolution, "Happiness is a new idea in Europe." The Declaration of Independence went on to assert that government exists only to protect the rights thus affirmed, and that when government failed in this function, the people "may alter or abolish it." They might then "institute new government" as they chose. This is a pure formula of revolution .

As a matter of fact, it was not the Declaration of Independence which first attracted attention in Europe, or which best illustrates the resemblances in ideas between America and Europe at the time. A complaint by disaffected provincials against the king of England, rehearsing his real and alleged misdoings, however adorned with familiar eighteenth-century generalizations, could have little universal appeal. The connection between the American and European revolutions is more apparent in the constructive part of the American program, the way in which the Americans "instituted new government." They instituted it, or "constituted" it, first of all in each of the thirteen states, each of which received a new written constitution (except that in Connecticut and Rhode Island the colonial charters were retained, being virtually republican anyway), and then by establishing the federal union with the Constitution written in Philadelphia in 1787, which, as amended, remains the Constitution of the United States today. For this purpose, at the state and federal levels, the Americans devised the mechanism of a special convention or constituent assembly, which was held to exercise the sovereign power of the people, and which characteristically did two things. First, it issued a declaration of rights, listing the "rights of man" in a series of numbered articles, and setting limits beyond which the powers of government could not go. Second, it produced a written constitution, one short single document, by which the people were supposed to create a government for themselves, all public power was held to be merely a revocable and delegated authority (as in the *Social Contract* of Rousseau), various political bodies and offices were defined, and the executive, legislative, and judicial powers were separated and balanced, so that abuse of government, despotism, or dictatorship might be prevented. The American constitutions and declarations of rights gave a practical embodiment to ideas of political liberty and legal equality, to the principle of representation by numbers rather than by classes or corporate groups, the rejection of hereditary office and privileged status, the opening of careers to merit rather than birth, and the separation of state and church, or at least of citizenship from religious affiliation.

This machinery and these ideas—the constituent convention, the declaration of rights, the written constitution, the separation of powers, the new basis for political representation, the equality of rights, the career open to talent, the separation of church and state—soon became common to the great European or "Atlantic" revolution, from the French Constituent Assembly of 1789 and the French Convention of 1792, through the new regimes in Holland, Switzerland, and Italy—that is, the Batavian, Helvetic, Cisalpine, and other republics that arose during the wars of the 1790's—to the French Constituent Assembly of 1848, the German Frankfurt Parliament, and other European developments of that same year.

Yet the American Revolution was very different from the European, and especially the French Revolution, for the good reason that America in the eighteenth century was a very different kind of country from Europe, more so than it is today. The astonishing thing is that any parallel in political behavior or ideology could exist at all. In the Thirteen Colonies, at the time of their revolution, there was no feudalism, no seigneurial or manorial system, and no peasantry—for the mobile and property-owning American farmers were hardly peasants. There were no lords or nobility, no magnificent and privileged church, and one might almost say no monarchy, though the distant king and his agents were long respected. Before the troubles with England the Americans lived virtually without problems of taxation, civil service, armed forces, or foreign policy. There were no craft gilds or other medieval economic survivals. The Americans had no developed capitalism, as in Europe, no banks, no corporations or trading companies, no great wealth, and no extreme poverty. The exceptions were the Negro slaves, who were numerous in the South but played no political role (except to give importance to their owners) and whose very existence accentuated the difference between the two continents. There were no large cities and no significant network of roads. There were a handful of small colleges but no universities; and although many Americans, such as Franklin, Adams, and Jefferson, were well read and well informed, there was in truth no intellectual class. Almost no books were written in America; the book trade was part of the import trade from England. There was as yet hardly any distinctive national culture or political unity. How could such a country give lessons to Europe, or even share in European ideas?

The answer, of course, is that for many revolutionary developments in Europe, America offered no parallel. It is obvious that the French Revolution was a vaster and more profound social upheaval, involving more violent conflict between classes, more radical reorganization of government and society, more far-reaching redefinition of marriage, property, and civil law as well as of organs of public authority, more redistribution of wealth and income, more fears on the part of the rich and more demands from the poor, more sensational repercussions in other countries, more crises of counterrevolution, war, and invasion, and more drastic or emergency measures, as in the Reign of Terror. From very early in the French Revolution the American Revolution came to seem very moderate. Thomas Jefferson, who was then in France, feared that the French were going to dangerous extremes as early as June 1789. For the advanced democratic leaders of France and Europe, from 1789 or 1793 down through the nineteenth century, the Americans seemed "Girondist" or "federalist." They failed to see the need of a powerful, enterprising, centralized, unitary, democratic state as a means not only of carrying on war but of reducing inequalities against strong opposition. Only in our own time, as the federal government intervenes locally, to protect the rights of Negroes, or to assure more equality in such matters as schools and highways, are Americans learning what has long been known to Europeans.

Yet the parallels between the American and European revolutions, as already indicated, remain. Apart from the fact of rebellion itself against an older authority, the parallels have mostly to do with constitutional principles, and with the essentially ethical goals summed up in the ideas of liberty and equality. At this level there was undeniably a transatlantic ideology common to the revolutionary era of Western civilization. The Americans thought like Europeans because they were transplanted Europeans. Their only culture was an English and European culture, modified and diluted by the experience of living in a new and simpler environment. They drew their ideas from the same sources as Europeans, from their own experience in affairs, from their churches in part, and from Greek and Latin classics read in school, from Cicero and Plutarch, from Livy and Tacitus, and from the modern philosophers of natural law, such as Grotius, Pufendorf, and John Locke. Social conditions, social structures, problems, and grievances were very different on the two sides of the Atlantic. But a political philosophy is not merely the product of specific social conditions, or an instrument devised to meet immediate practical needs. There are many kinds of restraints from which a desire for liberty may arise, and many kinds of inequalities or injustices from which equality may be made an ideal. Different though the circumstances were, the American Revolution could announce a revolutionary program for Europe.

By the same token, the American Revolution has its relevancy to the contemporary anticolonialist movements, despite immense differences in circumstances, not only between the United States today and the ex-colonial countries, but between the Thirteen Colonies of 1776 and the British, French, Dutch, and Portuguese "colonies" in Asia and Africa of some twenty-odd years ago. These differences are very great, and involve first of all a difference of meaning in the word "colony" itself. "Colony" in recent usage has meant no more than a "possession." The colonies which became the United States were colonies in the classical and Latin sense, new communities established by the migration and settlement of persons from a mother country, with which they shared the same language, culture, inheritance, and race. In this respect, the parallel of the American Revolution might be to the Europeans in Algeria before its independence, or to the white population in Rhodesia today. The white Rhodesians, in fact, in their unilateral assertion of independence of 1965, adopted some of the language of the American Declaration of Independence, though carefully avoiding any reference to human equality. There is actually no significant parallel here. In the American colonies of the eighteenth century the whites were not newcomers among a much larger indigenous population. The native Indian population of eastern North America had always been very sparse. The attitude of the white population to these Indians may be called ruthless, but the two million whites in the Thirteen Colonies in 1776 probably outnumbered the aborigines by some magnitude such as ten or twenty to one. There were also the Negroes, some half million in number, almost all slaves. Like the whites, they were immigrants or the descendants of immigrants. Deprived of their African culture by the slave trade and by the daily experience of enslavement, and not yet sharing significantly in the European culture of the whites, they formed a large passive element in the population. Neither slavery nor racial questions were ever at issue between Britain and America at the time of the Revolution, as they might have been if the white Americans had rebelled a half-century later. It may be noted in passing that many white Americans were already uneasy about the enslavement of Africans and that they suppressed the question in order to maintain unity among themselves. It was not the Americans, but the French, at the height of their own revolution in 1794, who were the first to abolish slavery. In this respect, as in others, the French Revolution went further than the American in equalitarian and humanitarian principles, though it was easier for the French to abolish slavery, which existed only in their colonies, than it would have been for the Americans to do so in their own country.

The point is that for practical purposes, at the time of the American Revolution, the Americans meant the white Americans of European and mainly English descent, and that these ex-Europeans, unlike those of Rhodesia, South Africa, or Algeria today, were far from being a minority in their own country. But of course by the anticolonial revolution today we mean the movements of the black Africans of Africa, the Arabs of North Africa, the peoples of Asia and the former Dutch East Indies and the technically independent republics of Latin America, especially those in which the aboriginal or non-European element is very large. How does this modern "anticolonialism" compare with the American Revolution?

Certainly the differences are obvious and considerable. For one thing, it is not clear how many such anticolonial revolutions, in a strict sense, there have ever been. Algeria is a special case, Mexico has had a real revolution, and Cuba entertains a revolutionary ideology. On the whole, however, and with exceptions as in Vietnam, the British, French, and Dutch liquidated their empires without waiting for revolution, and not many Africans or Asians have actually had the American experience of rebellion and war to obtain their political independence.

In any case, the problems are different. In the Afro-Asian-Latin American world the problems are poverty, overpopulation, economic underdevelopment, and exploitation by foreign capital or the forces of a world market. There are difficulties of language and communication, and a lack of trained personnel for positions in government and the economy. There is the cultural problem posed by Western civilization—is this foreign culture to be rejected, resisted, made use of, or imitated? And there is the racial problem, inflamed by the humiliation of having been condescended to, segregated, or ostracized by a white ruling class.

On these matters, parallels to the American Revolution are shadowy or nonexistent. The Thirteen Colonies did not suffer from poverty. The average American at that time probably enjoyed better food, lodging, and conditions of work than the average European. There was no overpopulation; quite the reverse. Though the British colonial system was operated for British commercial and strategic advantage, and though Americans had begun to chafe at certain restrictions, the Thirteen Colonies had not been exploited. The Americans had always enjoyed a large measure of genuine self-government, and could draw on their own political experience after independence. The Thirteen Colonies were economically undeveloped, though in some cases they rivaled England itself, as in fisheries and ship-building; but in any event they had the means of rapid develop-ment in their human and natural resources and in their institu-tional setting, a development aided in the generations following the Revolution by the continuing investment of British capital and influx of European immigration, which brought skilled labor and professional talents to the new country. This influx was made possible by the racial and cultural affinity between white Americans and Europeans. For Americans, Europe with its older and richer civilization, and more elaborate social classes, might pose a psychological problem. Americans might at times suffer from an "inferiority complex" toward Europe, or complain of European condescension. But there was hardly the same social distance as for Asians or Africans. America was the daughter of Europe, never its slave girl or its captive.

Given such differences, what can be the parallels? What rele-vancy can the American Revolution have for non-Europeans and for the anticolonial movements of the twentieth century? Per-haps it might be wise to give up the very idea that there are any such parallels or resemblances. Americans today might have a more realistic view of the world, and more real sympathy, under-standing, and tolerance for other peoples, if they expected no resemblance whatsoever to the American pattern. Perhaps, for some peoples in Africa, the revolution of the 1790's in Haiti offers a more significant precedent than the revolution which produced the United States. At that time the blacks of the French colony of San Domingo, in conjunction with the French Revolution, established the second oldest independent republic in the Americas. But the subsequent history of Haiti was very troubled, and the precedent would be a discouraging one, except for the fact that the Africans of today are more advanced than the slaves of eighteenth-century San Domingo, and enjoy far more support from the white man's world than the blacks of Haiti ever obtained.

Yet, in conclusion, something can be said for resemblances between the American Revolution and the twentieth-century anticolonial revolutionary upheavals. The independence of the United States did signify, after all, the first case of breakup of a European empire. It set a precedent for the act of rebellion; it showed men fighting, living dangerously, and dying for their rights. The Americans, after their independence was recognized, were the first "new nation" in a certain modern sense of the word, and they faced the problems of a new nation. Emerging from the old British Empire, they soon embarked on a successful economic development. They also had to establish their national unity and identity, and they did so with difficulty, for in the early years of the federal constitution it seemed that the country might fall apart into separate fragments, and all compromises broke down in the great Civil War of 1861. If formal unity was thereafter restored, it was at the expense of the Negroes; but as all the world knows, the movement for Negro rights has been renewed in recent years, and the Americans, in attempting to create an interracial society, are still at work on a problem of national unity of a kind, in general, which other "new nations" also face.

But it is at the highest level, that of abstract ideas, that the American Revolution has something to say to the anticolonialists of the twentieth century, as to European revolutionaries at the time of the great revolution in France. The Americans justified their independence by the grandeur and universality of a revolutionary message. The idea that peoples should choose their own government, and determine the forms and powers of this government by constituent assemblies, is not yet exhausted. The old eighteenth-century "rights of man," though much criticized by philosophers from that day to this, and now known more tamely as "human rights," are still very much alive. As a matter of fact, a more lucid and balanced statement of these rights was given in the French Declaration of the Rights of Man and Citizen of 1789. Some of the first American state constitutions likewise expressed the idea in more definite form. But for the belief that all men are "created equal," and have an equal right to life, liberty, and the pursuit of happiness, whose protection is the function of good government, we still turn, with good reason, to the American Declaration of Independence.

BIBLIOGRAPHY

The place of the American Revolution within the general revolutionary movement of the eighteenth century may be seen in more detail in my *Age of the Democratic Revolution: A Political History of Europe and America, 1760–1800* (2 vols.; Princeton, 1959, 1964). See especially Vol. I, Chapters 7 through 9, and the various places in Vol. II for which indications are assembled in Vol. II, p. 523, n. 13. The conception of an eighteenth-century revolution involving both America and Europe is developed also by Jacques Godechot, *France and the Atlantic Revolution of the Eighteenth Century,* trans. Herbert Rowen (New York, 1965). Arguments by various scholars for and against the validity of this conception are provided in a student's manual, ed., Peter Amann, *The Eighteenth-Century Revolution, French or Western?* (Boston, 1963).

For the impact of the American Revolution in France, see Durand Echeverria, *Mirage in the West: A History of the French Image of American Society to 1815* (Princeton, 1957). Jefferson's conservatism toward events of 1789 in France is examined in my article, "The Dubious Democrat: Thomas Jefferson in Bourbon France," *Political Science Quarterly* LXXII (Sept. 1957), 388–404. The fact that in America the urban and merchant classes opposed the French Revolution, which similar classes in France generally favored, and that in America it was the agrarians who favored the French Revolution, which agrarians in Europe generally opposed, is developed in my essay, "The Great Inversion: America and Europe in the Eighteenth-Century Revolution," in Richard Herr (ed.), *Ideas in History: Essays Presented to Louis R. Gottschalk* (Durham, N.C., 1965). The comparative relationship of the American Revolution to modern anticolonialist revolutionary movements is explored by the sociologist, Seymour Martin Lipset, in *The First New Nation: The United States in Historical and Comparative Perspective* (New York, 1963), an important and widely ranging book, in which the net effect is to stress the resemblances at a fundamental level rather than the differences.

My reference to Friedrich von Gentz is to his *The Origin and Principles of the American Revolution, Compared with the Origin and Principles of the French Revolution,* first published at Berlin in Gentz's *Historisches Journal* in 1799, then in English at Philadelphia in 1800. It was reprinted with an introduction by Russell Kirk (Chicago, 1955). For Barruel see his *Memoires pour servir à l'histoire du jacobinisme*

(5 vols.; Hamburg, 1798–1799), or its English translation of the same date (London), and my *Age of the Democratic Revolution,* Vol. II, pp. 251–55. The reference to a recent study of the American state legislatures before and after the Revolution is to Jackson T. Main, "Government by the People: The American Revolution and the Democratization of the Legislatures," *William and Mary Quarterly* 3rd. series, XXIII (July 1966), 391–407. The literature on the American Revolution, general and monographic, is of course too abundant for comment.

The "Newness" of
the New Nation

SEYMOUR MARTIN LIPSET

One of the most fruitful comparative approaches to American history has been one that emphasizes the ways in which the conditions facing new societies, new nations, and new or open frontiers have affected subsequent developments. I want to point to some of the ways in which such perspectives have enriched our understanding of American society.

In recent years, a number of studies have sought to specify the conditions facing the contemporary new nations of Asia and Africa which seek to establish legitimacy, to find a basis for national linguistic and value consensus so as to have a stable national society which does not rest on force, or which will not come apart during the strains of major crises. Some studies concerned with these issues have included the early United States in the category of new states and have sought to re-examine early post-Revolutionary history in the context of such concerns. The United States may properly claim the title of the "first new nation" because it was the first major overseas colony successfully to break away from European imperial rule.

Concern with the social requisites of new nationhood has inspired the work of some historians, such as Robert Lamb and

Richard Merritt, in dealing with colonial America. Both recognized that the creation of a new nation, or even united colonies in rebellion, required, as Lamb put it, a new *national* elite, the members of which had to be in communication with one another, and which had a consciousness of kind. Lamb traced through the interconnections that emerged in personal, family, and business ties among members of the elite in Virginia, Pennsylvania, New York, and Massachusetts. Merritt has shown that a national consciousness emerged before the Revolution through his analysis of the symbols in the colonial press, which showed a steady increase in the use of the term "Americans" to refer to the colonists. Both studies, it should be noted, were consciously concerned with general processes of national development. Thus Lamb addressed himself to "those interested in the role of elites in the formation of new nation-states," and Merritt suggested that "the evidence provided by the American experience is useful in testing current ideas about nation-building . . ."

The approach to American history that seeks to fit the United States into the rubric of new nations, and to formulate or elaborate propositions about the conditions for nationhood from its experience, has been challenged by other historians who argue that the American Revolution did not establish a new nation in the contemporary sense of the term, since it was led by the established elites of the colonies, essentially transplanted Englishmen, who had political rights and power before the Revolution.

Louis Hartz, one of those who argue that the Revolution basically represented more continuity than discontinuity in ideas and institutions, has urged that the appropriate comparison is not with the new states but with the various nations that have been formed from overseas societies settled by Europeans—the nations of the Americas, Australasia, and South Africa. Hartz has introduced the concept of the "fragment" society to refer to such cultures, since they were formed by immigrant groups that constituted fragments of the mother culture. Despite all their variations, these societies represent for Hartz a common body of experience in being "fragments" of Europe which developed differently from the mother societies since they did not embody the European "whole." Many important European values and institutions, usually associated with the privileged strata, never reached the "new societies." Each left behind in Europe an ancient source of conservative ideology in the form of the traditional class structure. Hence Enlightenment doctrines could predominate.

In applying this approach to the United States, Hartz contends that the American national ethos which embodies liberal Enlightenment doctrines is derivative from its origin as a fragment culture, a new society, which never had a conservative elite-dominated social structure. For him, the Revolution was a relatively moderate event sociologically. It was not a basic source of the American value and institutional system, and hence did not raise problems comparable to those faced by modern-day new states. In line with this thesis, the chapter on Canada (written by Kenneth McRae) in his book treats English Canada as a liberal Enlightenment society, not very different from the United States. The varying political experiences of the two North American nations that emerged out of the two sides in the Revolution did not differentiate them socially and ideologically, since, according to Hartz, they shared the common experience of never having had an aristocracy.

This issue of evaluating the relative significance of the Revolution and new nationhood may be faced by comparing American experiences with other Enlightenment, late-eighteenth-century revolutions in Europe, and with Canada. Robert Palmer in his treatment of the late-eighteenth-century revolutions presents a striking contrast to Hartz in his assumption that the American Revolution was a major dynamic event which greatly changed the course of American society, its social structure and values. He has attempted to trace strong similarities among the American and European revolutions.

To a considerable degree, issues such as these often involve evaluating the same fact as meaning "as much as" or "as little as." Comparative analysis sometimes permits us to place a given result in contrast with a comparable event elsewhere. For example, if we accept the French Revolution as a standard for a "real revolution," then the fact that there "were twenty-four émigrés per thousand of population in the American Revolution, and only five émigrés per thousand of population in the French

Revolution," suggests, as Palmer says, that "there was a real revolution in America." For those who argue that it was easier to emigrate from the United States than from France, Palmer has a second standard of comparison, the compensation paid for confiscation of property by the British government and the French Bourbon Restoration. The sums were similar, holding population size constant.

Hartz also compares the American and French Revolutions to evidence his opposite thesis that the American Revolution had *relatively* little effect. He points out that contemporary American conservatives hail the Revolutionary heroes, while in France "the royalist still curses the Jacobin." Palmer would reply (in fact the two ignore each other in print) that the French émigrés returned to their native land after the Restoration while the Americans never did, that this fact made for great differences between the two countries, since the American loyalists, unlike the French royalists, are forgotten. "The sense in which there was no conflict in the American Revolution is the sense in which the loyalists are forgotten," writes Palmer. "The 'American consensus' rests in some degree on the elimination from the national consciousness, as well as from the country, of a once important and relatively numerous element of dissent."

More directly to the issue of the relevance of the concept of new nationhood to the analysis of American development have been the efforts to account for structural differences between Canada and the United States by means of comparative historical analysis. A number of Canadian scholars, such as S. D. Clark, Frank Underhill, and A. R. M. Lower, have suggested that Canada has been a more conservative or traditional country culturally because it is a nation which emerged out of a successful "counterrevolution," whereas the United States has been more liberal, more egalitarian, more universalistic in its orientations as a result of processes stemming from its successful "revolution." They point to the fact that two nations emerged out of the American Revolution, the United States *and* Canada. And if one looks at developments north of the American border after 1783, it is clear that the success or failure of the Revolution had major consequences on the core national values which informed behavior, on the nature of class relations, on the spread of education, on the type of religious organization, and the like. In each case, Canada has sustained a more conservative pattern showing greater respect for authority and law and order, greater emphasis on elitism and hierarchy, more conservative religious behavior, and a lower level of economic development. Canadians writing on these topics have tried to show that the maritime provinces of Canada, which before 1783 were essentially part of New England, fostered traits endemic in the Tory image of society, while the new United States extended many of the egalitarian and universalistic emphases which were inherent in the dogmas proclaimed in the Declaration of Independence.

According to this interpretation, the two traditions, revolutionary in the United States and counterrevolutionary in Canada, have had continuing influence. Thus Clark points to the fact that the failure of the effort to annex Canada to the United States in the War of 1812 represented a second defeat for the democratic or revolutionary forces in Canada. The frontier farmers, there, were pro-American. And this defeat unleashed a second series of internal events which reinforced the conservative values and institutions in Canada. Again, during the Jacksonian period in the United States, Canada had its Mackenzie-Papeneau rebellions which were defeated. The achievement of Canadian independence occurred in 1867, not as a result of a triumphant democratic movement, but rather under the leadership of the Canadian Empire-oriented Conservatives. It reflected Britain's desire to reduce her overseas commitments.

Subsequent American reform movements such as Populism and Progressivism had their parallels in Canada, but in the north they had much less effect on the national ethos and values. And the period which witnessed the American reformist left hailing the triumph of the New Deal found his Canadian compeer resorting to the creation of a third party (now called the New Democratic party), which has remained small. To preserve a national *raison d'être*, Canadians have been forced to denigrate the egalitarian American democracy, to hold up as a positive model various aspects of the more elitist British society. Thus S. D. Clark and Frank Underhill have argued that while the predominant political tradition in the United States has been a leftist and populist one, Canadians live in a country which has had to justify its refusal to join the American Revolution and praise the values of political moderation, cultural conservatism, and respect for authority. And various Canadians have interpreted comparative trends in Canadian literature, in education (far fewer Canadians attend university than Americans), in the family (lower divorce rate), in attitudes toward law and order (lower crime rate), toward elites (greater respect), and religion (less sectarian innovation), as derivative in large part of the differences in the political events forming the two nations.

The United States shares with many of the present-day new nations a national identity which is linked to revolutionary, egalitarian, anti-imperialist ideas. Most struggles for independence have employed leftist ideologies, that of equality in revolutionary America, that of socialism in many of the new states. The political tendencies identified with conservative values have been considerably weakened as a result. The franchise is to be extended to everyone, the people being regarded as the source of power and authority. The efforts of conservatives to resist the linkage between national identity and left-wing values have failed in most of these societies. In the United States, the early end of the Federalist party meant that all American political parties were to be egalitarian in overt ideology.

Comparisons with developments in the emerging nations of Asia and Africa point to a number of other similarities with the early United States. Like latter-day new nations, the new American polity was unstable because it lacked traditional legitimacy (a built-in title to rule stemming from historical continuity). In the first three quarters of a century of American existence as a nation, it was uncertain as to whether the complex balance of forces would swing in the direction of an institutionalized opposition party system, or even whether the states would remain together. It took time to institutionalize values, beliefs, and practices, and there were many incidents that revealed how fragile were the commitments to democracy and nationhood, as Arthur Schlesinger, Sr., has pointed out. Almost every group in America threatened at one time or another to secede when faced with the possibility of defeat. There were major plots to prevent the duly elected from taking office, the passing of laws that gave the party in power the right to persecute its political opponents, and virtual one-party rule for some decades.

Among the strong similarities is the extent to which many of the new nations have relied on some version of charismatic legitimacy to secure loyalty to the new regime. They have erected cults of personality which attribute heroic qualities to the national leader. Charismatic justification for authority may be seen as a mechanism of transition, an interim measure, in which the hero helps bridge the gap to legal-rational legitimacy, acceptance of the rules of the game. There is considerable evidence to indicate that George Washington played such a role in the early United States. We tend to forget today that George Washington was idolized in much the same terms as various leaders of contemporary new states.

It may be argued that Washington was more successful in his conscious effort to give the country time to establish a legal-rational system of legitimacy, because, unlike many of the latter-day leaders of new states, he refused to act out his charisma to its full potential. He not only resisted efforts to make him a king, but, perhaps as important, he abstained from imposing his will on conflicts among other leaders, and withdrew from the presidency while in seeming good health, thus permitting the first succession conflict to occur while he was present to legitimate the precedent of peaceful turnover of office to an elected successor. This particular halfway type of charismatic leadership probably had a critical stabilizing effect on American political development.

The parallels which some writers have drawn between the experiences of the United States as a new nation and those of contemporary states are not meant to imply that those states will have comparable histories. It is fairly obvious that conditions in the early United States were quite different in many ways, that it faced a much simpler set of problems and had more resources to deal with them than do the new states of Africa and Asia. In particular, the weight of ancient traditions and institutions antithetical to a modern economy and polity which is present in almost all the contemporary new states was largely absent in early America. As Hartz has stressed, it was not only a new nation, it was a new society, far less bound to customs and values of the past which serve to inhibit economic development than any of the present-day new nations. In fact, America's most important "traditional" institution, religion, far from inhibiting economic growth, helped in its Calvinist and Armenian forms to facilitate positive orientations toward saving and hard work. Political traditions, also, were conducive to establishing a stable regime, since the common traditions of the American colonists included the concept of the rule of law and even of constitutionalism.

The thesis that aspects inherent in being a "new society" contributed to various characteristics of American society has been long argued in the form of the frontier hypothesis. Frederick Jackson Turner and others have suggested that the key aspect to understanding American society has been the way in which the experience of colonizing an open frontier resulted in individualism, egalitarianism, and strong political participation.

This approach also calls for elaboration in a comparative context, since there are a number of other pioneer settlement countries. Students of the Australian frontier, for example, have pointed to the fact that the frontier experience of the Australians was quite different from that of both North American countries. In America, each individual attempted to find his own plot of land. The Australian agricultural frontier, on the other hand, was much less hospitable in terms of climate, and family agriculture was less practicable. Many of the Australian frontier enterprises involved large-scale cattle and sheep grazing, both of which required considerable capital if the enterprise was to be worthwhile. According to Russell Ward, "The typical Australian frontiersman in the last century was a wage-worker who did not usually expect to become anything else."

There are, of course, other differences which have been suggested to account for the varying nature and influences of the Australian and American frontiers. Thus the absence of strong aboriginal resistance in Australia as compared with the Indian wars in the United States may have weakened the need for strong local community life in Australia. And the frontier, regardless of the institutions and values which it fostered, necessarily had much less impact on Australia than it did on the United States, since the relative size of the frontier population as compared to the urban one was much smaller in Australia because of geographic factors.

Although frontier geographic conditions in the two North American states were quite comparable, these frontiers also differed greatly, in large part for reasons derivative of their varying political histories discussed above. Inasmuch as Canada had to be on constant guard against the expansionist tendencies of the United States, it could not leave its frontier communities unprotected or autonomous. As Edgar McInnis has indicated, "It was the established tradition of British North America that the power of the civil authority should operate well in advance of the spread of settlement." Law and order in the form of the centrally controlled Northwest Mounted Police moved into the frontier before and along with the settlers. This contributed to the establishment of a much stronger tradition of respect for the institutions of law and order on the Canadian frontier as compared with the American.

The pervasiveness of government legal controls on the Canadian frontier seriously weakened the development of an excessive emphasis on individualism which characterizes the United States. There has been no particular glorification of the frontiersman in Canadian writing as there has been in the United States.

An effort to explain why Brazil, the largest, most populous, and most richly endowed of the Latin American states has developed so much more poorly economically than the United States also emphasizes the varying nature of frontier settlement in the Americas. Vianna Moog points to the differences between "bandeirantes" and "pioneers" as a key source of the varying patterns of development in his native Brazil and in the United States. As Adolf Berle summarizes his thesis:

> "Bandeirantes" ("flag-bearers") were the explorers and settlers of the interior of Brazil, as "pioneers" were the conquerors and colonizers of the great unoccupied heartland of the United States. The difference lies in their motives and ideals. The Brazilian bandeirantes were perhaps the last wave of colonial conquistadores. The American pioneers, though of all kinds, were predominantly Reformation settlers. The resulting civilizations set up by the two groups of wilderness-conquerors were therefore quite different, despite many elements common to both.

Moog relates the varying nature of the Brazilian and United States frontiers to the fact that for three centuries in Brazil the main motive for going to the frontier was to get rich quickly, to find gold or other precious minerals, that labor, whether in urban or rural occupations, was denigrated as fit only for slaves; while the English and later American settlers looked for new homes based on their own work. These differences are linked to varying cultural traits and motives for seeking new opportunity on the frontier. In Brazil the bandeirante is credited with the geographic enlargement of the country, much as the pioneer is in the United States. Moog points out that "In the United States a thing, to be capable of arousing enthusiasm, must bear the label of pioneer; in Brazil . . . it must merit the epithet of *bandeirante*."

The history of Argentina offers yet another example of the way in which the social structure of an American frontier was determined by the predominant structure and values established in colonial times. Values and structures endemic in the settlement of an open frontier did not either serve to influence the social organization of the rural community or help shape a national democratic outlook. Argentine agriculture developed in a way much like that of Australia, with large cattle and sheep ranches which used many workers either as hired help or as tenants, and preserved a hierarchical status system. Various efforts to encourage small landholding, after independence, failed because of the power of the large landowners. And subsequently, in the latter part of the nineteenth century, it proved to be impossible to apply meaningful homestead legislation to Argentina, although there was a general belief among Argentine experts that United States prosperity and development were attributable to its policy of encouraging land settlement in the form of family homesteads. The Argentine pampas, which closely resembled the prairies of the United States and Canada, remained in the hands of a small class of large landowners. According to James Scobie, "Churches, schools, and clubs did not develop in rural Argentina for the simple reason that settlement was dispersed and often temporary." And as in Australia, the urban centers, particularly Buenos Aires, became the focus for immigrant settlement. "Rather than a frontier, Argentina had a city."

A comparative approach to the way in which the various "new" aspects of American development, as society, as state, and as frontier, affected subsequent development clearly cannot resolve conflicting interpretations about causal processes. It does, however, add significantly to the kinds of data which historians and other social scientists can use to test out and elaborate their hypothesis. Clearly, any interpretation which rests on assumptions that certain factors played a key role in determining a particular result is limited if the analyst cannot point to alternative consequences when the variables are absent. Although the plethora of differences between nations prevents us from making any conclusive statement that any one difference has been crucial in accounting for other variations, pointing up such differences does help. To compare the American and French revolutions helps to explain much about each; similarly, the understanding of United States and Canadian history is sharply enriched by dealing with both. The concern with the conditions which affect developments in contemporary new states has already led a number of historians to ask new questions about old and familiar aspects of the American past.

Although much comparative research remains to be done, it seems already clear that a considerable part of the success of the early United States as a developing society lay in the fact that it was a "fragment culture" which became a new nation and possessed an open settler frontier. Each of these elements has been present in other nations; no other one has combined all three.

BIBLIOGRAPHY

Since this essay touches on themes which are dealt with more elaborately in the chapters by R. R. Palmer and Ray Billington on the Revolution and the frontier, it should be noted that much of their bibliography is relevant here as well.

Concern with the role of the United States as a new or fragment society has been laid down by Louis Hartz, *The Founding of New Societies* (New York, 1964). Relevant treatments of the Revolution in comparative perspective are R. R. Palmer, *The Age of the Democratic*

Revolution: The Challenge (Princeton, 1959), and Crane Brinton, *The Anatomy of Revolution* (New York, 1938).

A number of works treat the United States as a new nation in the sense in which this term is used for the new nations of Africa and Asia. These include various writings of Robert Lamb, such as his "Entrepreneurship in the Community," *Explorations in Entrepreneurial History* (March 1950), pp. 114–127; "The Entrepreneur and the Community," in William Miller (ed.), *Men in Business* (Cambridge, Mass., 1952), pp. 91–119; and a "Memorandum," in Karl W. Deutsch, *Nationalism and Social Communication* (New York, 1953), pp. 18–20. In this last-named book, Deutsch also treats the conditions for the emergence of integrated nationhood in comparative perspective. Together with a group of historians, Deutsch, a political scientist, has analyzed the conditions which made for successful efforts to create new confederations out of previously separate units in the early United States and a number of other countries, in Karl W. Deutsch *et al.*, *Political Community and the North Atlantic Area* (Princeton, 1957). Richard Merritt, *Symbols of American Community, 1735–1775* (New Haven, 1966), seeks to analyze the emergence of national consciousness as a condition for new nationhood.

Two books which attempt to treat in detail comparable processes in the early United States and the contemporary new nations are William N. Chambers, *Political Parties in a New Nation, 1776–1809* (New York, 1963), and Seymour Martin Lipset, *The First New Nation: The United States in Historical and Comparative Perspective* (New York, 1963). An interesting treatment of the charismatic aspects of Washington's role may be found in Marcus Cunliffe, *George Washington: Man and Monument* (New York, 1958).

A number of books by Canadians point, in a comparative North American context, to differences between the United States and Canada that are related to their different relationship to the Revolution. These include S. D. Clark, *Movements of Political Protest in Canada, 1640–1840* (Toronto, 1959); A. R. M. Lower, *Colony to Nation: A History of Canada* (Toronto, 1946); J. M. S. Careless, *Canada: A Story of Challenge* (Cambridge, England, 1953); Frank Underhill, *In Search of Canadian Liberalism* (Toronto, 1960); S. D. Clark, *The Developing Canadian Community* (Toronto, 1962). I have sought to integrate much of the literature bearing on this topic in my essay, "Revolution and Counter-Revolution—The United States and Canada," in Thomas Ford (ed.), *The Revolutionary Theme in Contemporary America* (Lexington, Ky., 1965), pp. 21–64.

There is an abundant comparative literature on the Turner frontier thesis which is relevant here. Some studies which are particularly pertinent to my discussion are: F. J. Turner, *The Frontier in American History* (New York, 1920); George R. Turner (ed.), *The Turner Thesis* (Boston, 1949); Marvin W. Mikesell, "Comparative Studies in Frontier History," *Annals of the Association of American Geographers,* L (March 1960), 64–74; Walker D. Wyman and Clifton B. Kroeber (eds.), *The Frontier in Perspective* (Madison, Wisc., 1957); Paul F. Sharp, "Three Frontiers: Some Comparative Studies of Canadian, American, and Australian Settlement," *Pacific Historical Review,* XXIV (1955), 369–77; and Herbert Heaton, "Other Wests Than Ours," *Tasks of Economic History,* Suppl. to *Journal of Economic History* (December 1949), pp. 50–62.

On other countries, see Russell Ward, *The Australian Legend* (Melbourne and New York, 1958); Carter Goodrich, "The Australian and American Labor Movements," *The Economic Record,* IV (1928); Brian Fitzpatrick, *The British Empire in Australia, An Economic History;* Frederick Alexander, *Moving Frontiers: An American Theme and Its Application to Australian History* (Melbourne, 1947); G. V. Portus, "Americans and Australians," *The Australian Quarterly,* XIV (June 1942), 30–41; Edgar W. McInnis, *The Unguarded* [Canadian] *Frontier* (Garden City, N.Y., 1942); Claude T. Bissell, "A Common Ancestry: Literature in Australia and Canada," *University of Toronto Quarterly,* XXV (1956), 133–34; John P. Matthews, *Tradition in Exile* (Toronto, 1962); S. D. Clark, *The Developing Canadian Community* (Toronto, 1962); Vianna Moog, *Bandeirantes and Pioneers* (New York, 1964); Charles Wagley, *An Introduction to Brazil* (New York, 1963); James R. Scobie, *Argentina* (New York, 1964).

6

Frontiers

RAY ALLEN BILLINGTON

To the hundreds of visitors from abroad who have recorded their impressions of the United States during the past two centuries, the Americans are a strange and inexplicable people. They are arrogantly nationalistic, and so blindly worshipful of democratic principles that they can recognize virtue in no other governmental system. They demand more economic freedom for the individual than is allotted in most urban-industrial countries. Whatever their wealth or social status, they refuse to recognize the existence of class lines or, if they do, proudly proclaim themselves in the middle class. They are forever moving about, exhibiting none of the attachment to place that lends stability to more mature societies. They are prejudiced against time-tested ways of doing things, preferring to experiment with the new when the old is still usable. They worship at the shrine of the Almighty Dollar, laboring so incessantly that the relaxing leisure enjoyed in other lands is not only avoided but scorned. They are shockingly wasteful, squandering their natural resources with an abandon incomprehensible to more frugal peoples.

That these traits are uniquely American is, of course, untrue; all are exhibited to a degree by the people of other nations. Moreover, national differences between inhabitants of industrialized nations are today rapidly disappearing; everywhere the rate of mobility is accelerating as men drift about from job to job, and everywhere wastefulness, hard work, and an inclination to technological experimentation are increasing as the urge for profits dominates behavioral patterns. But one fact remains clear. These characteristics have for more than two centuries appeared in such exaggerated form in the United States that travelers have branded them as distinctly American. When an Englishman remarks, as many have, that despite the language difference he feels more at home in Paris than Chicago, he reveals that the Americans do think and act differently from their cousins beyond the seas.

These differences are the product of a multitude of factors. The mingling of peoples from many lands has helped to create a distinct culture differing from that of any of the ethnic groups who have contributed to its growth. The relative isolation from the remainder of the world during the nation's formative period stimulated the evolution of unique traits and institutions. So did the lack of an enervating feudal tradition that would serve as a brake on change. Social experimentation also was encouraged by the abundance of natural resources; the high level of prosperity demanded new value judgments and new techniques. But of the many forces helping to create a distinct American culture, none was more important than the existence of a frontier during the three hundred years needed to settle the continent.

Because of that unique experience, the term "frontier" has been endowed with a new meaning in the United States. Suggest the word to a European or Asian or African and you conjure up in his mind a vision of customs barriers, passport controls, and other troublesome hindrances to his freedom of movement. Propose the term to an American and he thinks at once of beckoning opportunity. That frontier was born when the first English settlers carved their homes from the wilderness in the early seventeenth century. Until the end of the nineteenth century it advanced steadily toward the Pacific, and was usually a broad geographic area in which a variety of pioneers applied their separate skills to subdue the wilderness. Some were fur trappers and missionaries roaming far beyond the settled areas; others were cattle herders, miners, small farmers, propertied farmers, and the speculators and merchants who laid out the first villages. They followed no sequential pattern but ranged haphazardly, sometimes led by town planters, sometimes by farmers, sometimes by miners. All were heralds of civilization, and as they marched westward civilization followed in their wake.

Their progress created a distinctive social environment within the frontier belt in which they labored. This resulted from a fortunate combination of men with an unusual degree of ambition and physical conditions uniquely suitable to that ambition's fulfillment. The first settlers helped establish the human phase of this equation; they came from an England in which an emerging capitalistic system and a relative degree of economic, religious, and political freedom whetted the appetite of individuals for self-betterment. On the successive frontiers they found a physical environment that furthered these ambitions, for there land was cheaper and labor dearer than in settled communities. Almost for the asking, pioneers could secure virgin fields for farming, lush grasslands for pasturage, and prospective fortunes in mineral and forest wealth. These attainable riches stimulated the urge for progress to a unique degree. With property easily obtainable, and with a fluid social order that placed few barriers before individuals eager to ascend the social pyramid, the ambitious found their ambitions heightened as they could not be in solidified societies where property was already distributed and class lines firmly drawn. The dominating impulse of the frontier social environment was individual self-betterment.

I

The combination of ingredients generating this impulse was virtually unique. Other among today's nations experienced a frontier past; Latin America, Canada, Australia, and Siberia were settled during a period roughly comparable to that of American expansion. Yet in no one of them was the physical environment conducive to exploitation by relatively propertyless individuals *and* the invading pioneers equipped by tradition to capitalize fully on that environment.

In Latin America dense jungles, semiarid plateaus, and rugged mountains rigidly restricted the areas suitable to individual conquest; only on the pampas of southern Argentina and the plains of Brazil did pioneers find a temperate climate, navigable rivers, and arable soils to encourage the lone farmer or herdsman. Expansion over a vast area through repeated pioneering was impossible. Nor were the people equipped to react to the opportunity for self-betterment as were Englishmen in North America. The settlers who peopled New Spain and New Portugal in the fifteenth and sixteenth centuries imported cultural habits reminiscent of the medieval rather than of the modern age. In Spain an absolute monarchy had recently imposed its authority over feudal orders, capitalism was in its infancy, church and state were united under an autocratic ruler, and a militant nationalism prevailed in the wake of the expulsion of the Moors. This authoritarian system was transplanted to the New World in only slightly altered form. Powerful viceroys curbed political freedom, the semifeudal *mita* and *encomienda* restructured economic activity, and a rigid mercantile system hindered the flow of commerce. In this social climate the explosive urge of individuals to better themselves was never allowed expression. The agents of expansion in Latin America were not opportunity-seeking pioneers as in the United States, but government-supported conquistadores in New Spain and community-minded bandeirantes in New Portugal. Nowhere did the reaction of men and nature generate a social environment that would stimulate the urge for self-improvement among individuals.

In Canada and Australia, by contrast, the first settlers came from nations well advanced in modern concepts of capitalism and middle-class values, but physical conditions precluded the emergence of a frontier spirit identical with that of the United States. In Australia frontiersmen during the 1850's and 1860's pushed through gaps in the coastal mountains as had American pioneers through the Appalachians nearly a century before; but instead of finding the rich plains of a Mississippi Valley, they encountered semiarid lands and uninhabitable deserts. With the pioneer pastoralist driven back by lack of water for farming, the continent's interior remained either unsettled or the province of wealthy capitalists whose resources could support the large-scale sheep-herding operations that alone were profitable there.

In Canada frontier expansion was blocked by the Laurentian Shield, a tangled mass of brush-covered hills and sterile soils that deflected migrants southward into the United States. Not until railroads penetrated this barrier in the later nineteenth century could settlers reach the lush lands of the prairie provinces; those who did so came directly from the East and brought with them established practices that had not been loosened by a recurring pioneering experience.

Only in eastern Canada during the seventeenth century and in Russian Siberia during the nineteenth did pioneers find a physical environment comparable to that of the United States. In each instance, however, the newcomers were so restrained by absolute rulers and tyrannical traditions that they were incapable of developing the "go-ahead" spirit that thrived on the American frontier. The pioneers of New France who occupied the St. Lawrence River Valley came from a land where feudal customs prevailed and all freedom was rigidly restrained; those of Siberia from a country where autocratic czars ruled unchecked and serfdom was a thing of the recent past. Yet so persuasive was the opportunity for self-advancement amid the unspoiled riches of the St. Lawrence Valley and the Siberian plains that institutional modifications resembling those on the American frontier occurred. Thus in New France church authorities were forced to modify the tithing system in order to check the flow of dissatisfied parishioners into the forests, while civil rulers virtually abandoned the *corvée* as a seignioral device to restrict freedom of movement among peasants. At the same time local authority was largely shifted from the governor or seignior to militia captains approved by the people. Among the five million peasants who migrated to Siberia between 1861 and 1914 a comparable transformation occurred when bettered economic opportunity there allowed the accumulation of landholdings roughly four times larger than those in Russia. Not only did they incline to innovate as they adjusted their customs to these larger farms, but they showed a tendency toward self-reliance and independence that cast fear into the hearts of their rulers. By 1910 a Russian prime minister could complain that frontier-like opportunity in Siberia had created an "enormous, rudely democratic country, which will soon throttle European Russia."

These halting steps toward self-rule and economic freedom in Siberia and French Canada underlined the gulf that separated American frontiersmen from their counterparts in other times and places. Elsewhere neither physical conditions nor cultural traditions were properly combined to create the same social environment that existed in the successive American Wests. Only in the United States did the frontiering experience, repeatedly operating as it did on individuals peculiarly susceptible to its influence, generate an atmosphere capable of altering popular traits and institutions. Only there was the urge for self-betterment elevated as a major motivating force in the lives of the pioneers.

II

Among these alterations, none was more important than the changed interpretation of democracy as it was practiced on the frontier. Frontiersman took naturally to self-rule, partly because aristocratic practices seemed outmoded in a land where the ambitious could readily acquire the possessions that stood for privilege in older societies, partly because a plastic social order allowed the humble to rise to posts of influence, partly because the unique problems faced in pioneering seemed to require local solutions. But the frontiersmen added something more; they wanted elected officials who would be of, not above, the people. Their wish, as one of them put it, was for leaders who "ain't too darn'd proud to shake hands with a poor man." This did not mean that ill-trained demagogues captured control in the successive Wests; men's instinct is to elevate those of proven ability to leadership posts, and this habit was too strong to be broken. Instead, the frontiersmen transplanted authority from a hereditary aristocracy to what one called a "natural aristocracy." Men entrusted with office were successful farmers, merchants, or lawyers who knew the wishes and could speak the language of their constituents. This shift symbolized the manner in which pioneers sought to reward the worthy who had proven themselves by earning economic and social success. The self-made man deserved a leadership post in a land where equality of opportunity, not proper lineage, allowed an individual to demonstrate his merits.

The frontier experience also helped redefine the theory and practice of social democracy in the United States, for in the successive Wests two basic concepts took on new meaning. One was "individualism." Seemingly the frontier was ill-suited for the individualist; group conformity and cooperation was essential there for defense, home-building, harvesting, and multitudinous other tasks. Yet while the pioneers were applying the principle of association in their daily lives, they were developing the philosophy of individualism in its peculiarly American sense. This held that property rights were immune from governmental or public control. Such a philosophy emerged naturally in a land where private property was easy to acquire; where every person was a potential capitalist, property assumed a new importance, even to the propertyless. "Here," wrote a visitor to the West, "a man looks upon the wealth of others as held in trust for himself, and will suffer no diminution of its sanctity." Westerners, even more than Easterners, were insistent on the right of every person to acquire possessions, and to use them as he pleased. Their beliefs have persisted in the United States; today the American is a social conformist, but he resists governmental meddling with his business affairs more persistently than his counterpart in other industrialized nations.

A second ingredient of frontier social democracy was faith in the equality of all men (excluding, unfortunately, Negroes and the red Indians and Mexicans who disputed Anglo-American advance westward). This faith, mounting almost to a passion, was universally noted by every visitor to the frontier. All recorded the prevalence of a self-assured "I'm as good as you are" spirit wherever they went. Only an American frontiersman, one wrote, could:

> Enter a palace with his old felt hat on—
> To address the King with the title of Mister,
> And ask the price of the throne he sat on.

These attitudes came naturally in a land where self-betterment was a fact of life, and where the most humble could rise to affluence by the turn of a shovel or a fortunate speculation. An underdog who would someday be a millionaire saw no reason to be servile to his temporary betters. Wrote an English traveler from the Kentucky frontier in 1819: "The clumsy gait and bent body of our peasant is hardly ever seen here; every man walks erect and easy." In the West every man was a "gentleman" and every woman a "lady," whatever their lineage. "It's what's above ground, not what's under, that we think on," wrote one pioneer.

Belief in equality was carried to fantastic extremes. Any form of ostentation was frowned upon and sometimes forcefully resented. One British traveler on the Mississippi Valley frontier had his ornate brass buttons rudely ripped from his coat, while a pioneer housewife who put on airs was told by a neighbor who had waited three years to call: "I woulda come before but I heard you had a Brussels carpet on the floor." Servants in the traditional sense were unknown in such an atmosphere; even the term was obnoxious, and those who worked for others were called "helps" or "hired hands." They demanded complete equality; visitors from more aristocratic lands were repeatedly amazed to see the serving maid join the family for dinner or the evening's conversation, or to witness the tavern waiter as he removed his apron to join the guests in a game of cards. In the successive Wests, where self-betterment was inevitable, all men felt equal, and acted the part.

III

The universally held belief that life on the frontier made progress inevitable for both the individual and the social order altered the behavioral patterns of the frontiersmen, and to a lesser degree of all Americans; persons who lived on an escalator that was carrying them to a higher social plane naturally developed different values and beliefs from those whose status could not be changed. With advancement inevitable, most became impatient to hurry the process. Many of the characteristics branded by travelers as uniquely American originated in this ambition.

The frontiersman, like his descendants after him, was inclined to be materialistic in his philosophy, and had less respect for aesthetic values or abstract thought than persons in more mature nations. Material tasks were essential on the frontier; the pioneer must clear his land, plant his crops, build his home, and enlarge his farm as a duty to society as well as to his own family. These tasks consumed all of his time and energy for years on end, leaving little opportunity for cultural pursuits. "There is," wrote one pioneer, "so much work to be done, and so few people to do it, that the idea of labor is apt to absorb the entire area of the mind." This attitude has persisted, and Americans today are more materialistic, more inclined to venerate the Almighty Dollar, and more neglectful of cultural goals, than their European neighbors.

Enduring, too, was the habit of wasting natural resources, so shocking to visitors to the frontier. Wastefulness came naturally to the pioneer, partly because he lived amid such an abundance of nature's riches that he could never envisage their depletion, but more because wasteful methods would hurry his self-advancement. With land cheap and both labor and fertilizers expensive, higher profits could be earned by exhausting the soil than by conserving the soil; farmers "mined" their fields and then moved on. Old-timers in the West, one story goes, bragged to younger men, "Why, son, by the time I was your age I had wore out three farms." Destruction became a habit with the frontiersmen. Millions of acres of stately forests fell before their axes; millions of acres of farm lands were despoiled by their wasteful methods. The translation of nature's riches into personal riches was more important than their preservation.

The frontiersman was as disdainful of tradition as he was of conservation; he was far more inclined to experiment or to discard time-tested techniques and implements than was his counterpart in more tradition-governed societies. This seemed logical to him, partly because the unique problems he faced demanded unique solutions, partly because the lack of manpower encouraged a search for mechanical devices that would do the work of men. This did not mean that the frontier was an area of invention; the leisure, the wealth, and the education necessary for the inventive process were lacking there. It did mean that the frontier created a market for inventions in America that was lacking in the Old World, and that the frontier's disdain for tradition generated a social atmosphere in which change was acceptable. In established societies obstacles had to be overcome before any new product could be accepted: the resistance of established producers whose profits were threatened, the opposition of organized workers whose jobs were endangered, the strong influence of habit which made anything new suspect. These barriers were lacking in the frontier's plastic social order, and innovation became the way of life there.

IV

Just as frontiersmen were willing to experiment in their pursuit of self-betterment, so were they ready to move about whenever opportunity beckoned; the true pioneer had no more attachment to place than to tradition. Many were perennial movers, changing residence seven or eight times in a lifetime as neighbors pressed in upon them or the dream of affluence failed to materialize. "Wandering about seems engrafted in their nature," wrote a Virginia governor in the eighteenth century; "and it is a weakness incident to it, that they should ever imagine the Lands further off, are Still better than those upon which they have settled." Charles Dickens, who visited the Mississippi Valley frontier in the mid-nineteenth century, saw the West as peopled by a great human army, ever on the march, and led by wandering pickets whose lives were dedicated to extending its outposts, leaving home after home behind.

Frontiersmen moved for many reasons, but one motive transcended all others: the desire for self-betterment. Farther west, they knew, were better lands, richer pastures, more productive farms or mines or ranches. They knew also that they could sell their land or "improvements" at twenty times the price they would have to pay for similar acreage on the outer fringes of settlement. So they drifted onward. The pioneer, noted a British traveler, "has always something better in his eye, further west; he therefore lives and dies on hope, a mere gypsy in this particular." Migration became a habit among frontiersmen precisely because wealth and status lay ahead.

This migratory compulsion heightened the exaggerated nationalism that prevailed in the successive Wests. Moving about broadened the vistas of the pioneers, weakened their provincialism, and eroded their loyalties to their homelands. On the frontier they tended to focus their loyalties on the national government, which alone could offer them protection from the red Indians, lands for expansion, transportation outlets, and other necessities. The results were a steady intrusion of national authority into spheres formerly reserved for state control, and a mounting fever of patriotism that was strongest in the newer regions. Visitors from overseas never ceased complaining of the spread-eagle boasting that they had to endure along the frontiers; one believed that the pioneers would soon maintain that the United States was not only the biggest, strongest, and best country in the world, but also the oldest.

Faith in progress for the nation among pioneers was paralleled by faith in progress for themselves. Optimism was one of their most obvious characteristics; they glorified what was to come in the same spirit that people in older cultures venerated what had been. What was more natural in a land where progress was the order of the day and the rags-to-riches myth a proven reality? Frontiersmen lived in the future, not the past, because the years ahead were certain to bring improvement: tomorrow a newcomer would buy his half-cleared farm at a speculative price; next week would bring an announcement that a railroad would be built nearby to open new markets. This was as foreordained as the succession of day and night. Wrote one Westerner: "One could as well gaze upon the rising sun and not foresee the splendors of midday, as live in these magnificent plains, and have no vision of their future greatness." Optimism sustained the pioneers and gave them hope as they sought the will-o'-the-wisp of fortune in their march westward.

V

These, then, were some of the traits identified by generations of travelers as particularly observable on the American frontier. Their significance lies in the fact that they have endured, for the social environment that fostered them proved to be transmittable in space and time. Frontier resources and frontier opportunity influenced not only the narrow band in which pioneering went on, but adjacent eastern regions immediately and more distant areas remotely. Thus the migratory impulse was quickened among New Yorkers and Scandinavians when railroad advertisements told them of free homesteads in Nebraska, just as the urge and opportunity for self-improvement were heightened in Massachusetts and Great Britain by the business and investment opportunities generated by the exploitation of frontier natural resources. Nor did these social attitudes expire with the passing of the frontier. They were transmitted to later generations, partly because the sequential development of frontier mineral and forest wealth through technological improvements continued to stimulate the economy well into the twentieth century, and partly because behavioral patterns fostered by the frontier's social environment were passed on from father to son to grandson. Frontier youths accustomed to frequent migrations would have less attachment to their own homes than children in more stabilized societies, and would bequeath this restlessness to their own offspring. Frontier characteristics have been eroded away by the industrialization and urbanization of the United States, but their vestiges remain to account for some of the traits that still distinguish Americans from peoples of nonfrontier countries.

One is the continuing practice of democracy. Politically today's Americans are more sophisticated than their pioneer ancestors, yet they still suspect a candidate for high office whose wit and wisdom are far superior to their own, and they still are slightly contemptuous of "politicians" who would be venerated as "statesmen" in older societies. Social democracy has also persisted in even more apparent form. The taxicab driver who addresses his passenger as "Mac" rather than "Sir" and the elevator operator who enters into easy conversation with the business magnates in his building are mirroring a frontier-like belief in the eventual equality of all men.

Closely linked with this attitude is the enduring belief in the possibility of upward mobility for all who are worthy. Comparative studies show that today men rise in social status at about the same rate in all industrialized countries, and that American society is as stratified as that in France or England. This the people refuse to believe. They hold that every man of proven ability is certain to scale the ladder of success, and that no class barriers will impede his progress. Pollsters who have asked a sizable segment of the population, "To what class do you belong?" have been answered "middle class" by an overwhelming majority, whether drawn from the ranks of day laborers or bank presidents. This is the substance of the American dream, and to a degree not found in capitalistic nations elsewhere, Americans believe in a one-class society and the inevitability of rags-to-riches progress for all who are competent.

Faith in social mobility stimulates physical mobility in the United States as people move about in quest of better jobs. The difference in the degree of movement is today diminishing; in all developed countries the increased employment opportunities created by industrialization, relaxing class distinctions, improved transportation, and the rise of cities send Europeans and Americans scurrying about at approximately the same rate. But in America people move more readily, and with a greater disregard for distance. Especially in the American West, where the frontier tradition remains strongest, migration is almost a compulsion; in northern California one out of every three persons changes his residence each year, and in southern California one in two. For the nation as a whole, of the 170 million residents in 1960, no less than 82 million had moved during the previous decade. Americans live on wheels. They watch motion pictures at drive-in theaters, deposit funds at drive-in banks, eat at drive-in restaurants, sleep in drive-away trailers, and kill each other at the rate of fifty thousand persons yearly on highways. "If," wrote a recent visitor from Latin America, "God were suddenly to call the world to judgment, He would surprise two-thirds of the American people on the road like ants."

The habit of hard work has also persisted to a degree unknown in more stabilized nations, even though this too is declining as machines which assume the tasks of men are endowing leisure with an unaccustomed respectability. In the United States no noontime siesta eases pressures as in Latin lands, no leisurely lunch period closes shops as in Britain, no lingering conversation at a sidewalk cafe provides an interval of relaxation as in France. Instead, the American works long hours, broken only by a hurried meal gulped down at a quick-lunch counter, and sometimes closes the day with a succession of martini cocktails designed to achieve a maximum degree of exhilaration in a minimum amount of time. Even his holiday periods are usually spent in competitive sports played with a grim determination to win rather than for pleasure. The respectability of labor was too firmly enshrined by the frontier experience to be easily discredited.

So was the habit of wastefulness. The United States is the land of the throwaway; paper towels and paper handkerchiefs, metal cans and plastic containers, disposable tissues and wear-once clothing are all made to be used and discarded. Thrifty visitors have pictured the American home as a reverse assembly line skillfully designed to reduce expensive objects to rubble, and the American factory as a creation cunningly contrived to produce gadgets that will disintegrate after a brief interval. The tall tale of the Texan who threw away his Cadillac car because the ash tray needed cleaning may not be true, but it could be told with appreciation only in the United States.

Americans continue to be unimpressed with tradition and prone to experiment to a degree lacking elsewhere, even in industrializing nations where the goad of prosperity and the stern fact of competition encourage improvisation. Only the optimism that sustained the pioneers has proven a victim of modern times. So long as a continent awaited conquest, so long as sheltering oceans protected their land from the political storms of the Old World, so long as democracy was the wave of the future everywhere, Americans sustained the buoyant faith in progress they inherited from their pioneering ancestors. The Great Depression of the 1930's and World War II altered their perspectives. The collapse of the economy during the 1930's, the years of conflict, and the unfamiliar experience of a cold war all shook their self-confidence. No longer were they masters of their fate. The protecting seas around them had been transformed into highways for aggressors. Their democratic beliefs were challenged by alien philosophies that unaccountably appealed to the emerging nations of Africa and Asia. Their monopoly on technological progress disappeared as they lagged in the race toward outer space and nuclear destruction. Faced with these unfamiliar conditions, Americans today are slowly substituting a philosophy of expectation with a philosophy of realism. But this alteration comes slowly and painfully to a people accustomed to frontier optimism.

That these vestiges of the frontier heritage alone shape the American character or even play a major role in determining the attitudes and behavior of today's Americans is obviously untrue. The modern United States is an industrialized-urbanized nation, controlled by the impulses that govern all developed countries, and little influenced by its rural past. Yet some influences remain, and these must be recognized in order that the differences that distinguish Americans from peoples of different backgrounds may be appreciated. Their materialism, their devotion to hard work, their veneration of democracy, their refusal to recognize class divisions, their faith in progress and the "go ahead" spirit, their excessive mobility—all these are relics of an era when frontier opportunity generated an excessive desire for self-betterment. The United States can be a good neighbor in a contracted world only if its people recognize that their beliefs and practices are uniquely based and cannot be applied to other nations, and only if other peoples realize that certain characteristics of the Americans—some of them irritating —are too firmly rooted in a frontier past to be easily discarded.

BIBLIOGRAPHY

Evidence to bolster the conclusions advanced in this essay is in Ray Allen Billington, *America's Frontier Heritage* (New York, 1966). The importance of the frontier in American history was noted in 1893 by Frederick Jackson Turner, whose germinal essays on the subject are in his *The Frontier in American History* (New York, 1920) and *The Significance of Sections in American History* (New York, 1932). Previously unpublished essays that shed light on his theories are in Wilbur R. Jacobs (ed.), *Frederick Jackson Turner's Legacy* (San Marino, Calif., 1965).

The uniqueness of the American experience is emphasized in the studies of comparative frontiers. Two convenient guides to the large body of books and articles on this subject are Dietrich Gerhard, "The Frontier in Comparative View," *Comparative Studies in Society and History*, I (March 1959), 205–29, and Marvin Mikesell, "Comparative Studies in Frontier History," *Annals of the Association of American Geographers*, L (March 1960), 62–74. Works of particular importance not summarized in these essays include Richard M. Morse (ed.), *The Bandeirantes* (New York, 1965), which deals with the Brazilian frontier, and H. C. Allen, *Bush and Backwoods* (East Lansing, Mich., 1959), which compares the frontiers of Australia and the United States.

The frontier hypothesis as stated by Turner was subjected to searching criticism during the 1930's and 1940's; since that time scholars in several disciplines have shown a tendency to test aspects of the thesis rather than either accept or reject uncritically. The extensive writings on the subject are summarized and appraised in Ray Allen Billington, *The American Frontier* (2nd ed.; Washington, D.C., 1965).

Among recent studies which evaluate the frontier's impact are Ellen von Nardroff, "The American Frontier as Safety Valve," *Agricultural History*, XXXVI (July 1962), 123–42, which shows that westward migration altered the wage structure; Stanley Elkins and Eric McKitrick, "A Meaning for Turner's Frontier," *Political Science Quarterly*, LXIX (July 1854), 321–53, and (Dec. 1954), 562–602, which demonstrates that expansion served as a democratizing influence; and Daniel J. Elazar, *The American Partnership* (Chicago, 1962), which reveals the manner in which the frontier served as a nationalizing force.

A persuasive defense of the frontier as a molding force is in H. C. Allen, "F. J. Turner and the Frontier in American History," in H. C. Allen and C. P. Hill (eds.), *British Essays in American History* (London, 1957), pp. 145–66. Walter P. Webb, *The Great Frontier* (Boston, 1952), advances the stimulating thesis that the American frontier was only part of a larger frontier of European expansion that existed between 1500 and recent years, and warns that the people of the globe must now adapt to a closed-space existence.

 7

Immigration

JOHN HIGHAM

In the late 1770's a well-to-do French farmer who had settled in the Hudson River Valley posed a question that has fascinated every subsequent generation and reverberated through American history. "What then is the American, this new man?" asked Hector St. John de Crèvecoeur in writing an affectionate sketch of his adopted country. Crèvecoeur's answer elaborated a claim already advanced by another recent arrival from Europe, Tom Paine. Paine's famous revolutionary pamphlet, *Common Sense* (1776), was the first stentorian call for independence from Britain. It declared, and Crèvecoeur heartily agreed, that the Americans are not transplanted Englishmen. They are an intermixture of many European peoples, a nation of immigrants.

The idea that all Americans (except possibly the Indians) once were immigrants has sometimes been sharply challenged. It has not appealed to everyone. It is not, as we shall see, entirely true. It partakes rather of the rich combination of reality and myth from which national legends arise. The idea is no less important for that, no less a shaping fact of American life. For almost two centuries it has provided one standard response to a collective need for self-definition. It persists today in the meanings that cluster around the Statue of Liberty. In a posthumous work written for and attributed to President John F. Kennedy, a little book entitled *A Nation of Immigrants* (1964), one can find a classic statement of the legend. The ideas summarized there influence more serious scholarship as well. The best survey of American immigration characterizes it as the nation's "historic *raison d'être* . . . the most persistent and the most pervasive influence in her development." Still more sweepingly, an eminent historian declared a few years ago that the immigrants *were* American history. An adequate description of the course and effects of immigration would require him to write the whole history of the country.

In view of such large conceptions of the matter, it is little wonder that American scholars have been hard put to specify what particular features of their national heritage derive in some distinctive way from the impact of the immigrant. In some senses, of course, immigration does ramify into every aspect of American experience. Conceived as the quintessential act of mobility, or as the starting point of the great American success story, immigration exemplifies conditions general to the whole society. But insofar as we meet it on that mythic scale—as a kind of *rite de passage* to an American identity—it eludes us as a historical variable. By visualizing the immigrant as the representative American, we may see him building America; we cannot see him changing it. Whatever significance immigration may have in some inclusive or representative way, it has also been a major differentiating force. It has separated those who bear the marks of foreign origin or inheritance from others who do not. The importance of immigration in this more limited sense—as a source of distinctions, divisions, and changes within the United States—remains as yet only dimly grasped. We shall have to disentangle the special effects of immigration from the encompassing legend; and that will require all the light comparative history can shed.

Let us begin with the word. In 1809 a traveler noted, "Immigrant is perhaps the only new word of which the circumstances of the United States has in any degree demanded the addition to the English language." So far as we know, the word materialized simultaneously with the creation of a national government. In 1789, Jedidiah Morse's famous patriotic textbook *American Geography* mentioned the "many immigrants from Scotland, Ireland, Germany, and some few from France" who were living in New York. Paine, Crèvecoeur, and earlier writers had referred only to "emigrants." But by 1789 our language was beginning to identify newcomers with the country they entered rather than the one they had left. Thus the term immigrant presupposed the existence of a receiving society to which the alien could attach himself. The immigrant is not, then, a colonist or settler, who creates a new society and lays down the terms of admission for others. He is rather the bearer of a foreign culture.

Morse explicitly differentiated the "immigrants" from the "original inhabitants," the Dutch and English "settlers." The Dutch had planted in 1624 the settlement on the Hudson River that became the province of New York forty years later when it fell into the hands of the English. At the time of the American Revolution, Dutch was still spoken fairly extensively in churches and homes in New York and New Jersey. By that time people of English origin composed the preponderant element, as indeed they did in all thirteen states. The best estimate identifies as English about 60 per cent of the white population of 1790. Like the Dutch in New York, the English in all of the colonies before the Revolution conceived of themselves as founders, settlers, or planters—the formative population of those colonial societies— not as immigrants. Theirs was the polity, the language, the pattern of work and settlement, and many of the mental habits to which the immigrants would have to adjust. To distinguish immigration from other aspects of American history, we shall have to exclude the founders of a society from the category of immigrant.

The English seizure of the Dutch settlements illustrates another mode of ethnic aggregation that does not belong within the scope of immigration. It should not include peoples who are forcibly incorporated into the host society. Those groups join the society on terms that shape their subsequent experience in special ways. Americans tend to forget how many alien groups joined them involuntarily. The great American success story features the saga of the immigrant, for the immigrant chose America, attracted by the prospect of a better life. In the process of immigration the alien seeks a new country; and it encourages his aspiration. Most of the captured groups, on the other hand, do not fit the success story because their entry into the Anglo-

American community did not depend on the real freedom and mobility that propelled the immigrant.

Two types of coercion have contributed to the peopling of the United States. The most obvious was slavery. The English founders imported African slaves who accounted in 1790 for about 19 per cent of the population of the new nation. Virtually from the beginning, Negroes constituted an inferior caste in the American social order. Immigrants were expected sooner or later to blend with the rest of the society or go back where they came from. But Negroes were positively forbidden assimilation, and they were unable to leave.

Meanwhile expansion and conquest engulfed many Indian tribes and other groups already established in the New World. Unlike the Negroes and the immigrants, these groups belonged to a particular place, to which they tried to cling in their encounter with the dominant American society. The Indians, after proving resistive both to assimilation and to enslavement, were driven steadily westward. Treated as foreign nations until 1871 and expected to die out, most of them became part of the United States only when they could not otherwise survive at all. With far less cruelty and destruction, the Anglo-Americans also overran various French and Spanish settlements. In 1755 they uprooted several thousand French Acadians from villages on the Bay of Fundy and dispersed them to other English colonies. Subsequent annexations took in, and left relatively undisturbed, the languid French settlements in the Illinois country, at St. Louis and, most importantly, New Orleans. As a result of the war with Mexico (1846–1848) the Anglo-Americans took possession of a considerable Spanish population in the Southwest. The "Californios" lost their patrimony and disappeared. In the Rio Grande Valley of New Mexico, on the other hand, the "Hispanos" still survive, ancient inhabitants of the place, proudly distinct from the "Anglos" around them and from the Mexican immigrants in adjacent states.

Altogether, the United States has participated in almost all of the processes by which a nation or empire can incorporate a variety of ethnic groups. It has acquired a diverse people by invasion and conquest, by enslavement, and by immigration. The one incorporative process America has not attempted is federation between contiguous peoples. When the individual American states federated into a single national community in 1789, the event was political and economic; it had no direct ethnic import. Elsewhere, as in Canada or Nigeria or the old Austro-Hungarian Empire, federation has given local ethnic majorities a threatening veto power against one another. In the American Union, however, the dominant group in every state sprang from approximately the same British ancestry. Union increased the variety of minorities; it did not alter the distribution of ethnic power.

After taking account of the English colonizers and their descendants, as well as the Negroes, and the more or less indigenous groups adopted in the course of expansion, what remains? Actually, a great deal. The 40 per cent of the white population of 1790 who were not English, plus the 44 million immigrants who have entered the United States since that time, have produced a very considerable part of the American people. For example, in 1920, the best authorities estimated, 15 per cent of the population of the continental United States might be ascribed to German immigration and another 10 per cent attributed to southern (i.e., Catholic) Ireland.

Yet these figures have very little meaning. The effort to assign all Americans to specific national origins was made at a time of unusual anxiety over the menace of immigration to the whole social order. Such statistics grossly exaggerate the proportion of people with any consciousness of belonging to a distinct minority. The essential fact about immigrant groups in America is their instability. They undergo steady attrition unless their cohesiveness is reinforced by powerful religious or racial peculiarities, as in the case of the Jews or the Chinese; and even then the difference in assimilation may be one of tempo or degree. In the typical process of ethnic development an increasing proportion of every generation after the first marries outside the group and ceases to be identified with it. A hard core, freshened by new immigration, can persist indefinitely. Yet the importance of the group as an ethnic minority declines sharply in the third generation and after. Those who lose meaningful contact with their immigrant origins become absorbed in the Anglo-American community; and this inflow continually widens its limits. That is why Americans have likened their society, not too inaccurately, to a melting pot. In Canada, where a more pervasive sense of ethnic separateness obtains, census takers regularly ask everyone to designate his or her ancestral nationality. The American census reflects a different set of values. It records the major racial divisions, but it has never tried to trace national origins beyond two generations—the foreign-born and their children.

We may now be in a position to correct the oversimple conception of the United States as a nation of immigrants. In addition to certain scattered indigenous groups and a hitherto segregated Negro minority, the United States has a fluctuating immigrant population and an expanding ethnic majority which I have labeled (too crudely) the Anglo-American community. That community was once predominantly English, and in times of ethnic conflict both its defenders and its critics have perceived it as "Anglo-Saxon" and exclusive. Actually, too many immigrant strains have fed into the majority group for it to regard itself consistently as anything but American.

The immigrant sector has at times been large, but not so large as in some other new countries. For example, Canada's people in 1911 were 22 per cent foreign-born. In Argentina 30 per cent of the population in 1914 was foreign-born. Foreigners outnumbered natives in some provinces of Canada and Argentina by two to one. Immigration in the United States never reached anything like those levels. At most, the proportion of the foreign-born was half as great as it was in Argentina. First- and second-generation immigrants combined never exceeded a third of the whole population.

In some states and localities at certain periods the impact of immigration has indeed been massive. At the time of the American Revolution, German stock alone comprised about a third of the population of Pennsylvania, to say nothing of the many Ulstermen in the same state from northern Ireland. At the time of the Civil War slightly more than half the population of Chicago, Milwaukee, and St. Louis was foreign-born. At the beginning of the twentieth century 75 per cent of the people of Minnesota, 71 per cent of Wisconsin, 65 per cent of Rhode Island, 63 per cent of Massachusetts, and 62 per cent of Utah had at least one parent born outside the United States.

In a larger view, however, the sheer size of the immigrant population has been less impressive than its truly extraordinary diversity. Other immigrant-receiving countries have tended to draw disproportionately from a few favored ethnic backgrounds. In a century of immigration to Argentina, for instance, 40 per cent of the newcomers came from Italy, another 27 per cent from Spain. The same nationalities, together with a large Portuguese contingent, made up 76 per cent of Brazil's immigration. Canada, between 1851 and 1950, got almost half its immigrants from the British Isles and a quarter of the remainder from the United States. Australia too recruited overwhelmingly from the British Isles. As recently as 1947 only 11 per cent of the Australian white population was traceable to other origins. In contrast, the United States during the period 1820–1945 recruited 12 per cent of its total immigration from Italy, 13 per cent from Austria-Hungary and its successor states, 16 per cent from Germany, 10 per cent from Russia and Poland, 6 per cent from Scandinavia, and a third from the British Isles. New England sustained a major invasion of French Canadians. Hundreds of thousands of Mexicans poured into the Southwest. About half a million Greeks reached the United States before World War II. Substantial concentrations of Japanese materialized in the San Francisco Bay area, of Finns in the lumber and copper towns of the Northwest, of Armenians in the orchards around Fresno, of Netherlanders in South Dakota and Michigan, of Portuguese in New Bedford, of Arabs in New York City. In some mining and mill towns one might find a dozen ethnic groups intermixed in more or less the same neighborhood. No other country has gathered its people from so many different sources.

The very diversity of the immigration makes its impact difficult to measure. In some ways diversity may have limited that impact. Where one immigrant culture predominates, it can impart its own distinctive flavor to an area and perhaps affect decisively the allocation of power. Thus Chinese immigration created a deep and lasting social cleavage in Malaya and Thailand, as East Indians did in Guiana. In Argentina, Latin immigration drastically reduced the importance of the Indian and mestizo elements. In Canada immigration has strengthened the English culture to the disadvantage of the French. But an influx as miscellaneous as that which the United States has received cannot easily alter pre-existing relationships. Competing against one another, immigrants have ordinarily found themselves on all sides of the choices America has thrust upon them. Except in relatively isolated, rural areas, no immigrant enclave—no close-knit neighborhood or favored occupation—has been safe from invasion by some newer, less advantaged group. Employers learned to set one group against another and thus manage their labor force more easily, a policy they called "balancing nationalities." Politicians learned to rally miscellaneous support, while exploiting ethnic divisions, by a strategy known as "balancing the ticket." Accordingly, the immigrants have never been arrayed solidly against the native population on economic issues and no political party has ever captured the whole "foreign vote."

All of this is not to say that immigrants have exercised only fleeting and localized influence before melting away into America's great majority. Neither the commanding position of the majority group nor the fragmentation of the immigrants into many disunited minorities deprives them of a major role in American history. To delimit the scope of their role is rather to make possible a judgment of its distinctive import. Even so, the crux of the matter still eludes us unless—concentrating on the process of immigration—we can somehow separate what it may have *made possible* from what it merely *reinforced*. No one has yet wrestled hard with that question. But we can make a tentative start by noting that immigration occurred in two large and quite distinct phases.

Beginning in the 1680's, the English colonies in America attracted a sizable voluntary inpouring of other ethnic groups, which continued without slackening until the American Revolution. This First Immigration followed a sharp decline in English fears of overpopulation at home and a consequent falling off of English emigration. The proprietors of the newer colonies, notably Pennsylvania and Carolina, turned to foreign sources for the people essential to their promotional designs. Prior to 1680 the occasional Scot, Irishman, or Jew had left no imprint at all on the long Atlantic seaboard except in the motley Dutch town of New Amsterdam. Now advertising, the promise of religious liberty, and other inducements attracted French Huguenots,

Irish Quakers, German pietists. Their coming started a wider movement—particularly from Ireland, Scotland, Switzerland, and the Rhineland—which soon acquired its own momentum. The colonies, dependent on local initiative and competing with one another for people, became so avid for immigration that their Declaration of Independence in 1776 charged the king with obstructing it.

Actually, Britain by an act of Parliament in 1740 had sanctioned in the colonies a latitude in the naturalization of foreigners that was inconceivable in the mother country or elsewhere in the world. The other great colonizing powers, Spain and France, admitted only native-born Catholics to their overseas domains, so immigration to those parts did not begin until after the end of the colonial era. The United States not only had a colonial immigration, but by 1776 a significant portion of the immigrants of the preceding century had been fully accepted in the new society. Consequently its "charter group" (to use a helpful phrase Canadian sociologists have coined) did not consist exclusively of the English founders of the society. The charter group was already becoming a blend—a blend not of races but of closely related ethnic strains.

This widening of the Anglo-American community took on a special ideological significance when Americans needed, in 1776 and after, to differentiate themselves from Englishmen. The immigration of the eighteenth century enabled Paine and other formulators of the national legend to claim that Americans, unlike Englishmen, are a truly cosmopolitan people, the heirs of all mankind. Thus the First Immigration engendered a universalistic and eclectic ideal of nationality. It set the United States on a course leading away from the English presumption that all groups should retain their own cultural distinctiveness and remain at a comfortable distance from one another.

The Second Immigration, like the First, lasted for almost a century. It ran from about the 1830's to the stiff immigration restriction law of 1924. This human flood vastly extended the diversity its predecessor had created. During the half century between 1776 and 1830, war and other restraints on emigration had kept the transatlantic movement at a low level. The proportion of the foreign-born in the American population fell by the 1830's to about 8 per cent. Then a transportation revolution made America accessible from more and more remote points, while a population crisis in rural Europe and the breakdown of the traditional agricultural system put millions of people to flight. The tide surged to a high point in the 1850's, to a higher one in the early 1880's, and to a crest in the opening decade of the twentieth century. Whereas the First Immigration had been entirely white and predominantly English-speaking, the Second brought a babel of tongues and an array of complexions ranging from the blond Scandinavian through the swarthy south Italian to the West Indian Negro. Whereas the First Immigration had been very largely Protestant, the Second was heavily Catholic from the outset; and by the end of the century it was increasingly Jewish and Eastern Orthodox.

Primarily because of immigration the Roman Catholic Church as early as 1850 became the largest single religious body in America; and so it has remained. In the course of the next century the immigrant religions domesticated themselves and came ultimately to share with the Anglo-Protestant churches more and more of a common ethos. By the 1950's informed observers of all faiths were ceasing to conceive of America as distinctively or predominantly a Protestant country. This in itself was a major consequence of the Second Immigration. Elsewhere in the Western Hemisphere immigration has tended to reinforce, rather than alter, the pre-existing religious pattern.

In the secular sphere the Second Immigration was perhaps most important in shaping an urban, industrial way of life. Obviously, it did not work alone. Many influences intermingled in transforming the United States from a decentralized, rural republic to a consolidated, industrial nation. But immigration converged with other circumstances in a peculiarly effective way. The immigrants supplied an industrial labor force and an urban state of mind.

Initially, the promise of land and the wealth it contained lured many of the 50 million people who poured out of Europe in the nineteenth and early twentieth centuries. Like the eastward migration across the Russian steppes, the overseas movement to North and South America, to Australasia, and to parts of Africa was in good part an occupation of empty land, an expansion of the Great Frontier of European settlement. Immigrants broke the soil and harvested the wheat of the Argentine pampas and the Canadian prairies; they cleared forests in southern Brazil; they dug gold in California and Australia; they spread rich farms over large parts of the American Middle West. Where they could acquire land, they took root. To a marked degree, however, the newcomers in all of the immigrant-receiving countries gravitated toward the cities. For example, 62 per cent of America's foreign-born lived in urban places in 1890, as against only 26 per cent of the native whites born of native parents. Through their concentration in and impact on the cities, the immigrants changed the countries they had come to build.

The economies of most of those countries were still quite primitive a hundred years ago. Consequently, the immigrants not only contributed the hard, casual labor that built the cities and the transportation network; they and their children also provided a very large part of the commercial, technical, clerical, and professional skills on which the cities thrived. In Argentina, for example, European immigrants may be said virtually to have created an energetic middle class in a nation that had been sharply divided between a creole aristocracy and the apathetic mestizo masses. The United States, on the other hand, already had its own mobile middle class. What its more highly developed economy lacked was an industrial working class. The Second Immigration coincided with the industrialization of the United States and furnished the bulk of the manpower for it. Irish and French Canadians gave a tremendous impetus to the textile industry of New England; Germans, Jews, and Italians transformed the clothing industry of New York; a dozen nationalities collaborated in the blast furnaces and rolling mills of Pennsylvania and the meat-packing houses of the Middle West. In these and other enterprises, a dependence on unskilled immigrant labor encouraged the introduction of automatic machines and processes in order to standardize the task and the product. Only in America did the immigrants constitute a mass proletariat engaged in manufacturing; and because they did, America was able to develop to the full a system of mass production.

In some respects the standardized, mechanized life of the industrial city was uncongenial to the older Americans. Their heritage from the eighteenth century included a deep distrust of consolidated power. They conceived of the big city as a dangerous, corrupting place. They associated virtue with nature, and freedom with open space. They cherished ideals of individualism that seemed incompatible with the impersonal, collectivized character of the new urban world. But the foreigners, or at least their children, had to accept that world—they had to make it bearable and secure—in order to be at home in America. This they were somewhat prepared to do, for their own cultures were far less individualistic than that of the Anglo-American community. Thus the immigrants, in reaching out for a place of dignity in America, took the lead in organizing trade unions. Moreover, the long struggle to create a welfare state for the protection of the poor and the unorganized depended at every step on immigrant votes, from Hazen Pingree's reforms in Detroit in the 1890's to Franklin D. Roosevelt's New Deal.

While coming to terms with the city in these ways, the immigrants were also forging a new urban mass culture to replace the traditions they could not transplant intact. It is hardly surprising that heterogeneous people, cut adrift from their past and caught up in the machine process, should have found the substance of a common life in the stimuli of the mass media. Beginning as early as 1835, when the Scottish-born journalist James Gordon Bennett started the raucous New York *Herald,* immigrants have pioneered in the production of mass culture. Hungarian-born Joseph Pulitzer modernized the sensationalism that Bennett began. Pulitzer's New York *World,* with its special appeal to immigrant readers, showed how a newspaper could speak for as well as to the urban masses. Meanwhile a transplanted Irishman, Robert Bonner, developed the promotional techniques that created in the late 1850's the first mass-circulation weekly, the New York *Ledger.* Of the four outstanding editors at the turn of the century who expanded the magazine audience still further, two— S. S. McClure and Edward Bok—were foreign-born. Other immigrants and their children have thronged the popular stage, the music shops of Tin Pan Alley, the film studios of Hollywood. Spyros Skouras created a theatrical empire; Edward L. Bernays professionalized the field of public relations. The early history of radio broadcasting is in large measure a story of struggle between David Sarnoff's R.C.A. and William Paley's C.B.S.—one of them a first-generation Jewish immigrant, the other a second. All of these were thoroughly urbanized, thoroughly uprooted men, who gained from the experience of cultural displacement and ethnic assimilation a special capacity to relate themselves to Everyman. In some measure the immigrants have taught the older Americans how to endure deracination and anonymity.

So we come finally to a paradox in assessing the impact of immigration. In general it has enhanced the variety of American culture. We can observe its diversifying influence in the American ideal of nationality, in the American religious pattern, and in the sheer presence of so many different human types. Yet the diversities seem in the long run to give way to an irresistible pressure toward uniformity. Through the systems of mass production and mass communications, America and its immigrants have assimilated one another within an urban, technological culture that overrides all distinctions of place, class, and ethnic type.

BIBLIOGRAPHY

The full sweep of immigration as a great theme of international as well as American history was first developed by Marcus Hansen, whose three posthumous books are the classics of the field: *The Immigrant in American History* (Cambridge, Mass., 1940); *The Atlantic Migration, 1607–1860* (Cambridge, Mass., 1940); *The Mingling of the Canadian and American Peoples* (New Haven, 1940). A great deal of additional information on individual nationalities was brought together by Carl Wittke in *We Who Build America: The Saga of the Immigrant* (New York, 1939). Oscar Handlin's *Boston's Immigrants: A Study in Acculturation* (rev. ed., Cambridge, Mass., 1959), is an outstanding special study; and his *The Uprooted: The Epic Story of the Migrations That Made the American People* (Boston, 1951), generalizes the travail of the immigrant in the American city. Maldwyn Allen Jones, *American Immigration* (Chicago, 1960), is an expert synthesis of the whole subject.

Writing from an international point of view, Brinley Thomas gives an important re-evaluation of economic aspects in *Migration and*

Economic Growth: A Study of Great Britain and the Atlantic Economy
(Cambridge, Mass., 1954). Will Herberg set forth an influential ap-
praisal of changing relations between religion and ethnicity in *Protes-
tant-Catholic-Jew: An Essay in American Religious Sociology* (New
York, 1955). Nathan Glazer and Daniel Patrick Moynihan collaborate
on a fascinating gallery of sociological portraits in *Beyond the Melting
Pot: The Negroes, Puerto Ricans, Jews, Italians, and Irish of New
York City* (Cambridge, Mass., 1963). Glazer's article, "The Immigrant
Groups and American Culture," *The Yale Review*, XLVIII (Spring
1959). 382–397, first suggested to me a link between immigration and
modern American popular culture; while J. Joseph Huthmacher,
"Urban Liberalism and the Age of Reform," *Mississippi Valley His-
torical Review*, XLIX (Sept. 1962), 231–241, indicates the kind of re-
form the immigrants supported. On anti-immigrant feeling see Ray
Allen Billington, *The Protestant Crusade, 1800–1860: A Study of the
Origins of American Nativism* (New York, 1938); and John Higham,
Strangers in the Land: Patterns of American Nativism, 1860–1925
(rev. ed., New York, 1963).

For a comparative approach, I found Louis Hartz *et al., The Founding of New Societies* (New York, 1964), an essential starting point. A
symposium sponsored by UNESCO, *The Positive Contribution by Immigrants* (Paris, 1955), offers expert appraisals of the experience of the
United Kingdom, Australia, Brazil, and Argentina. Additional suggestions appear in the collected essays of William Petersen, *The Politics
of Population* (Garden City, N.Y., 1964). *Immigration in Latin America*
(Washington, D.C., 1964), by the Brazilian sociologist, Fernando Bastos
de Avila, S. J., is a reliable study emphasizing the period since World
War II.

For Argentina, I have relied heavily on Ysabel F. Rennie, *The
Argentine Republic* (New York, 1945), and on James R. Scobie, *Revolution on the Pampas: A Social History of Argentine Wheat, 1860–1910*
(Austin, Texas, 1964), a much broader book than its title suggests.
Irving Louis Horowitz, "The Jewish Community of Buenos Aires,"
Jewish Journal of Sociology, IV (Dec. 1962), 147–171, throws added
light on the process of assimilation. T. Lynn Smith's *Brazil: People
and Institutions* (2nd ed., Baton Rouge, 1963), has an informative
chapter on immigration. John Porter's *The Vertical Mosaic: An Analysis of Social Class and Power in Canada* (Toronto, 1965), includes a
masterly analysis of migration and ethnicity. It should be supplemented
with the essays in *Canadian Society: Sociological Perspectives*, Bernard
R. Blishen *et al.* (eds.) (New York, 1961). For Australia there are two
discriminating monographs: Wilfrid D. Borrie, *Italians and Germans*

in *Australia: A Study of Assimilation* (Melbourne, 1954); and Charles A. Price, *Southern Europeans in Australia* (Melbourne, 1963). Michael Banton, *White and Coloured: The Behavior of British People towards Coloured Immigrants* (New Brunswick, N.J., 1960), is written with a perceptive eye for national character.

8

Mobility

GEORGE W. PIERSON

One day, several years ago, a single-engine Cessna airplane, flying from New Haven to Rhode Island, ran out of power, came down safely on Expressway 95, and was promptly hit by a mobile home.

About the same time a team of youth researchers discovered that, out of more than a thousand boys and girls whom they had been studying, 70 per cent remembered their families' having moved once, twice, three, or even four times, and 13 per cent remembered their families having moved five or more times. Eighty per cent did admit to having lived in the same house for one year, but only 50 per cent for as long as five.

Again in 1964 the American Petroleum Institute announced that we Americans, using 55 million oil credit cards, drove 86 million motor vehicles some 38 billion miles and lost some 43,000 lives on the road. Meanwhile at a single oil company it was taking 650 trained employees to keep track of the credit transactions—and on a routine day they had to handle four thousand changes of address: which figured out to a *residential* mobility of 30 per cent in a single year.

We live, it has been said, in a state of perpetual transportation —and as a not surprising consequence it appears that 25 per cent of all the revenues of all these fifty United States now derives from the automobile.

But let us not suppose that we are the only highway nomads,

the only people on the move. Englishmen have been notorious world wanderers. And even the French are learning about automobility. A few years ago, for example, the Paris automobile show generated such traffic that Parisians had to be advised to go by subway: *Pour aller au Salon de l'Auto, prenez le Métro.*

So Europe too has this restlessness, this mobility fever. Indeed Europe has long had it, much longer than we. Europe has known mobility in all its forms, great or small, organized or individual, rational or irrational, for hundreds, even thousands of years. But we've had this motion sickness worse. Ours has been the great spatial carelessness. We've been the footloose folk—and the scars of the experience show on our land. It has even warped our national character.

So now I have stated my theme. My theme is that mobility, as a cultural triumph or failure, is a human achievement—not strictly American. In *all* its varieties and consequences mobility was known to, or invented by, Europeans long before this country was settled. Yet nowhere has free movement been so unrestrained, or reached such extreme forms, or generated such drastic consequences, as with us. So it is here that it can best be studied, here that we can perhaps begin to understand what has been happening to us and what may in some degree happen to our friends in the wider world tomorrow.

Let us scrutinize the two halves of the proposition—and in the process perhaps catch sight of some of the advantages and disadvantages, the illuminations and deceptions, of historical comparisons.

Mobility, we ventured to say, is an ancient invention, and has appeared in many guises. Indeed it has been an extraordinarily complex phenomenon, varied in its forms, confused in its motivations, and often contradictory in its results. On many of man's migrations in the past we have no statistics and only the most general recorded observations. Mobility as a psychological phenomenon or even as a social act is only just beginning to be studied systematically. Yet perhaps we do know enough to distinguish certain major categories and identify the most important kinds of human movement.

There was first the gradual, unplanned, prehistoric migration now known as *Dispersion*—the slow outward drift into empty or sparsely occupied country: what Franklin D. Scott calls the "creeping expansion." The first occupation of Europe by primitive man, the invasion of North America by the Indian aborigines, were examples of this creeping expansion. Perhaps also the peaceful infiltration of the Roman Empire by the tribal Germans in their *Volkerwanderung,* or, in modern times, the massive percolation of the Chinese into Southeast Asia and Manchuria, have partaken in some degree of this primitive mobility we call Dispersion.

There have been next the more rapid, organized, and hostile migrations which we call *Conquest.* Conquest is deliberate armed migration, and may result in empire building or in empire collapse. It may take the form of a massive expansion, as with the Moslem conquests or the Golden Horde, or it may be mounted in what Scott calls the "sharp thin thrust," as with the Vikings, or the Spaniards in Mexico. Conquest appeals to soldiers and adventurers, but also to priests. The Crusaders belong in this class.

Resembling such armed migrations, but often with a friendlier, more peaceful, and beneficent intent, is *Colonization.* America was created by colonization from Europe. But the Europeans have practiced it on each other. And the motives and methods, as we know, have taken many different forms.

A fourth and rather different kind of international migration has been *Forced Migration:* the driving out of the heretics, the expulsion of the aristocrats in the French Revolution, the persecution of the Tories in ours, and in more recent times the repatriation of the Greeks or the pogroms against the Jews. The slave trade was another species of forced migration, in which both sides of the Atlantic shared. And the men and women who were pushed out or carried off or bought and sold can hardly have regarded this transport of human livestock as did the ambitious conquerors or the hopeful colonists.

One might mention next what we call *Nomadism,* the practice of perpetual motion, the inability to sit still. The imprisonment of small clusters of people within a never-ending cycle of movement—as with the desert folk driving their flocks from oasis to oasis, or the mysterious comings and goings of the gypsies, or the seasonal circuit of the Mexican fruit pickers up and down the West Coast—have been variations on this theme.

But there has been still a sixth major category of international mobility, and for modern times the most important. This is *Immigration and Emigration:* the free, voluntary, private transfer of individuals, families, congregations, even villages or whole countrysides from one country to another. Here the sending and receiving states are largely passive, and the initiatives rest in private hands. But these same initiatives derive from a kaleidoscope of experiences and spring from the widest range of human motivations. Thus we know that a man may take ship for the new world, or move from Italy to France, or even move about within the United Kingdom, because he is looking for adventure or change or something new—or because he is a refugee from starvation, or persecution, or is running away from the law—or because he is a man with a mission, a message to carry—or because he is a student with something important to learn—or because he is an expert with a professional skill to impart—or because his health forces him to seek a better climate, or his doctor prescribes the waters, or he wants to rest his nerves and recharge his emotional batteries—or he may move because he has just married a stranger, or must get his first job, or has been retired from active work. Moreover, the move may not satisfy, so that he moves again and in so doing joins that large company of emigrants and immigrants who are "birds of passage," who may return home, or instead may try moving again.

Among all the motivations for migration, of course, the economic has often seemed by far the most influential: the search for a job, the hope of bettering oneself. Yet here too the variety of incentives is almost beyond counting. A man may be looking for El Dorado, for gold in the streets—or he may be an inventor seeking ears that are more open—or he may be a fugitive craftsman with industrial secrets to sell—or a skilled operative looking for still better pay—or he may follow a trade from country to country, or take advantage of an industry his fellow countrymen have already organized and pre-empted, and migrate with the Cornish miners to Pennsylvania, or become an Italian bootblack in New York, or sell flowers with his fellow Greeks. But let us not forget that these occupational systems of movement had already been organized and long practiced in Europe. As Frank Thistlethwaite has pointed out, the *padroni* system was already shipping workers about the Mediterranean before it attracted and organized its immigrants over here.

And there are many other things about European emigration that are worth American notice. The "push" factors were European and were often stronger than the "pulls." With the decline of feudal localism people were freed for moving. With the agricultural revolution the peasant was forced off the land. With the industrialization of Europe many farm folk simply had to go to town or seek a free farm in the new world north or south. So once again we are driven to recognize the priorities of Europe. For essentially it was the modernization of the continent (not the discovery of America) that freed men from their bondage to place and invited or even forced them to move: from the soil to the city, from province to province, from country to country, from the Old World to the New. It was the breakup of the old order again that incited men to move up in society, to climb the social ladder, by changing occupations, and locations too. As Lewis Mumford long since so cogently observed: the wishful dreamer and the businessman, these were types that appeared in old Europe long before they made their conquest of America. We may almost all seem to be middle class in the U.S.A., but we hardly invented the breed. Nor even did the marginal man, the hobo and the wobbly, the alienated personalities or the beatnik temperaments, originate over here. The cities of Europe have long known these furtive folk. For drifters the *quais* and *quartiers* of Paris had served as resort.

All of which should remind us of still a seventh most important category, the *Internal Migration* which each of our nations has known. Internal migration, let us recognize, is very like emigration and immigration. It is largely private and voluntary. It is caused by the same hardships, energized by the same emotions, respondent to the same occupational opportunities, economic drives, social impulses or frictions of change. A peasant may cross the Atlantic or simply move into town. A miner is offered opportunities in Colorado but also closer by. For the ailing or melancholic there will be continental spas and health resorts more accessible than the Fountain of Youth. Tourists can make a pilgrimage to the natural wonders of their own country. Men of enterprise can resort to the nearer centers of capital. Indeed for two centuries the modernization of Europe has been setting its populations into internal migrations more thoroughly, more massively even, than into emigration abroad.

So I think we must recognize that the great transatlantic migration has not been unique either in its motivations or in its personnel. Indeed it has not even been the largest fraction of Europe's modern restlessness. For every man who moved out of Europe, many stayed and moved or are moving at home. As Frank Thistlethwaite so perceptively argues, we should regard the great transatlantic dispersion "not as the dominant demographic factor of the nineteenth century, but as a subordinate feature of demographic trends within Europe."

The students of population do tell us that Europe and Africa between them sent in the neighborhood of some 75 million persons across the Atlantic, of whom more than half came to settle in the U.S.A. And only one-third of these North American settlers later returned home. So the 25 million net migration to our shores did constitute the single largest, most spectacular, and most successful folk movement of the nineteenth century. But it was not a new human experience. It was not unique. It did not equal in volume the cumulative movements going on elsewhere. Let me say again: all the kinds of mobility our immigrants practiced had long been known in Europe. And I think it can or will be shown that most of the causes of their crossing the Atlantic were European, not American.

So if we would inquire into human mobility, its ninety-nine varieties and its group secrets, and if we become curious about the psychological or social incitements to restlessness and their spatial cures, it is to the Old World we may turn. And it is in Europe that there is surely much to learn.

And yet. And yet.

It is here, in America, that free mobility can best be studied. For not only was the whole American movement carried on within the horizon of visibility and the time span of the written record, but it is here that mobility has been most widely practiced, carried to its furthest extremes, even, as it were, house-broken and domesticated. We Americans have taken what I call the M-Factor into our lives, into our vocabulary, into our homes, into our public institutions, into our private and social psychology, to such an extent that mobility has become an essential ingredient in the American way of life. Mobility has been and is something special here, something so different in degree as to approach a difference in kind. Our comparisons with Europe must therefore be in part contrasts as well as likenesses.

Can it really be proved that ours has been the mobile society par excellence? I believe it can. Or it will be, when we unearth and assess what can be known. Let me here try to make just a beginning. I believe the mobility of our people was and is greater per man, and proportionately a much more important element not only in the fabric of our expectations but in the structure and balance of our society. And I argue this on the following grounds.

1. We all began as immigrants. Whether our first American ancestors arrived in 1607, 1848, 1907, or since World War II, our origins were unanimously immigrant and have been these 360-odd years—whereas of the awakening masses who stayed in Europe only some left their village or province or patrimony behind.

2. In the second place, once the settlers had landed, it proved difficult to settle down. Their sons and their sons' sons spread out from the seaport towns, moved along the coast or up river, and filled in the vacant back country from colony to colony. Thereafter came the assault on the mountain barriers, and the drive West. The conquest of the continent became the obsession of our successful revolutionists, and of many nineteenth-century immigrants too. It came to be expected that the young folks would strike out on their own. In a word we found ourselves committed to movement. The trip across the Atlantic had been but the first stage of our journey. And if in Europe more people were beginning to move about than had ever left for America, in America the movements westward surpassed in frequency, distances, and varieties of participants anything that had yet been seen.

Frederick Jackson Turner caught the vision of what had been going on, but in a limited and partial way. The frontier meant movement, he said, movement over and over again. What he failed to notice was that as early as 1830, perhaps even as early as 1790, the elements of our society who ever saw the wilderness, or participated in the frontier experience, were a declining percentage of our total population. Were the rest sitting still? Far from it. They were filling in the intermediate country. And they were going to town. From as far back as 1830, at least, more Americans moved to other destinations than to the frontiers. And when the frontiers fused and were gone they kept on moving, more regularly, more feverishly, more miscellaneously than ever before. So whereas the census figures of 1850 and 1870 had caught some 24 per cent of the population living in states where they had not been born, and by 1900 that figure had dropped to 20.6 per cent, by 1930 it was back to 24 per cent, by 1950 up to 26.5 per cent, and by 1960 up to 29.6 per cent.[1] Turner's frontier was the spectacular cutting edge of our westward movement. It created a myth. It confirmed the expectation and the habit of movement. But so did our cities. And today even the interstate migrations, like the emigration across national boundaries in Europe, turn out to be but a small fraction of the internal movement that is actually taking place. Statistical samplings confirm these facts. And today our demographers, notably Everett Lee of the University of Pennsylvania, assert without fear of contradiction that, residentially speaking, ours is the most mobile population of which we have reliable knowledge.

3. But there are other witnesses, and have been since our

[1] The estimates of current mobility vary slightly, but agree in emphasis. Thus it is reiterated that 18 per cent, or one out of every five persons over one year old, or one out of every five families, seem to move every year. The 1960 census indicated that, out of 159 million persons five years of age or older, 75 million had changed residence since 1955 (an annual rate of 10 per cent per year *not counting repeaters*). Of these 75 million some 14 million (8.8 per cent) had moved to another county and a second 14 million (8.8 per cent) had moved to another state. If such were the returns for just five years, it staggers the imagination to contemplate how many will ultimately abandon the state of their birth before they die. The *Statistical Abstract of the U.S.* shows that about 3.3 per cent of the total population one year of age or older are moving across state lines in a single year, and F. D. Scott has noted that 40 per cent of all Americans over the age of fifty now live in states other than those of their birth. (The student will find confirmation and illumination in F. D. Scott, "Migration in Dynamics of History," Municipal University of Omaha, 1965; and in Everett S. Lee, "The Turner Thesis Re-examined," *American Quarterly*, Spring 1961.)

national beginnings, to testify to this strange propensity, even peculiarity, of our nation. Foreign traveler after foreign traveler was struck, not only by the restlessness and mobile tendencies of the Americans, but by the way it was reflected in or was affecting our character, and by the way it was aided by or giving shape to our institutions. From Alexis de Toqueville and Sarmiento and Francis Lieber to Rudolph Heberle or André Siegfried and André Maurois, the astonishment and the puzzlement have been the same. We don't seem anchored to place. Our families are all scattered about. Our loyalties are to abstractions and constitutions, not to birthplace or homestead or inherited associations. We share an extraordinary freedom to move and to move again. No locality need claim us long. In 1847 Sarmiento imagined the trump of doom surprising us out on the road like ants. Today we are on the road still. And perhaps more than ever. We have a love affair, they say, with the motorcar. The automobile has even become our chief status symbol.

True, the American people may have known few persecutions or deportations, and no flights from famine. But in the planting of new territories and colonies, in the cross-country pursuit of economic opportunity, in travel for curiosity or health or recreation, or in almost all of the kinds of free movement that Europe pioneered and has long known, we have had and still have no equals. Small wonder that pursuit of happiness in this spatial way has had such profound effects.

But before I say just a word about these far-reaching consequences, let us ask: *Why?* How did it happen that we became so footloose and fancy-free? What freed us to keep wandering? Here it seems to me we are on more difficult ground. But perhaps a few tentative answers can be hazarded.

A first answer is surely that, for a number of reasons, we attracted the mobile temperaments. Out of Europe came settlers who, by and large, were more willing to move.

A second answer may be that the transatlantic passage represented such a drastic cutting of ties—such a catastrophic abandonment and so difficult a return (psychologically as well as physically)—that the New World Europeans became, as it were, permanently uprooted, without immemorial and instinctive attachments to any patricular company or spot.

To these exiles came then the invitation of the great open spaces. The rich free lands and resources of the continent beckoned. So in America there was not only more space, there were not only more places to go, but more opportunities and more wealth to be got by the going.

Still a fourth powerful push came from an accident: the accident that during the 360-odd years of our history, and most particularly during the nineteenth century, the whole structure of Western society on both sides of the Atlantic was undergoing a series of tremendous transformations. The old systems were breaking up, the old authorities were being challenged. What we call the political, commercial, agricultural, and industrial revolutions not only destroyed the static rigidities which had held men in their places so long, but provided the means of escape and offered rewards for those who would step out and seize them. Our national development, it hardly needs be repeated, owed much to the new democratic participation, but much also to the new capital and to the industrial revolution. Without the new means of transport and employment, without steam engines and steamboats and better roads, we would hardly have been so ready to take advantage of the discovery of oil and of the European invention of the gasoline buggy.

Yet Europe, it will quickly be observed, had these new tools and opportunities too. Why did not the people of the continent also cut loose from their fixed abodes?

To this question there must be a whole catalog of answers—yet many of them, I think, can be summed up in one word: barrier. In Europe there were too many difficulties. The old structures of church and state, the old authorities of family and class, the old commitments to field or to shop, the old attachments to village and countryside—these were all being eroded, but they could not melt away overnight. Nowhere were the military frontiers far distant, and these frontiers remained hard to cross. Everywhere the inherited prejudice of province and language still obstructed the way.

Whereas over here there soon came to be one language and one limitless expanse. Nowhere in our freer society were there the same high fences. No states could imprison their citizens or keep them from wandering. No systems of authority had survived the Atlantic passage still strong enough to keep men in their place. And no government could be made strong enough afterward to prevent the hunters and pioneers, the squatters and the speculators, the traders and the lawyers and the missionaries from seeping West.

To sum up my argument or explanation: we have been more mobile, it seems to me, because we attracted out of Europe the mobile temperaments, because these wanderers found themselves uprooted and unattached, because there were so many places to go, because there were so many means of going and rewards to be had for the venture, because the transformation of the old agrarian order now freed us for going, and because there were not and are not today the traditional social barriers to fence us in.

The results? Surely if we have been so mobile, that mobility must have had some very obvious and visible effects on our society and on what we please to call the American character. I am convinced this is true. I think the effects of our playing so fast and loose with locality can be seen everywhere. The moving has put many marks on us. Let me name just a few.

The marks or scars of our experience can be seen in almost all our attitudes, and in our institutions too. Our family life has been relaxed, broken up, even dangerously disintegrated by the habit of moving. Our language has been filled with mobility metaphors and the slang of get-up-and-go. Our casual friendliness to strangers and facility for forming voluntary associations owe much to the same influence. Our economic institutions have been distorted in favor of transportation, communication, and the mass market, in part by the practice of an almost constant interchange. Our inherited institutions of church and state were first strained, then disintegrated, in favor of congregations and town meetings that could be carried everywhere. One can almost say that no institution that wasn't portable or that couldn't be made portable could survive. Our very temperament was forever being reinjected with hope but also with the acids of restlessness and anxiety, by each fresh journeying. We got the habit of movement and the expectation of change in our blood. Change freed us for moving, but moving then made change seem easier and more natural. We became enamored of the new, we became wedded to change.

But let me cease this random catalog to fix on one point, one peculiar feature of our historical development, that might be illuminating to our brothers in Europe. It has been remarked again and again, and often with no little astonishment, that ours is now one of the three oldest governments in the world. For some reason or reasons, we have experienced only one revolution, and one civil war, and the first was less drastic than the great revolutions in Europe. How could such things be? How is it that our younger generation, or our disadvantaged groups, have not raised the flag of rebellion, not once, but over and over again?

A common answer is that we left feudalism behind, and so did not have to destroy before we could build anew. Another has always been that ours has been a country of such rich opportunities and such vast free spaces that rebellion was unnecessary. Still a third has been that democratic participation made rebellion unnecessary. And in all these explanations there is the power of truth. But how was it that we could so easily take advantage of the opportunities and the open spaces, whether of frontier or of town? Was it not that we could always get away? The dissatisfied or the dissenter temperaments could always pack up and go.

Which brings me to a still more significant question. Ours has been the land of equality, but of liberty or free opportunity too. How have we been able to reconcile equality with an individualism which gave opportunity for quite unequal achievements or rewards? In the corporate sphere, the sphere of large economic organizations, it is clear that we have striven to counter the grosser evils of inequality by legislation, by the regulation of trade, by antitrust and antimonopoly laws, by a public redistribution of wealth through income and inheritance taxes. But for the individual American, has it not also been the freedom to move which has made possible the symbiosis of equality and individual initiative in our effervescent society? If our youth, or our unsuccessful, had had to sit still and watch the hopeless piling up of the inequalities of power and wealth, either revolution or a crushing state socialism could hardly have been avoided.

Whereas, as things have been, an ambitious man could always get away from the "big shot" at home and perhaps even become a "big shot" himself in some other place. Even when all the empty spaces had long since been in part occupied, a man still had a second, or even a fifth, chance. And in a society as mobile as ours, no man's empire was apt to sit quiet under him. The M-factor, so to speak, has been our great American permit to be both more free and more equal than our contemporaries could manage to become in many a more static European society.

I am sure the effects of mobility, both good and bad, can be exaggerated. Mobility has been but one factor among many, one powerful stimulant among others no less powerful. But I am persuaded we should not ignore it, or take it for granted as perhaps we have done. And when we examine it, and discover in how many different ways it has facilitated change, and has helped give shape to our world of the twentieth century, it may be that we will agree that the apparently neutral act of moving is not without a broad social significance. America has been the *locus classicus,* perhaps I should say the *dislocus classicus,* of mobility. So a comparative study of human movement here and abroad will help us to understand what Americans are today. Perhaps it will even give us some hints of the direction in which the people of Europe are now turning, and an inkling of what they will be like in the years to come.

BIBLIOGRAPHY

For the better understanding of the moving European neither the ancient memories nor the modern folklore and statistics of mobility seem to have been adequately organized and studied. What we do have are some monumental works on the macro-migrations of times past, plus a modest profusion of special studies focusing most often on the refugee problem, or the economics of migration, or the exceptionally informative Swedish population statistics. Examples of the larger historical treatment are A. and E. Kulischer, *Kriegs und Wanderzüge: Weltgeschichte als Völkerbewegung* (Berlin and Leipzig, 1932); and Maximilien Sorre, *Les migrations des peuples: Essai sur la mo-*

bilité géographique (Paris, 1955). The tragic displacement of Europe's nationality groups in the present century is recorded in Dudley Kirk, *Europe's Population in the Interwar Years* (Geneva, 1946), and in Eugene M. Kulischer, *Europe on the Move: War and Population Changes, 1917–1947* (New York, 1948). Meanwhile a small regiment of writers on both sides of the Atlantic have insisted, often perhaps mistakenly, on the primacy of the acquisitive instinct, or the irresistible push-pull of prosperity and depression, or the rhythmic cycles of economic growth. See, for example, H. Jerome, *Migration and Business Cycles* (New York, 1926); C. Goodrich *et al.*, *Migration and Economic Opportunity* (Philadelphia, 1936); Pierre Fromont, *Démographie économique: Les rapports de l'économie et de la population dans le monde* (Paris, 1947); J. Isaac, *Economics of Migration* (New York and London, 1947); and Brinley Thomas, *Migration and Economic Growth* (Cambridge, England, 1954). By contrast the often decisive intermingling of religious or social motivations with the economic in Swedish mobility has been developed by such scholars as John S. Lindberg (1932), G. M. Stevenson (1932), Florence E. Jansen (1934), and notably by Dorothy Swaine Thomas in her *Social and Economic Aspects of Swedish Population Movements, 1750–1933* (New York, 1941). With Rupert B. Vance and others in the depression years, Thomas also helped inaugurate a new line of American statistical inquiry into migration differentials and population redistribution (Social Science Research Council, Research Bulletins 42 and 43, 1938).

For American students it was Marcus Lee Hansen who first persuasively argued the importance of Old World conditions and feelings in generating New World immigration; see his *The Atlantic Migration, 1607–1860* (Cambridge, Mass., 1940). Eleven years later Oscar Handlin published his classic—a most sympathetic and moving but in some ways misleading work of art—*The Uprooted* (Boston, 1951). Other studies of particular importance have been carried forward in this country by Robert E. Park on culture transfer and the marginal man (1921, 1928); H. L. Shapiro on migration and environment (1939); Nathan Glazer and Daniel P. Moynihan on the persistence of ethnic cultures (1963, etc.); and by John Higham on patterns of American nativism (1955).

The pioneer theorist of voluntary mobility, using Anglo-Irish statistics, was E. G. Ravenstein, writing in two papers on "The Laws of Migration," *Journal of the Royal Historical Society*, XLVIII (1885) and LIII (1889). Now Everett S. Lee, on wider American demographic data, is carrying forward the statement of theoretical probabilities in his "A Theory of Migration," *Demography*, III (1966), 47–57.

My own interest and inspiration derived originally from the American experiences of Alexis de Tocqueville, from dissatisfaction with Frederick Jackson Turner's frontier hypothesis, and from three pioneer interpretations developed in the 1920's: P. Sorokin, *Social Mobility* (1927; rev. ed., 1959); Rudolf Heberle, *Über die Mobilität der Bevölkerung in der Vereinigten Staaten* (Jena, 1929); and Ellsworth Huntington, *The Pulse of Progress* (New York, 1926) and "The Selective Action of Migration" (Zbiór Prac, Lwów, 1943). My personal debt is also great to Frank Thistlethwaite, who most perceptively suggested some of the unique features of American mobility in *The Great Experiment* (Cambridge, England, 1955), and followed this up with a review of the European foundations in "Migration from Europe Overseas in the Nineteenth and Twentieth Centuries," in *Rapports, V,* XIᵉ Congrès International des Sciences historiques (1960). Those interested in further exploration of the causes, character, and consequences of American mobility may consult George W. Pierson, "The Moving American," *Yale Review,* (Autumn 1954); "The M-Factor in American History," *American Quarterly* (Summer 1962), Supplement—also in Ludwig-Maximilians-Universität, *Amerikanische Gelehrtenwoche, 1961* (München, 1962); "Under a Wandering Star," *Virginia Quarterly* (Autumn 1963); "A Restless Temper . . . ," *American Historical Review* (July 1964); and " 'Goin' Some,' " *South Atlantic Quarterly* (Autumn 1964).

9

Slavery

DAVID BRION DAVIS

Of all American institutions, Negro slavery has probably been the one most frequently compared with historical antecedents and foreign counterparts, and with the least benefit to systematic knowledge. Quite understandably, modern scholars have been so impressed by the long submission and degradation of southern Negroes, as well as by the extraordinary prevalence of racial prejudice in the United States, that they have often pictured American slavery as a system of unique and unmitigated severity that stands in marked contrast to other forms of servitude. Yet Thomas Jefferson could confidently assert that in Augustan Rome the condition of slaves was "much more deplorable than that of the blacks on the continent of America," and list barbarities and cruelties which were commonplace in Rome but presumably unknown in Virginia. Apologists for American slavery were always fond of comparing the mildness of their own institution, supposedly evidenced by a rapidly increasing Negro population, with the harshness of slavery in the West Indies or ancient Rome, where a constant supply of fresh captives made up for an appalling mortality. Yet abolitionists were always inclined to argue that the slave system of their own country or empire was the worst in history. Foreign travelers were not only subject to nationalistic prejudice but tended to rank various slave systems on the basis of fortuitous impressions or the biased accounts of hospitable planters. When we recognize how often comparisons have been influenced by ulterior motives and have been directed to the fruitless question "Which nation's slavery was the worst?" we might conclude that the subject can most profitably be studied in geographical isolation.

Yet American slavery was a product of the African slave trade, which was itself an integral part of both European commercial expansion and New World colonization. Most of the components of the slave-trading and plantation systems were developed in the thirteenth and fourteenth centuries by Italian merchants who purchased Circassians, Tartars, and Georgians at commercial bases on the Black Sea and then transported them to markets in Egypt, Italy, and Spain. As early as 1300 the enterprising Italians were even working Negro slaves on sugar plantations in Cyprus. In the fifteenth century, when the Portuguese adopted similar practices in trading with West Africa, Negro slaves displaced the Moors and Russians as the lowest element in the labor force of Spain. Negroes were shipped to Hispaniola as early as 1502; and as the Spanish colonists gradually turned to the cultivation of sugar, the rising demand for labor became an enormous stimulus to the Portuguese African trade. By the seventeenth century the Atlantic slave trade had become a vast international enterprise as the Dutch, British, French, Danes, Swedes, and even Brandenburgers established forts and markets along the West African coast. On both sides of the Atlantic there was close contact between merchants, seamen, and planters of various nationalities. In addition to competing and fighting with one another, they borrowed techniques and customs, cooperated in smuggling, and gathered to buy slaves at such entrepôts as Curaçao. If the British planters of Barbados looked to Brazil as a model, Barbados itself provided the impulse for settling Carolina. There was, then, a high degree of institutional continuity which linked the European maritime powers in a common venture. A trade which involved six major nations and lasted for three centuries, which transported some 10 to 15 million Africans to the New World, and which became a central part of international rivalry and the struggle for empire, cannot be considered as a mere chapter in the history of North America.

The unpleasant truth is that there could hardly have been

successful colonization of the New World without Negro slaves, since there was no alternative source of labor to meet the needs required by the cultivation of sugar, rice, tobacco, and cotton, and since even the more diversified colonies were long dependent economically on the markets and earnings of the staple-producing regions. It must be emphasized that this common dependence on Negro slavery was never universally recognized or welcomed. From the first Spanish in Hispaniola to the British in Barbados and Virginia, colonists were slow and hesitant in committing themselves to a labor force of foreign captives. Among the frequent dreams of New World Utopias and second Edens, no one envisioned a model society of several thousand free Europeans overseeing the life and labor of several hundred thousand Negro slaves. From the beginning, racial antipathy was reinforced by the much stronger emotion of fear; and the dread of insurrection and racial war would always balance the desire for quick wealth through a reckless increase in slaves.

Nonetheless, from sixteenth-century Mexico to eighteenth-century Jamaica and South Carolina, colonial administrators were unable to maintain a reassuring ratio between white immigrants and Negro slaves. In regions where tropical or semi-tropical staples could be cultivated, it became clear that investment in slave labor was the key to expanded production and spectacular profit. The Negro slave played an indispensable role in the conquest and settlement of Latin America, and in the clearing and cultivation of virgin land from Trinidad to the lower Mississippi Valley and Texas. And as the possession of slaves became itself a symbol of affluence, prestige, and power, the demand for Negroes spread to urban and temperate zones. Important leaders in New England and French Canada seriously argued that only Negro slaves could meet the labor needs of their colonies. From 1732 to 1754 Negro slaves constituted more than 35 per cent of the immigrants entering New York City; by mid-century they were owned by about one-tenth of the householders of the province and accounted for 15 per cent of the total population. Meanwhile, the slave trade and American Negro slavery were sanctioned by treaties and the law of nations, by the acts and edicts of kings and parliaments, by the Spanish Council of the Indies and the great trading companies of England, Holland, and France, by the Catholic Church and the major Protestant denominations. All the colonies of the New World legalized the institution, and many competed with one another for a supply of labor that was never equal to the demand. For more than three centuries the Negro slave was deeply involved in imperial wars, revolutions, and wars of independence. Insofar as the Western Hemisphere has a common history, it must center on a common experience with Negro slavery.

But did slavery mean the same thing to the various colonists of the New World? The fact that Dutch slave traders imitated the Portuguese and that a Dutch ship brought the first Negroes to Virginia did not mean that a Negro's status would be the same in Virginia as in Brazil. In England, unlike Italy and the Iberian Peninsula, true slavery disappeared by the thirteenth century. On the other hand, English jurists perpetuated the legal concept of unlimited servitude, and English judges recognized the validity of enslaving and selling infidels. We still have much to learn about the character of servitude in the sixteenth century and the later evolution of slave status in the British, Dutch, and French colonies. In making future comparative studies it would be well to keep in mind two points which should prevent hasty generalizations. First, in many societies the slave has only gradually been differentiated from other kinds of unfree workers, and his status, rights, and obligations have been defined in practice before receiving legal recognition. Second, although the actual condition of slaves has varied greatly even within a single society, there has been a remarkable persistence and uniformity in the legal concept of the slave. Since this last point has often been disregarded in comparative approaches to American slavery, we shall elaborate on it here.

The status of slavery has always been surrounded with certain ambiguities that seem related to the institution's origins. To be enslaved as a result of capture in war or punishment for crime implied total subordination to coercive authority. Yet bondage for debt or as the result of self-sale suggested merely a reciprocal exchange of labor and obedience for sustenance and protection. When a bondwoman's offspring were claimed by her owner on the same basis as the natural increase of livestock, the status was assimilated to that of movable property. In societies where slaves have largely been recruited from the native poor and have performed no specialized economic function, as in ancient China, Egypt, and the Near East, the element of reciprocal rights and obligations has taken precedence over the elements of punishment and ownership. Nevertheless, the slave was legally defined as a thing not only in the Southern United States but in ancient Egypt, Babylonia, Greece, and Rome. And the Roman conception of the slave as at once a person and a piece of movable property prevailed in medieval France, Italy, and Spain; it was extended to Latin America and was incorporated in the Code Noir for the French colonies; and it reappeared in the laws and judicial decisions of British North America. A Virginia court merely affirmed the ancient Latin concept of chattel slavery when it ruled that "Slaves are not only property, but they are rational beings, and entitled to the humanity of the Court, when it can be exercised without invading the rights of property." And when an American master claimed the offspring of his female slaves or asserted his right to move, sell, trade, bequest, or give away his chattel property, he added nothing to a legal notion of slavery that had persisted in Europe for more than two thousand years.

The definition of the slave as chattel property implied a condition of rightlessness on the part of the slave. In neither Europe nor the Americas could a slave testify in court against a free person, institute a court action in his own behalf, make a legally binding will or contract, or own property. There were, to be sure, minor exceptions and variations. Slaves were sometimes allowed to testify in certain civil cases or give evidence against a master accused of treason. In North America at various times Negro bondsmen were permitted to plead benefit of clergy and to give evidence in capital cases involving other slaves. As in Rome and Latin America, they were accorded limited rights over personal property, including horses and cattle, and might act as a master's legal agent, though never with the freedom and complex prerogatives of the Roman slave. But what stands out above the exceptions and variations is the fact that from pre-Christian laws to the slave codes of the New World the bondsman had no civil capacities and was considered only as an extension of his master's legal personality.

Even in Puritan Massachusetts slaves were, in the words of Cotton Mather, who was simply echoing Aristotle, "the *Animate, Separate, Active Instruments* of other men."

One of the few significant differences in the legal status of slaves was that bondsmen were denied legal marriage in ancient Rome and in Protestant America, whereas slave marriages were recognized in Carthage, Hellenistic Greece, and in Catholic Europe and America. Largely to prevent the sin of fornication, Catholic theologians even ruled that a slave might marry against his master's will. Yet according to St. Thomas Aquinas, slavery was an "impediment" to marriage, comparable to impotence, and a slave's first obligation must be to his master, not his spouse. If a master had a moral duty to try to preserve the integrity of slave families, he still had a legal claim to all slave children, and might of necessity divide husband from wife or children from parents. Since there is evidence that Latin American masters often did little to encourage or respect slave marriages, and that North American masters often recognized such marriages and tried to keep families intact, one may suspect that actual differences were more the result of individual personality and economic pressure than of legal and moral rights. The main point is that in no society have slaves had a legal claim to their wives and children.

Religious conversion has always complicated the question of a slave's status. The Muslims and ancient Hebrews drew a sharp distinction between enslaving infidels and temporarily holding servants of their own faith who had been deprived of freedom by economic necessity. Although the first Church Fathers ruled unmistakably that baptism should have no effect on the temporal status of slaves, medieval Christians showed an increasing reluctance to enslave their fellow Christians and came to think of perpetual bondage as a punishment suitable only for infidels. But the authorities who condemned the sale of Christians and yet preached slaving crusades against the infidels were ultimately faced with the problem of the baptized infidel. In 1366 the priors of Florence explained that it was valid to buy or sell slaves who had been baptized so long as they had originally come "from the land and race of the infidels." This was, in effect, the same test later applied in Virginia and other North American colonies.

Baptism was to have no effect on a slave's status unless he had been a Christian in his native country. And if the Catholic colonists felt a much greater obligation to have their slaves baptized, North American laws encouraged conversion and recognized that the Negro had a soul that might be redeemed. After a century of inaction, the Protestant churches slowly began their work of spreading religion among the slaves, and by the mid-nineteenth century the proportion of converted Negroes was probably as large in parts of the United States as in Brazil. It is doubtful, however, whether the mass of slaves in any country ever enjoyed a meaningful religious life.

There was little that was distinctive in the police regulations and penal laws restricting the lives of North American slaves. Throughout the ages, and in virtually all parts of the Western Hemisphere, slaves were prohibited from carrying arms, traveling at night or without permission, and acting with disrespect toward a freeman. Fairly typical was a law of 1785 for Spanish Santo Domingo which ordered one hundred lashes and two years in jail for any Negro who raised his hand against a white man. The penalties for such crimes as theft and assault were everywhere more severe for slaves than for others. During the eighteenth century there was a tendency in most New World colonies to abandon the most sanguinary punishments, such as mutilation, dismemberment, and burning at the stake. Harsh restrictions and terrifying punishments persisted longest in the West Indies, where the disproportion of Negroes to whites was the greatest. But even in the West Indies the long-term trend was toward more humane punishment and an extension of the slave's legal protections.

It is misleading to say that Anglo-American law never recognized the Negro slave as a human personality whose rights to life, food, and shelter were protected by law. There was ample precedent for the 1846 ruling of a Kentucky judge that "A slave is not in the condition of a horse. . . . He is made after the image of the Creator. He has mental capacities, and an immortal principle in his nature. . . . The law . . . cannot extinguish his high born nature, nor deprive him of many rights which are inherent in man." Although a master might kill his slave with impunity in the ancient Near East, the Roman Republic, Saxon England, and under certain circumstances in the Iberian Peninsula and Latin America, and although in much of British America the murder of a slave was thought to merit only a modest fine, by the early nineteenth century the slave states of North America had put the killing or maiming of a Negro bondsman on the same level of criminality as the killing or maiming of a white man. In both the British Caribbean and the Southern states, courts sometimes held that slaves were protected by common law against such crimes as manslaughter or unprovoked battery. Georgia and North Carolina both held that slaves had a right to trial by jury, and North Carolina went so far as to recognize a slave's right to resist unprovoked attack. Of course it was one thing for American states to threaten punishment for cruelty to slaves, and to make masters legally obligated to give their bondsmen adequate food and shelter and to provide for their care in sickness and old age, and it was another matter to enforce such laws when Negroes were barred from testifying against white men. Nevertheless, one can plausibly argue that in terms of legal protections and physical welfare American slaves by the 1850's were as favorably treated as any bondsmen in history.

Yet one of the paradoxes of American slavery was that the laws protecting the physical welfare of slaves were accompanied by the severest restrictions on manumission. This brings us to the most important distinction between the legal status of slaves in British and Latin America. It should be stressed that taxes and other restrictions on manumission were common in antiquity, particularly in Rome, and that freedom suffered from prejudice and legal disabilities even when the stigma of slavish origin was not associated with race. There were discriminatory freedmen's laws, for example, in medieval Spain and Italy, and in Latin America as well. But only in the Southern United States did legislators try to bar every route to emancipation and deprive masters of their traditional right to free individual slaves. It is true that thousands of American slaves were manumitted by their owners, many after buying their freedom in installments, as was far more common in Latin America. It is also true that in some areas of Latin America a slave had no more realistic chance of becoming free than did his brother in Mississippi. Nevertheless, one may conclude that slavery in North America was distinctive in its efforts to build ever higher barriers against manumission. And there is evidence that this had less to do with slavery as such than with social attitudes toward racial integration.

Although the questions are of compelling importance, we cannot begin to determine whether slavery was a source of racial prejudice or prejudice a source of slavery, nor can we explain why prejudice became more dominant in the United States than in other parts of the New World. One may briefly state the principal facts that are relevant to a comparative study of slavery. Without denying the significance of racial difference as an aggravation to American bondage, we may note that throughout history slaves have been said to be naturally inferior, lazy, cunning, thievish. lascivious, fawning, deceitful, and incapable of life's higher thoughts and emotions. When not differentiated by race, they have often been physically marked off by shaven heads, brands, tattoos, and collars. There is unmistakable evidence of racial prejudice in Italy and the Iberian Peninsula, where colored slaves generally suffered from various indignities and disabilities. In Latin America Negro bondsmen were long denied the privileges and protections of Indian workers. Nonetheless, while Latin America was by no means immune from racial prejudice, even against freemen of mixed blood, there was a gradual acceptance of racial intermixture and a willingness to accept each stage of dilution as a step toward whiteness. In the British colonies, although the first Negroes had an ill-defined status and worked side by side with white servants, there was never any tolerance of racial blending. White fathers seldom acknowledged their colored offspring, and a mulatto or quadroon was still legally classed as a Negro. These differences may have been related to religion, sexual mores, social stratification, or the proportion of white women in a colonial population. But whatever the reason, prejudice against Negroes seems to have grown in the United States with the advance of popular democracy. It can be argued that this had less to do with slavery than with the status of the free Negro in an unusually mobile and unstratified white society. In other words, differences in slave systems may not account for the fact that while the Negro in the United States today has far more economic and educational opportunities than the Negro in Latin America, he also suffers from more overt discrimination from whites who feel superior but are unsure of their own status.

By focusing thus far on the legal status of slaves, we have given an oversimplified picture of institutional homogeneity. In actuality, of course, American slavery took a great variety of forms that were largely the result of economic pressures and such derivative factors as the nature of employment, the number of slaves owned by a typical master, and the proportion of slaves in a given society. Thus we correctly categorize North American slavery as plantation and staple-crop slavery, but tend to forget that in 1820 Negro bondsmen constituted 20 per cent of the population of Southern cities and that in 1860 there were a half million slaves working in factories, on railroad construction, as stevedores, as lumberjacks, on steamboats, and in numerous other jobs unconnected with agriculture. As in ancient Athens and Rome, and as in Latin America, slaves in the Southern states were employed as valets, waiters, cooks, nurses, craftsmen, and prostitutes. In spite of these well-known facts, most comparisons of slavery in British and Latin America have assumed that the institutions were virtually monolithic. We still lack comparative studies of the domestic servant, the slave artisan, the rented worker, and the slave in manufacturing establishments.

It has been said that the latifundia of southern Italy and Sicily provided an ancient precedent for the gang labor, the rationalized system of production, and the absentee ownership of the Caribbean plantation. But one must be careful not to lump all plantation agriculture in an undifferentiated class. Since the production of sugar, for example, was a long and continuous process that could be ruined by a delay in cutting, milling, boiling, or curing, the rhythm of plantation life was probably much the same in parts of Brazil as in Jamaica and Louisiana. The cultivation of sugar and rice required heavy capital investment, and in the West Indies and South Carolina led to slave gangs of several hundred being divided for specialized tasks under constant surveillance. Slavery in colonial South Carolina, though less characterized by absentee ownership, had more in common with slavery in the West Indies than either had with the institution in Virginia and Maryland. By 1765 South Carolina's forty thousand whites were outnumbered by ninety thousand slaves;

eight years later Jamaica's sixteen thousand whites kept uneasy watch over two hundred thousand slaves. In neither society could a field slave be in close or frequent contact with white men. In Virginia, on the other hand, the proportion of Negroes and whites was roughly equal, and the typical tobacco plantation employed less than twenty slaves. Unlike any of the previously mentioned staples, cotton did not require elaborate stages of preparation and processing, and could be profitably grown on small-scale farms. It was thus not uncommon for a cotton farmer to own less than ten slaves and even to work beside them in the field. Even by 1860, after a long period of rising slave prices, nearly one-half of the Southern slaveholders owned less than five Negroes apiece; 72 per cent owned less than ten apiece and held approximately one-quarter of the entire number of American slaves.

Compared with the plantation agriculture of the West Indies and Brazil, the striking features of the American South were the wide dispersal of slave ownership and the relatively small units of production scattered over immense areas. This may have led to a greater variation and flexibility in the relationship between master and slaves, although we still lack comparative research on such vital questions as labor management, the social roles and subculture of Negroes, and the relation of plantation life to social structure. It seems plausible that if American Negroes sometimes benefited by a close relationship with white families, they were also denied the sense of massive solidarity that was probably essential for revolt. In the West Indies slaves not only had the opportunity to plan and organize revolts, but they were seldom tied by the close bonds of loyalty that led so many North American slaves to divulge plots before they were hardly formed.

This is not to suggest that North American slaves were less oppressed than those of other times and regions, but only that there were different forms of oppression. As comparative studies move ahead toward finer distinctions and a typology of slave systems, it is likely that less attention will be paid to legal status than to stages of economic development. It would be absurd to claim that all slave economies must pass through a pre-set cycle of boom and depression. Nevertheless, regardless of cultural differences and other variables, there are striking examples throughout the Americas of a pattern which began with an unmitigated drive for quick profit, a rapid expansion in slaves and land under cultivation, and a subsequent overproduction of staples. Whenever slaves were worked under boom conditions, as in the West Indies in the mid-eighteenth century and the Brazilian coffee plantations in the nineteenth, the institution was one of grinding attrition. A more relaxed paternalism tended to appear when prices had fallen, when there was little incentive to maximize production, and when planters in longer-settled regions looked to social and cultural distinctions to differentiate themselves from new generations of hard-driving speculators. Thus in the mid-nineteenth century there is evidence that in such states as Virginia and Maryland a more easy-going, paternalistic pattern of slavery was emerging, not unlike that of the depleted sugar plantations of Brazil. In Maryland and Delaware there was even a rapid decline in the proportion of slaves to freedmen, though this was partly a result of interstate migration. At the same time there was a heavy drain of slaves toward the expanding cotton areas of the Southwest, where the price of labor kept rising and slaves became more concentrated in the hands of a relatively few planters.

The question of stages of economic development is related to the much larger question of the place of slavery in the evolution of industrial capitalism. And here, though historians have long acknowledged the dependence of the world's cotton textile industry on the slave systems of North and South America, there is an astonishing lack of systematic and comparative analysis. The whole complex relationship between capitalism and slavery is still in the realm of suggestive speculation. Scholars still debate whether slavery was profitable and whether the forms it took in America can be termed capitalistic. We do not yet fully understand why so many areas where slavery flourished were stultified by soil depletion and a lack of capital formation, by an absence of internal markets, of urbanization, and of technological innovation. And finally, if we are really to comprehend the significance of slavery and the burdens it has entailed, comparative history must explain the great challenge posed to the institution by an emerging urban, bureaucratic, and capitalistic civilization, which led to a bitter conflict between England and her Caribbean colonies, to a sharp struggle between the Brazilian coastal cities and the interior valleys, and to an epic contest between the North and South in the United States.

BIBLIOGRAPHY

The pioneering work in the comparative history of slavery is Frank Tannenbaum, *Slave and Citizen, The Negro in the Americas* (New York, 1947). Stanley M. Elkins, in *Slavery: A Problem in American Institutional and Intellectual Life* (Chicago, 1959), surveys much of the relevant literature and synthesizes the generalizations of Tannenbaum with concepts from the modern behavioral sciences. The Tannenbaum-Elkins thesis regarding the uniqueness of slavery in North America is challenged by Arnold A. Sio, "Interpretations of Slavery: The Slave Status in the Americas," in *Comparative Studies in Society and History*, VII (April 1965), 289–308; and by my own *The Problem of Slavery in Western Culture* (Ithaca, N.Y., 1966), which also analyzes attitudes toward slavery from antiquity to the early American abolitionists.

The most comprehensive study of North American slavery is still Ulrich B. Phillips, *American Negro Slavery* (New York, 1918), which needs to be supplemented by Kenneth M. Stampp, *The Peculiar Institution: Slavery in the Ante-Bellum South* (New York, 1956). John Hope Franklin, *From Slavery to Freedom* (2nd ed.; New York, 1956), offers a general survey of the Negro in America.

More specialized studies which shed light on important aspects of American slavery are Eugene D. Genovese, *The Political Economy of Slavery* (New York, 1965); Richard C. Wade, *Slavery in the Cities: The South 1820–1860* (New York, 1964); Eric Williams, *Capitalism and Slavery* (New York, 1944); and Leon F. Litwack, *North of Slavery: The Negro in the Free States* (Chicago, 1961). The debate over the profitability of slave labor is summarized by Harold D. Woodman, "The Profitability of Slavery: A Historical Perennial," *Journal of Southern History*, XXIX (August 1963), 303–325.

Elsa V. Goveia, in *Slave Society in the British Leeward Islands at the End of the Eighteenth Century* (New Haven, 1965), presents a detailed study of West Indian slavery. Negro bondage in the French colonies is described by Gaston Martin, *Histoire de l'esclavage dans les colonies françaises* (Paris, 1948) and Lucien Peytraud, *L'Esclavage aux Antilles françaises avant 1789* (Paris, 1897). For other valuable material on slavery in the New World, the student should consult J. Harry Bennett, Jr., *Bondsmen and Bishops: Slavery and Apprenticeship on the Codrington Plantation of Barbados* (Berkeley, 1958); Frank Wesley Pitman, *The Development of the British West Indies, 1700–1763* (New Haven, 1917); Lowell Joseph Ragatz, *The Fall of the Planter Class in the British Caribbean, 1763–1833* (New York, 1928); Gilberto Freyre, *The Masters and the Slaves: A Study in the Development of Brazilian Civilization* (New York, 1946); Arthur Ramos, *The Negro in Brazil* (Washington, 1951); Stanley J. Stein, *Vassouras: A Brazilian Coffee County* (Cambridge, Mass., 1957); C. R. Boxer, *Race Relations in the Portuguese Colonial Empire, 1415–1825* (Oxford, 1963), and *The Golden Age of Brazil, 1695–1750* (Berkeley, 1962).

The best survey of the slave trade is Basil Davidson, *Black Mother: The Years of the African Slave Trade* (Boston, 1961). The monumental work on slavery in medieval Europe is Charles Verlinden, *L'Esclavage dans l'Europe médiévale* (Brugge, 1955). While one cannot begin to indicate the vast literature on slavery in various societies, three titles which should not go unmentioned are William L. Westermann, *The Slave Systems of Greek and Roman Antiquity* (Philadelphia, 1955); Isaac Mendelsohn, *Slavery in the Ancient Near East* (New York, 1949); and Moses I. Finley (ed.), *Slavery in Classical Antiquity: Views and Controversies* (Cambridge, England, 1960). Finally, one should note that the volumes of the *Journal of Negro History* contain a mine of information for anyone interested in slavery in the Western Hemisphere.

10

Civil War

DAVID M. POTTER

It has been the curious fate of the United States to exert immense influence in the modern world, without itself quite understanding the nature of this influence. Major trends of the modern world—both constructive trends and socially injurious ones—have repeatedly become apparent in the United States before they became evident elsewhere. But though the United States has often been a step ahead in the process of social change, it has frequently been a step behind in its awareness of the meaning of new developments. The shape of things to come often became visible in America earlier than it did elsewhere, but American preconceptions about the frontier, the classless society, and the agrarian basis of democracy prevented Americans from perceiving this shape as realistically as it was perceived by social thinkers in other countries. If Americans have failed effectively to interpret their experience to people in other societies, it is in part because they have not always been able to explain it to themselves. Further, the distinctive qualities of life in America have caused a good many forces which were generically universal to take forms which seemed more restrictively peculiar to the New World than they really were.

Thus in the late eighteenth century, America executed the first democratic political revolution of a democratic age, but American society was already so equalitarian that the revolutionary implication was muted. Without any great social over-turn, the American War of Independence seemed conservative when compared with the socially cataclysmic forces released in France a decade later. In the twentieth century the United States developed what was perhaps the first mass society, but the American cult of equality and individualism prevented Americans from analyzing their mass society in realistic terms. Often they treated it as if it were simply an infinite aggregation of Main Streets in Zenith, Ohio. America has witnessed episodes of extreme industrial conflict, but these have not been interpreted in the class terms which a Marxist society would invoke. America has experienced a sweeping revolution in sex behavior, but has not incorporated this change into the system of values by which it explains itself. Ironically, the United States has cherished a belief in its mission to spread a democracy for which it has had difficulty in finding converts, while it has led the world in technological changes which produced social transformations that it had no especial desire to bring about.

The reader need not be astonished, therefore, if the Civil War has been interpreted in terms which disguised its broader meaning. If, as some Americans asserted, its chief importance was in putting an end to chattel slavery, this could hardly be regarded as a leading development in the history of Western civilization; for slavery had disappeared from western Europe, except vestigially, while it still flourished in the Americas, and it had disappeared from most of Latin America, except Cuba and Brazil, while it still persisted in the United States. The American republic was almost destroyed therefore in a struggle over an institution which world opinion regarded as an anachronism.

If, on the other hand, the Civil War was, as some other Americans asserted, important chiefly because it preserved the American Union, this statement also was framed in restrictive terms which failed to reveal its broader implications. Beginning with the mystic phrase, *E pluribus unum,* the republic had not been able for two generations to resolve the question whether it was, in the last analysis, *pluribus* or *unum.* The Civil War gave *unum* the upper hand, and the importance of this fact became visible in world history in 1917 and again in 1941 when the strength of a consolidated American republic impinged decisively on two world wars. But at the time, in a literal sense, there was not much significance for other nations in the fact that the United States waited for fourscore years and ten to settle a question which other nations settled at their inception. There seemed little universality of significance in a war fought to find, or at least determine, a clear meaning for a cryptic federal system such as no other nation had ever had, and such as was deliberately made ambiguous in the first place in order not to lose the support which it certainly would have lost if its meaning had been clarified.

While the war was in progress, European policy makers tended to think of it simply in terms of whether it would leave the United States weaker or stronger than before. After it was over, the only people who examined it closely were military historians, looking for the lessons of strategy and tactics that might be derived from the first major conflict in which repeating arms, ironclad vessels, trench warfare, and railroads as supply lines were used on a significant scale.

Thus, while the campaigns of Lee and Grant have fascinated English and European readers, just as the campaigns of Napoleon have fascinated Americans, and while the personality of Lincoln has held an appeal for men everywhere, writers have scarcely asked the question: what was the role of the American Civil War in the history of the modern world? Did it have historical significance for anyone except Americans?

If we are seeking an answer to this question, it may be useful to begin by asking ourselves, simply, what were the prevalent tendencies of the nineteenth century, and what did the Civil War contribute in causing these tendencies to prevail? Historians have neglected the latter part of this question, but have repeatedly given an answer to the first part. They tell us, over and over, that the nineteenth century was an era of liberalism and nationalism. The basis for the generalization is obvious. Nationalism, as we know it in its modern form, scarcely existed before the French Revolution; but by the end of the nineteenth century Britain, France, Germany, Italy, and Japan had become prototypes for modern nationality, sometimes after great travail. Nationalistic forces were fermenting throughout other parts of Europe, and even in the colonial world of Asia and Africa the premonitory stirrings of a latent nationalism could already be detected. The Monroe Doctrine had done its bit to make the Western Hemisphere safe for nationalism, and the Latin Americans had responded by erecting eighteen separate nationalistic republics. Likewise with liberalism. It was scarcely more than an ideology in the minds of British and French rationalists before the French Revolution, but by the beginning of the twentieth century representative government and other liberal institutions prevailed in Britain, France, and Italy, and to some extent even in Germany and Austria-Hungary. The Hapsburgs, the Hohenzollerns, and the Romanoffs were still on their thrones, but they stood on the defensive before the onslaughts of Social Democrats, Social Revolutionaries, and other militant reformers.

All these facts are familiar to the point of triteness and it would be parochial to exaggerate the importance of the American Civil War in connection with them. But if we are to define the place of this war in terms of world history, rather than merely of American history, there are two aspects in which it exercised a crucial effect in shaping the tendencies of world history. These aspects may or may not have served the long-range welfare of human society, and it may be argued that, ultimately, their effect was pernicious. But for good or ill, here are two things which the Civil War did: first, it turned the tide which had been running against nationalism for forty years, or ever since Waterloo; and second, it forged a bond between nationalism and liberalism at a time when it appeared that the two might draw apart and move in opposite directions.

Because of the ultimate triumph of nationalism as a worldwide force by 1900, it is easy to forget how seriously nationalism appeared to have failed at the time when the Civil War occurred. After establishing firm bridgeheads in Britain and France, it had met with disaster after disaster in its efforts to spread into southern and central Europe. Britain had moved successfully to suppress nationalism in Ireland, and Russia had taken the most repressive measures in 1830 to crush it out in Poland. After the galaxy of nationalist revolutions of 1848 the dreams of a United Italy had ended with disaster at Custozza, those of a United Germany with the anticlimax of the Frankfurt Parliament, those of Czechoslovakia with the overthrow of the Pan-Slavic Congress, and those of Hungary with the defeat of Louis Kossuth. Simultaneously, in America, the steadily rising tensions between North and South seemed increasingly likely to destroy the feeling of national unity which had appeared completely triumphant during the first two decades of the century. The forces of nationalism reasserted themselves successfully in the Italian peninsula in the two years preceding the American Civil War, but otherwise nationalism and especially liberal nationalism in Europe seemed a lost cause. Louis Napoleon had made himself emperor of France in 1852, and within another decade was busily planting a Hapsburg imperialist regime in Mexico.

Viewed from the standpoint of appearances only, the forces which opposed nationalism in Europe were entirely unlike those which opposed it in America. In Europe, one might say, the forces which thwarted nationalism were those of universalism—of the Catholic Church and of the Hapsburg and Romanoff empires, for which the nationalist impulse seemed too localizing and disruptive. In America, one might say, the forces which thwarted it were those of localism and of sectionalism, for which the nationalist impulse seemed too consolidating and centralizing. In Europe, imperial forces sought to stamp out nationalism from above; in America, particularistic forces sought to resist it from below. It is perhaps because the opposition was centripetal in Europe and centrifugal in America that historians have tended to overlook the parallel triumphs of national unification, all within a period of twelve short years, in Italy, the United States, and Germany.

But the contrast between universalism and localism, as the forces which opposed nationalism, is perhaps more apparent than real. In both Europe and America, the forces of tradition and privilege tended to be arrayed against nationalism, while the forces of liberalism and democracy tended to support it. In America, the succession of the Southern states has been accurately described as a conservative revolt—a revolution by men who were not revolutionists, and who justified their revolution less by a philosophical defense of the right of the self-determination of peoples than by refined, legalistic arguments upon the intent of the Constitution of 1787. These "Rebels," instead of advocating change, were rebelling against it and were the champions of a traditional, relatively static, hierarchical society. They feared, with some reason, as we may now conclude, the transformations that might be wrought by an industrial society. They feared the destruction of a familiar social order and defended the evil institution of slavery less because they believed in human bondage as such than because they could not conceive of their social order without slavery.

In a certain sense, then, the landed planters of the South who opposed American nationalism were not unlike the landed proprietors in central Europe who opposed German or Polish or Italian or Hungarian or Bohemian nationalism. All of them were traditionalists. All feared that nationalism was linked with a democracy which they distrusted. All feared to release from the bottle the genii of manhood suffrage, of democratic equality, of social mobility, of universal education—and in the South, of emancipation for almost four million slaves. In this sense, European and American conservatism shared much in common, and the issue in the war between North and South carried implications considerably beyond the mere question as to whether the American states should form one republic or two.

The uprising of the North in 1861, and its decision to wage a war to preserve the American Federal Union, coming in the same year in which Victor Emmanuel was crowned king of a united Italy, marked a turning of the tide which had been running against nationalism for the preceding forty-five years. For better or worse, the course was set toward a world of sovereign nation-states, subject to no ultimate control in their conduct toward one another. The process of forging additional nations would reach out, within another century, from Europe and the Americas to Asia and Africa until by 1966 there would be more than 130. As the number of "nations" increased, the beneficial effects of nationalism became increasingly uncertain, for all too many of the new sovereignties regarded the possession of nuclear destructive power as the crowning sanction of their nationhood.

Nationalism today seems something of a curse because of the paradox that while the people of the earth have been growing more and more functionally interdependent socially and economically, they have also simultaneously grown more and more irresponsibly independent of one another politically. The fragmentation of empires and other forms of supranational political authority has proceeded in ironic parallelism with increases in the cohesion of the peoples whose political relationships are being fragmented. At the same time, nationalism has shown that it can have a hideous side, undreamed of by such idealistic nationalists as Mazzini, and Lamartine, and Daniel Webster. Hitler is the supreme example, but even at the present moment a number of tyrants whose authority would command no more respect than that of a gangster if it were not sanctified by the mystique of national inviolability—a number of such tyrants have given us cause to doubt that the advancement of nationalism is necessarily a contribution to human progress. Suppose Lincoln did save the American Union, did his success in keeping one strong nation where there might have been two weaker ones really entitle him to a claim to greatness? Did it really contribute any constructive values for the modern world?

To answer this question, it may be necessary to recognize not only that Lincoln sought to save American nationalism, but also why he sought to save it. To him, as to other idealistic nationalists, the Union—that is, the nation—was not an end in itself but a means to an end. He might affirm that "my paramount object . . . is to save the Union," and he might wage one of the most deadly wars ever fought up to that time to achieve his object. But he thought of the Union primarily as a context within which freedom might be preserved and extended. Moreover, he thought that survival of a liberal nation in America was vital as a test of the survival capacity of liberal nationalism anywhere. Thus, although personally he was distinctively and uniquely and even restrictively American—the only one of the great presidents who never went outside the United States—he thought of American democracy in the least restrictive of terms. Many years before his Presidency, he eulogized Henry Clay as one who "loved his country partly because it was his own country but mostly because it was a free country." When the Civil War came, he asserted that it involved "more than the fate of these United States" and was of concern "to the whole family of man." The Union mattered to him not because of the question of authority at Washington, but because of the "necessity that is upon us of proving that popular government is not an absurdity." In his supreme moment at Gettysburg, this American nationalist did not once use the word American, or United States. He spoke, to be sure, of the nation "which our fathers brought forth," but this one nation conceived in liberty and dedicated to equality was linked in his thought with "any other nation so conceived and so dedicated." He wanted the war to result, for his own nation, in a "new birth of freedom," but this goal was not for America alone; it was to assure "men everywhere" that "government of the people, by the people, and for the people shall not perish from the earth."

It has been well said that Lincoln fused the cause of Union with the cause of freedom, which is equivalent to saying that he fused the cause of nationalism with the cause of liberalism. A number of idealistic nationalists of the nineteenth century made this same equation, and impressed it upon the public mind so vigorously that, even a century later, when we have had fairly numerous as well as traumatic illustrations of how completely antagonistic liberalism and nationalism can sometimes be, most of us respond affirmatively to claims made in the name of national integrity. We do so because our own thought still moves in the grooves cut by the great liberal nationalists of the nineteenth century.

This equation of liberalism and nationalism is not, of course, without logical foundations. Nationalism and liberalism both share certain common assumptions. Both depend upon the awakening self-consciousness of the individual—in the one case awakening to his membership in the political community, in the other awakening to his rights to participate in the decisions of the community and to enjoy its advantages. But while logic might impel nationalism and liberalism to go hand in hand, history often violates logic, and today we have copious proof that nationalism can flourish in separation from any liberal counterpart. It did so in Fascist Italy and Nazi Germany. It does so in Red China, and in Soviet Russia (though these countries theoretically reject nationalism), and it is doing so in various dictatorships in the "emerging" nations. But if one kind of logic would prove nationalism and liberalism to be twin offspring of the idea of the free individual as patriot and as citizen, there is another logic which declares liberalism and nationalism to be opposites, since liberalism regards the state as existing for the individual and nationalism regards the individual as existing for the state.

This is only to say that the nineteenth-century conjunction of nationalism and liberalism was by no means inevitable. To regard it as inevitable is to lose the larger meaning of the Civil War, for the war was one of the important historic developments contributing to a conjunction which, in other circumstances, might never have occurred. Lincoln's dedication of nationalistic means to liberal ends went far to produce this conjunction in the cosmos of American values. But at the same time when Lincoln was fusing nationalism with liberalism in America, another of the great figures who made the nineteenth century a century of nationalism, Count Otto von Bismarck, was carefully disassociating liberalism from nationalism in Germany. Having watched how the debacle of liberalism wrecked all hopes of German unification at Frankfurt in 1848, Bismarck wedded his nationalism to a concept of power and not to ideas of freedom or popular government. He signalized this position by publicly embracing a policy of "blood and iron" when he came to the head of the Prussian ministry in the year of Lincoln's Emancipation Proclamation. Nine years and three wars later, while President Grant, as the head of an imperfectly reunited nation, was struggling to reconcile the liberal principle of home rule for the South with the liberal principle of citizenship rights for the Negro, Bismarck made his monarch emperor of a Germany which was at last firmly united under authoritarian controls.

Bismarck and Lincoln were, perhaps, the two foremost exponents of nineteenth-century nationalism, after Napoleon. No two exemplars of the same force could have been more dissimilar, and no dramatist could have designed two figures better suited to point up contrasting styles of nationalism. The Gettysburg Address would have been as foreign to Bismarck as a policy of "blood and iron" would have been to Lincoln.

The contrast, perhaps, points the way to what was significant, in world perspective, about the American Civil War. The significance lay not in the fact that it was a triumph for nationalism (though the war forged the North as well as the South into a nation larger than any in western Europe), not in the fact that it was a triumph of liberalism (though Lincoln vindicated government of the people, by the people, and for the people, and proved that democracy, with all its weaknesses, can withstand the shocks of war). The significance lay rather in the fact that the Civil War, more perhaps than any event in Europe, fused the two great forces of the nineteenth century—liberalism and nationalism. It fused them so thoroughly that their potential separateness was lost from view. The fusion gave to nationalism a sanction which, frequently since then, it has failed to deserve, and gave to liberalism a strength which, since then, it has frequently not known how to use.

Meanwhile, Americans remained in confusion as to what their war had signified for the world. Some thought they had proved the strength of democracy, forgetting that the Confederacy which they defeated was also democratic and shared democracy's weaknesses. Others thought that they had vindicated the principle of nationalism, forgetting that the loyalty which Southerners gave to the Confederacy was no less nationalistic than the loyalty which Yankees gave to the Union. Few perceived that one of the most sweeping consequences of the war was to identify with one another these two forces which were not necessarily linked. This partially fictitious identification may, in the final analysis, have done great harm by giving a spurious sanction to modern nationalism, with all its potential dangers for the larger human society. But in a more immediate sense, it was perhaps the most constructive identification made during the nineteenth century, for it gave significant moral purpose to the force of nationalism, which, without such purpose, was always in danger of degenerating into mere group egocentrism or chauvinism. At the same time, it also gave significant institutional support to the principle of freedom, which without such support would have had only the ideals of reformers to sustain it.

BIBLIOGRAPHY

While the bibliography of the American Civil War is, of course, enormous, the bibliography strictly applicable to this essay is composed largely of books that are yet to be written. It is in fact one point of the essay that the significance of the Civil War for world history, and particularly for the history of nationalism, has been generally neglected by historians.

A good bibliography of the general literature on nationalism up to the date of its publication is Koppel S. Pinson, *A Bibliographical Introduction to Nationalism* (New York, 1934). An interesting interpretative treatment is Boyd C. Shafer, *Nationalism: Myth and Reality* (New York, 1955), and a somewhat older one is Hans Kohn, *The Idea of Nationalism: A Study of Its Origins and Background* (New York, 1943). Carlton J. H. Hayes, *Essays on Nationalism* (New York, 1926) and *The Historical Evolution of Modern Nationalism* (New York, 1931) are still of interest.

The theme of nationalism in American history is treated in Hans Kohn, *American Nationalism: An Interpretative Essay* (New York, 1957). On the impact of nationalism on the historiography of the American Civil War see David M. Potter, "The Historian's Use of Nationalism and Vice Versa," *American Historical Review*, LXVII (1962), 924–950. For rather random samples of foreign views of the Civil War see Belle B. Sideman and Lillian Friedman (eds.), *Europe Looks at the Civil War* (New York, 1960).

A good critical assessment and analysis of Civil War historiography is Thomas J. Pressly, *Americans Interpret Their Civil War* (Princeton, 1954). Of the thousands of works on the subject, two of the most important are J. G. Randall, *Lincoln the President* (4 vols.; New York, 1945–1955; Vol. IV completed by Richard N. Current) and Allan Nevins, *The Emergence of Lincoln* (2 vols.; New York, 1950) and *The War for the Union* (2 vols.: 1959–1960, with more to come).

For the idea of the comparison of Lincoln and Bismarck, I am indebted to Denis W. Brogan, *The Free State* (London, 1945).

11

Reconstruction: Ultraconservative Revolution

ERIC McKITRICK

I

It has been understood for some time that the American Civil War was a revolution. But more than a hundred years have had to pass before Americans can finally begin to understand what sort of revolution it actually was. Not so many years ago our historians were still arguing that the Civil War—"the Second American Revolution," as the late Charles Beard called it—represented the final victory of Northern capitalism in its relentless aggressions against the agrarian economy of the South, and that slavery was in no true sense the central issue. Such a point of view was first encouraged by Marx and Engels, who observed the war and followed its course with great interest, and arguments based on some version of that same viewpoint have not entirely disappeared from the discussions of historians even today. Other writers in turn have argued that the Civil War should not be considered as a Marxian revolution of North against South, but rather as a revolution of the South against the United States—that slavery *was* indeed the central issue, and that in order to preserve slavery the Southern states were willing to undertake a war of liberation. The true revolutionary act, then, was the South's effort to achieve separation from the Federal Union. And yet by viewing the Reconstruction that followed the Civil War, and by considering it and the war together as parts of the same process, we begin to see that perhaps the North was, in a larger sense, the revolutionary aggressor after all. Moreover, by connecting these events with the events of today as part of an even larger pattern, we may see at last what sort of revolution it really was. We may see that its deepest, most pressing, most fundamental issue was, and still is, the proper place of the American Negro in American life. And we may even wonder, as we consider the experience of Reconstruction, whether the American political and constitutional structure itself provides a truly adequate framework within which the revolution may be brought to a satisfactory as well as peaceful close.

It has been very difficult for historians or anyone else to view all this as a single revolutionary cycle. One reason is that the cycle has been so long: it began at least a generation before the Civil War and has not yet ended. But the more important reason is that its central problem—the Negro's place in American life—was one which Americans were never willing to confront directly, even at the most critical phases of the revolution, those of the Civil War and Reconstruction. This confusion, this ambiguity, this reluctance to face the implications of a problem of such magnitude, have had curious effects on Americans' very habits of historical thought. Despite the enormous and persistent interest in the Civil War, and despite the lesser but still considerable interest in Reconstruction, the latter period has become intellectually encapsulated. It has been isolated within the national consciousness and the national memory in a very unusual way, considering the things that a revolution does to a nation's life. With regard to the objectives of the Reconstruction, even of the Civil War, the quality of our writing, our thought, and our public discourse has been very diffuse and has shown a remarkable lack of precision. Nevertheless, the demands of the 1960's have made it clear that the revolution is not yet finished, that it has not gone nearly far enough, and that the original character of the revolution must be considered all over again.

The problem, indeed, was systematically quarantined from the very first, even while society was beginning to concede its urgency. In a way this is understandable. In almost every ordinary sense the United States on the eve of the Civil War was politically, socially, and economically one of the most stable countries in the world. A political and constitutional system had been established which was acceptable to virtually the entire population. It was characterized by universal white manhood suffrage and a level of citizen participation not seen since the days of the Greek republics. Its electoral practices may have included strong elements of demagoguery and vulgar carnival appeal, but the result was a system of party government which was in many respects the most sophisticated in the world. And whereas most European countries at mid-century were permeated with the ferment of social revolution, the United States was perhaps the one nation in the Western world where the overwhelming bulk of the population was profoundly committed to laissez-faire capitalism. It had no tory class, no tory socialism, no aristocracy with traditions of noblesse oblige or a sense of responsibility for checking the excesses of laissez faire. American society, as Tocqueville had discovered a generation earlier, had become intensely egalitarian and intensely committed to the ideal of equal opportunity and careers open to talent. It would be difficult for most Europeans to understand that those values normally regarded elsewhere as "bourgeois" were in 1860 the values of the American farmer, the American workingman, and the American entrepreneur.

All of these values were embodied in the career and person of Abraham Lincoln, who was to be the leader of the "revolutionary" party of 1860. Lincoln, rising from the poorest possible origins, largely self-educated, a leader in politics while still a young man, becoming a successful railroad lawyer, and emerging from state politics in Illinois to become the Republican nominee for the Presidency, insisted again and again that there was no real gulf between capital and labor. "There is no permanent class of hired laborers amongst us," he announced in one of several speeches he made on this subject in 1859. "Twenty-five years ago,

I was a hired laborer. The hired laborer of yesterday, labors on his own account today; and will hire others to labor for him to-morrow. Advancement—improvement in condition—is the order of things in a society of equals." Probably few men of any class who heard these words would have thought of doubting their essential truth. For most Americans living in the North, this highly satisfactory state of affairs had come to be directly connected with the continued stability of the Federal Union. The one great flaw in it, as Lincoln reminded his audiences in each of these speeches, was the continued existence of a very rigid system of chattel slavery.

Americans had inevitably been brought to confront this problem. But they did so reluctantly, despite the steady growth of antislavery feeling which had already begun to force itself into national politics by the 1840's. This feeling could only be admitted into the realm of political discourse and contention by placing all stress upon the Union and virtually none upon the Negro, in order to maintain some sort of unity even in the North. It was done not by a direct assault upon slavery, but through the formula of "Free Soil": not by challenging slavery where it was, but by declaring that it should not be carried into new places where it did not yet exist. In short, men did face the issue, but they deliberately avoided facing it directly as long as they possibly could.

Even after the war broke out, they continued to avoid it. In order to prevent the alienation of a sizable portion of the Northern people, to say nothing of the border states which had not seceded, the administration felt it necessary to declare that its sole purpose in waging war was to restore the Federal Union. Lincoln announced this on many occasions in the most solemn tones. "I would save the Union," he insisted; "I would save it the shortest way under the Constitution. The sooner the national authority can be restored, the nearer the Union will be 'the Union as it was.'. . . My paramount object in this struggle is to save the Union, and is *not* either to save or to destroy slavery." And yet the man to whom this was written—Horace Greeley, editor of the influential New York *Tribune*—himself represented a growing sector of public opinion which was insisting that emancipation should be made one of the objects of the war. It had already become obvious to Lincoln by the summer of 1862 that without the support of this sector the continued vigor of the war effort might itself be undermined; and although he had told Greeley, "If I could save the Union without freeing any slave, I would do it," he also conceded that if he "could do it by freeing all the slaves," he would do that. But if he conceded this much, he was hardly prepared to go the whole way, because he too understood public opinion, probably better than Greeley. The Emancipation Proclamation (which, according to one of our historians, "had all the moral grandeur of a bill of lading") was presented not as a statement of high purpose but as a measure of military necessity.

It was the same with regard to the use of Negro troops in the Union Army. Two objectives might be served by accepting Negro enlistments. One of them directly concerned the Negro himself: "Once let the black man get upon his person the brass letters, U.S.," as the Negro abolitionist Frederick Douglass expressed it, ". . . and there is no power on earth which can deny that he has earned the right to citizenship in the United States." The other was that Negro soldiers might augment the declining strength of the army and thus assist in suppressing the rebellion. Of the two objectives, the Northern public would accept only the second. Even this could occur only after the war was well under way, and after many discouraging military reverses. Few concessions were made to the Negro's representing any more than a matter of military policy. Negro regiments could have no Negro officers, and the United States Congress refused to grant them equal pay with white troops until the war was nearly over. The Negro's proper role, even in the society of wartime, could not be considered on its own terms but only in the interest of some other objective. Even the President, despite his "oft-expressed personal wish that all men everywhere could be free," could still think of no more satisfactory way of dealing with slaves who had been freed than to encourage them to leave the country. His "first impulse," he had stated in 1854, "would be to free all the slaves and send them to Liberia"; eight years later, on the very eve of emancipation, he was earnestly urging a committee of Negro leaders to colonize themselves and their families in Central America, as the best example that could be offered to American Negroes everywhere.

II

Once the war was over, the problem of dealing both with the Negro and with the readmission of Southern states to the Federal Union dominated all else. But all emphasis was placed upon the latter. And again, the first instinct was to change as little as possible. By constitutional amendment the Negro had been given his freedom, but few steps were taken to adjust him to his new status. At the same time elaborate efforts were made by the administration of Lincoln's successor, Andrew Johnson, to re-establish state governments in the South which would be more or less identical with those in existence before the war. Certain things were rejected almost out of hand. There was to be no redistribution of land, either with or without compensation. There was no insistence that Negroes be accorded rights of citizenship. Federal responsibility for education and welfare was regarded as being only of the most temporary and limited kind. Legislation to expand even the minimal services of this sort that did exist—those performed by the wartime Freedmen's Bureau—was opposed by the President, and there were not enough votes in the national Congress to enact it over his veto. It is certainly true that the President's position on these questions lagged behind that of the Republican majority in Congress, and perhaps even somewhat behind the center position in public opinion. But the differences, in 1865 and 1866, were hardly more than differences in degree.

The revolution was destined to go considerably further than anything Andrew Johnson had in mind. But its conservative nature would still be such, even at its height, as to make it hardly comparable to any other revolutionary or counterrevolutionary movement known to modern Western history. Not one political prisoner, for example, was ever put to death. The political head of the rebellion was kept in prison for two years and then set free, while the rebellion's military chief was never molested at all. The President of the United States spent much of his time during the first year of peace over matters of amnesty and pardon; and a few years later, while Congressional Reconstruction was still in full force, an act of general amnesty in effect removed that problem from further contention altogether. The government of Soviet Russia was executing enemies of the Revolution years after the Revolution itself was over. Even in England, whose revolution was one of the earliest and mildest, the revolutionary party felt it expedient to execute the head of the state, after having done away with his two chief advisors, and to massacre priests, women, and children in Ireland. With the Restoration, only the genial disposition of the king himself prevented a blood bath of vengeance and limited the number of executions to a dozen regicides.

The political, constitutional, legal, and administrative changes effected in the United States through the Civil War and Reconstruction were almost invisible compared with those that remained in France from the French Revolution, even after the restoration of the Bourbon monarchy. There, the provincial boundaries of the Old Regime were eliminated forever (in the America of 1865 and 1866, the very thought of such a thing made men turn pale with consternation); while the new geographical boundaries were designed in such a way that the resulting "departments" could be uniformly administered through the central government in Paris. (In the American South, even today, mere "interference" by the central government is the issue most likely to unite the entire population.) The most sweeping changes in property, class, fiscal, and jurisdictional relationships throughout French society, effected by the Revolution and codified by Bonaparte, were never reversed despite all efforts by the Bourbons to turn back the clock. The American "Bourbons," as the South's post-Reconstruction leaders were called, hardly needed to turn back the clock at all. No changes on this scale had been effected in the first place. As for the emancipated slaves, far less was done for them by the United States government in the way of land redistribution and social planning than was done during that very same period for the emancipated serfs of autocratic imperial Russia.

By 1867 the extraordinary refusal of President Andrew Johnson to cooperate with Northern leadership on any of the problems of readjustment, plus the determination of the South to resist even the minimal implications of change, had brought the North—still reluctantly—to see the need for stronger measures. The result was called "Radical Reconstruction." These measures, designed to protect Negroes and those Southern whites who had supported the Union, represented the high point of revolutionary action. The military occupation, followed by the enfranchisement of the entire Negro male population, the temporary disqualification of former Confederate leaders from suffrage and officeholding, and the establishment and support of state governments heavily dependent upon Negro votes and operated by pro-Union whites and Negroes constituted the closest thing to a revolutionary situation that was reached.

This situation, which began deteriorating almost at once, lasted no more than a few years. By 1877 all of the so-called "Radical" state governments had been expelled, mostly through the force of local pressure. Two general criticisms of this experiment may be made, not counting the traditional one that the Southern white people had been forced for a time to accept regimes which they did not want. One is that this relatively radical political program was not accompanied by anything systematic in the way of social and economic welfare. Much of what was accomplished in matters of education, for example, had to be undertaken through private efforts by Northern philanthropic groups, and in the face of enormous local resistance. There was no confiscation of estates, and no systematic effort to aid the freedmen in acquiring holdings of their own. Thus it might be said that the true priorities were reversed: that the Negro was given the vote before he had either the education or the economic power that would enable him to make effective use of it. The other criticism is that, even if it were granted that political rights ought to have come first after all, the federal government was still unprepared to undertake the massive commitment of long-term supervision, combined with continuing force, that would have been needed to preserve those rights.

Thus in the face of corruption, inefficiency, and chronic local aggression and unrest, the federal government gradually withdrew its support and allowed the white community in each state to re-establish full control. By 1877 the political, social, and economic systems of the South had become remarkably similar to what they had been in 1860, except that now the Negro was a landless laborer rather than a legally bound slave. A final stage of reaction remained. In the general effort to reconstitute the structure which had been disrupted by the Civil War and Reconstruction, even the Negro's small political gains—to say nothing of the minimal social rights he had acquired, in no way commensurate with the total effort and sacrifices implied in that war —were systematically removed. One by one, and with no interference whatever, the Southern states now began by law to impose systems of social segregation and disfranchisement which set the Negro entirely outside the mainstream of Southern civic life. By 1900 the process was virtually complete.

III

Without a clear center of gravity, historical discussion of this entire problem has had a somewhat erratic character. For the most part, it has been considered well within the context of the American constitutional system, and with very cautious assumptions, quite orthodox and traditional, as to where the boundaries of that system are located. One line of thought, probably more persistent than any other, regards the whole episode of Reconstruction with the most profound distaste, because it prolonged into peacetime the internal conflicts and alienations which had driven the American people into fratricidal war. The Civil War and Reconstruction thus represented a breach that must above all be healed, smoothed over, reknit. Perhaps the definitive statement of this position was made by Paul Buck in his *Road to Reunion, 1865–1900*. Yet it may also be significant that the terminal date of Professor Buck's study coincides with that very point in time at which the Negro's own exclusion from American society had been made all but complete.

My own study of Andrew Johnson's role in Reconstruction, published seven years ago, also assumes reunion to be a primary value, without questioning the limits of the system as it then existed. I argued, perhaps somewhat conservatively, that within those limits, and without violating the basic assumptions and values of the most enlightened men of the time, far more might have been done toward solving the problems of reconstruction, as well as of reunion, than was in fact done. And yet these assumptions might themselves be questioned. An English historian of great perception and intelligence, William R. Brock, has recently looked at the subject of Reconstruction through the eyes of an outsider. He concludes that the very system of federalism, as established by the Constitution and construed by two generations of pre-Civil War Americans, was simply not adequate for the containment of a problem of such dimensions and magnitude.

As the problem confronts us all over again in the 1960's, we might well consider the bare possibility, at least, of Brock's being right. It could be argued that the decision to commit federal power to reconstruction would not have been taken at all but for the abnormal stimulus of a crisis between the executive and legislative branches of the federal government. Then, as the will to maintain that commitment began to wane, there remained to the states—thanks to the federal "balance"—all the power they needed to expel with relative ease those features of Reconstruction they found not to their liking. By the turn of the century the states, using the authority of their state governments to render federal law inoperative, could place restrictions on the political and social rights of Negroes which the judicial branch of the federal government could overlook only by allowing the law to be construed in a highly strained and dubious way. These restrictions—virtual disfranchisement and complete social segregation—remained until World War II almost wholly unchallenged. As late as 1964 the Assistant Attorney General in charge of civil rights, Burke Marshall, was not optimistic about the future of federal law enforcement. At that time Mr. Marshall devoted two public lectures at a major university to the inherent restrictions imposed by the very structure of the federal system. Even the guarantee of voting rights, despite a series of federal laws beginning in 1957 which simply attempted to enforce the Fifteenth Amendment, had been for practical purposes frustrated in innumerable Southern communities.

Thus in view of what is minimally indispensable to complete

the revolution begun with emancipation and Reconstruction, the restrictions of the federal structure do indeed seem formidable. The minimum obligations go well beyond political rights. They include full employment and whatever is necessary to guarantee it: special programs of training, the full opening of union membership, and the elimination of job discrimination. They include massive support for education, recognizing that the need for special compensatory instruction enormously complicates a problem complex enough already. They include a vast expansion of municipal recreation facilities, and automatic government responsibility in all cases of major social disturbance. They include adequate housing, which means not simply a great deal more low-cost public housing but open access to all housing, even to the point of public guarantees of property values. Whatever the present restrictions of the federal structure, it seems imperative that any real movement toward realizing these aims requires a national government with the power to act.

And yet this is hardly as utopian as may now appear, nor need one be so quick to assume that the governmental structure of federalism is the truly critical factor. History itself shows us otherwise. It is rather a question of the community's will to use what powers its federal government already has. Mr. Marshall's pessimism in 1964 over Negro voter registration, for example, was rendered to a considerable extent out of date after two more years of focused federal legislation and effort, and resistance to Negro registration is no longer the major issue it was then. Or, to go back a full century: although there was not the remotest constitutional precedent for the Reconstruction legislation of 1867, the majority found a constitutional sanction for it anyway, strained though it may have been, in the obligation of Congress to guarantee to each state a republican form of government. During the New Deal period of the 1930's, federal intervention in state affairs went beyond anything most men would have thought possible a few years before. And this was nothing to the vast scope which federal power allowed itself for the purposes of fighting World War II. Controlling and directing the entire national economy, and in effect regulating the lives of millions of people, both military and civilian, the federal government impinged itself on the rights of the citizenry to a degree vastly exceeding anything that would be required to fulfill every demand of the Negro revolution. The difference was that in its objectives the government had the overwhelming support of the entire society.

It is a matter not so much of the government's defining its powers as the community's defining its needs. Even the "revolutionary" terminology I have been using up to now may be more confusing than enlightening. The problem of the Negro's place in American life was one which, despite the upheavals of emancipation and Reconstruction, had by 1900 been solved in a way that a majority of Americans found satisfactory. A majority today is finding that same "solution" not only unsatisfactory but intolerable. Times have changed, and it is not simply the moral weather that has changed; the very conditions of community life have changed.

The "revolution," if we wish to go on calling it that, has shifted to the Northern cities, and thinking on federal civil rights policy has shifted from voting rights to matters of much broader social and economic significance. The problem of race relations is now of such a nature that it can no longer be encapsulated as it could be in post-Reconstruction times. Moreover, the problem is inexorable; its dynamic element is an increasing concentration of Negroes in urban areas, and the lives of a majority of Americans are coming to be tied in more and more ways to the condition of the Negro community. Whatever the immediate vicissitudes of the question—the "backlash" vote in the 1966 elections, the continued preference of Southern communities for segregationist candidates, the failure of the 1966 civil rights bill—the problem will not go away. It is there, and there it remains; no one living in an American city can escape it.

The situation contains elements today which it did not have in Reconstruction, and broadening the battleground to include the Northern cities has perhaps for the first time provided a base upon which the problem can be—as indeed it must be—truly nationalized. In such a setting there is no longer any way to avoid dealing with the Negro as a functioning part of the community's economic, social, and political life. It is here that the pressure and energy needed to sustain a high level of federal concern are most likely to be generated, and as a more and more substantial portion of the decision-making community accustoms itself to acting systematically and conceiving policy in massive terms, the sooner a base will be built upon which permanent national standards may be formed.

The complexities of the federal system have often functioned in an inhibitive way, and pockets of regional resistance have traditionally operated to undermine the national will. And yet whenever standards of national necessity have had majority support, and where majority will has been present for insisting upon such standards, the abstract rigidities of the federal system have had a way of becoming surprisingly fluid. History does provide us tests for this. They are, as I have said, such as may be found in the depression years of the 1930's, in World War II, in the Civil War, and even—though in a form we can now see as much too temporary—in Reconstruction.

BIBLIOGRAPHY

On Reconstruction policy, as it took shape amid the extraordinary conflict between President Andrew Johnson and Congress, see W. R. Brock, *An American Crisis: Congress and Reconstruction, 1865–1867* (New York, 1966); Eric L. McKitrick, *Andrew Johnson and Reconstruction* (Chicago, 1960); and LaWanda and John H. Cox, *Politics, Principle, and Prejudice, 1865–1866: Dilemma of Reconstruction America* (New York, 1963). They may be contrasted with two other works, representing between them the best case anyone is likely to make for Andrew Johnson: George F. Milton, *The Age of Hate: Andrew Johnson and the Radicals* (New York, 1930); and Howard K. Beale, *The Critical Year, 1866: A Study of Andrew Johnson and Reconstruction* (New York, 1930).

On Reconstruction as a whole, embracing both Presidential and Congressional Reconstruction as well as the actual experience of the Southern states under their Reconstruction governments, there is no single comprehensive modern account. William A. Dunning, *Reconstruction, Political and Economic, 1865–1877* (New York, 1907; Torchbook ed., 1962), is an overall synthesis reflecting the state of thinking which prevailed with regard to that subject in the early years of this century. Kenneth Stampp, *The Era of Reconstruction, 1865–1877* (New York, 1965), does not claim to be a "history," but it is an excellent short introduction to the subject and a statement of the issues of Reconstruction as seen by scholars of the present day—among the most authoritative of whom is Professor Stampp himself. James G. Randall and David Donald, *The Civil War and Reconstruction* (Boston, 1960), devotes 165 pages to Reconstruction and has an excellent bibliography.

Among the numerous state studies, those well worth consulting include James W. Garner, *Reconstruction in Mississippi* (New York, 1901); C. Mildred Thompson, *Reconstruction in Georgia, Economic, Social and Political, 1865–1872* (New York, 1915); Francis B. Simkins and Robert H. Woody, *South Carolina during Reconstruction* (Chapel Hill, 1932); Vernon L. Wharton, *The Negro in Mississippi, 1865–1890* (Chapel Hill, 1947, 1965); Willie Lee Rose, *Rehearsal for Reconstruction: The Port Royal Experiment* (Indianapolis, 1964); Joel R. Williamson, *After Slavery: The Negro in South Carolina during Reconstruction, 1861–1877* (Chapel Hill, 1965); and Alan Conway, *The Reconstruction of Georgia* (Minneapolis, 1966).

Four other works whose focus is on the Negro, rather than on other aspects of Reconstruction and its aftermath, are James McPherson, *The Struggle for Equality: Abolitionists and the Negro in the Civil War and Reconstruction* (Princeton, 1964); Otis A. Singletary, *Negro Militia and Reconstruction* (New York, 1963); William Gillette, *The Right to Vote: Politics and the Passage of the Fifteenth Amendment* (Baltimore, 1965); and C. Vann Woodward, *The Strange Career of Jim Crow* (2nd rev. ed.; New York, 1960). The last named has a supplementary chapter dealing with events of the decade ending in 1965.

12

The Negro since Freedom

JOHN HOPE FRANKLIN

It has often been remarked that the history of the Negro in the United States is, in many ways, unique in world history. Those who make this assertion point out that in no other country of the world has such a large and distinctive Negro minority persisted for such a long period of time. Indeed, with the exception of Nigeria, which became independent only in 1960, Negroes are in no other state as numerous as they are in the United States. To advance further their argument that Negro Americans are unique they point to the fact that in no other country of the world has the position of the Negro been so clearly defined in law and custom. It should be pointed out, of course, that in few countries of the world is there such preoccupation with racial desegregation of the various elements of the population. Only in the United States is a Negro regarded as any person having a *known* trace of "Negro blood" in his veins—no matter how far back it was acquired.

If the definition was so precise, it could be used quite effectively in defining the place of the Negro in American life. By an elaborate ideology of white supremacy and through a complex apparatus of segregation and discrimination, the Negro's place in American life has, for a full century, been clearly, if tragically, defined. The argument is further advanced that only in the United States has there been such vigorous and sustained resistance to any and all moves to extend equality to all persons regardless of race.

But those who contend that the race problem is unique to the United States run the risk of overdrawing their case. It is well to remember that something resembling a race problem, arising from the institution of slavery, existed in Britain in the eighteenth century. To be sure, it was largely dissipated by Lord Mansfield's celebrated decision in the Somersett case in 1772; but it was to return in the twentieth century with such ugly manifestations that one may well wonder if it had ever actually disappeared. The race problem existed in other parts of the world, moreover, wherever slavery existed. A part of the apparatus of slavery was the rationalization and defense of the subordination of one race by another. And the racial ingredient was ever present in any discussion, philosophical or practical, of the institution of slavery.

A favorite argument supporting the claim that the problem of the Negro in the United States is unique has been advanced by several historians who have compared slavery in English America with slavery in Latin America. In 1947 Frank Tannenbaum, in a stimulating volume *Slave and Citizen, The Negro in the Americas,* suggested that, thanks largely to the influence of law and the church, the condition of the slave in Latin America was considerably better than that of the slave in English America. In his book, *Slavery: A Problem in American Institutional and Intellectual Life,* published in 1959, Stanley Elkins emphasized and reinforced the Tannenbaum thesis. Herbert Klein explored this view further and sought to document the way in which the situation actually worked out in favor of the Latin American slave. His findings were published in 1966 in *Slavery in the Americas: A Comparative Study of Cuba and Virginia.* The implication of all of these studies was that because of his degraded status in slavery, compared with the more elevated status of the Latin American slave, the Negro in English America would continue to suffer a degraded status in freedom.

While there can be little doubt that the comparative approach is fruitful and assists in the effort to understand many things about the status of the Negro in both areas, these pioneer and praiseworthy efforts leave something to be desired. As David B. Davis has pointed out in his study *The Problem of Slavery in Western Culture,* published in 1966, national and cultural differences have been exaggerated; and the superior moral and legal status of a slave, if such was the case in Latin America, did not inevitably lead to his better treatment. It is true that the Spanish model law, *las Siete Partidas,* recognized freedom as man's natural state and granted the slave certain legal protections, but it is also true that the same law not only made the person and possessions of the slave totally subject to his master's will, but even gave owners the right to kill their slaves in certain circumstances. Slavery was not so different in Latin America that it eliminated such barbarous practices as boiling slaves alive and roasting them in furnaces. There were enough of these practices to raise serious doubts about the nature of the differences between slavery and the status of Negroes in the two cultures.

The question of the place of darker peoples in the social order exists today, not merely in the United States but in numerous other places. While the most notable examples are in such countries as South Africa and Rhodesia, there are other examples in Australia, Malaysia, Indonesia, and other places where a rationale is needed to bolster and justify the exercise of power by a white minority or by some other group whose orientation rejects the sharing of political power and social acceptance on a basis of equality. Sensitivity about color differences is a phenomenon that is virtually world-wide. Whether it has to do with essentially different races, as in South Africa, or different shades of the same race, as in India and Japan, the practices and experiences are almost universal and can be instructive in the effort to understand and solve the problem of the rights of Negroes in the United States or darker peoples elsewhere.

Among those who insist that the so-called Negro problem is not unique, even in the United States are, curiously enough, some Americans themselves. Looking back on the history of their own country, they point to the continuing difficulties of assimilation of a succession of ethnic and national groups that have migrated to the United States. After reviewing the difficulties that the Irish, the Poles, the Jews, and the Italians have experienced, they claim that the struggle of the Negro for his rights is but a repetition of the experiences of other groups. This, of course, overlooks the very important point that the very nature of the Negro's difficulties is different. This is so not merely because the newly assimilated groups themselves often take the lead in denying the Negro his rights, but also because history, tradition, and even law have conspired to deny the Negro his rights in a way that has not been the case for any other group. Negroes themselves have often remarked that the really unique feature of their own struggle for equality has been the vehemence of the opposition of those who arrived in the New World one, two, or even three centuries after Negroes began to make their own contributions to American civilization.

One of the striking similarities between slavery in Latin America, English America, and wherever else it existed was the unwillingness of the enslaved to accept the status of slavery as a permanent arrangement. Negroes in the United States were no exception. The means and methods of expressing their opposition varied, of course, with circumstances as well as with the resources and temperament of the slaves. Some slaves took their own lives rather than remain the chattel of an owner. Others murdered their masters or destroyed the property of their masters. Where possible some purchased their own freedom and the freedom of their wives, husbands, or children. Some of those who ran away were not content merely to enjoy their own freedom, but then proceeded to assist others to escape. A smaller number resorted to revolting; and even if their plot was discovered, it clearly indicated the desperate nature of their plight as they viewed it. One can never know how many of the four million slaves in the United States took some action to secure their own freedom. Even without such precise information the record is clear that they were sufficient in numbers to establish a firm tradition of freedom and equality that would survive emancipation.

Negro slaves had insisted that they had the same right to freedom as other Americans. During the American Revolution they advanced their claims under the natural rights philosophy by which the colonists justified their fight for independence from England. They were a part of the later activist movement to end slavery; and their writings and speeches contain some of the most impressive arguments produced by the abolitionist movement. They further strengthened their claims to freedom by joining wholeheartedly in the fight against the Confederacy during the Civil War. The 186,000 Negroes who fought as soldiers during the Civil War wanted to save the Union; but they doubtless viewed emancipation as an objective that was at least equally worthy.

Perhaps the difference between Latin America and English America in the manner of achieving freedom for the slaves is more striking than the difference between slavery itself in the two areas. When Haiti secured her independence from France in 1803, a very important and immediate consideration was the emancipation of all the slaves on the island. All through the mainland of Latin America the sentiment against slavery increased as the sentiment for independence grew. When the five small countries of Central America federated themselves into one nation, the assembly passed an act ending slavery in 1824. Five years later the President of Mexico issued an emancipation proclamation. Soon the slaves were free in Bolivia, Uruguay, Colombia, and Argentina. By 1855 all the slaves in Latin America were free except those in Cuba and Brazil.

The independence sentiment in the United States also stimulated a movement to free the slaves; but only in the Northern states was it sufficiently strong to lead to an effective emancipation movement. Meanwhile, slavery had become even more deeply entrenched in the Southern states, and the resistance to emancipation was strong and widespread. When Northern antislavery leaders, Negro and white, sought to extend their movement into the South, they were rebuffed. And even those Southerners who had spoken out against slavery were silenced and, in some cases, ordered to leave the South. There ensued a period of increased tension between the two sections, North and South, that eventually led to the Civil War. Thus, the end of slavery in the United States came after a bloody and costly war that lasted for four years. This was never the case in Latin America. When slavery was finally abolished in Brazil in 1888, a five-day holiday was proclaimed to celebrate that historic event. Small wonder that the United States minister to Brazil at the time remarked that "what had led to a devastating struggle in the United States was the cause of merriment and rejoicing in Brazil."

Emancipation in Latin America did not lead directly or inevitably to full equality. The freedman there enjoyed some advantages that his counterpart in English America did not share, however. Even if it did not work out in practice, free Negroes had substantially the same rights before the law as whites. Race mixing, a common practice in both areas, was not viewed with the same abhorrence in the Latin countries as in the area to the north. But, as David B. Davis has indicated, racial prejudice persisted in Latin America, despite the frequency of intermixture. Spanish colonial law barred a freeman of Negro descent from bearing arms, holding public office, entering craft guilds, appearing on the street after dark, or associating with Indians. Many of these practices survived general emancipation. An important consideration, however, is that there was a steady improvement in the status of slaves and free Negroes before emancipation; and this had a profound effect on the consequences of abolition.

Freed Negroes did not become a political issue in Latin America, and there was no special legislation on the subject of Negro-white relations or on the status of Negroes in the social order. No ideology of white supremacy had developed, as it had in the United States, to justify and rationalize the institution of slavery. Consequently, the problem of adjustment to freedom was much less complicated for both the slave and his master. In his *Modern and Contemporary Latin America*, Harry Bernstein observed that after emancipation miscegnation, assimilation, and socialization made immense strides. Color differences persisted, however, and the color distinctions in customs and practice, if not in law, testify to the persistence of some of the vestiges of an earlier era.

It would seem that the history of the Negro American since freedom is rather more distinctive than his history before freedom. This was due to several important factors. In the first place, the effort to justify slavery and defend it against its assailants had resulted in the development of an ideology of white supremacy that easily survived war and emancipation. If, as the defenders of slavery claimed, the Negro was innately inferior, his lowly status was the result of divine ordination; and the development of a superior civilization required the Negro to remain in a servile status. No mere proclamation by the President or an amendment to the Constitution could change that "fact"! Southern whites and a good many Northern whites held to that view long after slavery had ended.

Indeed, by the end of the nineteenth century the view that the Negro was innately inferior seemed to be as widely held as it had been a half century earlier. The social Darwinists justified the Negro's lowly position on the ground that in the full competition to survive, the Negro had only barely done so. Public servants, politicians, writers, and even philanthropists subscribed to this view and acted accordingly.

In the second place, the first group that had an opportunity to define the freedman's place in the American social order was, to a large extent, the same group that had resisted the abolition of slavery and had fought the United States in the Civil War. In the two crucial years following the war, the governments in the Southern states were in the hands of the former slaveholders and their allies who had fought to retain their way of life. Having lost the war, the vast majority of white Southerners were almost immediately restored to full citizenship. With little interference on the part of the federal government and with Negroes having no voice in the proceedings, they expressed through the laws they enacted their view that Negroes should occupy a permanently inferior place in society. With the exception of a few concessions regarding the Negro's right to own property, make contracts, and testify in courts under certain limited circumstances, these Black Codes, as they were called, undertook to place the Negro in a state of permanent subordination. Although they were not successful in the long run, the experience of enacting these laws provided Southern whites with an opportunity to think through and formulate a position that they would not readily or willingly relinquish.

Finally, few people in the federal government seemed to have any clear notion of what the place of the Negro should be and what the role of the government should be in establishing a place for him. The result was several false starts and no effective program to assist the Negro in his transition from slavery to freedom. The government in Washington set up an agency to assist the Negro's subsistence and education, but at the beginning it did not even provide funds for the operation of the agency. It finally conferred political rights on the Negro, with little machinery to protect him in the exercise of those rights. Thus, it was in no position to combat the Ku Klux Klan and other lawless elements that drove Negroes from the political arena and wantonly violated their civil rights. Soon, the semblance of political rights that Negroes had momentarily enjoyed disappeared almost altogether. Outside the government, few citizens showed any interest in elevating the Negro to a position of equality. There ensued a really long, dark night of segregation, discrimination, and degradation.

By the end of the century Negro Americans had been segregated most effectively in the Southern states where some 90 per cent of them resided. States seemed to vie with one another in developing ingenious segregation legislation and practices. There were laws separating Negroes and whites in factories, exits, entrances, and toilets on railroads and streetcars, in public parks, drinking facilities, telephone booths, county jails, stockades, convict camps, institutions for the insane, hospitals, and cemeteries. The meticulous care with which the races were separated caused one Arkansas Negro to observe that if whites did not want to associate with Negroes there should be laws to divide the streets and sidewalks so that Negroes could go on one side and whites on the other. He said that there should be an end "to all intercourse between white and colored people by day, and especially by night."

In the treatment of Negroes before the law, the practices of discrimination matched those of segregation. The Negro car on the train was not merely separate, it was a part of the baggage car, and there were no first-class accommodations whatever. If Negroes frequented public auditoriums, they occupied dark galleries to which they gained access by side or rear entrances. They were consigned to the basements of hospitals and to the least attractive portions of public parks. For them education was not only critical but indispensable. Yet, public support of their segregated schools was the very epitome of discrimination. The view prevailed that virtually any expenditure on schools for Negroes was a waste not merely because Negroes were unable to learn anything important but also because the very effort would give Negroes false notions of their capacities and spoil them for their "place" in society. Thus, by 1916 the per capita expenditure for the education of white children in Southern counties was $12.67 whereas it was $3.90 for the education of Negro children.

Although Negroes generally lacked the skills to participate in the new industrial order that was emerging, the opportunities to acquire the skills, through apprenticeship and membership in the unions, was generally denied them. Here and there, an organization, such as the United Mine Workers, opened its doors; but the opposition to Negroes' becoming a part of the general labor market was fierce. All too often, their only opportunity for industrial employment was to serve as "scabs" during a strike by one of the unions. On such occasions they became the objects of attack, as people who had no appreciation of the problems of organized labor, by the very unions that had excluded them. In the new industries of the South, Negroes had no opportunity to become operatives in the textile mills or foundry hands in the iron and steel works.

Their brightest opportunities lay either in following the advice of Booker T. Washington and becoming farmers and artisans or in seeking domestic employment with the white industrial workers.

As a group suffering disfranchisement, segregation, and discrimination of every kind, Negro Americans had no defense against the violence and intimidation that were heaped upon them with impunity. In the final decade of the nineteenth century, lynchings of Negroes reached an average of more than one hundred per year. The spirit of the times was exemplified in 1892 by Governor Benjamin Tillman of South Carolina, who, in condoning the lynching of an alleged Negro felon, merely instructed a county official to "preserve the proprieties." The new urban phenomenon, the race riot, took shape with an outbreak in Wilmington, North Carolina, in 1898. In the following decade there would be several major race riots in such Southern communities as Atlanta, Georgia, and Brownsville, Texas, and in such Northern communities as Greensburg, Indiana, and Springfield, Illinois. In the year following the close of World War I there was another rash of riots that caused one writer to describe the summer of 1919 as "the red summer."

Despite their apparent helplessness, Negroes were not passive; and they reacted in a variety of ways. As long as possible they resisted, through political action, their consignment to a subordinate status. After disfranchisement they argued their case with uncommon, though ineffective, eloquence. They wrote histories to show that from the beginning they had contributed to their country's development. At the Atlanta Cotton States Exposition in 1895 Booker T. Washington, the founder of Tuskegee Institute, urged his fellow Negroes to seek a place in society where they could make an acceptable contribution. At the same time he sought the good will and tolerance of the whites. W. E. B. DuBois conducted and published a series of studies on Negro life in the belief that if whites knew more about Negroes they would be more willing to accept them as equal citizens. Negroes founded schools, edited newspapers, strengthened their churches, organized businesses, and even founded towns in the effort to counteract their rejection. While it was difficult for them to agree among themselves regarding the line of action they should pursue, few would disagree with the prediction of DuBois that the problem of the twentieth century would be the problem of the color line.

Negro Americans employed a direct method of attack by establishing organizations whose primary function was to fight for equal rights. In 1890 more than 140 Negro delegates from twenty-one states and the District of Columbia met in Chicago and organized the Afro-American League of the United States. In its constitution the league called for a more equitable distribution of school funds, a fair and impartial trial for accused Negroes, resistance "by all legal and reasonable means" to mob and lynch law and tyrannical usages and abuses by railroad, steamboat, and other corporations. Branches of the organization were established in many parts of the country. Among them were the Pennsylvania Equal Rights League, the Georgia Suffrage League, and the New England League for Equal Rights.

In the face of increasing disfranchisement, segregation, and lynchings in the 1890's, the league's method of protesting and memorializing proved ineffective. Articulate, aggressive young Negroes liked neither the conciliatory approach of Booker T. Washington nor the moderate approach of the league. Led by W. E. B. DuBois and William Monroe Trotters, they met at Niagara Falls, Ontario, in 1905 and set forth their views in a declaration of principles. In part they said, "We believe that Negroes should protest emphatically and continually against the curtailment of their political rights. We believe in manhood suffrage; we believe that no man is so good, intelligent, or wealthy as to be entrusted wholly with the welfare of his neighbor."

These young men were in the process of developing a program of action when they accepted the invitation of a group of whites who also wanted to take some action in response to the race riot in Springfield, Illinois, in 1908. Together they founded the National Association for the Advancement of Colored People. As the first important interracial organization in the United States since Reconstruction, the N.A.A.C.P. pressed for justice in the courts, equal rights laws, and decent employment for Negroes. Thus began a successful assault on inequalities in American life that ranged from the outlawing of discrimination in voting to the outlawing of segregation in public schools. Meanwhile, the National Urban League, another interracial organization, had entered the fight, concentrating its attention on housing and employment. Soon, Negroes and whites were developing the techniques of picketing, demonstrating, and negotiating that were to prove so effective in the civil rights revolution of the 1960's.

Many factors contributed to the intensification of the drive for equality that culminated in the civil rights revolution of the 1960's. The two world wars increased awareness on the part of Negroes and many white Americans of the disparity between the principle of equality and the actual practice. Millions of Negroes migrated from the rural South to the urban South and North. By 1960 more than one-third of the nation's 20 million Negroes lived in twelve metropolitan areas of the United States. Disappointed by the lack of adequate housing, employment, and educational opportunities in their new surroundings, Negro Americans became more determined than ever to fight for their rights.

While the example of the emergence of new states in Africa was inspiring and even stimulating, it would not be correct to conclude that the vast numbers of Negro Americans who were fighting for equality were seeking to emulate the Africans whom they admired. Black nationalism in the United States was not new. It extended back for more than 150 years, to 1815, when Paul Cuffe took a group of his fellow Negroes to settle the west coast of Africa. Whether it was Cuffe or his successors, such as Martin Delany, Henry McNeal Turner, Marcus Garvey, or Elijah Muhammed, the black nationalists of the United States were essentially voicing their protest over what one of them called the absence of any "manhood future" for Negroes in the United States.

Perhaps more to the point was the effect of developments in Africa and Asia on public opinion and policy in the United States. The insults that representatives of Asian and African states experienced in the United States were a source of great embarrassment to the United States. Meanwhile, the segregation and discrimination against Negro Americans convinced many peoples in Asia and Africa that the United States was not prepared to lead the world toward greater human justice. Along with domestic pressures of several kinds, this was indeed a factor in the reversal of national policy that led Congress to enact new civil rights legislation and that caused the executive to take steps to secure equality in numerous phases of American life.

The revolution of rising expectations was marked by several events that underscored the increased pressure for equality on the part of Negro Americans and their allies. In 1955 a Negro seamstress in Montgomery, Alabama, refused to move to the back of the bus. When she was arrested, Negroes, led by Dr. Martin Luther King, undertook a boycott of the bus company that continued until the company agreed to desegregate its buses. In 1960, four young Negro college students initiated the first sit-in, when they were refused service at a lunch counter in Greensboro, North Carolina. Soon, young people—white and Negro—were sitting in lunch counters, libraries, hotels, and other public places in many parts of the United States; and they succeeded in desegregating many establishments. In 1961, an even more dramatic attack on segregation and discrimination was undertaken when "Freedom Riders" from the Congress of Racial Equality toured the South to test segregation laws and practices in interstate transportation. By the end of the summer the jails of Jackson, Mississippi, were virtually filled with Freedom Riders. It was the actions of these persons that the dean of the Yale University Law School called "a generalized moral demonstration of the nation's failure" in the area of civil rights.

The mass demonstrations were yet to come. In the spring of 1963 hundreds of Negroes were jailed in Birmingham for demonstrating against segregation and discrimination in housing and employment. Shortly thereafter, the President of the United States called for legislation that would put an end to such practices. In August 1963, more than two hundred thousand white and Negro Americans "marched on Washington," called on the President, and received assurances from him that he would support their drive for equality. In the following years, there were other mass demonstrations in Cambridge, Maryland, Selma, Alabama, and Chicago, Illinois. The Civil Rights Acts of 1964 and 1965 undertook to satisfy the most urgent demands of Negro Americans; but *de facto* school segregation in the North, the continued discrimination in housing and employment, and the intransigent opposition to political equality for Negroes in the South, merely meant that the struggle for equality had just begun.

If mere color distinctions continued in Latin America several generations after emancipation, much more remained as vestiges of slavery in the United States. By 1966 more than a score of states had joined the federal government in enacting legislation looking toward equality. But discriminatory practices based on race continued to be rather commonplace both in public and private life. Miscegenation continued to be unthinkable for most white Americans—and indeed for many Negro Americans—and a score of states continued to enforce laws against the intermarriage of Negroes and whites. The revolution had merely begun to affect the private sector, but it had turned government, for the most part, toward the support of the demand for equality; and even the laws against intermarriage have recently been challenged in the courts, with still undetermined results. This affirmative position of the government of the United States had the effect of removing it from the dwindling list of nations, such as South Africa and Rhodesia, that continue to adhere to a national policy of segregation and discrimination.

BIBLIOGRAPHY

In addition to the works cited in the text, the reader would do well to examine the classic work by Gunnar Myrdal, *An American Dilemma: The Negro Problem and Modern Democracy* (2 vols.; New York, 1944). A briefer historical and sociological treatise is E. Franklin Frazier's *The Negro in the United States* (New York, 1949, 1957). John Hope Franklin's *From Slavery to Freedom: A History of American Negroes* (New York, 1947, 1956, 1967) treats the Negro in Latin America, the West Indies, and Canada as well as the United States. Other general histories of the Negro American include Lerone Bennett, *Before the Mayflower* (Chicago, 1961, 1964); Rayford W. Logan, *The Negro in the United States* (Princeton, 1957); August Meier and Elliott Rudwick, *From Plantation to Ghetto* (New York, 1966); Benjamin Quarles, *The Negro in the Making of America* (New York, 1964); J. Saunders Redding, *They Came in Chains* (Philadelphia, 1950); and Carter G. Woodson, *The Negro in Our History* (Washington, D.C., 1922).

Recent works, in part historical, that deal with various aspects of the Negro in American life are numerous, and it is impossible to mention more than a selected number. Among the outstanding are Margaret J. Butcher, *The Negro in American Culture* (New York, 1956); Louis Lomax, *The Negro Revolt* (New York, 1962); Herbert Hill (ed.), *Soon, One Morning: New Writing by American Negroes* (1963); Milton R. Konvitz, *A Century of Civil Rights* (New York, 1961); Jack Greenberg, *Race Relations and American Law* (New York, 1959); Oscar Handlin, *Race and Nationality in American Life* (Boston, 1957); and C. Vann Woodward, *The Strange Career of Jim Crow* (New York, 1966).

Other works specifically dealing with recent developments of Negro life and the civil rights revolution include James Baldwin, *The Fire*

Next Time (New York, 1963); Martin Luther King, *Why We Can't Wait* (New York, 1964); Merrill Proudfoot, *Diary of a Sit-in* (Chapel Hill, 1962); Talcott Parsons and Kenneth B. Clark (eds.), *The Negro American* (Boston, 1966); Thomas F. Pettigrew, *A Profile of the Negro American* (Princeton, 1964); Robert Penn Warren, *Who Speaks for the Negro?* (New York, 1965); and Whitney M. Young, *To Be Equal* (New York, 1964).

# 13

Industrialization

THOMAS C. COCHRAN

An economic explanation of the rapid and massive industrialization of the United States can be given in terms of natural resources, but such an answer is far too simple. Other nations that did not rapidly develop industry have also had great resources, while Japan, with little coal, iron, or oil, astonished the world with the speed of its industrial revolution. Aware of such apparent contradictions, some leading American economists have maintained that the most important elements in economic growth are noneconomic. Granting that these economists may be right, let us take a broad view of both economic and "noneconomic" factors that seem to have been important in making the process of American industrial development differ from that of other nations.

Two alternative types of comparison come immediately to mind: first, comparison of the historical experience of America as an underdeveloped area with that of other underdeveloped nations of the world; and second, comparison of American development with that of the leading industrial nations of Europe. The latter is rather the more fruitful exercise as it can be done by contemporaneous comparisons, whereas comparison with underdeveloped nations of the present day requires study spanning long time periods involving radically different surrounding circumstances. For example, the flows of information at present from advanced to less advanced nations are often much larger than those from Europe to America in the nineteenth century, but the information is vastly more complex and difficult to absorb.

In one important respect America's history had differed from that of any other underdeveloped nation, in that early American society was composed almost entirely of immigrants from the British Isles, France, Germany, and The Netherlands. These early settlers brought with them some familiarity with the world's most advanced business and industry. Holland led the seventeenth-century world in most types of technology; England was close behind; and the Huguenots, who were the chief French immigrants, were highly skilled artisans. The settlers had only to reproduce the kind of society with which they were familiar in order to begin industrial development. Furthermore, the mere fact of immigration, the risking of the terrible ocean voyage and of settlement in a country of savage climatic variations, indicated a strong motivation for self-betterment.

In America, the immigrants found no indigenous culture that could dilute or postpone their drive for both self-preservation and economic advance. The Indians were too few and too remote on the culture scale to mix with the Europeans. Consequently, no local customs or traditions stood in the way of practical solutions to economic problems.

In contrast, as the English historian Charles Wilson has written of his own country, "always the forces of mobility and growth were balanced against the forces of inertia, the forces of enterprise without those of custom." Men struggling to establish themselves on the edge of a wilderness were unlikely to suffer from inertia, and the customs were only those they brought with them and found useful. Outside the Southern plantation areas, the immigrant and his children did not develop a farm with the idea that it would become a hereditary homestead; rather, they saw their labor as a means of acquiring capital through subsequent sale of the property at a profit. Such businesslike attitudes were, of course, not lacking in western Europe, but in the Old World there was less expectation of increasing land values and no cheap land a few miles farther out which could, in turn, be developed and sold. European land operations required expert knowledge and considerable capital, as well as time and good fortune, whereas Americans were primarily profiting from a continuous process of population growth, and meanwhile the farmer created additional capital values through his own efforts.

The colonial period, however, had ended and thousands of settlers had crossed the mountains to the great interior river valleys, before modern machine and factory industrialism began its rapid spread. The importance of the early period was in its heritage of an interest in ways to save labor and devotion to the goal of economic progress, a legacy lacking in most areas of the world other than northern Europe. The very shortage of men willing to leave farming for factory work, that held back American industrialization in the early decades of the nineteenth century, was ultimately to be an asset because it forced entrepreneurs to take a greater interest in labor-saving machinery than was the case in Europe. Inventor Eli Whitney said that Americans sought to substitute machine operations for the hand skills of Europe, which in turn led to more interest in the possibilities of new processes. Thus, the principle of interchangeable machine-made parts, learned from the French, was brought to commercial profitability in American armories. Similarly, the sewing machine that scarcely seemed worth perfecting because of the availability of cheap seamstresses in Europe was pushed to commercial success by the stimulant of America's high wages. This process of borrowing from the science and technology of Europe for new commercial applications in America was repeated over and over again.

Underlying the ability of the American economy to divert men from farming to transportation or industry was a low ratio of population to arable land, especially to land that lent itself, better than in western Europe, to extensive cultivation by machines. Tilling broad level acreages of new soil by machines such as wheelharrows, seed drills, and even horse-drawn reapers, the farmers of the mid-nineteenth century produced large surpluses. A smaller and smaller percentage of the population not only supplied all domestic needs for food but also exported large quantities of agricultural products. Some economists see the export surplus of staple crops in the early nineteenth century as the initial stimulant to rapid economic growth. Cotton, tobacco, and, later, wheat and meat were exchanged for machine tools, railroad iron, and other sinews of industrialism.

By 1850, when great waves of German and Irish immigrants ended the shortage of labor on the east coast, Americans had already formed the habit of thinking in terms of machinery. Furthermore, Americans, ever on the move, wanted cheap useful goods that could be left behind without too great loss. Equipping new, frequently inaccessible farms, they could not afford fine finish, artistic elegance, or durability in furniture or tools, if the last required too much bulk or solidity. The growing home market, that is, demanded the kinds of simple goods that could be turned out even by primitive methods of mass production. Hence, the increased availability of unskilled labor did not noticeably retard the processes of mechanization.

Immigration, of which the United States was the only major recipient during most of the nineteenth century, obviously benefits the receiving nation by supplying workers whose upbringing has been paid for elsewhere. In less tangible ways, however, the continuing process of migration, either from abroad or within the nation, stimulates economic growth. Migrants are predominantly young people at the height of their intellectual and physical vigor. Lacking the support of the extended family, of relatives and friends, the virtually anonymous migrant has to rely on his own ability to get ahead. He tries both to conform to his new environment and in subtle ways to change it. Thus, the process of adjustment to new surroundings stimulates innovation. Areas of rapid immigration, such as the frontier or the growing city, are therefore competitive markets for customs and ideas. The migrant detached from old friends also makes decisions more pragmatically and impersonally than is possible in a settled, traditional community. Thus, he becomes more an "economic man" and less a social or communal one.

Yet, the needs of new farms and towns also required cooperation. The American learned to apply a utilitarian calculus to the problems of competition and cooperation, rather than one based, as in many other nations, on family, social prestige, or tradition. The value of this cooperative attitude increased as business grew larger. Americans merged their firms, gave up ownership to become officers in larger corporations, and generally submerged their egos in collective ventures with a readiness lacking in most cultures. Studies of Latin American business, for example, have shown the resistance of family-owned firms to loss of identity through mergers, even when the struggle to survive meant continuing financial loss for all involved—whereas in America what Thorstein Veblen and others have called technological behavior was emphasized and ceremonial behavior minimized.

The process of large-scale migration in the United States has never ceased. In the old cities of the east coast in recent times, when total population may scarcely change from decade to decade, a continuous shifting of people still goes on. Every decade, a third or more of the population moves elsewhere and their places are taken by as many newcomers. Thus, apparently, static or settled areas are, in fact, ones of both in-and-out migration. This type of movement has also become obvious in Europe, particularly since World War II, but the evidence suggests a marked contrast between the two continents and also between America and the rest of the world during the nineteenth century. In all, both continuous in-migration and internal population movement undoubtedly represent elements more important in nineteenth-century American than in European or world industrialization.

To say that in the United States, more than in other nations of the late eighteenth century, government was created and operated to suit the popular will is a historic platitude, but the implications of this statement for economic growth are often overlooked. Governments in state and nation were created by and for those most attentive to politics, and many of these were businessmen. The new governments were shaped by the needs of merchants, craftsmen, and commercial farmers. Such government was not a rigid structure run for the traditional interests of a clerical or lay aristocracy, but rather a utility set up by enterprising citizens to provide order and aid cooperative endeavor. If a bank, canal, factory, or railroad that seemed economically desirable could not secure adequate private financing, government was called upon to make up the deficiency. Not until well into the nineteenth century was there a feeling of division of purpose between the professional politician and the private capitalist. In contrast, a state like Prussia, dominated by a landed aristocracy, did almost nothing prior to 1848 to encourage railroads or other forms of social overhead capital needed for economic development.

Another facet of this relationship between business and government was confidence on the part of the investor that government and the common law would protect his property. Aside from a few old metropolitan areas where hereditary merchant society tried to maintain its grip, no distinction or mark of prestige was denied the self-made man and in no place were the social fruits of material success denied his sons. Unlike England, where successful businessmen were likely to neglect their mill for the greater prestige of cultivating gentility on a manor, or France, where a modest and secure position in a small market was preferred to the hazards of continued growth and where aristocratic status seemed too remote to be a common goal, most American industrialists lived simply and used their earnings to expand their businesses, secure in the belief that business success was the sure road to social acclaim.

The fact that in this continental American market, supplied from great natural resources, personal wealth came to be more of a possibility for anyone with a little training and commercial acumen than anywhere else in the world, led to a striving for success that colored child-rearing, family life, education, and religion. Parents taught their children that work was a duty and idleness a sin. School readers increasingly carried success stories and emphasized the necessary values. Many of the same admonitions were present in European education—they were the universal values of the rising industrial middle class—but some examination of English and other school texts indicates that success was not emphasized to such a degree; and in addition, as the nineteenth century progressed, American secondary and higher education became more utilitarian than in most other leading nations, although probably no more so than in parts of Germany.

The nineteenth-century atmosphere of enterprise and progress pervaded the northern Protestant religious denominations. Ministers cast their sermons in the language of business and wrote homilies on success, while their business parishioners, who provided support for the church, brought the language of divine guidance to the market place. A later age may see self-delusion in the piety of a John D. Rockefeller, Sr., but to him, his religion was a compelling reality. This language of justification by God's law and faith in a divinely ordained American mission continued to bolster entrepreneurial morale until, at least, World War I.

The interaction of all these economically favorable forces produced a type of personality in the United States peculiarly suited to developing its resources. This normal American entrepreneur was willing to take moderate risks because he was optimistic regarding success, in contrast to the entrepreneur, common to most underdeveloped parts of the world, who sees so little to be gained by venturing further in the face of competition that he is content with what he has. This spirit of optimism, this continuing dream of high returns from further investment, put a premium on saving for the future rather than spending for present consumption. As a result, few Americans developed the gracious living of Europeans or wealthy Latin Americans, and leisure, even among those who could amply afford it, produced a feeling of guilt.

While many may see noneconomic factors as differentiating American development from that of various nations in Europe and Asia, no one will deny that social and cultural characteristics were closely related to the economic situation. No two geographic areas are identical and no one can measure the force of resources and climate in conjunction with other factors shaping human personality. All these assumptions regarding average American business behavior might be derived originally from geographic and economic conditions in the more advanced areas of the country; nevertheless, they come in the course of generations to exist as forces in themselves.

The United States developed as a series of regions often economically related to each other in ways similar to those of the nations of Europe, yet always brought a little closer, after 1789, by lack of tariff or other barriers to domestic trade. New England, with its poor soil and good water power, was the first to industrialize; and lacking raw materials at home, it invested its surplus profits in building transportation and exploiting resources in other areas. On their fast-flowing small rivers, the middle states of the Eastern seaboard quickly followed New England with factory industry; but the burgeoning overseas and domestic trade of New York and the great natural resources of Pennsylvania, by providing more local use for their surplus capital, lessened their early investment in distant areas.

Lack of both agricultural and mineral resources sent the people of New England, as well as their capital, westward. This region became the educator of the interior in business practice and, inevitably, carried along the language and habits of an enterprising Puritanism. In a sense, New England played the role in America that Old England played in Europe, pioneering industrial technology and spreading it to other areas, which ultimately became overly strong competitors. But in the wide-open American market the spread of industrial technology was more rapid than in a partly feudal and politically divided Europe. New York and Pennsylvania were only slightly behind New England, and industry moved across the Appalachian Mountains with surprising ease.

Only the slaveholding South failed quickly to embrace the industrial business system. Historically, the South illustrated many of the problems of present-day underdeveloped areas. An agrarian society did not educate young men to be alert to manufacturing opportunities. Local banks did not understand industrial risks and preferred to lend money only on land, crops, or animals. Land ownership had an aura of respectability and stability not attached to a new shop or factory. Consequently, as long as it was possible profitably to invest in agriculture or urban real estate Southerners continued to do so, as did most other people outside of northern America and western Europe. By the 1880's, however, declining agricultural prices were making investment in Southern agriculture unattractive, and a growing surplus of rural labor was tempting both Northerners and local capitalists to invest in Southern textile mills, furniture factories, tobacco processing and other industries for which the region was well suited. But after three-quarters of a century of such development, speeded greatly by World War II, there are striking differences in the degree of industrialization between the deep

South and the Northeast or Midwest. The gradual pace of this development suggests that agricultural regions, receiving manufactured goods on reasonable terms from readily accessible outside areas, will not suddenly be changed into mature industrial states by the injection of some capital and technicians.

In the process of building a national industrial market, transportation has, in all other areas of the world, been more of a problem than it was in geographically small and thickly populated Europe. Once the Appalachian Mountains were reached in America, navigable rivers were far apart. Extensive canal building between 1815 and 1840, largely government financed, was the initial solution. Water transportation was greatly aided by the steamboat, which could penetrate the fast-flowing rivers of the Mississippi system and navigate the treacherous Great Lakes. It has been argued that transportation by river, canal, and lake could eventually have knit the interior markets together; but before this could happen, the railroad intervened.

Between 1830 and 1851 a rail network was built covering the region east of the Mississippi River, and in the decade of the 1850's railroads, penetrating still farther west, had as much track as those of all western Europe. In 1870, the United States had about 50,000 miles of railroad tracks; the United Kingdom was next in the world with 15,000, followed by Germany with 12,000 and France with 10,500. But the United States, with more track than all of these leading nations of Europe, was also substantially greater in area. The fact that by 1890 the capital invested in the United States railroads was larger than that in all forms of manufacturing showed the magnitude of the problem for which the railroad had been the solution.

Aside from the cost of overcoming distance, American industrialization was retarded by the usual problem of new areas: lack of buildings. Throughout American history, building construction has been the great consumer of savings. As population moved westward, families needed new homes, manufacturers new shops, and retailers new stores. Meanwhile the expansion of American agriculture and mining drained capital away from trade and manufacturing.

The pinch of scarce capital was eased in the case of transportation by substantial foreign investment, largely British,

Dutch, and German, which released domestic funds for more risky ventures such as factories. It is notable that except for the ownership of agricultural land, foreign investment almost never carried with it the control of American enterprise or forced the receivers to buy goods from the lenders. In this respect investment in America differed from most other European investment in underdeveloped areas. The British stake in Argentine railroads, for example, carried with it British management and control. Much of the early foreign investment in the United States was in state securities, whose proceeds were used to build or subsidize transportation. As absentee owners or creditors, the Europeans suffered the usual disadvantages when it came to defaults, receiverships, and reorganizations.

So far relatively little has been said about the exact timing of American industrialization. Did the United States have a "take-off" period in the sense used by W. W. Rostow? He selects 1840 to 1860 as the time when investment in industry in the United States reached a magnitude that promised sustained growth. If one must pick a twenty-year period, there is much to be said for this one. Waves of German and Irish immigrants, after 1845, provided an adequate labor supply; completion of the central railroad net created a true national market; gold discoveries in California gave the nation a new attractiveness to foreign investors and an added ability to meet trade deficits; railroad corporations provided training for Americans in the management of large enterprises; and vast mineral discoveries guaranteed what appeared to be limitless raw materials. But these developments may be seen as either fortuitous or continuing factors, promising sustained growth, but not indicative of why other nations should necessarily conform to the Rostow model or thesis.

To summarize, American industrialization was rapid from the early nineteenth century onward. In view of American interest in technology and vast natural resources, there never seemed any doubt that industrial progress would reproduce the steady advance of Great Britain. Speeded by the characteristics of American personality and culture, the United States of 1900 was on a par with the world's industrial leaders. Stable government and favorable law continued to encourage high rates of saving and investment. In overcoming massive problems of distance and the high cost of the development of new areas, America was aided by European capital. By 1900, the American domestic market had become the largest in the world and this, in turn, encouraged a larger scale of operations in business with increasing economies in production, management, marketing, and research.

BIBLIOGRAPHY

The usual elements involved in industrialization are discussed by economists in books on economic growth or development. Among the many such volumes, Albert O. Hirschman's *The Strategy of Economic Development* (New Haven, 1958) is unusually well written and appealing to the layman. Barry E. Supple, an English scholar, has collected the views of a number of recent writers in *The Experience of Economic Growth: Case Studies in Economic History* (New York, 1963). W. W. Rostow presented an interesting theory that attracted worldwide attention in *The Stages of Economic Growth* (Cambridge, England, 1960).

Noneconomic factors in American industrialization have not been analyzed in any comprehensive historical studies. For a theoretical discussion of the importance of migration and new environment see H. G. Barnett, *Innovation: The Basis of Cultural Change* (New York, 1953). Several essays by Thomas C. Cochran in *The Inner Revolution* (New York, 1965) discuss the conjunction of social, psychological, and economic factors in growth. An early effort to synthesize industrialization with the social history of the United States is Thomas C. Cochran and William Miller, *The Age of Enterprise: A Social History of Industrial America* (rev. ed.; New York, 1961).

Two recent books deal succinctly with the early phase of American industrialization. Douglas C. North in *The Economic Growth of the United States, 1790–1860* (Englewood Cliffs, N.J., 1961) emphasizes the export trade in staple crops as an important element in initiating rapid growth. Stuart Bruchey, in *The Roots of American Economic Growth, 1607–1861* (New York, 1965), takes a broad historical view of the factors that helped to speed industrialization.

The Economic History of the United States (New York, 1947–) is designed to cover the period from the first settlements to 1960 in ten volumes, of which all have appeared except the first on the colonial period and the last on the period 1940–1960. The authors are among the leading economic historians of the older generation. The work of a number of younger men, often referred to as the "new economic historians" because they are reapplying economic theory to historical data, is illustrated in William N. Parker (ed.), *Trends in the American Economy* (Princeton, 1960). An institutional rather than a statistical approach to economic development in the mid-nineteenth century is David T. Gilchrist and W. Davis Lewis (eds.), *Economic Change in the Civil War Era* (Greenville, Del., 1965). H. J. Habakkuk's *American and British Technology in the Nineteenth Century* (Cambridge, England, 1962) is an interesting study because it is specifically comparative.

The monographic and textbook literature on American economic, business, and relevant social history is far too large to describe in a brief essay. Each of the volumes of *The Economic History of the United States* has a detailed bibliography. Bruchey has a bibliography that covers most of the important books and much of periodical literature up to the late nineteenth century. Cochran and Miller have a fairly comprehensive bibliography on industrialization in material published before 1961. The reader anxious to keep up with American scholarship in this field should see *The Business History Review, Economic Development and Cultural Change,* and *The Journal of Economic History.*

14

Urbanization

RICHARD C. WADE

When the United States was born, less than 5 per cent of its people lived in cities; today over 75 per cent live in two hundred metropolitan areas. From the standpoint of the urban historian, these simple figures comprise the single most important fact about our historical development. In less than two centuries, the country was transformed from a simple agrarian society to a highly complex urban one.

The urbanization of the continent, perhaps more than any other aspect of our past, accounts for the "comparability" which the chapters in this book attempt to assess. For we all now live in an increasingly metropolitan world where we occupy a common environment. Thus a Chicagoan quickly feels at home in London, Paris, Milan, or Amsterdam despite differences in nationality, language, and custom. Even first impressions of distinctiveness of architecture, age, and street scenes do not conceal for long the shared urban attributes of the world's important cities. To the tourist, the airport at Madrid, the hotel in Vienna, the restaurant in Sydney, or the museum in Mexico City are more like the same facilities in cities everywhere than they are like a small town or a rural village anywhere. Not only have Western countries undergone the same urban growth, but they have also had to grapple with the same consequences—slums, traffic, congestion, pollution, disorder, and the other ills usually lumped

187

together as "urban problems." This sameness springs from the emergence of the modern city, which has not only reduced differences between nations but has muted regional peculiarities within the same country .

I

Urbanization in the United States is not so recent a force as is often believed. In fact, cities have played an important role from the very beginning. Carl Bridenbaugh's two books *Cities in the Wilderness* and *Cities in Revolt* develop this urban dimension of colonial life, demonstrating that the port towns exerted a disproportionate influence in the seventeenth and eighteenth centuries. Not only did they create a kind of life that contrasted sharply with conditions in the countryside, but their strategic location made them the special workshops of the revolution. Moreover, it is suggestive that the figure so often called "the first American," Benjamin Franklin, was not a farmer, a frontiersman, or even a planter, but rather a middle-class city dweller whose life was bound up with the world's great cities. He grew up in Boston, lived his adult life in Philadelphia, and spent a large part of his career in London and Paris.

The early influence of the city is at odds with conventional expectations, for the popular symbol of the young republic's growth has been the frontier with its emphasis on the discovery and settlement of the West. Frederick Jackson Turner was the historian most responsible for shaping this perspective of the nation's past. He argued that the distinctiveness of American development was to be found in the existence of free land in the West and in the collision of "barbarism" and "civilization" along the thither side of the frontier. Thus he sought the keys to national development in the exploration of the new country, in the taming of the Indians, prairies, and plains, and in the log cabins and sod huts of the pioneers.

Turner's perspective—indeed his poetic vision—became deeply embedded not only in the popular mind but in serious scholarship as well. It was quickly challenged, however, by an apparently contradictory framework developed most persuasively by Charles

A. Beard. This approach saw the development of the country as a function of industrialization, and in the broadest sense a transformation from an agrarian to an industrial society. Hence, the clues to American growth were to be found in the introduction of the factory system, the appearance of an entrepreneurial class, the development of the labor movement, and in the expansion of technology. Unlike Turner's, this scheme emphasized the comparability of American experience with that of the Western world rather than its distinctiveness.

Turner and Beard looked at American history in quite different ways. But from the viewpoint of the city, they presented a curiously similar outlook. For in both schemes the city came at the end of the evolutionary process; in both, significant urban growth was assumed to be a very modern development. Turner saw the continent occupied in waves: first came the pathfinder, then the fur trader, then the extensive farmer, then the intensive farmer, and, as the final stage, the "factory and the town" appeared. In Beard's analysis the nation began as agrarian, but industrial forces slowly changed its character and produced a new and modern society. In this perspective the city's influence became a commanding fact only toward the end of the nineteenth century.

Turner and Beard not only located the rise of the city in comparatively recent times, but they also reinforced, if they did not introduce, a persistent confusion in the analysis of modern America. For they equated industrialization and urbanization, assuming that the two were integrally related and were simply two sides of the same coin. Thus such phrases as "urban industrialism" and "industrial urbanism" entered the language and became a kind of shorthand to describe modern society. Actually, the two movements simply happened to coincide in American history; in other places the timing was quite different. In Europe, for example, very large cities existed long before the industrial revolution; and in the underdeveloped nations of our time substantial metropolises have developed in essentially pre-industrial societies. The coupling of the two forces in one historic period was peculiar to the United States, yet this unusual conjunction led to analyses which attributed to industrialization things which were essentially urban, and attributed to urbanization things which were essentially industrial. Nor was the confusion confined to historians alone—it has characterized the work of political scientists, economists, and other social scientists. Just as importantly, it has inhibited the serious study of early American cities, which were commercial rather than industrial but which laid the foundation for the urban growth of the last century.

II

The rise of cities in the nineteenth century deepened the historic division between town and country; yet it also had, ironically, a profoundly nationalizing effect. In the first place, they appeared very rapidly in every part of the country, providing each section with important urban centers. When the "line of settlement" barely reached across the mountains in 1800, towns had already sprung up along the Ohio Valley and as far west as St. Louis. By the time the farm areas were opened up along the middle border, Denver, San Francisco, and Seattle had already begun their rise to regional dominance. In the West, Josiah Strong observed in 1884, "The city stamps the country, instead of the country stamping the city. It is the cities and towns which will frame state constitutions, make laws, create public opinion, establish social usages, and fix standards." Even the South, so often thought of as overwhelmingly rural, developed a ring of cities at its perimeter which played a disproportionate role in the life of Dixie.

Second, this spread of urbanization fostered the growing nationalism by providing each region with enclaves of a similar environment. For nineteenth-century cities had much in common. They all stemmed from commercial necessity; they all developed similar political and social institutions; they all created local governments which found the same range of urban problems. Moreover, their mercantile communities dealt with each other, and their local officials consciously borrowed ordinances and techniques for dealing with city affairs from other urban places. Thus American cities tended to look alike, to foster common characteristics, and to breed a texture of life that differed sharply from farm and plantation. While many historians dwell on the regional flavor of a "Southern," "Western," or "New England" city, they usually overlook the overarching similarities.

This nationalizing influence of urbanization was facilitated, paradoxically, in part because the capital of the United States was not located in its commercial, financial, or cultural center. Unlike the Old World, where capitals dominated the nation because of their mixture of public and private functions, the American pattern has been dispersal rather than concentration. New York, to be sure, has had an unchallenged supremacy in many fields, but it lacked the political dimension which could have given it the national dominion of a Paris, London, Rome, or Berlin. The pattern meant, too, that while other places suffer from a "second city" psychology, they have escaped the "provincial city" relationship. In every part of the country the regional capital, like Chicago, Atlanta, Houston, San Francisco, or Detroit, is self-contained enough to exercise an independent influence over a large hinterland.

III

The eighteenth- and nineteenth-century American city, however, was quite different from the modern metropolis. It was most importantly a compact city. The rich and poor lived close together; residential and commercial uses of land were mixed; industrial facilities were located amid shops and homes. It was a "walking city." The boundaries were determined by the distance one could walk—to work, to shop, or to visit. This limitation governed both the size and the shape of the early city.

A new revolutionary agent, however, entered this historic setting. No incendiary ever looked so poorly suited to the task of creating such far-reaching change as this awkward object moving down Broadway in 1829. It was simply a large carriage drawn by a single horse. But it carried a dozen people over fixed routes, on a rough schedule, and for a single fare. Though primitive, this "omnibus" embodied the principle of mass transportation. This uncomplicated innovation blew asunder the casement of the old city and made possible the emergence of the modern city. Now it was possible for people to live quite removed from downtown and still work there. Moreover, the new system permitted greatly increased internal circulation, the ability of people to get around in a much expanded commercial center.

Soon the omnibus was replaced by the horse-drawn railway; in turn that gave way to the cable car, the street railway, the elevated, subway, the motorbus, and ultimately the automobile. Each new mode enhanced the area of urban settlement by accelerating the movement of people throughout the metropolis. Just as importantly, the introduction of mass transit gave the modern city its shape. What would later be called "urban sprawl" was the result of the transit revolution which made it possible to live miles outside municipal limits and still be part of the same metropolitan community.

The first consequence of the introduction of mass transit was an enormous expansion of the city, both in its physical limits and in the growth of its population. The old confinement of the historic city was broken, and urban residents spilled outside into the neighboring countryside. The extent of the city was now determined by commuting time. The radius of Boston settlement in 1850 was two miles; by 1900 it had grown to ten miles; by 1960 the metropolitan area would stretch as far as the expressways could tap the commuter. Everywhere, the population flowed over the old boundaries, the surrounding countryside fell to the developer, and old villages and small towns were overwhelmed by the "exploding city."

This urban expansion came at just the right time, for the mounting number of immigrants had begun to reach the shores of this country. Not only was there now room to accommodate the newcomers, but the enlarging metropolis created thousands of jobs for untrained labor. In the latter half of the nineteenth century, most cities constructed their basic municipal plants— streets, bridges, commercial facilities, schools, water and lighting systems, and industrial capacity. Most of these installations had to be built by hand, and largely by unskilled labor. The new environment was thus fashioned by the immigrant and in part shaped to his needs.

But the primary beneficiary of the modern city was the urban middle class, for the second consequence of the introduction of mass transit was the sorting out of people according to resources and taste. Since it was now possible to live outside the city and work in its downtown, those with the greatest wealth were given the widest options of where to live. Generally they very quickly abandoned downtown, with its commerce, noise, and different kind of people, in favor of pleasant residential neighborhoods. There they built large houses on generous lots and carved out an area of genteel and comfortable living. Those with fewer resources had fewer options. They built more modest houses nearer to the city center, or moved into newly erected two- and three-story flats. Those with few resources had to take whatever kind of housing they could find. They occupied large old houses which had been cut up for multifamily dwellings, or were jammed into old commercial buildings converted for residential use, or they could fill up the newer tenements designed to house the immense new numbers.

The third consequence of the mass transportation revolution was the acceleration of the inherent instability of the American city. With the growth of urban areas and the immensely increased population came a constant residential mobility. Every urbanite was involved. Not only was there obvious transiency in the congested center, but even the beneficiaries of the new city were on the move. The wealthier members of the middle class who moved out from downtown soon discovered that the city followed them; they picked up again and built farther away. Other middle-class groups expressed their rising success or expectations by moving into a better neighborhood a little more removed from the congestion and expanding commercial and industrial areas. Thus every section was in motion. This instability became characteristic of growing American cities. Indeed, it would be hard to overestimate its extent. In Omaha, Nebraska, for example, a tracing of 450 families between 1880 and 1890 demonstrated that only fifty-two lived in the same house over ten years; many had lived in two or three places within the city during that time.

Present planners and urban critics now yearn for the "old stable neighborhoods" that they think once comprised American cities. Yet what has been the most significant fact about urban neighborhoods is their historic instability. Even the "ethnic neighborhood," which has been invested with such nostalgia, was part of the constantly changing system. The "Italian," "Irish," or "Jewish" areas were always in motion; what kept them apparently stable was the fact that the same kind of people who moved out also moved in. When one group replaced another, the neighborhood would be characterized as in "transition." But it had in fact been in constant movement all the time, though a constant ethnic flavoring had observed the persistent turnover. All sections have witnessed the same mobility and no plans, zoning, or regulations have ever been able to still them.

The sorting out of people residentially by numberless individual decisions provided the new city with its characteristic social profile. The outer edges of the city were occupied by the older inhabitants, usually wealthier than others. These pleasant neighborhoods tended to be Protestant in religion and northern European in extraction. At the center were the newcomers, fresh from foreign lands, Catholic and Jewish, lower class in occupation and income. Between the two were the "zones of emergence," increasingly comprised of second- and third-generation immigrants on their way out of the central city and on their way up socially and economically. But the situation was never static; each area was enlarged as the urban population mounted and as the metropolitan area expanded.

The social profile of the new American city was quite different from that of Old World cities. For the early European development found the wealthy in the center of the city, near the public and religious buildings, with the poor huddled at the outskirts. Moreover, this tradition was brought to the New World by the Spanish and Portuguese, who built their new cities around the traditional plaza. The American urban shape was less planned and depended on a relatively free market in real estate and a largely unrestricted practice of land use. And it was the function of a highly mobile society where upward movement dissolved fixed class lines. In the twentieth century, especially since World War II, cities around the world have begun to assume this American shape. Mexico City and Paris, for instance, are witnessing the flight to the suburbs, the problems of decay at the center, and the frustration with "urban sprawl."

IV

This new city refashioned American society and increasingly dominated national affairs. Not only were immigrants from abroad attracted to it, but young people from the farms and country were also caught in the urban undertow. The census takers, of course, could measure quantitatively the numerical shift from country to city, but the novelist Harold Frederic saw the change on a more sensitive gauge. "The nineteenth century is a century of cities," he wrote bitterly. "They have given then one twist to the progress of the age—and the farmer is as far out of it as if he lived in Alaska. Perhaps there was a time when a man could live in what the poet calls daily communication with nature and not starve his mind or dwarf his soul, but this isn't the century." The end of rural supremacy, symbolized by the searing discontent of the Populists, took place long before the census bureau counted over half the people living in "urban places"—a watershed not reached until 1920.

Indeed, the conflicts within the new urban society soon displaced the old city versus country antagonism. For the metropolis had its own divisions. The process of growth had divided the city. The newcomers appropriated the inner city, in areas where people were afflicted with great congestion, irregular jobs, and pervasive and persistent poverty. Strangers in a new land and new environment, they struggled to keep some kind of social organization and identity. None of their old institutions seemed wholly relevant to their new predicament; but they utilized what they could, and through voluntary associations they met some of their important needs. Still the newcomers remained economically weak and socially insecure.

But they found some protection in numbers. These numbers were in most cases a curse; housing never caught up with demand, the job market was always flooded, the breadwinner had too many mouths to feed. Yet in politics such a liability could be turned into an asset. If the residents could be mobilized, their combined strength would be able to do what none could do alone. Soon the "boss" and the "machine" arose to organize this potential. Feeding on the vulnerability of the neighborhoods and the hostility of the outside world, the boss system became a distinctive feature of American politics. It succeeded because it was rooted in the realities of block life—the clubhouse, the saloon, the cheap theaters, and the street. Moreover, it met certain specific needs. The boss helped recent arrivals to find housing, secured them jobs, mediated with public authorities, managed families through bad times, and somehow gave the recent arrivals a sense of belonging to their new land. To be sure, the cost was not small—laws were bent and broken; officials corrupted; funds embezzled; the franchises sullied. Essentially, however, the boss system was simply the political expression of inner city life.

Conditions, were, however, much different in the pleasant residential areas which ringed the new city. Here the residents lived in detached houses on large lots or in new two- or three-story flats within commuting distance to downtown. Neighborhood life revolved around churches, schools, and voluntary societies. The men hurried for the streetcar every morning and joined the business and professional life of the expanding city. Political organization in these white-collar residential areas was as much an expression of the neighborhood as the boss system was of the congested center. "Reform associations" grew up to protect and advance the concerns of the middle-class constituents of the outlying wards. Thus the characteristic instrument of reform was "the committee of one hundred," or the "committee of seventy-five," etc. Since the neighborhoods were scattered and the interests diverse, unlike the more compact and monolithic center, the periphery found the broadly based committee more appropriate than the "boss."

As the machine scored increasing successes around the country in what one writer described as "the Irish captivity of American cities," reform groups gathered forces in an effort to reclaim the city. Initially, urban reform centered on an attempt to clean up municipal corruption and to find some better means of coming to grips with a wide range of pressing local problems. Only later was this impulse translated into a national movement. The enemy of this civic uprising, of course, was the city boss and his machine. Local business interests which had working arrangements with this political system also came under attack, especially traction magnates, gas rings, and utilities companies. The connection between "bad" politics and "bad" business became one of the most significant problems for urban reformers; indeed, little was said later by national progressives on this question that had not already been argued in the metropolis. But in the municipal context, the central target was the boss and his control of city hall.

The drive for improvement began sporadically in the seventies; toward the end of the century reform administrations appeared with increasing frequency. Though this municipal agitation contributed to the general discontent of the period, it grew independently of the rural protest embodied in Granger and Populist activity. It addressed itself to different objectives. Moreover, when the agrarian revolt failed in 1896 and new conditions calmed the countryside, urban reform activity continued at an accelerated pace. The years between the failure of Bryan and the accession of Theodore Roosevelt, so often left dangling awkwardly between Populism and Progressivism, were in fact filled with significant successes on the municipal level. When the twentieth century opened, the basis for a new surge of national liberalism was present in cities all across the country.

Progressivism in this phase was an intra-urban conflict, and, although not without economic overtones, it was essentially political. Reform found its major spokesmen and greatest support in middle-class residential areas on the outer ring of the city. These were the wards occupied by the older inhabitants who had abandoned downtown for the more pleasant, less congested spots. Ethnically these sections were white and heavily Protestant. The boss's strength was in the city's core where the newcomers had settled. These were the tenement, tenderloin, and transient precincts. Low income, irregular employment, and overcrowding prevailed. The people were predominantly immigrants; neighborhoods developed strong ethnic flavorings; large proportions of the residents were Catholic or Jewish. Hence, reform was a movement of the periphery against the center.

The two camps divided over many questions. The formal issues usually had to do with "charter reform" and attempts to change existing structures of municipal government. But the real cleavage went much deeper. The contest was to determine whether the oldest residents or the newcomers would shape the life of the metropolis. Behind the attack on the boss lay thinly disguised hostility to the hyphenated population of the central city. The drive for a civil service system always carried an implied attack on immigrant leaders and their modest educational qualifications for public office. Charges of corruption in city hall, whether true or not, usually suggested that the natives and foreign-born had different standards of conduct and honesty. And the sporadic raids on vice and gambling, generally directed at saloons and beer halls, carried a judgment on the private habits of the downtown neighborhoods.

The attack usually strengthened the boss and the machine, permitting them to pose as the protectors of oppressed segments of the city's life and the defenders of persecuted minorities. Nor was this wholly a pose. At a time when others preached self-help and limited government, the boss practiced paternalism and municipal service. People in his area felt they needed help—getting housing, jobs, relief, leniency in court judgment, even exemptions from the law. Reformers thought assistance in these fields was harmful both to those who received and to the public agency that provided it. The boss had no such inhibitions. He did what he could, and when successful he expected recipients to show their gratitude by supporting him. When a city-wide showdown came, they seldom disappointed him. To the people of the neighborhood he had become a symbol of both their predicament and their hope. His enemies were somehow theirs; his triumphs would also be theirs.

Political patterns in the Progressive era reflected this split between the middle of the city and its outer edges. Voting results could be plotted on a map; reform majorities dwindled, then disappeared, as they crossed over the lines demarcating the oldest parts of town. The balance between the forces was close enough to afford victories for both sides and to make no defeat permanent. In the first decades, reform succeeded often enough to make improvements in municipal government. Boss rule, however, was so deeply rooted in the needs of the neighborhood and the requirements of newcomers that it could only be tamed, not killed. Yet the battle itself had led to a valuable discussion of city problems. The competence of local government was greatly widened and the standards of municipal service measurably raised.

These internal urban political struggles had a broad significance for national Progressivism. Reformers active in local affairs often moved onto a wider stage, and they carried the same attitudes into the national arena that informed their approach to municipal problems. Hence, Progressivism found it difficult to appeal to the crowded center of the cities. Historians have observed, usually with some surprise, that neither labor nor immigrant groups responded very enthusiastically to progressive programs or leaders. The answer to this riddle is not only that Progressivism was essentially a middle-class movement, but also that it was led by the same people whose local activities had been directed against the residents of the downtown neighborhoods. Having rejected such leadership in the city, tenement dwellers could scarcely be expected to embrace it in the nation.

The gap between the center and the periphery remained a constant factor in local and national affairs for nearly three decades. The first major figure to build a bridge across this chasm was Alfred E. Smith of New York. Himself a product of the tenement and immigration section, he had a claim on the support of the machine; but he also developed strong ties with the reform community. His extraordinarily successful career in New York reflected an ability to join the traditional antagonists. What Smith accomplished within one state, Franklin Roosevelt was able to accomplish on a national scale. Standing prominently in the famous New Deal coalition were the boss and the reformer, neither exactly comfortable, but together making very formidable what political scientists came to call the "urban consensus."

V

The 1920's, however, brought to the cities a much more disturbing element than any which exercised the public life of the decade—the automobile. Initially a plaything of the rich, then a mode of incidental travel, it became the common carrier for subsequent generations of urban dwellers. As it did so, it altered the face of the metropolis. Previously, growth had a kind of controlled development, since the means of transportation had governed the shape of the city. The spread was concentric, or nearly so, depending on the capacity of public conveyances to handle increased demands. Even suburban expansion had hugged railroad lines and radiated out from the commercial focus. But the automobile destroyed even this semblance of order. The old restraints burst; the age of megalopolitan sprawl had arrived.

But not quite yet. The depression of the 1930's did not deprive Americans of their cars, but it did inhibit wide-scale building outside of the established cities. Later, wartime shortages further prevented any substantial residential construction. With the coming of peace, however, the pent-up pressure was suddenly released. Almost uninterrupted prosperity provided an affluent economic base; the automobile brought the remotest spots within reach of the bulldozer. A sharp rise in the birth rate gave an added impetus to these centrifugal forces. For fifteen years, virtually without interruption, suburban development dominated American economic, social, and political life.

The term "exploding metropolis" scarcely seemed to encompass the full range of changes. Not only did the surrounding countryside fall to the suburbs with all that that meant, but the old city faced a series of drastic crises. Its physical plant needed repairs that bad times and war had deferred; public transportation no longer competed with the private vehicle; downtown had somehow to service an immensely increased area and population. Furthermore, all these problems had to be met on a shrinking revenue base, for many of the well-to-do had led the flight into the green ghettos beyond municipal boundaries, taking shopping centers and even some industry with them.

To be sure, some of the old elements were still there. Particularly the historic antagonism of the center and periphery broke out again. Though somewhat obscured by the spillage of population outside the town's formal limits, the new battle lines were simply the older ones on a larger scale. Within the metropolitan area, the urban-suburban clash was essentially the one which had characterized the city alone for a half century. Now, however, the core had moved out toward the boundary. The flow of low-income newcomers from abroad had been stopped, but the movement of Negroes from the South and Latins from south of the border replaced it. As a result, the old ethnic bitterness was heightened by racial divisions. Dreams of metropolitan government became the analogue of the old charter reform hopes of an earlier time.

Suburban growth reduced markedly the previous domination of the city in Presidential politics. In the 1950's, Republican majorities outside municipal boundaries overwhelmed traditional Democratic urban successes. Though Eisenhower's personal popularity magnified this shift, observers understood that the conditions which produced the Roosevelt and Truman victories no longer existed. Any Democrat who hoped to win would have to penetrate the crabgrass curtain which surrounded every urban center. The genius of the Kennedy campaign of 1960 lay in its appeal to the inner ring of communities just beyond the city line where it either divided the vote with Nixon or contrived small margins. The New Frontier's and later the Great Society's domestic programs, with their emphasis on urban problems, represented attempts to consolidate and extend these gains.

The rise of metropolitan power brought a new orientation to national politics. The states, once the focus of local government, lost much of their influence, and the new axis ran between Washington and the cities and suburbs. Congress established the Department of Housing and Urban Development and a Department of Transportation designed to give coordination to old federal programs and to invent new ones that meet the new issues. The Supreme Court's reapportionment decision gave a firm political underpinning to the new arrangement by reducing the disproportionate representation of rural areas in legislatures. The new relationship has not always been happy, and disputes over local control are frequent. And a new drive to strengthen state government, perhaps by returning some federal revenues to the states, represents a reaction against the new system. Yet the Washington-metropolitan axis reflects the changing demographic facts of life and is not likely to be broken.

Despite new federal help, the "urban crisis" still bears down on the country. Most of the problems are neither new nor unsolvable. Indeed, in general the contemporary metropolis is a cleaner, safer, and more pleasant place to live than its predecessor fifty or a hundred years ago. The complaints against the city stem less from worsening conditions than from rising expectations; and for nearly all questions, American society already has the resources—the technology and the money—for alleviation or correction even if it lacks the will at the moment.

But one problem which is new and dangerous is the development of large Negro ghettos in American cities. The ghetto itself was not new, for every immigrant group had historically occupied similarly congested and confined neighborhoods. However, for white newcomers the ghetto was temporary, and second and third generations escaped and dispersed around the metropolis. For the Negro the situation is quite different. The ghetto does not break at the edges, few even successful residents can find housing outside all-colored areas; instead, Negro districts simply expand block by block. White neighbors either resist incursions or flee to other parts of the metropolitan area.

Meanwhile the ghetto festers. Middle-class Negroes resent the hostility which prevents them from moving into the pleasant white communities with better homes and schools, and they turn back into the ghetto to organize the more deprived. And among the young there is a growing despair and hopelessness. They can see that even if they do everything that is asked of them, they will still be confined to the ghetto. Immigrant slum dwellers had often known poverty, joblessness, and deprivation as bad as this, but they also know that with ambition, drive, and some luck it was possible to get out. The young Negro, however, finds the walls higher and the prospect of escape slim. Thus motivation is low, energy wasted, and the alienation deepens. From time to time the ghetto erupts in riot and terror, not only as a signal of bitterness but as a warning of a more formidable explosion.

The growth of the ghetto is the central domestic problem of American life. Not only does it stand mockingly as a symbol of the unfulfilled promise of equality, but it also frustrates the attack on other metropolitan issues. For decisions on such questions as education, housing, and poverty are caught up in the controversy over civil rights and are often deflected or postponed.

VI

Despite the persistent problem of the ghetto, American cities have witnessed a general renaissance in the past decade. Critics might speak of the "sickness," even death, of the city, yet the facts belie the pessimistic diagnosis. Nearly every major metropolis is working on a new skyline, with higher skyscrapers, larger apartments and office buildings, enlarged suburbs, and usually a civic center. Urban renewal, for all its faults, has removed some of the worst slums, while new construction and better code enforcement has substantially reduced the proportion of substandard dwellings. Many people who had once given up on the city are returning, bringing back not only their wealth but considerable talent as well.

The urban renaissance, however, is simply the American expression of the "modernity" which has characterized the postwar world everywhere. The new technology harnessed to a new economic vitality has greatly altered the pace and texture of life. In the old capitals new glittering (and sometimes garish) glass and steel structures rise over the city, dwarfing established landmarks and puncturing familiar skylines. The new forces extend around the globe—into Soviet Europe as well as into many of the new nations—creating a new metropolitan world which will be the common environment of a large part of every future generation.

BIBLIOGRAPHY

American historians have arrived at the study of the city by slow freight. Some nineteenth-century authors, such as Richard Hildreth and John Bach McMaster, had an appreciation of the role of the city in national development, but until recently it has been the lost dimension of American history. The intense investigation of urbanization was in the hands of sociologists, political scientists, and geographers. Now, however, a growing number of young scholars are taking the city as the major focus of their work. Indeed, over the last ten years or so, more books have been published on the subject than in all preceding years.

Two collections of essays provide a good introduction. Oscar Handlin edited *The Historian and the City* (Cambridge, 1964), which includes material on ancient as well as modern cities and a helpful bibliography. Philip Hauser and Leo Schnore (eds.), *The Study of Urbanization* (New York, 1965), assesses the state of scholarship in the social sciences.

The City in History: Origins, Its Transformation and Its Prospects (New York, 1961) by Lewis Mumford has sweep and synthesis. *The Growth of Cities in the Nineteenth Century* (New York, 1899) by Adna Weber is still important for the rise of the modern city, and Jean Gottman's *Megalopolis, The Urbanized Northeastern Seaboard of the United States* (Cambridge, 1961) is informative and suggestive in the present and future. John W. Reps' *The Rise of Urban America: A History of City Planning* (Princeton, 1965) is not so broad as the title indicates but is a good survey and includes a large collection of wonderful plates, maps, and plans. *American Skyline: The Growth and Form of Our Cities and Towns* (Boston, 1955) by Christopher Tunnard and Henry Hope Reed is a brief but interesting survey of the physical growth of cities from an architectural point of view. Charles N. Glabb's *The American City: A Documentary History* (Homewood, Ill., 1963) is a convenient collection of contemporary accounts. Constance McLaughlin Green's *The Rise of Urban America* (New York, 1965) is short but useful.

There is an increasing number of histories of individual cities, nearly all of which add importantly to our growing knowledge, but some have special distinction. Constance McLaughlin Green's two volumes, *Washington, Village and Capital, 1800–1878* (Princeton, 1962) and *Washington, Capital City, 1879–1950* (Princeton, 1963); Blake McKelvey's four-volume history of Rochester, New York, *Rochester, the Water Power City, 1812–1854* (Cambridge, 1945), *Rochester, the Flower City, 1855–1890* (Cambridge, 1949), *Rochester, the Quest for Quality, 1890–1925* (Cambridge, 1956), and *Rochester: An Emerging Metropolis, 1925–1961* (Rochester, 1961); Byard Still's *Milwaukee, the History of a City* (Madison, Wisc., 1948); Bessie Louise Pierce's three volumes on Chicago, *The Beginning of a City, 1673–1848* (New York, 1937), *From Town to City, 1848–1871* (New York, 1940), *The Rise of a Modern City, 1871–1893* (New York, 1957); and A. Theodore Brown's *Frontier Community, Kansas City to 1870* (Columbia, Mo., 1964) indicate both the distinctiveness of the experience of a single community and its connection with national development.

Other scholars have illuminated very significant facets of urbanization by studies of special topics. Sam B. Warner, for example, opens up the critical connection between transportation and urban growth in his *Streetcar Suburbs: The Process of Growth in Boston, 1870–1900* (Cambridge, 1962). Stephen Thernstrom reassesses the question of mobility in an urban context in *Poverty and Progress: Social Mobility in the Nineteenth Century City* (Cambridge, 1964); and Oscar Handlin analyzed the relationship between immigration and urbanization in *Boston's Immigrants, 1790–1865* (Cambridge, 1941). Robert Albion explains the economic origins of New York's primacy among American cities in *The Rise of New York Port, 1815–1860* (New York, 1939).

15

Political Parties

RICHARD HOFSTADTER

In a certain sense American political parties were the first modern parties. They had, of course, their predecessors in the British Whigs and Tories of the eighteenth century. But if we define political parties not simply as aggregates of men who share certain interests or points of view, nor simply as coalitions of notables, but rather as broadly based social structures that mediate between public opinion and the processes of parliamentary decision-making in a fairly regular manner, the United States was the pioneer nation in the development of the modern political party. The phrase "His Majesty's Opposition," when first used in the House of Commons by Sir John Cam Hobhouse in 1826, was employed in a spirit of levity and greeted with laughter. At that point Americans had had more than a quarter century of fitful experiment with partisan opposition, and their two-party politics was even then in the process of being resuscitated after the lapse of a decade. In Britain the modern procedure for a change of ministry dates from 1830. The American precedent for the peaceful transition of power from a government party to an opposition party dates from the election of 1800–1801. If we take mass participation as our primary criterion of the modern political party, the priority of the United States in party development is still more impressive. Under the broad suffrage of the early American states, popular participation in elections in the United States reached a high degree of development well before the Reform Bill of 1832 brought about a modest extension of the British electorate. A remarkable thing in the history of this dynamic country is the stability of the American constitutional system and of its two-party structure.

Stability and blandness are much talked about as qualities of American political life. The relative blandness and the unpolarized character of contemporary American two-party politics need not blind us, however, to the fact that sharp conflict has been a recurrent fact of American political life, with a fairly severe crisis taking place about once in a generation. The most important of these crises, of course, was the unresolvable issue of slavery and the nature of the Union which led to civil war in 1861. The Civil War represents the great failure of American political history. It is true that the Union was saved and the slaves were freed, but this was at a terrible cost in lives and anguish, and the resolution of the crisis was not otherwise successful. The legacy of sectional antagonism remained, the rural South was not really lifted out of the miasma of poverty, backwardness, and oppression, and the emancipation of the Negro was not followed by his absorption into the civic order on any satisfactory basis or by his achievement of human rights. The country is still, one hundred years later, haunted by the consequences of its failure. In good part this failure was the result of a breakdown in political leadership and party unity. So long as there had been two intersectional parties making their own internal compromises, the grave tension between the North and South had been manageable. The breakdown of the system came about when one of these parties, the Whigs, was replaced by a wholly sectional party, the Republicans, and when the internal breakup of the Democratic party made it possible for the new sectional party to take power. However, the terrible example of the Civil War may have been one of the historical forces behind the modern development of the basically conciliatory machinery of American political life. It is noteworthy, for example, that when the disputed election of 1876–1877 created a crisis grave enough to bring about violence, anarchy, or a *coup d'état* in many polities, it was settled by conservative business and political leaders in an enormously conciliatory fashion calculated to

bring out a minimum of public excitement. As C. Vann Woodward remarks, "The Compromise of 1877 marked the abandonment of principles and of force and a return to the traditional
ways of expediency and concession."

American experience in handling other crises has been far
more successful. Even during the first decade of the Union the
Alien and Sedition Acts were challenged by the legislators of
Kentucky and Virginia in such a way as to suggest that the Union
might crack over the unwillingness of some state governments to
enforce a federal law which the state legislators held unconstitu-
tional. This crisis, which was intimately involved with the
European war and questions of foreign policy, was finally settled
peacefully when Jefferson's party took over from the Federalists.
Less than a decade later, in 1814, the New England Federalists,
despite the embargo and war policies of the Republicans,
assembled at Hartford, Connecticut, and turned the tables on
the Jeffersonian leadership by again invoking the principle of
state intervention against federal authority. This crisis was
truncated by the simultaneous end of the war. Less than twenty
years later another serious crisis was precipitated by the threat
of the legislature of South Carolina to nullify the tariff of 1828.
The crisis did not come to a head, partly because the state
leaders found themselves isolated and threatened by an armed
President and partly because the tariff issue was soon com-
promised in Congress. Since the solution of the crisis of 1876–
1877, no Union-shaking crises of this order have occurred, and the
number of truly bitter and significant elections is not great. However, one such election was that of 1896, in which the domination
of Eastern capital, at least insofar as its banking and currency
policies were concerned, was threatened by the Democratic uprising under William Jennings Bryan. Another came in 1936,
when the various reforms and recovery measures instituted by
Franklin D. Roosevelt were challenged almost in their totality
by Republicans who saw in them the end of the American
system. Finally, the civil rights crisis of the 1950's and 1960's
came to a head in another polarized election in 1964. It is worthy
of note that each of these efforts on the part of an opposition to
take what was regarded by many contemporaries, either rightly
or wrongly, as an "extremist" position has resulted in a relatively

decisive defeat. Bryan, although he waged a vigorous campaign, received the lowest percentage of any Democratic candidate from 1872 to 1896. The defeats of Landon in 1936 and Goldwater in 1964 stand out for their devastatingly decisive results.

Its temporal priority hardly made the United States a model for other two-party systems. The comparative study of party systems is still in its infancy, but at this point, when it is still so difficult to generalize with precision, the overwhelming impression one gets is that of the differentness of party systems. The American way was never followed by other nations, and even those nations that have arrived at competitive party systems have reached them by different paths. The American system remains unique, distinguishable even from the British system to which it owes so much.

Indeed, the whole idea of an effective party system rests upon the immensely sophisticated notion of a legitimate opposition. Historically, the normal procedure of governments dealing with oppositions has been, quite simply, to suppress them, using whatever measure of force was deemed necessary and expedient. As Robert A. Dahl has observed; "Of 30 countries having in 1964 opposition parties, widespread suffrage, and governments based on relatively recent elections, only 8 would be considered two-party systems in the usual sense." Of these eight, all but two (Austria and Uruguay) were either English-speaking or were launched politically under the influence of Britain or the United States. The development, then, of effective and responsible opposition, is an unusual growth, and something not to be taken for granted. By an effective opposition, I mean a cohesive opposition party that forms a real alternative to the one in power— that is, a body which is itself capable of taking power and governing. By a responsible opposition I mean one that does not just outbid the government party in promises but that has a real alternative program actually capable of being executed under the historical circumstances in which it is set forth.

It is apparent, moreover, even upon superficial observation, that not all two-party systems are alike. They vary in several respects, in their competitiveness, cohesion, discipline, orientation toward ideology, and in their strategies. They are profoundly shaped by the institutional systems in which they emerge and by class structure and the social order. To make detailed, many-sided comparisons between the parties of the United States and those of other countries is impossible here. It may be enough to concede that the American party system, even when we grant certain broad similarities shared by almost all parliamentary systems with legitimate opposition parties, is quite unique, and to enumerate some of its distinguishing characteristics.

The American party system is a *two-party* system which is unlikely to become anything else. It is not just that the two-party polarization has the weight of tradition behind it but also that the two-party polarization is built into and underwritten by our constitutional and legal system. Our entire electoral arrangements, the absence of proportional representation, the exorbitant cost of political campaigns, the legal difficulties in getting on and staying on the ballot in many states, even the quasi-official role of the majority parties as supervisors of elections—all these things work against the rise of minor parties. Also the single-member legislative district, the division of power between the nation and the states, the method of electing a president with the winner-take-all system in the electoral college, the very leadership function of the Presidency itself, work to keep power in the hands of the two major parties. Major parties (like the Federalists and the Whigs) have broken up and been replaced as new parties have emerged in the past. But no minor party has ever gradually risen to achieve the stature of a major party, and no third party has lasted very long in any prominent capacity.

All this is not to say that third parties do not have a function in the American system. However, their function is largely that of pressure groups, and in this respect they are a curious combination of European ideological or special-interest parties and American interest groups. They have at various times been useful in bringing to the fore the interests of neglected or especially outraged groups in the public at large. The Populist party of the 1890's was a notable case in point. What happens characteristically, however, is that as soon as third parties begin to make their mark, one or both of the major parties appropriates enough of their principles or program to absorb the discontent on which they were flourishing. For this reason it has been said that third parties are like bees: once they have stung they must die.

Another characteristic of American parties is their lack of ideological orientation. They aim at the position of power, particularly through the Presidency, and at the distribution of patronage. The focus of major parties on capturing the Presidency impels the politicians to think of the processes by which they can forge a majority coalition. Such a coalition will inevitably embrace antagonistic interests and prejudices. It thus becomes the function of the major party to mediate between the clashing elements in its own ranks. Hence it is compelled to blur profound differences, to avoid espousing too sharply or clearly a particular ideology or point of view, and to try to stress the cohesive ideas and sentiments that bind its following together. In the United States both major political parties have to try to make some appeal to the working classes, to the farmers, to the business interests, to Catholics and Protestants, to ethnic new immigrants and to Anglo-Saxon old Americans, to Negroes and whites.

A third characteristic is decentralization and the concomitant lack of party discipline. It is often said that each of the major parties is composed of fifty state parties. Some of the state parties show a high degree of internal discipline while others do not, but in any case they make up a national aggregate that is extremely undisciplined, and the problem is complicated by the principle of local as well as state political machines. The national committees of the Republican and Democratic parties have very little real power, and even their efforts to draw up programmatic statements have at times been futile and widely resented. The Presidential nominating convention can thus be understood as a sort of diplomatic congress of all the local forces in the American political party. The political convention in the United States has developed a whole series of techniques which must seem strangely ritualistic to those who do not understand their function, not merely in nominating candidates but in developing institutional rituals by which the various machines and factions that constitute the parties can persuade themselves that it is possible for them to remain united. One of the curious features, for example, of an American Presidential campaign is the drafting of lengthy and elaborate platforms, programmatic statements which nobody reads. The symbolic function of such program drafting, however, is extremely important. Among the programmatic commitments, there are a few central ones which are likely to be controversial within the party itself. The capacity of the political leaders to arrive at an agreement as to what they want to *say* about such issues is a token that they do not have to fight the issues out or to arrive at clear statements of plans and policy. When a party falls into a bitter and prolonged platform fight, as in the case of the Democrats in 1860 and 1924 and the Republicans in 1964, this is a token of a fatal lack of unity.

Also, it is important for the winning candidate to develop placatory devices to hold his party together. In the choice of a Vice-presidential running mate, for example, he may pick a leading opponent, as Kennedy did in 1960, or he may turn to someone who represents the main opposing tendency in the party. Failing this, he may go far out of his way to arrive at an understanding; as Eisenhower did with Taft in 1952, or Nixon with Rockefeller in 1960. When he delivers his acceptance address to his party he tends to dwell on conciliatory themes, to stress the commitments and sentiments that unite the party, and to slur over those that divide it. Such stratagems, repetitive and tiresome when one sees them in operation, are nonetheless profoundly important manifestations of the American capacity for compromise.

The absence of cohesion and discipline that prevails in intraparty affairs is also manifest in Congress. Party lines are frequently broken in Congressional fights on legislation, and sometimes with decisive effect. So uncertain is the disciplinary pattern in Congress that the political scientist James M. Burns purports to find in fact four parties at work, the Presidential Republicans and Presidential Democrats and the Congressional Republicans and Congressional Democrats.

The Presidential Republicans have been led by such men as Willkie, Dewey, Eisenhower, and Rockefeller; the Presidential Democrats by Roosevelt, Truman, Stevenson, Kennedy, and Johnson. Leaders of the two Congressional parties are very often men whose names mean little or nothing outside the United States, but who are great powers on Capitol Hill, particularly great in their powers of obstruction. They control the Congressional machinery, the committees, caucuses, promotions, the progress of legislation on the floor. They are usually too obscure—though Robert A. Taft was an exception—and too devoid of glamor to hope to win the Presidential nomination, though they are often given the Vice-presidential nomination as a placatory gesture toward party unity. The two Presidential parties are the popular parties and they usually have the big political stars. Their more liberal and international orientation usually has more appeal in the big urban states which the party must have in order to gain the great prize of the Presidency. But their Presidential candidates, once elected, often find their powers of leadership hampered, their ability to get their legislative programs adopted hamstrung, by the power of the Congressional parties, whose leaders, coming from rural constituencies where the parties are so often noncompetitive, have longer tenure in their seats, hence vastly greater power than transient legislators under the seniority system.

Burns expresses a discontent with the rigidity of the American national government under the present two-party system which is by no means uncommon among American political scientists. In 1950 a select committee of the American Political Science Association published a report, *Toward a More Responsible Two-Party System,* in which it criticized the results of the absence of national cohesion in the parties. Its members remarked that, "as a result, either major party, when in power, is ill-equipped to organize its members in the legislative and executive branches into a government held together and guided by the party program. Party responsibility at the polls thus tends to vanish. This is a very serious matter, for it affects the very heartbeat of American democracy. It also poses grave problems of domestic and foreign policy in an era when it is no longer safe for the nation to deal piecemeal with issues that can be disposed of only on the basis of coherent programs." Some critics have even urged, rather impracticably, the adoption of the British system of cabinet government as a remedy. The advancing industrialization of the country, the increasing proportion of urban and competitive constituencies, and the reapportionment of elective districts recently required by the Supreme Court, may do more to remedy some of the rigidities in the American system than any such blueprints.

The degree of competitiveness of the American party system is another quality that demands attention. On the national level, and when we are considering only Presidential elections, the American parties can be regarded as highly competitive since the division between them is normally rather close. A Presidential contest in which one candidate gets as much as 55 per cent of the majority party vote is likely to be called a "landslide," and only three times in history (1920, 1936, 1964) has any candidate received as much as 60 per cent of the popular vote. Moreover, the alternation of the parties in power after eight- or twelve-year intervals is usually taken for granted. Even such a long period of one-party predominance in the Presidency as that enjoyed by the Republicans with only two breaks from 1861 to 1913, when examined closely, shows that the parties are not far apart in their command of voter loyalties.

When we look at the state level, however, the competitiveness of the American party system is not so impressive. In 1956 Austin Ranney and Wilmoore Kendall, surveying the state patterns, concluded that ten of the states—all rural, and, with the exception of Vermont, all Southern—showed a pattern of pure one-party politics. They also found that twelve of the other states, most of them with a relatively high rural composition, had a modified one-party system. To a large degree party competitiveness in the United States has been a product of urbanization. In recent years the tendency has been for competitiveness to increase in some of the previously noncompetitive areas, but the pattern observed by these two scholars has not been shattered.

Competitiveness may be regarded from another angle: how competitive are the two parties in the legislative process itself? My earlier observation that they lacked parliamentary discipline will suggest part of the answer: the two parties, though highly competitive in Presidential elections, behave in a more complex way in Congress. There their pattern of behavior, which involves a curious institutionalized system of mixed competition and cooperation, will readily be understood by people familiar with multi-party systems, such as those of France and Italy, where party cooperation is essential to government, but will not be so readily understood by those more familiar with the British system, in which party behavior in Parliament is strictly competitive and highly disciplined. Many of the greater legislative measures in American history—much of the legislation of the progressive era and of the New Deal, for example—have been bipartisan measures which would not have been possible if a national consensus had not been reflected in the ranks of both parties.

Foreign observers ever since the days of Lord Bryce have habitually asked about the American major parties what the difference is between them, and most of them have been content with Bryce's answer that the differences are negligible. In fact this is not quite the case. It is true that the class composition of both parties has always overlapped and that the programmatic differences have rarely been profound. Today both in Britain and on the Continent, where the programmatic commitments of parties are no longer so remote from each other as they once were, the American situation will no longer seem so strange. Yet American parties too can be distinguished in their history and composition, their form and leading ideas. To any outsider these differences may not seem consequential, but they are of lively interest to most Americans. A few things may be said about their general configuration. The Democratic party, which is the oldest of the world's modern political parties, enjoys the declared allegiance (with varying degrees of intensity) of about 50 per cent of the American electorate. This is in part a consequence of steady gains made over the last three decades. The Republican party, once the majority party, now enjoys the declared allegiance of about 25 per cent of the electorate, with the remaining 25 per cent classifying themselves as independent. The Republicans therefore find themselves in the unenviable position of having to attract a high proportion of the independent voters and a significant fraction of the Democratic voters in order to capture the Presidency—an achievement which they can pull off only with an exceptionally attractive candidate, as their experience with Eisenhower shows, or presumably when there has been a striking Democratic failure in domestic or foreign policy, or when both circumstances occur simultaneously.

The major parties have different regional sectional bases. The cities, both large and medium-sized, are, and long have been, Democratic strongholds in the main. Among the Representatives of the fifteen largest cities, for example, Democratic Congressmen usually outnumber Republicans about five to one; and Republican urban strength, when it can be found at all, usually turns out to depend chiefly upon suburban areas. Outside the South, rural America is almost as Republican as urban America is Democratic—a fact which accounts for many of the loyalties and sentiments of the Republicans as well as for some of the differences in their rhetoric. The Republican party is much more infused with nostalgia for the older America of the small towns and the countryside and the small business entrepreneurship and unregulated life of the nineteenth century.

Though "class" has always been an unacceptable term in American public discussion, it is beyond dispute that the parties do have a different class basis. Very roughly, business, particularly large corporate business, is overwhelmingly Republican, while labor, particularly organized labor, is strongly Democratic, and farmers outside the South lean Republican but show a high degree of independence. Party allegiances are reflected in socioeconomic breakdowns. Very roughly again, the upper and upper middle classes in the United States (comprehending the top 20 per cent of the population on the socioeconomic scale) will show a Republican allegiance that runs from 75 per cent to 85 per cent, while the lower middle class tends to be about evenly divided between the parties. The lower 45 per cent of the population has a normally Democratic allegiance, commanding from about 60 per cent to 80 per cent and increasing as one moves down the socioeconomic scale. The Republican allegiance of the executives of the largest corporations and of successful small businessmen gives the Republicans a financial advantage which has plainly been inadequate to overcome the distribution of popular loyalties. Today, though the outcome remains uncertain, the allegiance of businessmen may be undergoing a moderate but significant shift. In 1964 President Johnson got more support from the ranks of business than any Democrat in history. In part this reflected Johnson's conciliatory manner and anxieties aroused in some quarters by grave uncertainties about his opponent. But in good part, and perhaps more significantly for the long run, it reflects the fact that the Democratic party has been the successful practitioner of the "new economics" just at the time when a significant portion of the business community has been persuaded that Keynesianism spells stability and prosperity for business. It has now become possible that many more businessmen will continue to support the Democrats or at least to feel less convinced and emotional about their Republican allegiance than businessmen once did, though it is hard to foresee the day when the Republicans will cease to be the preferred party of the business class. What is more likely is that after some future Republican administration has practiced the new economics with somewhat the same effectiveness and confidence as the Democrats have done since Kennedy, the new economics will come to be considered an absorbed and ratified part of the national consensus—very much as those basic reforms of the New Deal that were unchallenged and untouched by the Eisenhower administration in eight years seem now to have become a part of the institutional structure of American life rather than a central issue.

Ethnic background and religious affiliation have also defined the American electorate. "New stock" ethnics from eastern and southern Europe have long been predominantly Democratic; but their Democratic allegiance was in some cases severely affected by World War II, when many Italians, Irish, and Germans defected from Franklin D. Roosevelt. Ethnicity is also associated with a lower-class position, and it has sometimes been difficult to decide whether, say, an Italian voter was Democratic more because he was Italian or because he was working class. Negroes have undergone a notable shift in the past generation. The policies of the New Deal took a majority of them away from the party of Lincoln and activated the political interests of many who had been apathetic. The civil rights issue has moved them increasingly into the Democratic camp, to the point at which in 1964 the Negro community was all but unanimous for Johnson.

There are differences between the parties in their historical associations and achievements. To go back no further than the post-Civil War-Reconstruction era the Republicans were the dominant party during the great age of the rise of American enterprise, the age of Carnegie, Rockefeller, and Harriman. During the moderate reform era that followed, under the leadership of Theodore Roosevelt and Woodrow Wilson, both parties showed a common sympathy for reform measures. More recently, of course, the Democratic party was the central formative party in the New Deal's attempt to democratize and reorder political and economic life after the Great Depression and to resist totalitarianism abroad. Since then it has also led in developing new instrumentalities by which the national government is expected to underwrite full employment and prosperity and in attempts to extend social reforms to new areas—to urban redevelopment, the campaign against the pollution of air and water, the extension of education and medical care, and other measures.

Historically, parties have been identified with great programs. The Republicans were the great party of high protective tariffs, bountiful grants to railroads, and (though here with decisive help from the Democrats in the era of Grover Cleveland) of sound money. In recent times Democratic votes in Congress have been more regularly cast for new welfare measures and for more regulation of business, Republican votes more consistently against such measures. The Democrats have also led the way in amplifying our foreign commitments. However, by the late 1940's the Republicans had to a very large degree swung over on foreign-policy issues, as the majority of them voted for confirming United Nations membership, for aid to Greece and Turkey in 1947, for foreign assistance under the Marshall Plan in 1948, and for NATO. But on innumerable details of foreign policy, as well as on welfare legislation, taxes, farm subsidies, the regulation of labor and business, issues between the parties have remained significant. The Democratic party tends to act as the avant-garde, with the majority of the Republicans following while resisting on many particulars and accepting changes only after their workability as well as their continuing acceptability to the majority of the public has been safely demonstrated.

BIBLIOGRAPHY

Clinton Rossiter, *Parties and Politics in America* (Ithaca, N.Y., 1960), provides a good brief account of the nature and function of American parties. More compendious accounts which I have found helpful are V. O. Key, Jr., *Politics, Parties and Pressure Groups* (New York, 1945); Austin Ranny and Willmoore Kendall, *Democracy and the American Party System* (New York, 1956); and C. E. Merriam and H. F. Gosnell, *The American Party System* (4th ed.; New York, 1949). An interesting recent critique is James M. Burns, *The Deadlock of Democracy: Four Party Politics in America* (rev. ed.; Englewood Cliffs, N.J., 1963). See also the older report of the Committee on Political Parties of the American Political Science Association, *Toward a More Responsible Two-Party System* (New York, 1943). On the comparative study of political parties, see Sigmund Neumann (ed.), *Modern Political Parties* (Chicago, 1956); Joseph La Palombara and Myron Weiner (eds.), *Political Parties and Political Development* (Princeton, 1966); and Robert A. Dahl (ed.), *Political Oppositions in Western Democracies* (New Haven, 1965).

16

The Coming
of Big Business

ALFRED D. CHANDLER, JR.

Big business has become an integral part of the economies of all major industrial urban nations where means of production and distribution are in private hands. There are great private business enterprises in all but the smallest of the non-Communist countries of western Europe, in Japan, and even in India. In the United States, however, there are more giant business enterprises than in any other national economy, and some of these are larger than the biggest businesses of other nations. In the United States, too, these great enterprises play a more significant role in the nation's economy than do similar private firms in other economies.

A few statistics reflect the dominating position which the giant business enterprises have achieved in the American economy. In 1960, 600 American corporations had annual earnings of over $10 million. These 600 constitute one-half of 1 per cent of the total corporations in the country; yet they accounted for 53 per cent of the total corporate income. The 100 largest industrials were responsible for 54 per cent of all profits made in the manufacturing sector. Statistics of employment tell the same story. In 1956 approximately 220 firms employed more than 10,000 workers. In the aircraft industry 10 such firms employed 94 per cent of the industry's total working force. In petroleum 15 such firms employed 86 per cent; in steel 13 hired 85 per cent; in motor vehicles 8 employed 77 per cent; in office machinery 4 used 71 per cent; in farm machinery 3 put to work 64 per cent.

Other sets of figures illustrate the same point, so let me just cite one more statistic to emphasize the scope and size of big business in the United States. In October 1965, *The New York Times* listed the world's largest units according to gross revenue in the following order: the United States, Russia, the United Kingdom, France, then the General Motors Corporation, followed by West Germany, Japan, and Canada. General Motors' revenues of just under $20 billion were more than the combined revenues of Japan and Canada and were very close to the United Kingdom's $21 billion and France's $20.5 billion.

In the United States the big-business enterprises differ from those of other nations not only in their size but also in the ways in which they are owned and managed. All the great firms are joint stock corporations. None is managed by a single man, not even by a single family. All employ senior officials who have no family relationship with the founder or his descendants and who have reached high executive position by working their way up the managerial ladder. In the United States the stock of nearly all of the large corporations is held by tens of thousands of individuals. Only rarely does a family still retain a controlling share in one of these large enterprises. As analysts of big business have repeatedly pointed out, the modern corporation in America is operated largely by professional managers who own only a tiny portion of its stock.

These professional executives have a major say in the management of the American economy. They are constantly making two sets of decisions. They determine what and how much their companies will produce and sell, and in what specific quantity, quality, and at what price. Second, they decide how the corporation's resources—capital, trained personnel, and machinery and equipment—will be allocated and used. In making the first set of these decisions, the managers of the giant corporations affect the pace at which the goods flow through the economy. In the second they play a large part in determining the direction of the nation's economic growth.

In the private sectors of other economies such basic decisions are still less centralized, and considerations of family and kinship still play a significant role in their making. In France, for example, family-owned companies still employ more than 70 per cent of all the workers involved in manufacturing and commerce. France's distribution system is particularly specialized and localized. As David Landes has pointed out, "This is a country of the family firm, the *boutique,* the artisan's shops, and the small factory." Significantly, the large enterprises in France are concentrated in the new, more technologically advanced industries such as chemical, electronics, automobile, and aeronautics. The smaller family firm predominates even more in Italy, Spain, and the Latin American countries. In Great Britain, Germany, and Scandinavia the professionally manned big business plays a larger part in the production and distribution of goods than it does in France. Nevertheless, the structure of the industries in these countries and the management of their enterprises are still in many ways more like those of France than of the United States.

In Asia the larger kinship group, rather than the individual family, continues to dominate the economy. In Japan the great business clans, the Zaibatsu, were the nation's "consciously chosen instruments" in the revolutionary transformation of the economy in the latter part of the nineteenth century. Despite rapid industrial and technological changes, despite war and defeat, and despite American attempts to break up these groups, the great clans still dominate the economy. In India, too, private enterprises stimulating industrial change have a similar strong clan orientation. The Dalmia-Jain and the Tata groups have almost as large and diversified holdings as those of the Mitsui and the Mitsubishi in Japan.

The story of the coming of big business in the United States should, then, indicate why and how the American corporations grew to such size, why and how they came to be operated by professional managers, and why and how these managers came to make the critical economic decisions. The giant enterprises which the professional managers came to command appeared suddenly and dramatically in many of America's most important industries during the last two decades of the nineteenth century. They came as the United States was reaching the climax of its drive to industrialism which made it the world's leading manufacturing nation before 1890 and producer of one-third of the world's industrial goods by 1913.

Before the rise of the new industrial giants—that is, before the 1880's—decisions affecting the flow of goods through the economy and the allocation of its resources were even more decentralized than they were in Europe. They were made by hundreds of thousands of small personal or family firms. These firms normally handled one product or one business function. The business decisions of their owners were affected by an impersonal market over which they had relatively little control, except possibly in nearby local areas. Price tended to determine the volume of output. Price also set the pace of the flow of goods from the producer of raw materials to the factory and then to the ultimate consumer via an intricate network of wholesalers. The great shift from decentralized decision-making to centralized coordination and control of production and distribution culminated in the years between 1897 and 1902, when the first and most significant merger movement in American history took place.

An understanding of this process of centralization calls for a look back to the 1850's and to the beginning of the modern corporation in American railroads. The railroads, as the nation's first big business, came to provide the only available model for the financing and administration of the giant industrial enterprises. They became so because their promotors, financiers, and managers were among the first businessmen to build, finance, and operate private business enterprises requiring massive capital investment and calling for complex administrative arrangements. American businessmen pioneered in the new ways more than did those of other nations, because American railroads were private rather than public enterprises and also because of the size of the system and of the individual roads themselves. By 1875 one American railroad corporation alone, the Pennsylvania, was operating a trackage equivalent to one-half the railroad mileage then in operation in France and over one-third of that in Great Britain. The only other privately built and operated railroad system, that of Great Britain, had only a little over 20,000 miles of track. By 1900 the American railroad managers were operating over 259,000 miles of track.

The financing of the American railroads required such large amounts of money that it brought into being modern Wall Street and its specialized investment bankers. The financial instruments and methods later used to capitalize large industrial enterprises were all employed earlier by the railroads. Financial requirements forced the use of the corporate form. An individual, partnership, or family firm simply could not supply enough capital to build even a small railroad. The sale of corporate stocks and bonds was essential. The modern holding company, too, had its start in the railroads, for the management of interstate business encouraged one railroad corporation to control others in other states by purchasing and holding their stock.

The railroads were forced to pioneer in modern business administration as well as in modern corporate finance. Their managers fashioned large functional departments to handle transportation, traffic, and finance. They set up central offices to supervise and coordinate the work of the departments and the railroads as a whole. They originated line and staff distinctions in business organization. They were the first to develop a flow of operating statistics used to control movement of traffic and also to evaluate the performance of operating departments. They, too, had to meet brand-new problems of modern cost accounting to make the distinctions between variable, constant, and joint costs, to differentiate between working and fixed capital, and to account for depreciation and even obsolescence.

The railroad thus provided the model for big business in industry. But the parent of the large industrial corporation was, of course, the factory. The modern factory with its power-driven machinery and its permanent working force, whose tasks were subdivided and specialized, appeared in the United States as early as 1814. Yet until the swift spread of an all-weather transportation network, including the railroad, the ocean-going steamship, and the telegraph, relatively few factories existed in the United States outside of the textile and closely related industries. Then in the late 1840's and 1850's factory production began for the first time to be significant in the making of sewing machines, clocks, watches, plows, reapers, shoes, suits and other ready-made clothing, and guns and pistols for commercial use. The same years saw the spread of the large integrated ironworks, using coal and coke instead of charcoal for fuel. The Civil War further stimulated growth in these industries. After the war the factory spread to still others. By 1880 the census of that year reported that of the three million people employed in industries using machines, four-fifths worked under the factory system of production. "Remarkable applications of this system," the census added, "are to be found in the manufacture of boots, shoes, watches, musical instruments, clothing, metal goods, general firearms, carriages and wagons, woolen goods, rubber goods, and even the slaughtering of hogs."

In the quarter of a century following the completion of this census, the family-owned factory was in many industries transformed into a vertically integrated, multi-functional enterprise. Let me explain what I mean by these terms. In 1880 nearly all manufacturing firms only manufactured. The factory owners purchased their raw materials and sold their finished goods through wholesalers, sometimes as commission agents and at others as jobbers who took title to the goods. By the first years of the twentieth century, however, many American industries were dominated by enterprises that had created their own distributing organizations, sometimes including even retailing outlets, and had formed their own purchasing systems. Often they had begun to control their supplies of semifinished and raw materials. The large industrial firm thus became a primary agent for large-scale distribution as well as large-scale production and, indeed, became a critical link connecting the two.

Many reasons have been suggested for this fundamental change. These include the impact of new technology, the influence of a shifting overseas demand for American goods, the development of the market for industrial securities, the desire for tighter market control, the tariff, and the personal motives of bad men, the robber barons. I would like to propose two specific and, I believe, more significant reasons for the growth of the large industrial enterprise. One was the inability of factory owners to enforce and so maintain cartels. If the American cartels had had some kind of legal support or sanction by the government as was true of those in continental Europe, the giant corporation would surely have been slower in coming. The other reason was the inadequacy of the wholesaler network to handle the high-volume distribution of goods required by a domestic or internal market far larger than that of any industrial nation in the world.

The manufacturers who pioneered in the building of the integrated firm were those who first found the wholesaler network inadequate for their needs. They were of two types. First, there were the volume producers of durable goods, who discovered that the wholesaler was unable to handle the making of the initial demonstration to customers, unable to provide the necessary consumer credit, and unable to ensure continuing repair and service of goods sold. Second, there were the producers of perishable goods for the mass market, who found the existing wholesaler totally inadequate for storing and distributing their products.

Among the first type were the makers of sewing machines, agricultural implements, typewriters, cash registers, carriages, bicycles, and most important of all, electrical machinery and equipment. The McCormicks in reapers, the Remingtons in typewriters, Edward Clark of Singer Sewing Machine, James Patterson in cash registers, Albert Pope in bicycles, William C. Durant in carriages, George Westinghouse and Charles Coffin in electrical machinery all pioneered in the creation of national and even international marketing organizations. Their new distributing networks usually included franchised retail dealers supported by branch offices which supplied the retailers with a flow of products, funds, spare parts and accessories, and with specialized repair and maintenance men. In order to assure supplies for the large volume of production needed to meet the demands of the new distributing system, these innovators also built large purchasing organizations, often bought or erected factories to manufacture parts and semifinished materials, and even came to own their own large tracts of lumber or iron and steel works.

In these same years, the 1880's and 1890's, the volume producers of perishable goods for the mass market created comparable distributing and purchasing organizations. Among these Gustavus Swift, a New England wholesale butcher, was probably the most significant innovator. In the late 1870's Swift realized, as had others, that the urbanizing East was outrunning its meat supply. Swift also saw the possibilities, which only a few others appreciated, of using the refrigerated car to bring Western meat to the East. The shipment of live cattle East, which since the 1850's had been the most lucrative eastbound trade for the railroads, was inefficient and costly. Sixty per cent of the animal was inedible. Cattle lost weight or died on the trip. As important, concentration of butchering in Chicago would assure high-volume operations and a much lower unit cost than the current method of shipping in small lots to wholesale butchers throughout the East.

Gustavus Swift's basic innovation was the creation of a distribution network. He realized that the refrigerated car was not enough. Carloads of fresh meat could hardly be dumped in Baltimore or Boston on a hot summer's day. So in the 1880's he began to build branch houses in every major town or city in the East and in many other parts of the nation. A branch house included a refrigerated warehouse, a sales office, and men and equipment to deliver meat to retail butchers and food stores. In carrying out this plan, Swift met the most determined opposition. The railroads were startled by the prospect of losing a major business, so the Eastern Trunk Line Association refused to carry his refrigerated cars. The wholesalers organized in 1886 the National Butchers Protective Association to fight the "trust."

But good meat at low prices won out. Once the market was assured, Swift then set up large packing houses in the cities along the cattle frontier and even bought into the stockyards. By the end of the 1880's wholesalers with more than ample resources realized that unless they quickly followed Swift's example they would have to remain small local enterprises. Armour, Cudahy, Morris, and the firm of Schwartzschild and Sulzberger (it became Wilson and Company in World War I) quickly built their networks and bought into stockyards. These remained the big five in the meat-packing industry until changes in transportation and refrigeration brought new challenges, particularly from supermarkets and other retail chain stores, who integrated backward to control their own wholesaling organization.

What Swift did for meat, Andrew Preston did in the same years for the mass distribution of bananas through the creation of the United Fruit Company. Also in the 1880's large brewers such as Schlitz, Blatz, and Pabst in Milwaukee and Anhauser Busch in St. Louis set up similar distribution networks based on refrigeration. In the same decade James B. Duke did the same thing for a new nonrefrigerated product—the cigarette.

These pioneers in high-volume manufacturing and distribution of both perishable and relatively complex durable goods demonstrated the clear economies of scale. They provided obvious examples for manufacturers who still found the existing wholesaler network quite satisfactory. Nevertheless, the factory owners in these industries were slow to follow the example of Swift, McCormick, and the others. They had to be pushed rather than attracted into adopting a strategy of vertical integration and with it the economies of mass production and mass distribution. It was the continuing oppressive pressure of falling prices between the mid-1870's and the mid-1890's that provided this push and forced many manufacturers to organize for the mass national and increasingly urban market. The price decline, in turn, had resulted largely from the coming of the factory itself. Far more efficient than hand or shop production, the widespread adoption of the factory after 1850, and particularly after the Civil War, had led to a sharply increasing output of goods and an excess of supply over demand.

In many American industries these falling prices resulted in a similar organizational response. The pattern was the same in producers' goods like iron, steel, brass, copper, rubber products, and explosives, and in consumers' goods industries like salt, sugar, matches, biscuits, kerosene, rubber boots, and shoes. This pattern—the second route to great size—was one of combination, consolidation, and then vertical integration. To meet the threat of falling prices and profits, the factory owners formed trade associations whose primary function was to control price and production. But these associations were rarely able to maintain their cartels. If the prices became stabilized, some manufacturers would leave the association and obtain business by selling below the established price. If prices rose temporarily, the members often disbanded until the downward trend began again. The association proved to be, in the words of the first president of the Petroleum Refiners Association, John D. Rockefeller, "ropes of sand." They failed for the same reason as did the railroad cartels, which collapsed in the 1870's and 1880's. The agreements could not be enforced. They did not have the binding effect of a legal contract.

While railroad men turned unsuccessfully to persuade state and national legislatures to legalize pools or cartels, the manufacturers devised ways of acquiring firmer legal control of the factories in their industries. They initially began to purchase stock in competing companies. Then came a new device, the trust. The stocks of the various manufacturing companies were turned over to a board of trustees, with the owners of the stock receiving trust certificates in return. Less cumbersome was the holding company, whose stock could be exchanged directly for that of an operating firm and could then be bought or sold in the security markets. Once New Jersey had passed a general incorporation law for holding companies in 1889, this instrument became the standard one by which a group of manufacturers obtained legal control over a large number of factories.

Administrative control and industrial reorganization often, though not always, followed legal consolidation. The managers of a few of the new holding companies, like the owners of government-supported cartels in Europe, were satisfied with assured legal control of their operating subsidiaries. Others saw that legal control permitted them to improve their market and profit position by rationalizing the production facilities under their control. In this they were encouraged by recent antitrust legislation, which discouraged the combination of companies under any legal form but did not yet penalize a single administratively consolidated firm.

So the holding company became an operating company. The factories it controlled were placed under a single manager with a specialized staff. The manager closed down the smaller, more inefficient plants and enlarged the more efficient ones. By running a much smaller number of much larger plants day and night, he quickly lowered unit costs. As a high-volume producer, the consolidated enterprise now found it could no longer rely on the fragmented distributing network of independent wholesalers. The enterprise therefore quickly moved into setting up its own wholesalers and occasionally even its own retailers and its own purchasing organization, after moving back to control of raw material.

The petroleum industry was one of the very first to combine, then to consolidate legally and administratively, and then to integrate, because it was one of the very first to overproduce for the national and international markets. In the early 1870's both refiners and producers of petroleum formed trade associations to control price and production. They were completely unsuccessful in enforcing their rulings throughout the industry. So in the mid-seventies Rockefeller, by using railroad rates as a weapon, was able to bring a large portion of the industry under the legal control of his Standard Oil Company.

However, legal control proved to be insufficient. Standard's primary market was abroad (for in the early 1870's close to 90 per cent of refined petroleum went to Europe). Rockefeller therefore had to develop an efficient operating organization at home if he was to compete successfully abroad. So his company tightened up legal control through the formation of the first modern business trust. Then between 1883 and 1885 the refineries were consolidated. Whereas the Standard Oil trust had operated fifty-five plants in 1882, it had only twenty-two in 1886. Three-fourths of all its production was concentrated in three giant refineries. As a result, unit costs dropped dramatically. By 1884, Standard's average cost of refining a barrel was already .534 cents as compared to 1.5 cents for the rest of the industry. Next, the trust moved to acquire its own distributing organization in the domestic market in order to assure a continuing outlet for its massive production. This move was stimulated by the expansion of the home market resulting from the rapid growth of American industry and cities. (By the mid-1880's, one-third of the illuminating oil and two-thirds of the lubricating oil products were going to the domestic market.) This creation of a distributing network meant an expensive investment in oil tanks and other storage areas, oil cars and wagons, offices, buildings, and facilities for making a wide variety of cans and other containers. Finally, in the late 1880's Standard Oil started to integrate backward, entering for the first time into the production of crude oil—that is, the taking of crude oil out of the ground.

In the late 1880's and early 1890's manufacturers in other industries began to follow the example of Standard Oil, Swift, and McCormick. Before the coming of the depression of the nineties, firms in rubber, whiskey, rope, cotton and linseed oil, leather, and other industries had moved beyond a combination to consolidation. The severe depression of the mid-nineties slowed the processes. Funds were hard to find to finance the new holding companies, to help them tempt other manufacturers into the consolidation, to pay for the necessary reorganization of production and distribution facilities, and to finance the purchase or construction of factories and mines producing raw or semifinished materials. Indeed, some of the newly formed consolidations failed to survive the depression. Then as prosperity returned in 1897 and capital became easier to obtain, industry after industry came to be dominated by a handful of large integrated corporations. The promise of handsome returns from mass production and mass distribution and the harsh memory of twenty years of falling prices made the prospect of consolidation and integration difficult to resist. The result was the first great merger movement in American history.

With the merger movement big business took its modern form. Externally the new consolidated enterprises competed in an oligopolistic way—that is, competed with only a few other giants. Internally they became managed in a bureaucratic manner—that is, through a hierarchy of offices and departments. In the early years of the twentieth century the managers of America's new big businesses experimented in the new ways of oligopolistic competition in which product improvement through research and development and product differentiation through advertising, trade names, and styling became as important competitive weapons as price. Pricing became based largely on costs. With better cost accounting the companies were able to set prices in relation to a desired return on investment. The managers of the competing giants had little to gain by cutting prices below an acceptable profit margin. On the other hand, if one firm set its prices excessively high, others could increase their share of the market by selling at a lower price and still keeping the expected profit or rate of return on investment.

The managers of the great consolidations also paid close attention to developing the internal organization of their enterprises. This task involved the building of departments to handle all the different functions—production, marketing, purchasing, finance, engineering, and research—and a central office to coordinate the work of the departments. Department building often required a massive reorganization of an industry's production and distribution facilities. The creation of a central office called for the development of procedures to assure a steady and regular flow of goods and materials through the several departments and regular and steady supply of working capital. It also required the formulation of systematic procedures to allocate the resources of the corporation as a whole.

The coordination of flow, particularly the control of inventory and working capital, came increasingly to be tied to detailed forecasts of short-term demand. The allocation of capital and the assigning of skilled personnel to existing or new ventures came to depend on a broad plan of company growth based on long-term estimates of demand. Appraising current performance as well as coordination of flow and allocating resources required the development of sophisticated cost-accounting methods and of formulas for determining long- and short-term rate of return on investment.

Because these procedures and techniques involved all aspects of the industrial process, they were of more significance and had a broader application than those developed earlier by the railroads or those formulated by Frederick W. Taylor and others for the "scientific management" of factories. These methods have, in fact, become one of America's most useful exports in an age when so many nations are seeking the material benefits of a mass-production, mass-distribution economy.

The United States pioneered in the techniques of mass production and mass distribution precisely because the consolidated, integrated enterprise replaced the small, family-owned and -managed, single-function firms and associations or combinations of these firms. Both economic and noneconomic differences made this change more rapid and more pronounced than in the other industrializing nations of western Europe and in Japan. The most important difference, as has so often and so rightly been stressed, was the existence of the large domestic market in the United States.

However, almost as important as its size was its newness. The existing forms of production and distribution were not so deeply entrenched in the United States as they were in Europe. The wholesale network only began to take form as the nation moved westward after the War of 1812; while the specialized wholesaling house, the key unit in the older distributing system, did not take root west of the Appalachians and south of the Potomac until after 1850. Nor, for that matter, did the modern factory begin to move south and west until after the Civil War. Significantly, the longest established industry in the country, the textile industry, was one of the last to accept the large integrated corporation.

In Europe the wholesalers had often existed for several generations, and factories grew out of industrial shops. So the business unit had become much more closely tied to family status and position than it was in the United States. The European preferred to remain the owner of his business, controlling price and production through a combination with other owners. By contrast, the American, having only just begun as a factory owner or as a wholesale merchant, found it easier to sell out to a proposed consolidation. He was less disturbed than his European counterpart at being transformed from an owner into a manager, particularly if the change increased his personal income.

The Europeans' preference meant that the older, more established industries—iron and steel, nonferrous metals, textiles, and agricultural processing—normally continued to be run by single-function, nonintegrated family firms, while the distributing side of the economy remained fragmented in the hands of many more, even smaller, family firms. In the newer industries, such as chemicals, electronics, petroleum, automobiles, and aeronautics, technological and market requirements made easier from almost the very beginning the creation of large plants and of national and international distributing and purchasing organizations. As in the United States, these same requirements forced the organizers of these firms to rely upon competent, specialized, highly trained managers. In Asia the dominance of the large clan in business enterprise has not hampered the growth of big business, but the favored position of family and clan has held back the development of carefully structured industrial enterprises administered by professional managers.

American attitudes and values may have provided an additional reason for the transformation of the cartel into a consolidated enterprise. To be effective, a cartel, in Europe or the United States, required at least tacit approval by the government. In the United States such combinations not only failed to receive governmental recognition but became explicitly illegal. The antitrust legislation reflected a powerful bias of Americans against special privilege, which had expressed itself earlier in the controversy over the Bank of the United States during the Jacksonian period.

In Europe, governmental support of special class and family interests was more acceptable. Moreover, the advocates of cartels could argue that their form of organization was essential if the nation was to compete in world markets. In any case, no other industrialized nation ever developed an antitrust movement similar to that of the United States. And, paradoxically, antitrust legislation and its interpretation by the courts, which made combinations of small units illegal but permitted the formation of large consolidated operating companies, actually encouraged the swift growth of big business in American manufacturing and distribution.

Antitrust legislation and the newness of existing economic institutions had a significant influence on the specific time when the giant industrial enterprise took its specific form. The more underlying causes for the coming of big business are the same as those that brought the rapid industrializing of the nation. These Thomas C. Cochran has listed in another essay in this volume. Vast natural resources, the large number of customers within the boundaries of a single nation, the ability to draw on European capital and labor, the success-oriented, utilitarian middle-class attitudes and values of a large portion of the population all created the basic opportunity out of which men could fashion an economy based on mass production and mass distribution and build the great enterprises that today carry on and link together this massive production and distribution.

BIBLIOGRAPHY

Part of this essay is taken from "The Large Industrial Corporation and the Creation of the Modern American Economy," given as a James A. Schouler lecture on May 3, 1966. The printed version of that lecture appears in Stepenen E. Ambrose (ed.), *Institutions in Modern America* (Baltimore, 1967).

Business histories are essential in providing the data on the activities of large transportation and industral firms. The most useful and dependable of the railroad histories is Richard C. Overton, *A History of the Burlington Lines* (New York, 1965); while Thomas C. Cochran, *Railroad Leaders, 1845–1890* (Cambridge, Mass., 1953) is the most perceptive and penetrating analysis of the thought and action of the men who created the nation's first big businesses. In the oil industry the most detailed history is the multi-volume, multi-authored *History of Standard Oil Company (New Jersey)* (New York, 1955, 1956, 1959). Thomas C. Cochran, *The Pabst Brewing Company* (New York, 1948); Charles W. Moore, *Timing a Century: A History of the Waltham Watch Company* (Cambridge, Mass., 1945); and Evelyn H. Knowlton, *Pepperell's Progress* (Cambridge, Mass., 1948) are all valuable. There are no histories based on the business records of firms in steel, rubber, chemicals, and other important industries. Nor are there many competent business histories on firms outside of the United States. Two impressive exceptions are Charles H. Wilson, *The History of Unilever* (2 vols.; London, 1954) and F. C. Gerretson, *History of the Royal Dutch* (4 vols.; Leiden, 1953–1957).

A very few biographies of businessmen have special value. They include Allan Nevins' *John D. Rockefeller, A Study in Power* (New York, 1953) and his three-volume study of Henry Ford (New York, 1954–1963); William T. Hutchinson's two-volume biography of Cyrus Hall McCormick (New York and London, 1930, 1935); and John A. Garraty's on George W. Perkins (New York, 1960). The autobiography of Alfred P. Sloan, Jr., *My Years with General Motors* (New York, 1964), provides an authentic inside view of big business in the automobile industry.

Often more useful than business histories and biography in tracing institutional and structural changes in the economy are the histories of industry. Excellent examples are Arthur H. Cole's *The American Wool Manufacture* (2 vols.; Cambridge, Mass., 1926); Harold F. Williamson and co-authors in the two-volume *The American Petroleum Industry* (Evanston, Ill., 1959, 1963); and Harold Passer, *The Electrical Manufacturers, 1875–1890* (Cambridge, Mass., 1953). My own studies look at a number of large corporations in a number of industries. *Strategy and Structure* (Cambridge, Mass., 1962) and "Le Rôle de la firme dans l'économie américaine," in *Économie appliquée* (Paris, 1964) include my analyses and hypotheses. Of the studies by economists, the most pertinent for the coming of big business are William Z. Ripley (ed.), *Trusts, Pools and Corporations* (New York and Boston, 1905); Hans B. Thorelli, *The Federal Anti-Trust Policy* (Baltimore, 1955); and Adolph A. Berle, Jr., and Gardiner C. Means, *The Modern Corporation and Private Property* (New York, 1934). Of the more general historical works, the best are Edward C. Kirkland, *Industry Comes of Age* (New York, 1961); Thomas C. Cochran and William Miller, *The Age of Enterprises* (New York, 1942); and William Miller (ed.), *Men in Business* (Cambridge, 1952).

The most useful analyses of the development of big business in other countries are in John H. Clapham, *An Economic History of Modern Britain* (3 vols.; Cambridge, England, 1926–1938) and *The Economic Development of France and Germany, 1815–1914* (Cambridge, England, 1921); Henry W. Ehrmann, *Organized Business in France* (Princeton, 1957); several essays by David Landes, particularly "Business and the Businessman in France," in E. M. Earle (ed.), *Modern France* (Princeton, 1951); Heinz Hartmann, *Authority and Organization in German Management* (Princeton, 1959); Thomas C. Cochran and Ruben E.

Reina, *Entrepreneurship in Argentine Culture* (Philadelphia, 1962); William W. Lockwood, *The Economic Development of Japan* (Princeton, 1954); James C. Abegglen, *The Japanese Factory* (Glencoe, Ill., 1958). The most valuable comparative studies are Frederick Harbison and Charles A. Myers, *Management in the Industrial World* (New York, 1954), and David Granick, *The European Executive* (Garden City, N.Y., 1962).

17

Socialism and Labor

DAVID A. SHANNON

With the exception of the United States, all the major industrial countries of the world—as well as many of the nations which are becoming industrialized only in the present generation—have some kind of Marxist political movement of significant proportions. These political movements embrace a wide range of the political spectrum, from various kinds of Communists (Soviet, Titoist, Maoist) to various kinds of social democrats, such as the British Labour Party, the West German Social Democratic party, and the Scandinavian socialists. National character, different traditions, and problems or conditions peculiar to a nation create some interesting variations, as in Mexico, for example. The differences between these parties and their programs are wide and important, but all of them derive in one way or another from the thought of Karl Marx. In most of these parties the trade unions or other organizations of industrial labor play an important role. In the United States, however, there is nothing quite comparable. There are many kinds of Marxist political organizations in America, from Maoists to mild social democrats, but none is politically important. In the highly unlikely event of their coalescing into a single party they still would be very weak. And these American political sects command the support of only a negligible part of the labor movement. American trade unions support the major political parties, mostly the Democratic party.

Why? How can we account for this American exception to the general rule? How did it come to pass that only in the United States did the labor movement fail to become Marxist oriented and that no politically significant socialist movement developed?

We must begin to consider the questions by noting that it is easy to overstate the contrast. There has been more of a socialist movement in America and more of a Marxist influence in the American labor movement than many people recognize; and labor and socialist organizations abroad sometimes behave less like ideological socialist models and more like American institutions than we often realize.

Early in this century the Socialist party, under the leadership of Eugene V. Debs, a Midwestern son of Alsatian immigrants who came to socialism after a youthful career as a leader of railroad unionists, appeared likely to become a major force in the nation's politics. In 1910, there were Socialist mayors in thirty-three American cities, the more important ones being Milwaukee, Wisconsin, Schenectady, New York, and Berkeley, California. Several state legislatures, mostly in New York and the Middle West, had Socialist members, and there were Socialist members of the lower house of Congress. Debs ran for President in 1912 and received 6 per cent of the popular vote. The Socialist party failed to continue to grow, however, and it suffered serious defections to both right and left during and immediately after World War I. Several prominent Socialists left the party because of its opposition to the war, and the party slipped further when the Communists split off in 1919. Thereafter, the Socialists never commanded enough votes to be a major political force, although Norman Thomas, who ran for President six times as the Socialist candidate beginning in 1928, impressed intellectuals with the clarity and incisiveness of his social criticism and developed a following among them.

It is more difficult to assess Communist than Socialist strength because the Communists put less emphasis on electoral activity, which is easily counted, and much more on the so-called fronts, which were designed to obscure Communist identification as well as to diffuse Communist programs. However, we know there were approximately 75,000 dues-paying members of the party during World War II, the peak of Communist popularity. New York City, which was the primary center of Communist strength, had two Communist members of the elected city council from 1941 until 1949.

Both Socialists and Communists have at times had a significant following in the American labor movement, but for the most part the unions in which they have been the leaders have not differed fundamentally from other unions in economic matters. For that matter, so far as economic issues are concerned, trade unions in basically capitalistic economies behave similarly regardless of their political rhetoric. Whether American or not, whether Communist, social democratic, or reformist capitalist in outlook, trade unions strive for control of the job market and a steady improvement in wages, hours, and working conditions for their members. French Communist coal miners, Swedish social democratic machinists, and American auto workers who vote the Democratic ticket do not differ fundamentally in their relations with corporation management. Samuel Gompers, the most important figure in the establishment of trade unions in America, advocated what is generally called "pure and simple unionism" or "business unionism," an emphasis on job and wage consciousness rather than class consciousness and ideological politics. Certainly, Marxist trade unionists do not follow the Gompers union philosophy faithfully, but in their routine dealing with employers over job conditions and job control they perform essentially as Gompers would have had them do. When ideology or political commitment conflicts with a union's short-term economic interest, the bread-and-butter approach usually prevails. For example, in 1949 and again in 1966 British dock workers went on strike because of job issues—wages, hours, and working conditions—even though their strikes embarrassed the political party with which they were affiliated, the generally social democratic Labour party, which at the time formed the government and was confronted with a serious balance of trade problem.

It is easy to overstate even the political differences between American and Marxist-oriented labor movements, at least of social democratic labor organizations of the British or Scandinavian type. The British and Scandinavian political arms of labor pay homage to socialism in the abstract, but they in fact have put their main emphasis on welfare state features such as unemployment insurance, old-age pensions, and national health plans. American labor, with only a few exceptions, has failed to pay homage to socialism in the abstract, but it has in fact put a major political emphasis on gaining welfare state objectives. One can even make too much of the absence of an American labor party such as Great Britain's. The federal system in the United States puts a greater emphasis upon the governments of the fifty states than is the case in most countries. In the heavily industrialized states, particularly those with basic industries that the CIO unions organized in the 1930's and 1940's, such as Michigan, the Democratic party's strongest element is organized labor. It is not true, as Michigan Republicans might argue, that the Democratic party there is a mere tool of the unions of the state; but then neither is the British Labour party a mere tool of the trade unions of the nation.

Nevertheless, despite these caveats about the dangers of overstating the differences, there are important differences between the labor politics of the United States and other industrialized nations. The rhetoric, the mystique, the symbols differ. The central fact remains despite the similarities: the United States does not have and never has had a politically powerful socialist movement, and in this respect it is unique. Why?

Let us make clear at the outset that suppression is not the answer to this question. To be sure, there has been both popular and governmental opposition to socialism. Senator McCarthy and McCarthyism were strong in the early 1950's. Leaders of the Communist party were imprisoned at about the same time, after trials in which they were found guilty of violating the Smith Act of 1940, which had been adopted during the period of the Nazi-Soviet Pact. The anti-Marxist measures of the McCarthy era, however, were not so strong or so popular as antiradicalism had been from 1917 until about 1920, and Marxists survived that storm and lived to flourish again during the Great Depression and the war. This is not to deny that antisocialist activity stunted socialist growth. Indeed, antisocialism developed in the United States from the very beginning of socialism, and the prevalence of anti-Marxist thought among American liberals as well as conservatives undoubtedly built strong resistance to socialist ideas in the minds of many people. But the blunt fact is that ideas and values and the social movements that derive from them are not capable of suppression short of physical extermination of all who embrace them. Whether in the United States or elsewhere, social movements that wither and die do so essentially because the basic conditions that fostered them change or disappear rather than because their enemies eliminate them.

One way of approaching this question of why there has been so small a socialist movement in the United States is to study in detail the history of the American socialists, and thereby to learn, among other things, what they did wrong. Several historians have worked in this field, and they have found an abundance of what in retrospect seem to be errors of judgment, cases of administrative inefficiency, unwise tactical decisions, occasional personal betrayal and venality, and ordinary human sloth and folly. Most of all, historians of American socialism have dwelt at some length upon bickering and conflict within the movement, the implication being that if only the opponents of capitalism had directed their energies against their enemy rather than one another they might have been more successful in their main objective. These "internal" histories of American socialism are often valuable for what they tell us about other things, but they fail to explain why socialism never was more successful in the United States than it has been. No one would seriously submit that American socialists were more inept or venal than British, Japanese, Swedish, Russian, or Australian Marxists, all of whom have enjoyed far greater success. Surely the explanation of the differences in the development of American, Japanese, and Swedish socialist movements lies in the differences among these societies generally rather than in the differences among their socialist movements. Almost certainly, a comparative approach to socialist movements will reveal that external rather than internal developments and conditions have been the more important.

One of the textbook answers to our question is that the political party system of the United States militates against the success of a socialist party or of any other minor party, and although the answer is too pat it still is relevant. For over a century, throughout the time a Marxist political party has been conceivable, control of the American government has resided with either the Democratic or Republican parties, each of which is a national coalition of local, state, and regional political organizations. Such coalition parties are a natural result of the American federal system and of the vast size and economic-geographic diversity of the nation. Neither of the major parties is ideological in nature. It is tradition and hope of political advantage rather than ideology that hold these coalitions together. Indeed, the range of ideological positions within each party is wide, and the degree of commitment to these many positions range from the deeply held to the lightly adopted for short-run political advantage. Although the center of ideological gravity within the Democratic party is a little to the left of that of the Republican party, a conservative Democrat, for example, is much closer in his thinking to many conservative Republicans than he is to many of his more progressive fellow Democrats. An ideological party such as Marxists organize just does not fit into the system and has little chance of moving either of the major parties aside. If Marxists should become powerful within one of the state or local organizations within a national major coalition, they would be only one of hundreds of local organizations within the big national party and without significant power. In fact, Marxists in the state of New York did something very much like this during World War II when they established the American Labor party. This group was an independent political entity, but it was part of the Democratic coalition nevertheless because it nominated the same national candidates as the Democrats did and endorsed many of the state Democratic candidates as well. The impact of the American Labor party on the national Democratic party was quite small. For any group to "capture" one of the national political coalitions is almost impossible because the coalitions are so decentralized. The two major parties also have a good defense against any minor party or third party that might develop enough strength to appear threatening:

merely appropriate for themselves the issue that makes the minor party popular.

Parenthetically we might note here that in some respects the two-coalition-party system is similar to the multiparty system in which no party achieves enough seats in parliament to form a government without forming a coalition with another party. In the United States the compromises that make the coalition continue to function are reached before the election; in multiparty systems the compromises that permit a coalition to function are made after the election. But the two systems are by no means identical even if they are not as unlike as they appear at first glance. American coalition parties command personal loyalty that can be quite intense, especially among those who aspire to high political office, and the interparty parliamentary coalitions of multiparty nations do not command any comparable response. The American coalition parties are thereby much longer lived. Indeed, the Democratic party traces its origins to the late eighteenth or early nineteenth century.

The Presidential system is still another feature of the American political structure that handicaps Marxists or any other dissident political group. In a nation with the cabinet system a bloc of Marxist votes in the legislature, even if well short of a majority, can have a greater effect upon national policy than a bloc of equal size within Congress. And Presidential elections, which no minor party can hope to win, dominate Congressional elections when they are simultaneous. It is no accident that all the members of Congress elected by the Socialist party were first elected in an off-year election, when there was no simultaneous Presidential poll.

But peculiarities of the American political structure do not explain the relative failure of socialism in the United States. American Marxists were certainly never denied political power, or even the role of minority opposition, because of the political structure. The simple fact is that there have never been enough Marxist votes to constitute an important political force.

An examination of social-economic class in America seems a promising way in which to seek an explanation of America's exceptional lack of a vigorous socialist movement. The matter is debatable because attitudes held by large numbers of people are not measurable, at least precisely measurable, but it does appear that there is less class consciousness in the United States than in other nations. This is not to say that socio-economic class does not exist in America; it obviously does. Nor is it to say that the American people are not aware of class, social distinctions, etc. Indeed, Americans seem to be remarkably anxious about social class and aware of complex and subtle class distinctions. But it is to say that Americans do not see themselves as divided along the class lines of classic Marxism. Among American wage earners there is less identification with the proletariat, less sense of solidarity with a working class, than among the wage earners of other nations. The evidence for this generalization is abundant even if not clear cut. Observers of many nations for almost two centuries have remarked upon a distinctively American attitude toward class. Public opinion polls also support the generalization. It is probably true that class attitudes in all nations with advanced economies are more complex than those described or assumed in classic Marxism, particularly as those economies become affluent, but it appears that social class in America is even further from the usual Marxist model.

Why are Americans' attitudes about social class exceptional, perhaps even unique? Why doesn't one find attitudes quite similar to those generally held in other industrial societies, particularly Western societies similar to America? Again the reasons are complex.

One rather obvious reason is that the people of the United States, particularly the wage earners, are unusually heterogeneous. Even by the time the United States became an independent national state in the late eighteenth century it had a more heterogeneous population than its mother country, Great Britain. The diversity of the population became more marked with the great migration to the United States that marked the industrial period of the nation's history. Although the population is mostly white, about 12 per cent of it is Negro. There are American Indians, Japanese, Chinese, Eskimos, and (in Hawaii) Polynesians. The Caucasians are from a wide variety of national and ethnic backgrounds, from all parts of northern, southern, eastern, and western Europe, all subdivisions of the British Isles, both French and English Canada, and all states of Latin America and the Caribbean.

Millions of Americans, particularly workers, have been unable to speak English beyond a few simple words. Even today, after a generation of relatively little immigration, many children in the United States learn English only after they start school. The population also divides along religious lines. Americans are Roman Catholic, Eastern Orthodox, Catholic, Jewish, and Protestant, and there is a bewildering variety of kinds of Protestant. The contrast with a nation like Sweden, for example, is striking. France, one of the least homogeneous nations of western Europe, is far more homogeneous than the United States.

This American ethnic and religious diversity has made a difference in social attitudes. Many Americans have tended to think of themselves as Negroes or as Irish Catholics or as East European Jews or as Puerto Ricans or as southern Baptists rather than as workers. Self-identification has tended to be along ethnic and religious lines rather than economic. Most of this heterogeneity and its results have been fortuitous, but there are documented cases of employers deliberately employing workers of different national backgrounds and languages in the hope of preventing their organization into unions.

This heterogeneity, plus the brevity of the nation's history as compared with that of most other nations, may well have handicapped the development of Marxian class attitudes in another and very subtle way. From early in their history, Americans have been acutely conscious of and anxious about their national identification in a way that is not manifest in more homogeneous and older societies. There has developed the concept of Americanism and its reverse, un-Americanism. The concepts are vague and do not mean precisely the same things to all people, but there is a fairly widespread feeling that to advocate socialist principles—or any principle that is not widely accepted—is "un-American." To pinpoint the reason for this nationalistic self-consciousness is difficult, but it probably has something to do with American diversity and lack of a centuries-old, commonly shared national history. At least, nations that are older and more homogeneous and therefore more confident about their nationhood do not have these concepts. There is no such thing as "un-Norwegianism," for example; and although there are many points at which outward manifestations of French and American patriotism are similar, still the idea that something is un-French would seem as strange to the ear of a Parisian as the idea of un-Americanism.

Still another factor that has blurred American views of social-economic class is the extraordinarily rapid and enormous growth of the American nation and its economy. At the time of the Sun King, what became the United States was a sparsely settled, economically backward area along the Atlantic seaboard of North America. A century after the death of Louis XIV, that is in 1815, the United States population was less than a third as large as that of France—approximately 8.5 million to France's 29 million—and its national wealth was probably in about the same proportion. By 1915, however, the situation had changed drastically. The American population was roughly two and a half times larger than France's—there were about 100 million Americans and about 40 million Frenchmen—and American wealth, however measured, had far outstripped that of France.

The implications of this fantastic growth are many, and some of them are relevant to our problem. Economic opportunity in the United States was greater than in economies that were expanding more slowly. Greater opportunity for significant economic advancement tended to minimize the feeling that the only way to improve oneself was through class action directed toward a revolution. The differing rates of economic growth in the United States and, for example, in France, made general satisfaction with the status quo more likely in America than in France. This is not to say that American industrial workers or poor farmers were satisfied nor that their objective conditions warranted satisfaction; it is to say that the economic pinch was less serious in America than it was in France and that a more optimistic view of the future was understandable. Economic optimism also tended to make conflicts between capital and labor less sharp. American employers were hardly noted for their generosity or encouragement of trade unions, but a general expectation of profitable, expanding markets made them hesitant about jeopardizing production with policies that would bring about work interruptions.

Another matter relevant here is that the United States, except for periodical economic slumps and regional lags within the country, has had a labor shortage as compared with less dynamic economies. This labor shortage, in turn, tended toward relatively high wages and toward relatively more job mobility. It also was a major factor in stimulating industrial managers to introduce labor-saving machinery to a degree unmatched elsewhere in the world, thereby increasing the gross national product, which, as we have noted, tended to blur class demarcations.

But fully as important as the astonishing growth of the American economy and its effects is the difference that existed between the New World and Old World economic and social structures even before the American economy reached the "take-off point." To be sure, the people who in the seventeenth and eighteenth centuries settled the land that became the United States brought British and Continental ways of life with them. American society, obviously, is a transplant of European society; but those who settled America did not transplant *all* of European society. Most important for the present discussion, feudalism— or, more properly, the residues of feudalism that remained in Europe and Great Britain in the seventeenth century—failed to make the transatlantic crossing. It is overstating the case only a little to say that the United States does not have a feudal heritage. To the degree that a clean break with the past is possible, America made a clean break with feudalism.

Surprisingly few of the observers who have made generalizations about America have noticed the absence of an American feudal past. One who did, Charles A. Beard, asserted that the "first" generalization that should be made about America was its lack of feudal origin. The United States, Beard wrote in 1935, "is not Italy, Russia, Germany or Great Britain; that is to say, it is not feudal and clerical in the roots of its economy and its thought. In land tenure, class arrangements and popular ideologies there are no feudal or clerical origins and remainders worthy of practical consideration. This is a fact of immense significance. . . ." Beard further argued that the political ascendance of the European bourgeoisie failed to extirpate feudalism and clericalism.

If the Old World, whether European or Asian, and the New World entered the modern industrial era with different attitudes and ideas about social-economic class as well as different practices, it is to be expected that their class arrangements would continue to differ as industrialism progressed. Because of the different traditions of class and resulting different political implications, it is natural to expect the Chicago workingman of, say, 1900, to have political ideas and loyalties different from those of his counterpart in Lyons, the Baltimore truck driver to think differently politically from the Newcastle shipyard worker, the St. Louis mechanic to have a political viewpoint different from that held by mechanics of Berlin.

Incidentally, it may well be that European and British class residues of feudalism are being eroded more rapidly by the developments of the last twenty years—by proletarian affluence, economic dynamism, and rapid social change—than by the bourgeois revolutions of a more remote age. In short, the so-called Americanization of Europe and Great Britain may be bringing about a significant lessening of the differences between American and European class arrangements. If true, we may expect significant changes in politics.

Kenneth McNaught of the University of Toronto in a recent provocative article has suggested still another way in which the lack of a feudal origin and consequent absence of a strong aristocratic tradition contributed to the failure of American socialism. Echoing Tocqueville, McNaught argues that "American liberalism is weak in its defense of dissent against majoritarian democracy precisely because it lacks an aristocratic legacy. American liberalism has been weakened and not strengthened by this lack, and the failure of the socialist phase of liberalism is the measure of the weakness." In the early twentieth century, he continues, "Whig-guided democracy was able to capture the bulk of the progressive movement and lead to the extinction of party-based dissent not because American society was essentially liberal but because that society lacked an aristocratic tradition of eccentricity and intellectual discipline." The subtlety and imagination of McNaught's thesis are exciting, and his further argument that the failure of socialism in America was by no means inevitable is certainly sound. But his thesis has nothing to say of many matters that seem relevant, and he comes close to a sophisticated version of the simplistic argument that the United States would have developed a strong socialist movement like other countries but for an essential illiberalism that brooked no dissent. The implicit assumption that underlies this argument is: America has no socialism; therefore, it must have been suppressed.

There is one big exception to the generalization that America from its beginnings was a modern society liberated from feudal strictures. That exception was slavery, which existed in the United States until approximately a century ago. Slavery and the agricultural economy based upon slave labor were not exact parallels of European feudalism, but they certainly were pre-modern. The class structure in the parts of the United States where slavery was strong was as close to feudal in character as anything in America's experience. This exception seems to be one of those that prove the generalization. Race complicates the situation—complicates it terribly—but if there is in America a case that corresponds to the classic models of class solidarity and consciousness it is among Negroes. And, logically, this solidarity and consciousness is mirrored among the whites in the former plantation areas when they are confronted with Negro demands for modernity. If America has a feudal heritage anywhere today, it is in those parts of the South, not yet industrialized, where cotton was king and the worker was black. Perhaps it is no accident that Europeans have felt more identification with Yoknapatawpha County than with the Chicago of James T. Farrell or Nelson Algren.

Chance, historical accident, may have more to do with an explanation of the unusual apolitical nature of American labor than we realize. If Eugene Debs and the American Railway Union had won the strike of 1894 as they had won their earlier strike against the Great Northern Railroad, each in the face of Samuel Gompers' opposition, perhaps the victory would have created a momentum that would have developed a significantly different labor ideology. American labor history might have been different if John Mitchell, the leader of the anthracite coal miners in their successful strike of 1902, had been more militant in victory and less eager to smooth over differences with management. Still again, if the left-wing Industrial Workers of the World, an anarchosyndicalist labor organization founded in 1905 which remained a threat to the Gompers-led American

Federation of Labor until World War I, had done a better job of maintaining its strength in basic industries, it might have accomplished a generation earlier what the CIO unions achieved in the 1930's. And if American workers had been organized at the beginning of the Great Depression as they were by its end, the political history of the 1930's might have been considerably different. One can only speculate. Speculation about what might have been, however, is not as promising as a historical-comparative approach to what in fact did happen.

BIBLIOGRAPHY

The most important works that address themselves, in whole or in part, to the problem posed in this essay are Selig Perlman, *A Theory of the Labor Movement* (New York, 1928); Daniel Bell, "The Background and Development of Marxian Socialism in the United States," in vol. I of Donald D. Egbert and Stow Persons (eds.), *Socialism and American Life* (2 vols.; Princeton, N.J., 1952); Louis Hartz, *The Liberal Tradition in America* (New York, 1955); Clinton Rossiter, *Marxism: The View from America* (New York, 1960); Werner Sombart, *Warum gibt es in den Vereinigten Staaten keinen Sozialismus?* (Tübingen, 1906); Kenneth McNaught, "American Progressives and the Great Society," *Journal of American History*, LIII (Dec. 1966), 504–520; and the last chapter of David A. Shannon, *The Socialist Party of America: A History* (New York, 1955).

For bibliographies on labor and Marxism in America see Maurice Neufeld, *A Bibliography of American Labor Union History* (Ithaca, N.Y., 1958); Gene S. Stroud and Gilbert E. Donahue, *Labor History in the United States* (Champaign, Ill., 1961); Fred D. Rose, *American Labor in Journals of History* (Champaign, Ill., 1962); Vol. II of Egbert and Persons, cited above, an extensive bibliography prepared by T. D. S. Bassett; and Fund for the Republic, *Bibliography of the Communist Problem in the United States* (New York, 1955).

Marxist parties have been the subject of several historical inquiries. Howard H. Quint, *The Forging of American Socialism: Origins of the Modern Movement* (Columbia, S.C., 1953), and Shannon, already cited, provide a survey of the Socialists' history, which can be supplemented with Ira Kipnis, *The American Socialist Movement, 1897–1912*

(New York, 1952), and Henry F. Bedford, *Socialism and the Workers in Massachusetts, 1889–1912* (Amherst, Mass., 1966). For the American Communists the best historical works are Irving Howe and Lewis Coser, *The American Communist Party: A Critical History, 1919–1957* (Boston, 1957); two important works by Theodore Draper, *The Roots of American Communism* (New York, 1957) and *American Communism and Soviet Russia, The Formative Period* (New York, 1960); and David A. Shannon, *The Decline of American Communism: A History of the Communist Party of the United States since 1945* (New York, 1959).

For standard general works on the history of unionism see John R. Commons *et al.*, *History of Labour in the United States* (4 vols.; New York, 1926–1935); Philip Taft, *The AF of L in the Time of Gompers* (New York, 1957) and *The AF of L from the Death of Gompers to the Merger* (New York, 1959). Shorter general histories of American labor are Foster R. Dulles, *Labor in America* (New York, 1949); Joseph G. Rayback, *A History of American Labor* (New York, 1959); and Henry Pelling, *American Labor* (Chicago, 1960).

18

Imperialism

ROBIN W. WINKS

"The depositary of power is always unpopular." Benjamin Disraeli knew this, and so did Theodore Roosevelt. Both contributed to their nation's power. Disraeli made Queen Victoria the Empress of India, while Roosevelt took Panama and built a canal there, by his own testimony. Both were imperialists.

But imperialism has proved to be an infinitely elastic term, one to be employed against all men who used power for expansion, consolidation, and conquest. Caesar, Alexander the Great, Genghis Khan, Suleiman the First at the walls of Malta, the Abraham Lincoln who crushed the drive for Southern independence (but not the Lincoln who freed the slaves), Dingaan and Shakar of the Zulu nation, even—according to English historian Christopher Hill—Oliver Cromwell, all were imperialists. As a result of such elasticity, the word is one which now carries almost exclusively a pejorative meaning, and since it has come to cover all those sins for which Western man is thought to be responsible, it is a particularly convenient form of verbal shorthand to demonstrate the gulf that separates the two worlds, the world of those who took and have and the world of those who lack and want. No one wishes to be called an imperialist, no nation wishes to admit to having undergone an imperialist past, and the new and emerging nations like to charge much of their current instability to the imperial tradition.

Many Americans have assumed that there was no period of American imperialism. Others admit to a brief imperialist past but prefer to clothe that past in other words. We were an expansionist nation, some historians argue, but not an imperialist one, a distinction more Jesuitical than useful. Yet other apologists suggest that since American growth was the direct result of a unique American sense of mission, of a Messianic impulse to set the world right which, even if wrongheaded, was sincere, humanitarian, progressive, and in general benevolent, the United States was apart from and above the ventures of the European scramblers for colonies. But most imperialisms have been rooted in a sense of mission, and the American sense differs from that of other nations chiefly in that the United States emphasized different characteristics. The British sense of mission sprang from a conviction of cultural superiority, the Japanese from a racial message thinly veiled in paternal rhetoric, the German from an impulse toward a preordained dialectic, and the Communist sense of mission from what was conceived to be a sure knowledge of the world's ultimate needs and ends. And to say that we all are sinners does not remove the necessity to see whether and how our sins have differed.

Imperialism was not always in ill-repute, of course. In Britain in the 1880's and 1890's, Chamberlain and Rosebery were proud to call themselves imperialists. They were helping unfortunate peoples around the world to come into the light; they were lifting Britain, and not at the expense of nonwhites but at the expense of other, highly competitive European powers. Whatever befell the subjects of imperial control was, on the whole, to their good. An advanced radical such as Charles Dilke and a conservative such as J. A. Froude could agree upon the righteousness of as well as on the need for imperial expansion; and while liberals and conservatives placed different orders of priority upon their respective rationales, they also agreed upon the basic mix: Britain must reform itself at home and make itself fit for an imperial role while expanding abroad in order to extend to the unenlightened the many benefits of a rationalized, ordered society. Improved sanitation and education, the equal administration of the law and the equal application of justice, the stamping out of slavery, debt bondage, suttee, polygamy, nakedness, and bride price—all seemed legitimate goals when viewed from within the liberal framework of the time. Theodore Roosevelt, too, thought that the vigorous Anglo-Saxon should carry forth the torch of progress; and, not unlike that hoary old radical and voice of the people, Walt Whitman, he wanted a race of splendid mothers.

Liberals, like conservatives, are always capable of highly selective indignation, and if they thought that the abolition of paganism and of slavery were of equal importance, if they thought the disruption of centuries of tribal alliances and of family stability was a small price for Africans to pay in exchange for monogamy, good roads, and a dependable market, they can hardly be blamed for thinking in the nineteenth century in nineteenth-century terms. Consider this statement, written at Brikama, in the Gambia, on the west coast of Africa, by a British traveling commissioner late in that century:

> There are higher purposes in life than merely living. Perhaps I shall die here, but I shall die a better man for having been here. These people are degraded, ignorant, swept by disease; how low, how low, they stand. Yet, they *stand*. I can help move them that inch higher, give them that direction they need, tell them of that truth that, once grasped, lived, proved, may one day make them right-thinking Englishmen, men with souls as white as any other, men I will have been proud to have known. Lift them, lift them. If I pass through the Gate before them, one day they too will pass through it, and I, there before them, will welcome them as men.

Such a sentiment may be found expressed by the *pakeha* among the Maori in the 1840's, by the Dutch in Java in the eighteenth century, by the Australians in New Guinea in the 1960's, and by the Americans in the Philippines in the 1920's. Indeed, one may find the same sentiment scrawled on postcards sent home from foreign parts by members of that most idealistic of all American organizations, the Peace Corps. Can we condemn this sentiment altogether, this amalgam of humanitarianism, of purpose, of drive, of sacrifice; this amalgam of arrogance, of self-righteousness, of superiority; this amalgam of progressivism, of Christianity, of Darwinism, of imperialism?

Imperialism was a practice; colonialism was a state of mind. Whether a powerful nation extended its control, its influence, or merely its advice over another people, those so controlled or so advised not unnaturally resented the controller. Indeed, we have all been colonies mentally at one time or another; no one likes, as they say, to be over a barrel. Much indignity lies in any subservient position, and yet there will always be the powerful and the powerless, and the people with the most power may not escape being the nation that is powerless, as Britain learned at Suez and as the United States is learning today. There is obvious indignity in never being the mover but always the moved, in waiting to see how a foreign capital or a foreign embassy will decide one's fate.

Behind the practice we call imperialism lay many strands of thought which were drawn together near the end of the nineteenth century to provide a rationale for expansive policies. The natural science, like the social organization of the time, emphasized selectivity, categories, hierarchies. There were natural orders of being, as there were natural orders of animal life, and nothing was more natural to political man than to assume that, as Walter Bagehot wrote, there were parallels between physics and politics. The new science taught "objectivity" and in the nineteenth century objectivity meant measurement, not cultural relativism but the opposite, the desire to place races, peoples, and cultures into classifiable categories. Cranial capacity, the length and width of heads, body odor, the color of the skin and the nature of the hair, all were measured, charted, and used to conclude that fundamental differences separated people. The vulgarization of the theories of Charles Darwin was combined with the romanticist's penchant for finding decadence wherever he looked, and the combination justified seeing the world as a jungle in which only the fittest might survive. The opening sentence of Count Arthur de Gobineau's *Essai sur l'Inégalité des Races Humaines,* published in 1853, spoke for the new pessimism that was, in fact, romantic: "The fall of civilization is the most striking and, at the same time, the most obscure of all phenomena of history." This pessimism was to run on through Spengler, through Toynbee, to the present. Arnold Toynbee was to write of the "natural dysgenic effects" that occur in societies; he was to find some groups—the Polynesians and the Jews, for example—suspended on plateaus where insufficient responses to overwhelming challenges had left them. The best men could hope to do was to turn back animality, or animality would take over the world. And to these strands of romance and science were added yet others—the Christian desire to save, to convert, and to enlighten, the commercial impulse to markets, the geopolitical and military notion of strategic values, the desire for adventure, the national thrust to a place in the sun, the national need for *la gloire*.

The very language of imperialism was all-pervasive. Neither the Maori in New Zealand nor the Navajo in America had any name for themselves until Europeans coined the words. Geographical terms of location—Near East, Middle East, Far East—were relative to a European map. Latin America became that portion of the New World where Spanish and Portuguese were spoken, because Americans decided this was so, oblivious of the fact that French Canadians considered themselves Latins too. Indonesia's Sukarno acquired a first name because American journalists refused to believe that a man could have but one. The names of the saints of European churches, like the names of European kings, run across the face of Asia, of Africa, and of the Pacific worlds as dictated by the whims of semiliterate men. The very geography of race itself is European, for it was Leclerc de Buffon who first classified the orders of life so that a later generation would have tools for distinguishing between peoples as well as plants. Long before Vachel Lindsay's vine-snared trees fell down in files along the Congo, Europeans had concluded that there, in truth, did lie a heart of darkness in need of both European goods and of European ideas. An imperialism of the mind preceded the imperialism of the gunboat, the adviser, and the investor.

The United States was part of this climate of opinion. American responses to some of the assumptions of European imperialists were bound to be negative, for the United States had grown, after all, out of a former colonial empire. The assumptions that Americans made about imperial responsibility were conditioned by an awareness of distance from the scenes of European conflicts, by a knowledge that the American people were an amalgam of many of the peoples of the world, some themselves representative of the victims of imperial struggles, and from an emotional predisposition to apply the basic tenets of republicanism to the imperial situation.

Perhaps here lies the most significant differences between the American empire and other imperial growths of a comparable time. Most Americans, including their overseas administrators, hoped to make the colonial societies over in the American model so that they could qualify for self-government or for admission into the Union itself. This assumption produced, as Whitney T. Perkins has pointed out, "a safety valve of sorts in an inherent bias toward the extension of self-government." This bias was more far-reaching than the British bias toward establishing representative institutions on the Westminster model, for it was there from the beginning, and republican principles were maintained for the so-called subject peoples as well as for the dominant nation. The territories acquired from Mexico whether by conquest or by purchase, became states of the Republic. So too did Alaska and Hawaii; and although the time needed to complete the necessary transformation before statehood became a reality was a long one, the assumption always was present that independence or statehood was the goal. The safety valve thus prevented the buildup within the colonies of a long-term ruling elite imposed from outside. It also decreased the intensity of local nationalist movements. While the British moved slowly toward their concept of indirect rule in East Africa, of governing through the already existing tribal structures, the United States applied a form of indirect rule almost immediately, and especially so in the Philippines, in Puerto Rico, and in Samoa. While the British anticipated that the Indians one day would be an independent people, as late as 1930 otherwise farsighted British spokesmen could suggest that such a day would not come for another century. Impatient, as usual, Americans presumed that their imperial role would be a short one, as indeed it was.

Unwilling to admit that dependency was more than a passing phase, American leaders were slow to think through the implications of having an empire. No permanent overseas civil service or military establishment, no educational system meant primarily to provide a continuing imperial tradition, arose to perpetuate imperial dogma. It is not without significance that American romantic novelists of empire, such as Richard Harding Davis, men of the same cloth as G. A. Henty, H. Rider Haggard, John Buchan, and Rudyard Kipling, wrote primarily of empires the United States did not hold, seldom using American colonial locales for their adventures. Perhaps the clearest proof that Americans assumed that their empire would be more transient than most may be seen in the fact that there was no Colonial Office, no Ministère des Colonies. The various territories were allocated to the Department of State, of the Interior, the Navy, and War; and when, in 1934, a Division of Territories and Island Possessions was created within the Department of the Interior, Guam and Samoa nonetheless were left to the Navy and the Panama Canal Zone to the Army.

The question is not, therefore, whether the United States or any other nation used power; rather, the questions are, how was this power first mobilized against the less powerful, and how was it ultimately employed? And in the answers to these two questions we may find some areas of contrast between American and, as an example, British imperial experiences.

The facts are clear enough. Most observers would agree in identifying two major periods of American expansion before 1939. The first of these, from perhaps 1803 until 1853, was a period of internal growth, of movement across the land from the eastern seaboard to the west coast, and of two wars—that of 1812–1814 with Britain and the Mexican War of 1846–1848—which, while not primarily concerned with the acquisition of new territory, nonetheless involved considerable and admitted expansionist interests. When in 1853 the United States purchased an additional corner of land from Mexico for ten million dollars, expansion within contiguous areas was complete.

Was this first period of expansion imperialistic? Perhaps. Certainly the rhetoric that accompanied it was so, and some of the same genuinely held and humanitarian if arrogant views were present in 1812 and in 1846 as sustained the British, for example, during their forward movement in Southeast Asia and Africa after 1870. In 1859 a Congressman from Mississippi envisioned the incorporation of the whole of Mexico, Central America, South America, Cuba, and the West Indies into the Republic, just as Cecil Rhodes later wished to see the entirety of at least the eastern sweep of the African continent painted red on the imperial maps. If the same Congressman also suggested that France and England might be annexed as well, while permitting them to retain their local legislatures for the regulation of local affairs, his hyperbole can be matched by much that Thomas Carlyle, Charles Kingsley, Sir Charles Dilke, or Lord Lugard wrote or said about various African kingdoms and reasonably viable Indian states.

Certainly the roots of the later period of American expansion overseas lie in the pre-Civil War past, for it was then that the American idea of a national mission developed. The secularization of the earlier Puritan concepts, the growing sense of the covenant the American people had made with themselves during the Revolution and within their Constitution, and the heightened awareness of and belief in a unique American destiny, led many Americans sincerely to support any of several arguments for expansion. Many believed they were liberating Canadians from British despotism in 1814 and freeing Mexicans from harsh and undemocratic rule in 1847. The doctrine of natural right, the European idea of natural boundaries to which a nation or a people naturally must expand, the desire to extend the "area of freedom" to those less fortunate, the thought that energetic, egalitarian Americans could better use the soil, even that they might regenerate people who too long had lived under effete and declining European institutions, including European churches—all these impulses toward reform lay behind the expansion of the pre-Civil War years.

Because the United States had a continent to conquer, it developed its first empire internally, incorporating territory into the body politic in a way that European nations having to seek overseas outlets for their energies, their people, their goods, their investments, and their doctrines, could neither understand nor attempt. If Britain's third empire lay in Africa, America's first empire lay at hand, merely across the wide Missouri. An imperial democracy might grow within the continent. Thus continentalism, not imperialism, occupied the driving American energies until near the end of the century. As Frederick Jackson Turner was to point out in his essay on the significance of sections in American history, the South and the West at differing times were to think of themselves as colonies of the North and the East.

The South was, after all, a conquered territory under military occupation between 1865 and 1877; and the West was, in its eyes and often in the eyes of Wall Street as well, a subject land. Further, Americans did not need coolies or castes in order to create an American *raj*. There always was the Negro to stand at the bottom of the social and economic scale, and there were the Indians to be pressed onto reservations.

The idea of mission was reinforced by the Federal victory in the Civil War. In 1867 the United States purchased Alaska from Russia. Following a period of internal concern for reconstructing Southern state governments, for reshaping the machinery of business, and for general domestic economic and social growth, Americans turned outward. The second major period of American expansion, and the first to propel America overseas, coincided with the world-wide wave of imperial annexations associated with the British, French, and German empires and with the awakening of Japan. If the earlier period were merely expansionist, as some contend, the growth between 1898 and 1920 was genuinely imperialist.

When Cubans renewed their periodic rebellion against the Spanish government early in 1895, *insurrectos* pillaged the land, destroying American and Spanish property indiscriminately, hoping to draw the United States into the conflict. The American Congress passed a concurrent resolution favoring recognition of Cuban belligerency, and anti-American rioting followed in Spain. Rioting in Cuba led the American government to send the battleship *Maine* to Havana Harbor to protect American lives and property; and on February 15, 1898, the *Maine* was sunk with the loss of over 250 lives. A month later a court of inquiry announced that an external submarine mine had caused the explosion, and the American public concluded, probably wrongly, that Spain had been responsible. War followed.

But war might well have followed even had there been no incident in Havana Harbor. A generation of Americans that had known no war was seeking adventure. Prosperity had returned to the land following the panic of 1893, and the nation's self-confidence returned with good times. Talk of regenerating Cuba, of driving European powers from the American hemisphere, and of the white man's burden mingled with the pseudo-science of the time. Populist frustrations arising from the defeat of William Jennings Bryan at the polls in 1896 were channeled toward the Cuban adventure, where reforms that had been blocked at home might have at least some compensatory outlet abroad. Free silverites thought that the war might bring remonetization. Businessmen saw the opening up of Eastern markets where, as one noted, if every Chinaman would buy but a single box of matches, the entire match industry would become rich. Unable to resist the many pressures upon him, President McKinley allowed the nation to be swept into war.

From the Spanish-American War flowed a train of events with a logic of its own. The United States won the war with ease; it acquired Cuba, under a pledge to make it free; it became the imperial overlord in Puerto Rico, Guam, and the Philippines. In the midst of the war, the United States agreed to a petition from the Hawaiian Islands to annex that kingdom. In 1899, Americans took Wake Island as a link with Guam; and, in 1900, Tutuila in the Samoan group was added. The Open Door Notes of Secretary of State John Hay followed.

Since a direct link with the Pacific was now needed for the Atlantic-locked American navy, Theodore Roosevelt hurried Panama toward independence from Colombia. Without question he connived at the Panamanian revolution, encouraging a puppet state which, in 1904, sold a strip of land across its isthmus so that the new imperial power might build a canal. Caribbean stability thus became important, and Roosevelt added his corollary to the Monroe Doctrine by asserting that America could intervene in any Central American or Caribbean state where financial or political instability threatened European actions. Haiti virtually became an American protectorate in 1915, and the corollary would be used to justify intervention in Nicaragua, Honduras, and the Dominican Republic. In 1917 Denmark sold her Virgin Islands to the United States, a clear example, even though by purchase, of the preventive annexation to which Britain had felt forced to resort in the Pacific and Indian oceans. The Corn Islands were leased from Nicaragua to protect the Caribbean entrance to the new Panama Canal, and tiny coral atolls in the Pacific were claimed for potential communications stations. The Caribbean became an American lake.

To say that these annexations were tempered by the American commitment to republicanism is not to say that they were not a form of imperialism. Clearly they were. But to say that the American empire that resulted was identical or even necessarily similar to other empires is to put one's premise before one's conclusion. At first glance one may find parallels between the cant of an Alfred Thayer Mahan and the pseudo-theories of a Halford John Mackinder, between the pledge made by President Lyndon B. Johnson in Honolulu in 1966 to use American power to defend the freedom of Southeast Asia and the promises made by Japanese leaders in the 1930's to create a Great East-Asia Co-Prosperity Sphere, between the *pax Britannica* and the *pax Americana*. But as pat as these parallels may seem, one cannot deny the presence of some differences between the British and American imperial experiences that are of significance. Mahan, after all, found his chief use not by the American but by the Japanese Imperial Navy, and Mackinder's geopolitical theories were most used not by Britain but by Nazi Germany.

However administered, three differences stand out between the American and other empires. Most British acquisitions between 1870 and 1920 were for the purpose of stabilizing already held possessions, arising from turbulent frontiers lying across some unoccupied and intermediate hinterland, turbulence that created vacuums into which the British feared other nations would rush. American annexations, largely consisting of islands, shared the strategic and preventive aspects of European imperialism, but in terms of scale alone the American holdings were relatively insignificant, and each acquisition did not to nearly the same extent create an ever-widening circle of new conflicts. Second, there was no grand design to American expansionism, no overall world strategy, no forward movement as in British Malaya, tied either to a containment policy, as Britain's island acquisitions were in part, or tied to an assumption of semi-permanence. The American occupations of both Haiti and the Dominican Republic were short-lived, seen from the outset to be temporary, with limited objectives in mind. This makes the occupations no less imperialistic, of course, but it does illustrate the makeshift nature of the American empire.

Most important, perhaps, is the by no means complimentary

fact that the American imperialism was more culturally in-
sidious than that of Britain or Germany, although perhaps not
more so than that of France. To qualify for self-government
among American states, colonial dependencies had to be utterly
transformed, and the Americans often showed very little respect
for Spanish culture in Puerto Rico, for Samoan life in Tutuila,
or for the structure of the old Hawaiian kingdom. The French,
with their *mission civilisatrice,* were equally willing to insist that,
to be civilized, the colonized must learn the language and customs
of the conqueror. The British, ever more pragmatic, were content
to administer through an elite, creating classes of Anglo-Indians
and other cultural hyphenates but leaving the fundamental
nature of the indigenous culture unchanged. Since they never
anticipated the day when India would become part of the United
Kingdom, and not until the 1920's did responsible officials give
serious thought even to the loose linkage now involved in Commonwealth ties, wholesale Anglicizing was unnecessary. Precisely because the Americans did anticipate rapid progress toward
assimilation did they insist upon such brutally fast Americanization.

As a British historian of empire David K. Fieldhouse has
pointed out, what set the American empire apart, then, was the
attempt to fit colonial possessions into the Procrustian bed of
republicanism. No one provided a theoretical base for permanent
colonialism, for the new territories were to be ushered into the
United States on the basis of the same machinery, already established by the Constitution, that was used for Kentucky and
Tennessee in the 1790's, for Colorado in 1876, and for Arizona in
1912. Congress extended full citizenship to the dependencies—
to Puerto Ricans in 1917, to the Virgin Islands in 1927, to
Guamanians in 1950. Representative government came quickly,
responsible government slowly, and Congress exercised over the
legislative bodies within the colonies the same kind of ultimate
veto that lay in Britain's Colonial Laws Validity Act of 1865.

A difference of considerable importance lay in the fact that
the American empire was the only one, other than the Russian,
which formed a single economic system. Alaska and Hawaii were
brought under the American tariff upon annexation, Puerto

Rico in 1900, and the Philippine Islands in 1909. The advantages of such a system accrued almost entirely to the colonies, for all were primary producers who would have found their chief markets in the United States in any event. That the colonies felt more economically benefited than exploited may be seen from the Philippines' rejection of an offer of independence in 1933 because it meant gradual exclusion from the American protective system. Nor did the United States gain economically from the colonies. In 1925, a high point, only 4.9 per cent of American exports went to any of the colonial areas, including those Caribbean states bound to the United States by treaty. Nor did the colonies become important for capital—by World War II, Puerto Rico and the Philippines together held only 2.5 per cent of total overseas American investment, a figure ridiculously tiny compared to the sums placed in independent nations such as Mexico and Canada.

Perhaps here we discover a large area of comparability between American and European imperialisms. France, still primarily concerned with agricultural problems, stands apart from many generalizations, but Britain assuredly also realized little direct economic gain from her colonies. The British also preferred to place investment capital in areas that need not be annexed. The British informal empire, an empire of trade, investment, and influence, extended into the Middle East, to Argentina, and to the Baltic states, just as an American informal empire existed in Latin America, in Canada, and in parts of China. But such nations also gained from such contacts, as any study of the growth of Canadian industry or of Argentine rails would show. Informal empires were a mixed blessing, but mixed they were, doctrinaire ideologies notwithstanding.

The American empire may be contrasted to those of the European powers in another way, however. The United States had grown out of an earlier empire, and having fought a revolutionary war to gain its independence of Britain, it continued to hold to certain principles which, as we have seen, injected republican assumptions into colonial relationships. Further, all of the colonial possessions acquired by the United States, with the exception of Hawaii, had belonged to another nation before.

They were not formerly independent states, they had not experienced a recent period of local autonomy, as Natal did under the Boers, as the Indian princely states had done before the British East India Company arrived upon the scene, or as the Malay States did under their sultans. Cuba, Puerto Rico, the Philippines, and Guam had been under Spanish control, the Virgin Islands under Danish, Alaska under Russian, Samoa under German and British, and the Canal Zone under Colombian. Former concepts of independence were not silenced and, in some cases, were introduced for the first time. The American imperial acquisitions might thus be best compared to those areas added to the British Empire at the Treaty of Versailles, as the spoils of war, not the spoils of trade. In effect, the American empire was not unlike the new colonial holdings of Australia and New Zealand—a ricochet empire, picked up as the by-product of other events, and ironically acquired by nations which themselves had grown out of former dependency status.

No European power gave any colony independence before the end of World War II. But the United States released Cuba from its administrative embrace in 1934 and promised in the same year to give the Philippines independence after a decade's transition period, a promise kept immediately following World War II. Puerto Rico was offered independence or statehood and chose neither, so that today it is a unique commonwealth, within the American nation, self-governing, and in part untaxed.

The United States rejected empire in 1945. Victorious, wealthy, clearly the most powerful nation on earth, the United States could have insisted upon retaining much, had nineteenth-century doctrines of power been operative. Perhaps it did not, as some of its critics say, because it recognized that through military occupation in Germany and Japan, through advantageous treaties with war-torn nations, and through the pervasive presence of American capital, there no longer was any need to build an empire in the old ways. Perhaps so; but if so, this was another kind of imperialism than was usually meant. It may be that American commitments overseas which arose in connection with Cold War diplomacy constituted another form of imperialism. But these are problems of comparability that will be dealt with in a later essay; for whatever imperial content the diplomatic and military events of the 1960's may hold, that content is not comparable with the events of the classic period of world imperialisms that fell between 1870 and 1920.

But then, has not the impact of the American way of life been so pervasive, so massive, so undeniable as to constitute a form of cultural imperialism? Canadians fear a cultural take-over, Africans and Asians alike refer to Americanization, and pseudo-intellectuals coin awkward terms, like Cocacolonization, to indict what they regard to be the essence of the American presence. Nonetheless, as most nations are coming to see, those manifestations they associate with Americanization are really nothing more than the coming of the industrial and urban age to their own shores. America has no monopoly on juvenile delinquency, a rising crime rate, or the automobile and its excesses.

What, then, have we said of American imperialism? That, like all imperialisms, it was contradictory and that it could make an entire people appear to be hypocritical. When Woodrow Wilson set out to make the world safe for democracy, he spoke for *Realpolitik* as well as for humanitarianism, for the kind of democracy for which he wished to make the world safe was American democracy. But if he thought that he must teach South Americans to elect good men, he also remembered himself sufficiently not to do so. "We can afford," he thought, "to exercise the self-restraint of a really great nation which realizes its own strength and scorns to misuse it."

We have also said that similarities in motivation do not prove similarities in execution. The imperial experience, whether viewed from the gunboats of the expanding powers or from the beaches of the colonized peoples, must involve more than the first part of the story. Because the United States had no established church, no class of permanent civil servants, no entrenched system of private and privileged education, and no well-established military tradition, the American imperial movement was reinforced by fewer institutions. While G. A. Henty rode *Through the Khyber Pass* and Henri Fauconnier sought out *The Soul of Malaya*, American novelists did not write of Samoa, Guam, or Puerto Rico. Racism, romanticism, pseudo-science, and

Christianity worked in roughly similar ways in British and American societies but they were projected into the colonies somewhat differently.

There are, perhaps, four questions which one might pose of any imperial relationship. What was the nature of the white settlers sent into the new country? What was the nature of the indigenous people? What was the degree of commitment on the part of the metropolitan power to retention of the territory and for what purposes? Within what geographical compass would the drama be played out? Since the United States sent few settlers into its empire, and since the areas, with the exception of the Philippines and Alaska, were quite small, the American answer to the first and last of these questions usually differed from the British, French, or Russian response. There rise the differences. In the answers to the second and third of the questions rise the similarities. One does not wish to reduce a complex problem to futile simplicities, but nonetheless one suspects that the American imperial experience is comparable to that of other nations only briefly, somewhat incidentally, and then but half the time.

BIBLIOGRAPHY

Despite the obvious invitation to comparative studies that lies within colonial and imperial history, few scholars have attempted to contrast the American experience with that of other nations. In the late nineteenth and early twentieth centuries, it was fashionable for students of empire to contrast the Roman with the British conceptions; but such contrasts usually were exercises in the irrelevant, conducted by those who wished to justify the latter by the civilization and longevity of the former. Too many changes in society, technology, and political thought across too many centuries have taken place to make the results of such speculations more than mere academic entertainment. I have made no comparisons here with the pre-nineteenth-century empires, of which there were many, because I do not consider them comparable.

But across time the word "empire" itself has taken on meanings which may be compared, even though the administrative structures that the word described may not be. Richard Koebner, in *Empire* (Cambridge, England, 1961), has shown how the nuances of the term changed. A. P. Thornton, in *Doctrines of Imperialism* (New York, 1965), has examined the nineteenth-century justifications for empire, although with little reference to the United States. The most effective, and also the briefest, attempt to show how American imperialism differed from other imperialisms within the same period of time appears in David K. Fieldhouse's excellent *The Colonial Empires: A Comparative Survey* (London, 1966). Whitney T. Perkins, in *Denial of Empire: The United States and Its Dependencies* (Leyden, 1962), implies a number of comparisons as well.

Monographs on American imperialism focus on the Spanish-American War, the Open Door Policy, and intervention in the Caribbean. The best of these works are Walter LeFeber, *The New Empire: An Interpretation of American Expansion, 1860–1898* (Ithaca, N.Y., 1963); Ernest R. May, *Imperial Democracy: The Emergence of America as a Great Power* (New York, 1961); Charles S. Campbell, Jr., *Special Business Interests and the Open Door Policy* (New Haven, 1951); and Dana G. Munro, *Intervention and Dollar Diplomacy in the Caribbean, 1900–1921* (Princeton, 1964). Other books which deal with the period of Anglo-American rapprochement in the midst of mutual imperialisms include Charles Campbell's *Anglo-American Understanding, 1898–1903* (Baltimore, 1957); Lionel M. Gelber's *The Rise of Anglo-American Friendship: A Study in World Politics, 1898–1906* (London, 1938); Alexander E. Campbell's *Great Britain and the United States, 1895–1903* (London, 1960); and R. G. Neale's *Great Britain and United States Expansion: 1898–1900* (East Lansing, Mich., 1966). Two books by Foster R. Dulles provide competent summaries: *America's Rise to World Power, 1898–1954* (New York, 1955) and *The Imperial Years* (New York, 1956). Perhaps the classic account, Julius W. Pratt, *Expansionists of 1898* (Baltimore, 1936), remains the best. The thesis that American expansionism was the result of a deflected and partially frustrated domestic drive for reform was stated in a somewhat extreme form by Richard Hofstadter in "Manifest Destiny and the Philippines," in Daniel Aaron (ed.), *America in Crisis* (New York, 1952). This essay, modified and with Cuba added to its title, has been reprinted in Hofstadter's *The Paranoid Style in American Politics and Other Essays* (New York, 1966).

Of the many books on the Pacific islands and Hawaii, the most useful are Merze Tate, *The United States and the Hawaiian Kingdom: A Political History* (New Haven, 1965); Earl Pomeroy, *Pacific Outpost: American Strategy in Guam and Micronesia* (Stanford, 1951);

and John Wesley Coulter, *The Pacific Dependencies of the United States* (New York, 1957). The standard authority on Samoa continues to be Sylvia Masterman, *The Origins of International Rivalry in Samoa, 1845–1884* (London, 1934), although much modified by recent articles. Particularly interesting is Francis J. West, *Political Advancement in the South Pacific: A Comparative Study of Colonial Practice in Fiji, Tahiti and American Samoa* (Melbourne, 1961). Most recently a journalist, E. J. Kahn, Jr., in *Reporter in Micronesia* (New York, 1966), has examined America's continued involvement in the lesser islands.

There are few theoretical studies. Of these few, the best are Albert K. Weinberg, *Manifest Destiny: A Study of Nationalist Expansionism in American History* (Baltimore, 1935); Julius W. Pratt, *America's Colonial Experiment* (New York, 1950); and Edward McNall Burns, *The American Idea of Mission: Concepts of National Purpose and Destiny* (New Brunswick, N.J., 1957). There are, of course, many books on Puerto Rico and American relations with Canada.

19

Social Democracy,
1900–1918

GEORGE E. MOWRY

When analyzing their own societies individuals often avoid certain emotion-laden words. "Social democracy" has been one such tabooed phrase in the United States, undoubtedly because of its association with social democratic and communist parties. Consequently, social legislation commonly described elsewhere as "social democratic" has been referred to usually by a variety of other terms, such as welfare, social service, or reform measures, and the parties proposing them as liberal or radical, or more often as progressive. The latter term stems directly from the progressive movement, which in essence was a reform mentality that animated both major political parties from about 1902 to 1918 and resulted in a series of significant political, economic, and social changes at all levels of the American government— city, state, and national. Since the progressive years most parties advocating widespread social reforms, including proposals for government ownership and operation of various enterprises, have been described as "progressive" but very rarely as "social democratic."

It is perhaps because of this semantic peculiarity that many Americans and probably more foreigners have believed that the

United States has lagged perceptibly behind other advanced democracies in the appreciation of the needs of its urban and industrial society. But if one looks at the record instead of the rhetoric, one finds, surprisingly, an almost simultaneous development of social democracy in the United States and Europe despite the differences in material conditions, relations between the social classes, and political traditions.

Although many of its roots lay in the late nineteenth century, American social democracy or Progressivism was largely a twentieth-century phenomenon. At about the turn of the century, spurred by such writings as Lincoln Steffens' *The Shame of the Cities* (1904), an urban reform movement led in good part by the upper middle classes and in some instances by individuals from the economic elite, first wrested political control from the old and corrupt political machines, which in the East at least were most often based upon the "purchased" votes of recent immigrants. Once in power in New York, Cleveland, Toledo, St. Louis, Minneapolis, San Francisco, and Los Angeles, these groups attempted to revamp city government and urban institutions. In the widespread experimentation with the form of city governments, the most significant efforts perhaps were directed toward divorcing the control of urban operations from the traditional politician and placing it, through the devices of a nonpartisan commission or a city manager, in the hands of experts or specialists.

Concurrently a host of housing, sewer, and tenement regulations, zoning codes, and health measures were passed, as well as provisions for playgrounds and parks. A demand for "gas and water socialism" resulted in municipal ownership and operation of street railways, water, electrical, and other utilities. Where municipal ownership did not eventuate, street regulation by municipal commissions protected the citizen from the private extortion hitherto often practiced. By such efforts the American large city, once described by Lord Bryce, the sometime British ambassador, as the worst governed political unit in the world, had become by 1917 a reasonably efficient social unit providing a somewhat more attractive environment for its inhabitants.

Almost simultaneously with this urban movement a reform

wave began in many of the states, with similar support but for wider and more generalized ends. Through the years 1900 to 1914 a number of nationally known state governors such as Robert LaFollette of Wisconsin, Joseph W. Folk of Missouri, Charles Evans Hughes of New York, Woodrow Wilson of New Jersey, and Hiram Johnson of California supported a broad spectrum of reform that ranged in scope from purely political devices making elected official and political decisions more reflective of the popular will to regulating and raising taxes of corporations, protecting unions from the more arbitrary actions of employers, and specifying the hours and conditions of labor for women and children. Other legislation provided for roads, longer schooling, and state payments for orphans and widows.

Among the major difficulties confronting modern reform movements at the state level has been the almost invariable drift of successful state politicians to the national government. Even more important, perhaps, than this brain or leadership drain has been the growing nationalization of social problems and the inability of the states individually to provide acceptable solutions. Thus it was predictable that the Progressive movement would invade the national government, a phenomenon that proceeded apace from 1900 to 1914 as successful state leaders such as LaFollette, Wilson, and Johnson went to Washington. When joined by other like-minded legislators their impact was remarkable. During the thirty years before 1900 not one amendment had been added to the Constitution. From 1910 to 1920 four major amendments were passed, providing for the direct election of United States senators, a national income tax, the prohibition of the manufacture and sale of alcoholic liquors, and suffrage for women. Under the presidencies of Theodore Roosevelt, William Howard Taft, and Woodrow Wilson, the legislative fruits of these years included the national regulation of interstate railroads, and to a lesser extent industries engaged in interstate commerce, protection for the consumer by the regulation of food and meat-packing plants and the producers of drugs, protection also for seamen, railroad workers, and to a minor degree working women and children, the rationalization and partial government control of the national banking system, the conservation of natural resources by the liberal creation of national forests and parks, and the freeing of labor unions from severe judicial restraints.

In attempting to compare the specific American advances in social democracy with those in other parts of the world, one is immediately struck by a coincidence in time. The progressive years in the United States were concurrent in time with the attempts of the Campbell-Bannerman-Lloyd George government to democratize Great Britain by attacking the power of the House of Lords and to secure more equality of opportunity by the taxation and land provisions of the famous 1909 budget. They were also coincident with the rapid rise of the labor and socialist parties in Great Britain as well as in France and Germany.

The extensive international borrowing of American Progressives in their reform programs is also striking. On the city and state levels the secret ballot was taken from Australia, the initiative, referendum, and recall devices from the Swiss provinces. As early as 1875, Parliament had granted British municipalities the power to own and operate their own trams and utilities. Many American arguments for like developments pointed to these experiments as well as to those in the Rhine Basin. On the other hand, in the field of city planning and building codes American legislation was surprisingly concurrent with European. The Pennsylvania State Planning Act of 1891 and various like measures in Boston, Chicago, and New York were not much antedated by similar legislation in Italy, Sweden, and Great Britain, although the British Act of 1909 was certainly the most comprehensive of all such legislation and became a model for city planners in the United States.

Nationally, Americans also borrowed extensively from abroad. Gifford Pinchot, the leading exponent of American conservation, studied forestry as a young man in Nancy, France, and was unquestionably also influenced by German forest and mineral policies. Faced with the complex task of revising the national banking system of the United States, the conservative Aldrich Commission presented a plan for a central bank dominated by private bankers and modeled on the existing British system, which the commission had studied extensively. Fortunately for subsequent developments, the original Aldrich scheme was modified by the Progressive forces under President Wilson to include a strong measure of government participation and control.

This compromise solution to the central banking problem reflected a rather characteristic American attitude to distrust the polar positions in any dispute as well as the attitude of the large element of reform forces from the more agrarian states, which feared unchecked centralized power in either government or private enterprise.

This spirit was also evident in the field of industrial regulation, in which both the antitrust laws curbing monopoly and providing for competition, and the instruments for the governmental regulation of business, were extensively strengthened from 1902 to 1914. By the frequent use of the old Sherman Anti-Trust Law and the new powers conferred by the Clayton Amendment (1914), the government prosecuted monopolies and cartel arrangements. At the same time, by the creation of the Bureau of Corporations, the thoroughgoing regulation of railroad rates, and in particular the passage of the Federal Trade Commission Act (1914), the ground at least was laid for the stringent control of business in the event of a future crisis.

A crisis did occur when the United States entered World War I. The subsequent effective and rapid mobilization of industry through stringent regulation, without major dissent from the industrial and financial world, indicated the extent to which the Progressives had weaned the average businessman away from the individualistic and almost anarchistic doctrines favored by the industrial barons of the 1880's and 1890's. And although American officials had the advantage of studying British industrial mobilization, the speed and effectiveness of American economic regimentation within the short span of eighteen months was nothing short of incredible. Field Marshal von Hindenburg's remark that Germany was defeated in good part by the efficiency of the American industrial mobilization is eloquent testimony both to the character of the war government and to the social-mindedness of the average American industrialist in accepting its dictates.

While such a factual approach as set out in the preceding

paragraphs may give the non-American some sense of the growth of social democracy from 1900 to 1920, it will convey neither its peculiar flavor nor the reasons for some substantive differences in comparison to similar developments abroad. These can only be brought into focus by a consideration of the rather distinctive American background from which it came.

As elsewhere in the world, social democracy in the United States was the obvious product of large-scale industry and modern urbanization. By 1900 a rapidly developing American industrialism had produced large combinations whose directors were as insulated from control by stockholders as they were from sympathy with and understanding of their workers. Conjoined with large-scale industry was the rise of the American metropolis. What London, Paris, and Berlin were to their respective countries in 1900, to a degree New York was to the United States. Philadelphia, Pittsburgh, Cleveland, Chicago, St. Louis, and the Connecticut River Valley cities also rapidly changed the character of their areas, representing in the changing social solution approximately what Birmingham, Staffordshire, and the Ruhr regions did to their own localities.

With some differences the results of large industry and urbanization in the United States approximated those in Europe. The financial panics of 1873 and 1893 produced unemployment and hunger in America as they did in Europe. And the American urban slums were, if anything, worse than the European, principally because of America's relative inexperience with large cities and the bewildering diversity of its urban peoples. From 1880 to 1910 a yearly average of almost one half million immigrants entered the country. Originating in practically every part of Europe and settling mostly in the Eastern cities, this complex human flood for a time at least made urban cohesion and unity all but impossible. It also gave a distinctive character to the cities, which from the point of view of the majority of old Americans still living on the land or in small villages, was distinctly alien, undesirable, and even un-American. The proposals for reform emanating from the East were consequently received by the remainder of the country with reserve. And the Socialist party, since it had most of its strength in the urban

East, was also viewed with suspicion by reformers in the South and West.[1]

As industry produced slums and urban poverty, it also created great wealth among the few. Europe, of course, had long been accustomed to marked economic inequality; but the United States, except in the South, had, as Tocqueville observed, made a reasonable degree of equality of circumstances a national ideal. The resulting tensions set up between this old article of faith and the rapidly developing differentiated society also gave impetus to the reform movement and colored its outcome.

The new urban-industrial complexes had already produced by 1886 the first permanently successful national labor union, the American Federation of Labor, remarkably the same year that witnessed the organization of the first successful national labor organization in France. But the mainstream of American organized labor, unlike the continental and British unions, was by aspiration, if not by economic standing, middle class in temperament, intensely interested in reform, and inclined against ideological radicalism and labor-inspired political movements. Thus in America the gulf between the major labor unions, the middle class, and the farmer was never so deep and politically unabridgeable as in most other countries of the world.

The American farmer, in fact, contributed greatly to the rise of American social democracy. Unlike most of his European counterparts, he had had essentially a radical political tradition since well before the Revolution. After the Civil War, increasing farm unrest, induced by falling farm prices, growing debts, and by the specter of transportation and industrial monopoly, had resulted in the Granger, Greenback, Anti-monopoly, and Populist reform movements. And though the ultimate objective of all this agitation was the preservation of the highly individualistic small landholder, to accomplish his ends the farmer supported political reform and, more important, felt impelled to call upon the regulatory power of state and national governments to curb the power of the railroads and industrial trusts. As John D. Hicks has pointed out in *The Populist Revolt*, the origins of modern American governmental economic regulation lay in the

---

1 For a short time after the death of the Populist party the socialist movement was rather strong in both Kansas and Oklahoma.

nineteenth-century demands of the free, small, independent farmer. And since the farmer and like-minded people in the villages and small towns constituted a majority until the 1920's, the objectives of American social democracy have until very recently been the compound ones—and to Europeans possibly contradictory ones—of attaining basic economic security for all, whether upon the land or in the factory, and at the same time preserving a large element of individual freedom to compete, and thus to maintain the traditional element of mobility in society. During the Progressive period and after, the nondoctrinaire American mind has never been unduly disturbed by the regulation of large business and the simultaneous taking of legal action against it to prevent monopoly and to preserve competition.

Among other factors which helped differentiate the growth of American social democracy from its development abroad were the lack of a rigid class structure, an attendant high degree of social mobility, and basic to both in modern times a widespread opportunity for higher education for both sexes, which by 1900 was already beginning to show considerable differences from that of Europe.

With the rapid rise of state universities during the last quarter of the nineteenth century, higher education in the United States was monopolized neither by the privileged classes nor by the male sex. Moreover, the period from 1880 to 1900 marked the beginning of an important tendency in the curriculum of most universities, public and private, away from the traditional classical studies toward the more modern, utilitarian, social, scientific, and technical ones. The result was the rise of a new class of specialists trained in the social sciences, particularly in economics and sociology, and in the more technical subjects of engineering, agriculture, and eventually business management. Some of the original impetus for the new studies, especially in economics, came from German seminars. But the rapid expansion of such courses as labor economics, urban sociology, and the fields of agriculture and business had few parallels abroad. Fifty years later many of these new subjects were still considered improper for inclusion among European university studies.

The vision of these new specialists was mainly directed away from the study of the past toward the problems of the present. The animus of the engineer and the business specialist was directed toward efficiency; that of the social scientist toward reform. As the credo of the newly organized American Economic Association proclaimed, its founding members regarded positive state action "as an indispensable condition to human progress." Although the collective influence of the American professoriat was to vary widely over the years, from that time on its voice was never completely stilled in its demands for reform.

The university education of many middle-class women also had an important effect upon the nature of social reform in the twentieth century. Denied entrance into politics, business life, and the professions, many trained women turned their attention to social work and moral reform, a portion of the latter being directed toward abolishing the double standard of conduct sanctioned by middle-class Victorian society. Some of their efforts were directed toward securing more freedom for women in and out of the institution of marriage; others toward limiting what they considered to be the license of the male. The resulting crusade against the consumption of alcoholic beverages, against commercial prostitution, and for the reform of marriage and woman suffrage, gave the progressive period in the United States a moral air unduplicated in Europe, save possibly for Great Britain.

In summary, while the major factors stemming from advanced industrialization and urbanization produced demands for social democracy in the United States at about the same time they did in Europe, many idiosyncratic factors in American society gave it a somewhat different character from its European counterparts. Because of its roots in both the farm and the city, American social democracy was far less labor oriented than most such movements. Because of its ponderable support from the middle class, it was also far less motivated by ideology from the traditional European left. By the same token, the answers it provided to existing social questions were probably centered more in the questions themselves than in political ideology. The part played by the educated woman gave the movement also more of a moral air. At least in the movements for the prohibition of liquor and prostitution, the feminine efforts resulted in sumptuary legislation, limiting the freedom of individuals to indulge some very human appetites.

Contrariwise, in the realm of industrial regulation and economics in general the American solution was usually more sensitive to the perils of an uncontrolled bureaucracy, whether located in a government agency or in a privately held monopoly. True to the American tradition, legislation often expressed a preference for the smaller social unit to the large, and seemed to rely more upon the process of competition and the relatively free market than upon the regulated monopoly and the cartel, in order to obtain a measure of economic equity.

If the character of American Progressivism was somewhat different from its European equivalent, American historians of the movement, including the present writer, have been quite similar to their European peers in their refusal to treat the institution of social democracy as an international one. Instead, they have viewed their own developments with a nationalistic monocular vision, and the comparative technique has been largely ignored. This in spite of the fact that the Progressive movement in the United States has attracted more than its share of able historians.

The interest of historians in progressivism is probably accounted for by two paradoxical elements in the rise of the movement. First, this widespread reform wave numbered among its leading supporters a large group of very wealthy men as well as an unusual number of hitherto conservative politicians. Second, the success of the reform movement in a period of relative prosperity is rather puzzling when juxtaposed against the numerous nineteenth-century failures of antecedent reforms born in periods of depression.

A variety of explanations and interpretations of progressivism have been advanced by American historians in answer to these seeming paradoxes. Some of the older historians have argued that progressivism grew out of populism and that its success was accounted for by the increasing disquiet of the majority of the population, which, faced with the great economic and social disparities created by large industry and finance capitalism, was determined to restore some of the pre-Civil War equalitarian conditions of American life. Thus Harold U. Faulkner in *The Quest for Social Justice, 1898–1914* (1931) emphasized the part of the rising labor unions, the white-collar worker, and the small manufacturer and merchant in the success of the movement. Russel Nye in *Middlewestern Progressive Politics* (1951) stressed the role played by the nineteenth-century agrarian reform tradition. A second group of the senior historians preferred to emphasize the less material and more psychic factors in accounting for the reform *élan*. The present writer, in *The California Progressives* (1951), noting the urban, upper middle-class, professionally educated character of the California Progressive leadership, ascribed the reform motivation largely to the fears of this particular class of being displaced in society by both the large industrial and financial classes and the rising labor unions. This and a sense of guilt among many of the very wealthy supporters he considered accounted for the reform spirit. In a later volume, *The Era of Theodore Roosevelt* (1958), he also emphasized the forces rising from the secularization of American Protestantism, the impact of the rise of the social sciences in the universities, and the obvious need of large cities for major operational changes if they were to be made reasonably decent places in which to live.

Eric F. Goldman in *Rendezvous with Destiny* (1952) stressed the part played in the creation of the will to reform by the impact on social thought of an evolving Darwinism and the new social sciences. Finally, Richard Hofstadter in *The Age of Reform, From Bryan to F.D.R.* (1955) argued that the old American middle classes threatened with a "status revolution" by the loss of power to both the business and labor elite had suffered a "psychic crisis" that motivated their reform zeal.

More recently a younger generation of historians have deemphasized the intellectual factors and have stressed the more material and more conservative forces at work during the period. Among the more valuable of these newer interpretations are Robert Wiebe's *Businessmen and Reform* (1962) and *The Search for Order* (1966). In his first volume Wiebe stresses the important part played by the non-Eastern and smaller businessmen and bankers in securing federal regulation of the railroads and such other reforms as the Federal Reserve Act. In the latter work, Wiebe contends that the United States after the Civil War was an unorganized society and that the new class of specialists, engineers, business and efficiency experts set about giving precision and order to the essentially anarchic institutions of the nation. This theme had been more than hinted at by Samuel Hays in *Conservation and the Gospel of Efficiency* (1955). Subsequently, in a series of articles in which the same author used the concept of a model so favored by modern economists, he has come close to denying that there was little real reform spirit among the leaders of the progressive movement other than a desire for efficiency and scientific management.

A recent interpretation of the reform movement, that by Gabriel Kolko, *The Triumph of Conservatism* (1964), is in some ways the most interesting since it perhaps throws more light upon the nature of the present mentality in the country than upon the period of history with which it is allegedly concerned. By a careful selection of data, Kolko contends that the so-called progressive years, instead of advancing social democracy, really fastened corporation control upon American economic and political life, and thus made the future achievement of any thorough and viable social democracy impossible.

Which, if any, of these contending interpretations will survive the onslaught of future historians is of course impossible to predict. The outcome will unquestionably depend upon the shape of the future and the mentality of the historians involved. Since, however, most of the basic American research has already been done and the facts fairly well established, it is very probable that future works will be more and not less polemical in tone. But one almost certain corrective will be the first publication of research that eschews the national viewpoint for an international and a comparative approach.

BIBLIOGRAPHY

In addition to the titles discussed in the text, other noteworthy books on American progressivism include Daniel Aaron's brilliantly written *Men of Good Hope* (New York, 1951); Arthur Mann, *Yankee Reformers in the Urban Age* (Cambridge, Mass., 1954), one of the few that explores in any detail the debt American progressives owed to

British liberals and socialists; Arthur S. Link's first two volumes of his impressive life of Wilson, *Wilson: The Road to the White House* (Princeton, 1947) and *Wilson: The New Freedom* (1956); Charles Forcey's thoughtful *The Crossroads of Liberalism* (New York, 1961); and the best study of the muckrackers, Louis Filler, *Crusaders for American Liberalism* (1950).

For the all-important European underpinning, H. Stuart Hughes, *Consciousness and Society: The Reorientation of European Social Thought, 1890–1930* (New York, 1958), and Peter Gay, *The Dilemma of Democratic Socialism: Eduard Bernstein's Challenge to Marx* (New York, 1952), discuss in a brilliant fashion both the formulation and the erosion of rational and liberal social democratic thought. Since the inspiration for many specific American reforms came from British socialists, G. D. H. Cole's classic, *A History of Socialist Thought* (5 vols.; New York, 1953–1960), should be consulted. For a more factual account of international developments C. W. Pipkin, *Social Politics and Modern Democracies* (2 vols.: New York, 1931), is useful.

The rather old but still valuable study, William H. Dawson, *Bismarck and State Socialism* (London, 1890), should be compared with A. J. P. Taylor, *Bismarck, the Man and the Statesman* (New York, 1955), for an understanding of the inception of German social democracy. Since after Bismarck German advances lay in the fortunes of the Socialist party, one should consult Carl Schorske's perceptive *German Social Democracy 1905–1917* (Cambridge, Mass., 1955).

For political developments most comparable to those in the United States, R. C. K. Ensor, *England, 1870–1914* (Oxford, 1936), gives a good summary of the origins of the new liberal collectivism. Two bibliographies of the leading British Liberal leftist, John Hugh Edwards, *David Lloyd George* (2 vols.; New York, 1929), and Thomas Jones, *Lloyd George* (Cambridge, Mass., 1951), account for the rise and decline of the modern British Liberal party. But since Sidney and Beatrice Webb and their Fabians had a profound impact upon most left-leaning British and American statesmen, liberals as well as socialists, Margaret Cole (ed.), *Beatrice Webb's Diaries 1912–1932* (2 vols.; New York, 1952–1956), and the subject's two autobiographical volumes, *My Apprenticeship* (London, 1926) and *Our Partnership* (1945), should be consulted.

For a comparative estimation of another part of the British world, Leslie Lipson, *The Politics of Equality* (Chicago, 1948), is a good study of social democracy in New Zealand. Margaret Cole and Charles Smith (eds.), *Democratic Sweden* (London, 1938), affords some of the background for an understanding of the spectacular Swedish advance from a reactionary society in 1914 to a present position of social democratic leadership. D. W. Brogan, *France under the Republic* (New York and London, 1940), and David Thomson, *Democracy in France* (London, 1952), recount the halting steps taken by the leading Latin country toward a democratic collectivism. A. W. Salomone, *Italian Democracy in the Making* (Philadelphia, 1945), contains the principal study of the prewar liberal impotence before the challenges of the left and the right. Additional insights into the liberal Italian mentality can be gained from Wayland H. Young, *The Italian Left: A Short History of Political Socialism in Italy* (London and New York, 1949). For the nearest comparable Asiatic development, in substance if not in time, see Evelyn S. Colbert, *The Left Wing in Japanese Politics* (New York, 1952), and Robert A. Scalapino, *Democracy and the Party Movement in Pre-war Japan* (Berkeley, 1953), studies centered upon the 1930's.

World War I

ARNO J. MAYER

In July–August 1914, Europe's statesmen faced the decision for war against a background of grave internal tensions and disorders, in some instances bordering on civil war. Parliamentary government was on trial, in Britain over Ulster and the strike threat of the Triple Industrial Alliance, in France over the draft law and the income tax, and in Italy over economic and social reform. Germany's semiparliamentary system floundered because, except for the far-right conservatives and nationalists, the major parties of the Second Empire pressed for the end of Prussia's three-class franchise and the institution of cabinet responsibility to the Reichstag. The power elite of both halves of the Dual Monarchy was confronted by explosive nationality unrest which itself was an expression of mounting political, economic, and social dysfunctions. In tsarist Russia, meanwhile, the counterfeit Fourth Duma was in no position to blunt the challenge of militant workers and of restless national minorities.

Throughout Europe the vital center, committed to the politics of accommodation, was being eroded in favor of the uncompromising extremes of the political spectrum. The extent to which these prerevolutionary conditions influenced the diplomacy of the Sarajevo crisis is still unclear. It seems safe to say, however, that with a few notable exceptions—Durnovo in Russia and Tisza in Hungary—ultraconservatives and protofascists advocated preparedness and were predisposed to exploit war, should it offer itself, as part of their struggle against the left. In turn, socialists and syndicalists, in conjunction with libertarian radicals, opposed the armaments race and urged appeasement in foreign policy in their battle with the forces of order.

Even though internal tensions never came close to the same level of intensity in America as in Europe, with regard to foreign policy the political line-up was comparable. Woodrow Wilson, not unlike Grey, was reluctant to go to war, convinced that it would further undermine the prospects for moderate reformism; and once he decided to intervene for reasons of power, prestige, and security, he, like Grey, felt compelled to provide his progressive followers with a moral purpose for combat. Moreover, in both countries, as also in Italy—these being the three major powers that had a diplomatic option—this decision for war was hailed by the right-oppositionists, who criticized its delay before themselves claiming credit for the intervention.

In setting about mobilizing and gearing America for battle and war production, the Wilson administration was able to draw on the experience of the European belligerents. But even without the benefit of this experience, which may have prevented some costly errors and delays, the institutions and procedures of the American warfare state would have paralleled those of its European counterparts. Government agencies were created to control and stimulate vital production; to fix and regulate prices of select scarce commodities; to plan and produce specialized war matériel; to encourage voluntary rationing; and to streamline railway transportation. The hallmarks of this emergency program were the Food Administration, headed by Herbert Hoover; the War Industries Board, headed by Bernard Baruch; the Fuel Administration, headed by Harry Garfield; and the Railway Administration, headed by William McAdoo. It is worth noting that, from the start, America's economic mobilization was designed to service not only its own but also the Allied war effort; that it was still in its infancy when Lenin, in September 1917, singled out the control measures with which the European belligerents regulated and developed their war economies, considering them possible guidelines for future socialist planning; and that because of prewar excess capacity as well as safety from enemy attack and blockade, even serious bottlenecks and failures in planning and production could not unsettle a war economy whose total life span was eighteen months.

As for the wartime labor policies, they too proximated the European pattern. In an effort to avoid labor unrest and attendant production setbacks, Wilson charted the National War Labor Board, under William Howard Taft and Frank Walsh, which he reinforced with a special agency, under Felix Frankfurter, charged with surveying labor needs and practices and also with promoting the standardization of wages and hours. Wartime prosperity and full employment underwrote a rapid increase in the membership of the American Federation of Labor, whose minimum peacetime program appeared headed for fulfillment, especially since in spite of inflation real income rose by some 20 per cent.

On the other hand, the syndical and political segments of the American labor movement were fatally mangled by the war. The Industrial Workers of the World became the special target of federal sabotage and sedition acts, subject to prosecution not only for strike activities but also for the expression of unpopular opinions about the war and the established order. As for the Socialist party, not unlike its European counterparts, it was split in two. But in addition to being weakened by the standard schism between the pro- and the antiwar factions, because its membership was so overwhelmingly foreign-born and non-English-speaking, the American socialist movement, notably its antiwar wing, became an easy target for superpatriots. Moreover, the staggering casualties, the spreading war weariness, the mounting consumer shortages, and the spiraling prices which in the other belligerent nations fostered the reunification and radicalization of the Allied left from mid-1917 to mid-1918, never materialized in America. No wonder that the reaction to Wilson's Fourteen Points was so enthusiastic in Europe while being so bland this side of the Atlantic. In Europe all radicals and socialists, except the Bolsheviks, hailed the President's war aims because they articulated and legitimized their own peace platform, thereby helping them challenge their own governments' vindictive and annexationist objectives. In America, where no disclaimers of annexationist aims were needed, the spirit of Wilson's pronouncements was suspect among leftists and libertarians precisely because they experienced firsthand the repressive policies of his administration.

In particular, Wilson set out to check the European belligerents' greed, which was a by-product of total—including spiritual—mobilization, with a built-in conservative thrust, at the same time that he himself presided over a similar mobilization in his own country. In England, H. G. Wells, who as early as September 1914 spoke of *The War That Will End War,* went to work for Crewe House. Similarly in America, left-oriented intellectuals and literati wrote ennobling propaganda pamphlets for the Committee on Public Information headed by George Creel, a well-known progressive journalist. But even though this committee was responsible to Wilson and enlisted the services of many men of good will, it mounted a *bourrage du crâne* which compared most favorably with France's. All Germans were portrayed as brutal Huns bent on world conquest; America was said to be swarming with German agents, operating out of the German-American communities; and any labor agitation or left-wing political dissent was denounced as disloyal and unpatriotic. This official campaign encouraged self-styled superpatriots in their sorties against German-Americans and antiwar radicals while also creating an atmosphere conducive to or supportive of violations of civil liberties by Congress, the Postmaster General, the Attorney General, and the judiciary, both federal and state.

This officially sponsored chauvinist tempest contributed to the conservative turn which Wilson himself had predicted and feared would be a by-product of intervention in war. Leaning on the precarious Democratic coalition of 1916, the President managed to steer a middle course with regard to war finance. But especially the Southern Congressmen, without whose support Wilson could not survive, backed him into a double bind. While teaming up with Western Progressives to impose a heavy tax burden on Northern and Eastern corporate and private wealth, the Southerners stubbornly insisted that cotton remain free at a time when the price of wheat was controlled. As a result, starting in mid-1918, conservative Republicans, under the clever guidance of Will Hays, launched a campaign charging the Southern agrarians with shifting the tax burden to the industrial states, with stifling the profits of Western wheat growers, and with supporting free trade.

Following the lead of the Tariff Reform League, conservative Republicans hastened to make an issue of free trade, which Wilson advocated in the third of his Fourteen Points. It was their contention that this third point attested to the hidden domestic design of the President's international project. Accordingly, Wilson was said to be seeking a settlement falling short of unconditional surrender and involving America in a league of nations as part of a campaign for another installment of the New Freedom, replete with free trade, graduated income taxes, and social legislation. In support of their allegation Republicans charged that Wilson's peace program, including his free-trade prescription, coincided with the foreign-policy platform of the Second Socialist International. They stressed, furthermore, that this program was being wildly cheered by Allied socialists who in addition to dragging their feet on the war were sworn to violent revolution.

And indeed, European socialists, both Allied and enemy, were Wilson's staunchest supporters, even as against their own governments, which eventually accused them of riding the President's coattails for selfish partisan advantage. Before America's intervention Wilson endeared himself to the European left with his peace-without-victory formula. Thereafter, especially once the Russian Revolution pried open the tsarist archives to expose the secret treaties, Wilson became their last hope for bringing this war to a judicious conclusion. The Fourteen Points suggested that their faith was not misplaced. Though the American President vowed to fight through to victory, he spelled out limited and principled political and diplomatic purposes in preparation for a negotiated instead of a dictated settlement.

Admittedly, in early January 1918, Lloyd George also abandoned his recently affirmed enthusiasm for the knockout blow in favor of clearly formulated and limited war aims. However, whereas the American President can hardly be said to have been under domestic political pressure to define and moderate the Entente's objectives, the British Prime Minister was under mounting labor, radical, and liberal conservative pressure to do so.

Of course, it was easier for Wilson than for Lloyd George, Clemenceau, and Orlando to propound a war-aims program which would be both self-limiting and ecumenical. Wilson did not inherit any secret treaties; he was not besieged by military and naval advisers urging security-motivated annexations; he did not have to reunite lost provinces or irredentas with the American nation; and he was spared annexationist pressures from independent dominions in arranging for the safety of the distant outposts of the American empire. Convinced that America's active involvement in world affairs was irrevocable, he resolved to thwart, restrict, or camouflage the territorial and colonial grabs of other powers in order to head off a chain reaction of crises which would culminate in another world war in which America would again be swept up. As a further hedge against future explosions, Wilson proposed a league of nations and a limitation of armaments to facilitate the processes of diplomatic accommodation.

Military victory produced the same political consequences in America as in the three Allied nations, with disastrous consequences for Wilson's grand design. Now that partisan politics was reconvened, conservative, reactionary, and protofascist parties, leagues, and newspapers zealously seized the offensive on a platform of inflammatory jingoism and Carthaginianism.

In the United States, Theodore Roosevelt, Henry Cabot Lodge, and George Harvey mounted a campaign for unconditional surrender against Wilson who, through his pre-Armistice exchanges with Vienna and Berlin, tried to make his peace principles the cornerstone and the touchstone first of the Armistice and then of the peace settlement. This clamor for unconditional surrender became a prominent aspect of the Congressional elections of November 1918, in which Wilson's domestic and foreign policy came under severe attack. Without denying the sectional, ethnic, local, and personal factors in the Republican victory, the fact remains that this victory registered a profound conservative impulse, and that it was so interpreted at home as well as abroad. In foreign policy it signified that Lodge, the new majority leader, who hated the President with a passion, was encouraged to organize the Congressional obstruction of a peace of reconciliation, even to the point of explicitly endorsing the exaggerated claims of Clemenceau and Orlando against Wilson. This obstruction in foreign policy was part and parcel of a general turn to the right which was reflected in the red scare, the anti-Negro riots, and the attendant drive for a return to "normalcy" which culminated in the election of Harding. Though there may well have continued to be broad popular support for the League of Nations, it was not sufficiently well organized. The *New Republic,* the *Nation,* the League of Free Nations Society, the Committee of 48, segments of organized labor, and internationally minded businessmen and financiers fought a rear-guard battle against conservatives, superpatriots, and anti-Communists within both major parties. Meanwhile this rising conservative temper encouraged the non-Progressive elements within the Wilson administration to press for the integral repayment of Allied debts, the instant termination of inter-Allied cooperation in supply, shipping, and finance, and the maintenance of a navy second to none.

At the same time that Wilson's political position was being undermined at home, his supporters were in disarray in England, France, and Italy. In the coupon election of December 1918, which followed in the wake of America's Congressional elections, laborites and radicals were routed by unionists bent on hanging the Kaiser. The new House of Commons was filled with hard-faced men determined to collect full indemnities and to block welfare legislation, tax reform, and home rule for Ireland. Heartened by the outcome of these American and British elections, Clemenceau vowed to follow a hard course at the Peace Conference, confident that the vast center-right coalition which dominated the French *chambre* was even less compromising than himself in both foreign and domestic affairs. In turn, Sidney Sonnino and his nationalist supporters so tightened their grip on the Orlando administration that in early January 1919, Leonida

Bissolati, Italy's foremost Wilsonian, resigned from the government.

This conservative-cum-jingoist upswing in the victor nations was the political context in which the Big Four negotiated the peace. The socialist and labor movements were too weak and fragmented to break this massive tide. Moreover, they were isolated because the center-left, including Wilson, hesitated to form a united front of the forces of movement for fear of encouraging and associating with extreme revolutionaries. Perhaps if the Ebert government had not contained spartacism so effectively and quickly—an outcome both welcomed and aided by the victors, notably by the United States—Wilson and his Allied supporters, eventually seconded by Lloyd George, might have frightened the conference into appeasing both defeated Germany and revolutionary Russia. As it was, whenever the conference seemed to stray from the straight Carthaginian path, the vigilant right exerted pressure to keep the Big Four on course. In any case, with Berlin and Vienna out of revolutionary danger and with Bela Kun safely isolated, the liberal conservatives, the Wilsonians, and the socialists in the victor nations were no match for their overbearing right-wing rivals. The best the forces of moderation could do was to curb the infractions of Wilson's principles; to secure the League covenant and the I.L.O. charter; and to limit—though not stop—the intervention in Russia.

All in all, the Versailles settlement and the intervention in Russia, which the peacemakers decreed and directed from Paris, were the foreign-policy manifestation of the triumph of jingoist conservatism in the victor nations. Admittedly, the rejection of the treaty and the covenant by the U.S. Senate was due to a host of factors: the irreconcilable antagonism between Wilson and Lodge; Wilson's disinclination to compromise; the absence of a tradition of bipartisanship in foreign policy; the opposition and concentration of the German-American vote; and the eruption of both nativist and Progressive isolationism. Even so, the impulse underlying the rebellion against Wilson and his twofold design was essentially conservative. Moderate progressives and internationalists in both parties were in headlong retreat. As for the advanced progressives and the socialists, even if they had not deserted Wilson because of his alleged sellout in Paris and his administration's retrograde policies at home, they were in no position to muster much strength. Besides, had they rallied to the President, there is every chance that such left-wing support would have galvanized the forces of order into still greater intransigence, as was the case in some European countries.

It would seem, therefore, that the same right-dominated amalgam of forces which, after criticizing the treaty for being excessively lenient, nevertheless voted to ratify it in London and Paris, threw it over in Washington. Throughout the victor world, not to speak of the defeated countries, the champions of Wilsonian and socialist internationalism were dissillusioned. But only in America, where these Progressive ideological warriors were least influential and powerful, did they become part of an unholy coalition bent on defeating the treaty. That they played an auxiliary and subordinate role in this outcome is evident from the sequel. Following the treaty's defeat, the successor Harding administration, checked by an astringent Congress, pursued an undisguised go-it-alone course, not isolationism, in international politics, while representatives of business and finance shaped its counterclockwise domestic policies. Certainly the power elites of postwar Britain, France, and Italy should have had full understanding and sympathy for this turn of events, which paralleled developments in their own countries.

BIBLIOGRAPHY

Arthur S. Link gives America's decision to intervene on the Allied side the most detailed and balanced treatment in the third, fourth, and fifth volumes of his continuing biography of *Wilson* (Princeton, 1960–1965). My *Political Origins of the New Diplomacy, 1917–1918* (New Haven, 1959) places Wilson's wartime diplomacy in its world setting, while my *Politics and Diplomacy of Peacemaking: Containment and Counter-Revolution at Versailles, 1918–1919* (Princeton, 1967) explores the interplay of domestic politics and foreign policy in the victor nations during the Paris Conference.

F. L. Paxson, *American Democracy and the World War* (3 vols.; Boston, 1936–1948), provides the most comprehensive coverage of the home front, to be read in conjunction with Frank P. Chambers, *The War behind the War, 1914–1918* (New York, 1939), which is transnational in scope. Economic mobilization is adequately discussed in Bernard M. Baruch, *American Industry in War* (New York, 1941); spiritual and ideological mobilization in George Creel, *How We Advertised America* (New York and London, 1920), in James R. Mock and Cedric Larson, *Words That Won the War* (Princeton, 1939), and in Horace C. Peterson, *Propaganda for War* (Norman, Okla., 1939); dissent and repression in Horace C. Peterson and Gilbert C. Fite, *Opponents of War, 1917–1918* (Madison, Wisc., 1957), in Zachariah Chafee, *Free Speech in the United States* rev. edn. (Cambridge, Mass., 1941), and in William Preston, *Aliens and Dissenters* (Cambridge, Mass., 1963).

The debilitating wartime and postwar conflicts within the socialist left are examined in David A. Shannon, *The Socialist Party of America* (New York, 1955), and in Theodore Draper, *The Roots of American Communism* (New York, 1957). Any study of the conservative, superpatriotic, and anti-Bolshevik outburst should start with Selig Adler, *The Isolationist Impulse* (London and New York, 1957); Robert K. Murray, *Red Scare* (Minneapolis, 1955), and John Higham, *Strangers in the Land* (New Brunswick, N.J., 1955).

For sketches of three of Wilson's principal opponents see Karl Schriftgiesser, *The Gentleman from Massachusetts: Henry Cabot Lodge* (Boston, 1944); Richard W. Leopold, *Elihu Root and the Conservative Tradition* (Boston, 1954); and Marian C. McKenna, *Borah* (New York, 1961). The best analyses of the rejection of the treaty and covenant are in W. Stull Holt, *Treaties Defeated by the Senate* (Baltimore, 1933); Denna F. Fleming, *The United States and the League of Nations, 1918–1920* (New York and London, 1932); Ruhl J. Bartlett, *The League to Enforce Peace* (Chapel Hill, N.C., 1944); and Thomas A. Bailey, *Woodrow Wilson and the Great Betrayal* (New York, 1945). America's role in the intervention in the Russian civil war can be pieced together from William A. Williams, *American-Russian Relations, 1781–1941* (New York, 1952); Frederick L. Schuman, *American Policy toward Russia Since 1917* (New York, 1928); Pauline Tompkins, *American-Russian Relations in the Far East* (New York, 1949); and Betty M. Unterberger, *America's Siberian Expedition, 1918–1920* (Durham, N.C., 1956).

This rejection of the treaty and intervention in Russia should be viewed against the background of the general trend of internal developments in the United States, accelerated by the war, which emerge from a critical reading of Henry F. May, *The End of American Innocence* (New York, 1959); William E. Leuchtenburg, *The Perils of Prosperity, 1914–1932* (Chicago, 1958); John D. Hicks, *Republican Ascendancy, 1921–1933* (New York, 1960); and George Soule, *Prosperity Decade: From War to Depression, 1917–1929* (New York, 1947).

21

The

Great

Depression

WILLIAM E. LEUCHTENBURG

Among the many things the Great Depression tumbled upside down, not the least was the relationship between the United States and the rest of the world. For two centuries, Americans had cherished the belief that they had developed a unique civilization which must be safeguarded against the contaminations of Europe. The Wall Street crash of October 1929 reversed these historic roles: the plague of the Great Depression began in the United States and spread to other lands. Europe, which in the 1920's had envied America its robust health, in the 1930's watched nervously for any new signs of contagion from the New World.

The disease took a far more violent form in the United States than in other countries. In nations such as France, the depression arrived later and was never so severe; unemployment, in particular, did not reach the appalling levels of joblessness in America. No other country in the world quite matched the United

States in the atrophy of industrial production. While net industrial output fell 47 per cent in the United States from 1929 to 1932, it dropped only 31 per cent in France, 16 per cent in the United Kingdom, 4 per cent in Japan; some countries—the Soviet Union, New Zealand, Denmark—actually experienced industrial growth in this period. Of the decline in industrial production throughout the world, more than half took place in the United States.

Unaccustomed to prolonged adversity, Americans experienced the depression as much more of a shock than did countries which had not enjoyed the boom of the 1920's. In a nation such as Brazil, where the masses were already sunk in poverty, or Norway, which had known a decade of falling prices, or Ireland, long acquainted with the grief of hard times, the depression did not have so dramatic an impact. In the United States, with its much higher levels of expectation, the contrast to the flush times of the New Era made the crackup especially painful.

When the depression struck, no major country in the world was so ill-prepared as the United States to cope with it. Long before the crash, Sweden had set up a State Unemployment Commission, and Ireland established an unemployment insurance scheme. The United States, on the other hand, lacking both instruments of control and a tradition of state responsibility, could not mobilize the machinery of government aid. Compared to other Western countries, the United States was, in these respects, a "backward nation."

The depression dealt a mean blow to America's confidence in the uniqueness of its civilization. It was hard to draw a contrast between America's good fortune and the misery of Europe when the United States had so many of the social ills it had long believed were endemic in the Old World. Daniel Boorstin has written, "The profoundest problems of American self-definition between the Great Depression of 1929 and the end of World War II arose from the obvious ways in which we now seemed to share the ills of Europe. There crept over us the sense that somehow we had been cheated of our uniqueness."

As Americans sensed that they were caught in Europe's predicament, they began to ask whether they were not witnessing the end of an era. "It may be true that, with the present breakdown, we have come to the end of something," observed Edmund Wilson. "The future is as blank in the United States today as the situation is desperate." On the day the Bank of England went off gold, Thomas Wolfe wrote his mother, "The trouble in England will affect the whole world, and we may soon be in as serious a condition ourselves—and perhaps we will not meet it as well as they have. . . . I think we are at the end of a period." A reporter in Washington found Colorado's Senator Edward Costigan in a black mood. Costigan told him, "Sometimes, of course, in history the door is finally closed." In America, as Roger Burlingame later noted, "destiny had ceased to be manifest."

The United States, which had long prided itself on being a "young" nation, now appeared to have aged suddenly and to have become as unadventurous as the Old World. "Is America growing old?" asked Anne O'Hare McCormick. "Have we—the young adventurers, the Innocents Abroad, the pioneers, the buccaneers, the racketeers—slumped into that sad maturity which submits to events, accepts the universe? . . . The great American nation is to be discovered in an attitude as elderly and unenterprising as that of Mr. Micawber. . . . We look a little like that fat comedian in the movies who sits in heavy contemplation after he gets tangled in his own gear." "It is nothing less than the American democratic tradition of 'free opportunity' which seems to us to have been in process of visible destruction," asserted a writer in a law journal. "The heroic age, in America, is past. We are no longer a nation of adventurers. Peer Gynt's philosophy is not ours."

As far back as 1893, Frederick Jackson Turner had pointed out that the frontier had disappeared; now men feared that the United States was finally paying the price. No longer able to expand into an undeveloped West, America was faced, as Europe had so long been, with "closed space." "Our country is older now," Henry Wallace stated. "We begin to feel some of the internal pressures which have pinched older nations for many centuries; and the problem of maintaining and governing democratically a land of the free becomes more complicated and challenging."

In the 1930's, businessmen became obsessed with the idea that an era of economic expansion had ended and the American economy had reached a point of "maturity." As the perceptive British historian Frank Thistlethwaite later observed, "So slow and halting was recovery that politicians, business men and economists, preoccupied with the problems of 'over-production' and contracting demand, came to fear that the long, dynamic expansion of the economy, the very foundation of the American way of life, might be at an end." The depression, *Fortune* magazine subsequently reflected, "did something that no foreign enemy, national disaster, or old-fashioned 'panic' had ever done: it paralyzed, for years, America's growth."

No event proved so decisive in creating a sense of the end of an era as the bank crisis of Herbert Hoover's last month in office. The collapse of the banks—those imposing Greek-columned edifices with their barred windows and impregnable vaults—undermined security and estranged the country from its financial leaders. It was pointed out that across the border in Canada not a single bank had failed, although Canada too had been hard hit by the world-wide depression. The panic, as Joseph Schumpeter later wrote, "completely demoralized all classes . . . The psychic framework of society, which till then had borne up well, was at last giving way. Nobody for the time being foresaw anything but continuing disaster, and everybody was resolved not to put up with it any longer."

For Hoover, the smash-up of the banks came as a crushing end to a long struggle he had waged to preserve America's confidence in its own uniqueness. Well before the crash, Hoover had argued that the United States had developed a civilization which had an emphatically non-European quality. "Ours is a system," Hoover claimed, "unique with America—an expression of the spirit and environment of our people—it is just American." In the 1928 campaign he asserted, "Our political system is unique in the world . . . Our social system is unique in the world. . . . From our unique political and social ideals we are evolving a unique economic system."

After the crash, Hoover recognized that if his claims for the American system were to be credible he had to explain how so remarkable a system had fallen victim to the Great Depression. After some oscillation, Hoover found his answer: the main causes of the collapse had come "not from within but from outside the

United States." He blamed the slump on Russian dumping, the creation of surpluses of raw materials in countries such as Peru and Java, "the political agitation of Asia; revolutions in South America and political unrest in some European states." In particular, he traced the depression to World War I, a "holocaust" born out of the "despotisms of Europe," and argued that the main blow delivered to the American economy had come "in 1931 out of the war-caused financial collapse of the area of former despotisms of Central Europe."

To combat the depression, Hoover relied on "American" makeshifts. He revealed that same pathological fear of direct relief which led some commentators to speak of the "soul-destroying dole," with a special shudder of horror at "the Debauch of the Dole" in Britain. At a time when writers described America's sharecroppers as a "peasantry" and compared New England's mill workers to the idle factory hands in Lancashire, Hoover was determined to avoid measures which would "Europeanize" American society.

Hoover's successor, Franklin Delano Roosevelt, had fewer illusions about America's uniqueness and was more willing to profit from Europe's experience. As early as the summer of 1931, when Roosevelt was governor of New York, his Industrial Commissioner, Frances Perkins, had spent six weeks in England in order to make recommendations to him on unemployment insurance. In 1934, Roosevelt urged Harry Hopkins to "make a trip abroad as soon as you can possibly get away and look over the housing and social insurance schemes in England, Germany, Austria, and Italy, because I think you might pick up some ideas useful to us in developing our own American plan for security." In 1938, Gerard Swope chaired a commission to study labor policies in England and Sweden.

The New Deal borrowed liberally from foreign experience. After closely observing the success of Britain and Sweden with abandoning the gold standard, the Roosevelt administration decided to pursue the same course. Securities legislation, while owing something to Belgian and German examples, owed even more to the British Companies Act. A crop control plan in Germany influenced the drafting of the Agricultural Adjustment Act, and both Denmark and Ireland provided models for farm security legislation. In framing his controversial plan to "pack" the Supreme Court, Roosevelt frequently recalled Asquith's threat to pack the House of Lords. The Mexican muralists, José Clemente Orozco and Diego Rivera, inspired the work of the Treasury's art project. Senator Robert Wagner found the Swedish prototype relevant when he drafted public housing legislation, and the Tennessee Valley Authority patterned its school system after Danish folk schools.

The New Dealers often turned to Scandinavia, and especially to Sweden, not only for specific models but also because these countries appeared to have found that democratic "middle way" Roosevelt was seeking in the United States. In June 1936, when the President dispatched three of his aides to Europe to study cooperatives, he explained to newspapermen:

> I became a good deal interested in the cooperative development in countries abroad, especially Sweden. A very interesting book came out a couple of months ago—*The Middle Way* [by Marquis Childs]. I was tremendously interested in what they had done in Scandinavia along those lines. In Sweden, for example, you have a royal family and a Socialist Government and a capitalistic system, all working happily side by side. Of course, to be sure, it is a smaller country than ours; but they have conducted some very interesting and, so far, very successful experiments. They have these cooperative movements existing happily and successfully alongside of private industry and distribution of various kinds, both of them making money. I thought it was at least worthy of study from our point of view.

The very next month, the Tennessee editor and historian George Fort Milton wrote Roosevelt that he was crossing the Atlantic "to study how the Scandinavians have made such an admirable synthesis of yesterday and tomorrow. . . . I am persuaded that the discoverable and usable analogies in Sweden and Denmark are substantially more than America can find in the more rigid autarkies such as Russia, Italy and Germany. . . . There has been consent as well as change. And it is extraordinarily important that we here in America find out how there can be change by consent rather than by conflict." Before he sailed, Milton was told by David Lilienthal that he should explore Swedish experience with the "yardstick" formula, "with particular attention to the possibilities of breaking the price log jam without complete public ownership."

Roosevelt and the New Deal helped break down the old antithesis between Europe and America. Boorstin has pointed out, "In many ways, some intended and some accidental, the New Deal helped assimilate the American to the 'European' political experience." In the 1930's class replaced section as the most important determinant of party disposition in America. By 1948, nearly 80 per cent of workers would vote Democratic, a higher percentage than had ever been recorded by left-wing parties in Europe. In the Roosevelt era, the lexicon of Americans expanded to include such "European" words as "planning," "intellectuals," and "the State," words which had been used before but had never had such wide currency. CWA, WPA, and EWR reminded one writer of Soviet Russia: "All the letters of the alphabet pranced about in the wildest jigs." When the Federal Arts Project recovered bayou chants and Appalachian folk melodies, it came up with the comforting intelligence that the United States, like older European cultures, had folk arts of its own.

In the 1930's, European observers noted, the United States developed, for the first time in its history, "a sense of state." Power gravitated to Washington as it long had to Paris and London, and financial authority moved from Wall Street to the national capital just as it did from São Paulo to Rio de Janeiro. The burgeoning government agencies offered exciting opportunities to the increasingly politicized intellectuals. In the United States, Franklin Roosevelt fulfilled the demand heard in so many lands in these years for a leader perceived to be in an intimate relationship with the people; Lázaro Cárdenas' tours to remote peasant villages had their counterparts in F.D.R.'s fireside chats. Yet Roosevelt's "sense of state" carried him beyond the tradition of *personalismo*. Far more than his predecessors, and especially than his immediate predecessors, he encouraged the development of the institutions of a twentieth-century state. As a South Carolina labor leader noted approvingly, "Franklin Delano Roosevelt is void of the laissez-faire personality."

American conservatives were shocked by this turn of events.

With Herbert Hoover as their main spokesman, they charged that the New Deal had introduced something "alien" into American life. Hoover warned, "The threat of the continuance of these 'emergency' acts is a threat to join the Continental retreat of human progress backward through the long corridor of time." But there was a curious ambivalence in this argument. At times, men like Hoover argued that, despite the depression, the United States was still the most prosperous country in the world. On one occasion Hoover asserted, "Even English Liberalism has today double the proportion of the people under the real poverty line that we have." More often, conservatives asserted that, because of the New Deal, the United States lagged behind every other nation in the world in achieving recovery. Exponents of uniqueness such as Hoover now found it useful to reverse national comparisons to point to the tardiness of American recovery, especially as contrasted with the performance of Great Britain, which was described, rather improbably, as the bastion of laissez-faire. After conceding that the British had both unemployment and old-age insurance, subsidized mass housing, and collective bargaining in industry, the writer for one financial journal contrasted the "British let-it-alone policy" with "the American policy of studied control." He asserted, "Britain has left recovery to private initiative; America has left nothing to private initiative."

Yet observers on both sides of the Atlantic were often too quick to find parallels which sometimes existed only in the eye of the beholder. When workers employed the weapon of the sit-down strike in American factories, writers traced the influence to Yugoslavian coal miners, Pondicherry textile hands, and above all to French unionists in the regime of Léon Blum. In fact, the practice was at least as old as an IWW folded-arms strike in Schenectady in 1906; and a three-day sitdown at the Hormel plant in Austin, Minnesota, in 1933 had preceded the episodes in Yugoslavia, India, and France. Mesmerized by European parallels, British leftists felt certain that the organization of the CIO had placed the American labor movement at the point where Britain had been with the "new unionist" movement of 1889–1891. Consequently, they anticipated that the United States would soon recognize the need for a labor party; the birth of the American Labor party in New York, and the activity of the CIO in the 1936 campaign, appeared to be hard evidence that America was following the British pattern. But far from creating a new party, the CIO was only introducing modifications into the traditional game of "reward your friends and punish your enemies."

If the New Deal bore resemblances to reform movements and governments in other countries, it also had qualities that stamped it "Made in America." It owed less to foreign examples than to the progressive tradition in the United States and to the experience of World War I, another "Europeanizing" phenomenon. Although social conditions in the United States in the 1930's acquired a more "European" complexion, American society continued to differ in important respects from that of other countries, and, as a consequence, the New Deal response was distinct.

Despite a rise in class animosity in the 1930's, the United States was not cleaved by internal divisions to the extent that other countries were, nor was the response of aggrieved groups either so violent or so antirepublican. Some commentators contrasted the eruption of farm strikes in the Midwest with the passivity of European peasants. Yet the strikers meticulously obeyed "No Parking" signs; and when they intercepted freight trains, they found, to their embarrassment, that they did not know what to do with them. The march of the bonus army and the demonstrations of the unemployed posed no threat comparable to that raised by the intrusion of the armed *Heimwehr* into Austrian towns in the summer of 1931 or the mobs that assembled in the Place de la Concorde in February 1934. Roosevelt did not have to cope with the threats of civil war that confronted Getulio Vargas: the Paulista uprising of 1932, the assault by the Communists on the Rio barracks in 1935, and the upsurge of the fascist Integralistas. His authority was not challenged by ambitious army leaders, a religious establishment, or a feudal caste, elements which, in different ways, proved fatal for democracy in Spain and Japan. In the United States, despite such deplorable incidents as the Republic Steel massacre, the right rarely resorted to violence. Indeed, the United States did not have a "right" in the same sense as did France with its *deux cents familles,* its entrenched civil service, and its Croix de Feu. While Roosevelt was subjected to vile verbal abuse, Blum was assaulted by a gang of royalists intent on killing him.

Thankful for America's good fortune, Roosevelt also believed that only decisive action by the New Deal had saved America from a similar fate. In 1936, in a chat with reporters, he ruminated:

> Suppose Brother Hoover had remained President until April, 1936, carrying on his policies of the previous four years; in other words, hadn't taken any steps toward social security or helping the farmer or cutting out child labor and shortening hours, and old-age pensions. Had that been the case, we would have been a country this past April very similar to the country that Blum found when he came in. The French for twenty-five or thirty years had never done a thing in the way of social legislation. Blum started in and he jumped right into the middle of a strike the first week he was in office. Well, they demanded a forty-eight hour week . . . and he put through legislation that did provide for shorter hours in industry. Then they demanded a one-week's holiday with pay and then they demanded, immediately, a commission to set up an old-age pension plan. Well, all of these Blum got through but, query, was it too late?

Roosevelt won election in the same year that the fall of the Inukai cabinet signaled the virtual end of parliamentary democracy in Japan, and he took office in the same month that Adolf Hitler received absolute power from the German Reichstag and Engelbert Dollfuss, claiming the need to govern by decree, destroyed democratic government in Austria. Throughout the 1930's, foreign observers predicted that in the United States, too, fascism would be the next stage. Since it was believed that the world faced but two alternatives—socialism or fascism—and since the United States had proved inhospitable to socialism, despite the fact that the "objective conditions" had never been better, Marxist sages assumed that fascism was inevitable for America. As proof, they seized on the rise of such groups as George Deatherage's Knights of the White Camelia, and Fritz Kuhn's German-American Bund, and the affinity of the Rev.

Charles Coughlin's movement for Austrian clerical fascism. Yet Mussolini's corporate state did not find the following in the United States that it did in the Quebec of Maurice Duplessis; Roosevelt never established an authoritarian government as did Vargas in Brazil; and the attraction of the Raucous Men such as Coughlin soon diminished.

When socialists were not forecasting fascism for the United States, they were condemning Roosevelt because his program had no ideological cohesion, a judgment which many historians subsequently accepted. Yet the United States was not the only country to approach the depression in an experimental mood. Even countries so well prepared as Sweden adopted *ad hoc* measures. The "socialist" leader Cárdenas, it has been said, "was at heart nothing more than a Mexican pragmatist." Nor did the more coherent plans adopted by some other nations always compare favorably with the New Deal. If Roosevelt's program lacked the unity of Australia's "Premier's Plan," it was also more humane. Furthermore, the New Deal proved to be more adventurous and less inhibited by capitalistic dogmas than some governments which were allegedly more radical. New Deal spending contrasted markedly with the drastic austerity program Labour approved in Australia, and with the retrenchment the Labourites Ramsay MacDonald and Philip Snowden imposed on Great Britain.

The achievements of the New Deal soon came to be not only admired but imitated; the United States became not merely the consumer of social experiments from other lands but the exporter. Even before the Popular Front took office in France, political analysts had labeled Blum's program the "French New Deal." When Paul Van Zeeland, a Princeton M.A. who had observed the Roosevelt operation while lecturing at Johns Hopkins in 1933, formed a government of national unity in Belgium in 1935, his program was criticized as "a slavish copy of the American New Deal." Social reformers in Uruguay and Colombia believed that they and the New Dealers were participants in a common cause, and the President of Mexico wrote Roosevelt to note that the New Deal coincided with his own policies and to express his admiration for "the magnanimous work of your administration in favor of the unemployed, the workers, and the forgotten man in general." From countries as distant as Russia and Arabia, foreign visitors flocked to the United States to study such innovations as shelterbelts and the Tennessee Valley Authority. In Moscow, H. G. Wells argued the merits of the New Deal with Stalin; he was disappointed when the Russian leader refused to concede the parallel between his program and Roosevelt's. A year later Wells, although more critical of the New Deal, thought that in some ways "America is still what, in the school geographies of my childhood, used to be called so hopefully the New World."

Although the British left continued to carp, many in Britain looked hopefully, if anxiously, toward the United States to demonstrate a way to bring democracy through the crisis. As early as 1933, George Bernard Shaw told an audience in the United States, "Possibly America may save human society yet by solving the great political problems which have baffled and destroyed all previous attempts at permanent civilization." At the end of that year, in an open letter to President Roosevelt, John Maynard Keynes wrote, "You have made yourself the trustee for those in every country who seek to mend the evils of our condition by reasoned experiment within the framework of the existing social system. If you fail, rational change will be gravely prejudiced throughout the world, leaving orthodoxy and revolution to fight it out." If the New Deal succeeds, agreed the *Sunday Dispatch*, "it will spread to every civilized country and there will in reality be a new earth. If it fails, then not only America but the world will have to begin all over again."

Save for the far left, advocates of change in Great Britain rejoiced that the New Deal gave them an example which they could hold up to their own government. In September 1933, at the Trade Union Congress, Walter Citrine, the general secretary, proposed a resolution criticizing the British government and praising "the vigorous efforts now being made by President Roosevelt." To a British radio audience early in 1934, Keynes said of Roosevelt that for the first time "theoretical advice is being taken by one of the rulers of the world as a basis of large-scale action." The American President was "trying new ways boldly and even gaily with no object but the welfare of his people." In July 1934, the "Next Five Years Group," which embraced members ranging from the young Conservative Harold Macmillan to Trade Union Congress leaders like Arthur Pugh, issued a manifesto stating, "The familiar paradox of dire poverty in the midst of plenty presents the sort of challenge to capacity for national organization which President Roosevelt has accepted, but our own Government has declined." In 1935 David Lloyd George offered a New Deal for Britain which was obviously inspired by the American experience; he even proposed a road-building program modeled on the WPA.

In 1935, Canada's Conservative prime minister, Richard B. Bennett, startled his country by advocating a series of reforms that became known as "Bennett's New Deal." Some thought his conversion was the result of the influence of his brother-in-law, William D. Herridge, Canadian ambassador at Washington and an intimate of the Brain Trust. The New Deal also served as a prototype for the program of Bennett's successor, Mackenzie King, who had studied at the University of Chicago and Harvard, and had spent a year at Hull House. Yet at the end of the Roosevelt era, one Canadian reformer, with some exaggeration, lamented:

> In Canada we had no New Deal, no A.A.A. or other measures designed to give agriculture a "parity" with urban industry, no Wagner Act for the trade unions, no great public housing schemes, no C.C.C. camps for unemployed youth, no T.V.A. to reconstruct a vast blighted area, no Federal Writers or Federal Artists Projects, no new parkways about our big cities and no new recreation camps among our lakes and forests, and—last but not least—no fireside chats.

Leaders of social democracy in other countries looked toward the United States to provide not only an example of resourceful liberal government but effective opposition to the expansionist designs of the fascist powers. During his first term Roosevelt accepted the fact that the depression had intensified isolationist sentiment in America, and he concentrated almost exclusively on domestic concerns. By his second term, however, the President was increasingly sounding the note of resistance to fascism which was so muted in the England of Neville Chamberlain and the France of Georges Bonnet. An English M.P. declared, "The moral leadership of the world may pass from Europe to the United States. Already my constituents on lonely farms . . . take the trouble to tune in to Mr. Roosevelt." When, in January 1939, Roosevelt warned that the dictators threatened civilization, one English newspaper commented, "Most Englishmen and women when they listened to President Roosevelt on the radio must have wished sadly that it was the head of their own Government who was saying those things."

Sir Isaiah Berlin later reflected:

> When I say that some men occupy one's imagination for many years, this is literally true of Mr. Roosevelt's effect on the young men of my own generation in England, and probably in many parts of Europe, and indeed the entire world. If one was young in the thirties and lived in a democracy, then, whatever one's politics, if one had human feelings at all, or the faintest spark of social idealism, or any love of life, one must have felt very much as young men in Continental Europe probably felt after the defeat of Napoleon during the years of the Restoration: that all was dark and quiet, a great reaction was abroad, and little stirred, and nothing resisted. . . .
>
> At a time of weakness and mounting despair in the democratic world, Mr. Roosevelt radiated confidence and strength. . . . He was one of the few statesmen in the twentieth or any other century who seemed to have no fear at all of the future. . . . In a despondent world which appeared divided between wicked and fatally efficient fanatics marching to destroy, and bewildered populations on the run . . . he believed in his own ability, so long as he was in control, to stem the terrible tide. He had all the character and energy and skill of the dictators, and he was on our side. . . . As the skies of Europe grew darker, in particular after war broke out, he seemed to the poor and the unhappy in Europe a kind of benevolent demigod who alone could and would save them in the end.

No longer did the British left indulge in *Schadenfreude* over the imminent doom of American democracy. In 1933, Harold Laski had written gloomily, "Once the last frontier had been crossed, it became the obvious destiny of America to repeat the classic evolution of European capitalism in a more intense form." By 1938 he was declaring, "If our age emerges satisfactorily from this period of blood and war, I believe that the Roosevelt experiment in America, with all its blunders and follies, will be regarded by the historian as having made a supreme contribution to the cause of freedom." In 1934, the year she married Aneurin Bevan, Jennie Lee wrote, "It is Fascism, not Socialism, which is most likely to overtake the American masses." In 1939 she was asserting, "There are flags of freedom flying higher and wider in America than anywhere else in the world."

Once again, the United States became a haven for the politically oppressed of other lands. To America in the 1930's came such remarkable figures as the novelist Thomas Mann, the painter George Grosz, the architect Walter Gropius, the physicist Albert Einstein, and the pianist Artur Schnabel. In New York, Alvin Johnson established a University in Exile which drew a distinguished faculty from foreign countries. The transit of refugee intellectuals to America, observed John Peale Bishop, meant that Europe's past was now entrusted to the United States, which alone could "prolong it into the future."

As the United States became a cynosure for social reformers, a leader of resistance to fascism, and a sanctuary for émigrés, Americans began to revive their faith in the uniqueness of their society. Alfred Kazin observed:

Now, as the tide of Fascism mounted higher and higher in Europe, and it looked as if Americans had been thrown back on their own resources as never before, the whole emphasis of the early depression literature on national self-scrutiny became a thundering flood of national consciousness and self-celebration. Suddenly, as if it marked a necessary expiation of too rapid and embittered a disillusionment in the past, American writing became a swelling chorus of national affirmation and praise. Suddenly all the debunkers of the past, who had long since been on relief, became the special objects of revulsion and contempt. Suddenly all the despised catchwords of the democratic rhetoric took on a brilliant radiance in a Hitler world; in the emotional discovery of America the country once more became, as Jefferson had long ago foreseen, "this government: the world's best hope."

In *Land of the Free,* Archibald MacLeish had voiced the doubts of the depression years:

> We wonder whether the dream of American liberty
> Was two hundred years of pine and hardwood
> And three generations of the grass
> And the generations are up: the years over
> We don't know.[1]

But in 1941, in *The American Cause,* MacLeish wrote that Americans were people "who had the luck to be born on this continent where the heat was hotter and the cold was colder and the sun was brighter and the nights were blacker and the distances were farther and the faces were nearer and the rain was more like rain and the mornings were more like mornings than anywhere else on earth—sooner or sweeter and lovelier over unused hills."[2]

Like American innocence, America's sense of uniqueness is forever being lost only to be regained. The bleak decade of the 1930's, which had raised such unnerving doubts, had also offered comforting reassurances. Yet if exceptionalism survived the Great Depression, it did not come out of the crisis unmarked. Many institutions in the United States remained "Europeanized." Even more important, Americans no longer felt the same buoyant optimism. It was dismaying to realize that such Old World misfortunes could visit the United States and that America, like other countries, had found recovery only through armaments and war. Nor was there the same confidence in the resilience of the American economy. *Fortune* found in 1946 that more than half of fifteen thousand leading business executives it polled expected an "extended major depression with large-scale unemployment in the next ten years." That same year, a recent Harvard graduate, John Fitzgerald Kennedy, responded to a class questionnaire: "I am pessimistic about the future of the country." After the shock waves of the Great Depression, America was no longer so certain that it was Fortune's favorite child.

[1] By permission of the publisher, Harcourt, Brace and World, Inc.
[2] By permission of the publisher, Meredith Press.

BIBLIOGRAPHY

The historian who attempts comparative analysis of so recent a period as the 1930's finds that so little has been written that he must rely heavily on his own research in scattered manuscript archives. Among the collections which proved fruitful for this essay were the papers of Franklin D. Roosevelt and Rexford Tugwell at the Franklin D. Roosevelt Library, Hyde Park, N.Y.; the papers of Newton Baker, John Frey, George Fort Milton, and William Allen White at the Library of Congress; the papers of Henry Stimson and Irving Fisher, Sterling Memorial Library, Yale University, New Haven, Conn.; Henry Morrow Hyde MSS, Alderman Library, University of Virginia, Charlottesville, Va.; W. Cameron Forbes MSS, Houghton Library, Harvard University, Cambridge, Mass.; George H. Earle MSS, Bryn Mawr, Pa. (privately held); Frank Gannett MSS, Cornell University, Ithaca, N.Y.; Blair Moody MSS, University of Michigan, Ann Arbor, Mich.; James F. Byrnes MSS, Clemson College, Clemson, S. Car.; Gerard Swope, Columbia Oral History Collection, Columbia University, New York, N.Y.; and the Edward Costigan MSS, University of Colorado, Boulder, Colo.

Although no historian has attempted a comprehensive comparative analysis of the Great Depression or the New Deal, there are suggestive observations in Daniel Boorstin, *America and the Image of Europe* (New York and London, 1960), and in Louis Hartz, *The Liberal Tradition* (New York, 1955) and *The Founding of New Societies* (New York, 1964). Foreign travelers frequently drew comparisons; especially noteworthy are two books by H. G. Wells, *Experiment in Autobiography* (1934) and *The New America: The New World* (London and New York, 1935), and two by Odette Keun, *A Foreigner Looks at the TVA* (New York and Toronto, 1937) and *I Think Aloud in America* (London and New York, 1939). George Bernard Shaw's *The Political Madhouse in America and Nearer Home* (London, 1933) is a droll commentary. The American depression and the New Deal were discussed widely in Europe. I have drawn on such works as E. M. Hugh-Jones and E. A. Radice, *An American Experiment* (London, 1936); editors of *The Economist, The New Deal: An Analysis and Appraisal* (London and New York, 1937); and such articles as Philippe Soupault, "La grande inquiétude des paysans et les calmes des cités industrielles américaines," *L'Europe Nouvelle*, XIV (1931), 1148–1151; Ludovic Naudeau, "Le Rooseveltisme ou la troisième solution," *L'Illustration*, XCCV (Nov. 28, 1936), 375; Aline Chalufour and Suzanne Desternes,

"Deux Théoriciens de la crise Américaine," *Revue des Sciences Politiques*, LVII (April 1934), 223–224; and "Interactions of American Depression: Britain and Scandinavia," *Midland Bank Monthly Review*, March 1938, pp. 5–8.

A helpful guide to foreign commentaries is Nicholas Halasz, *Roosevelt through Foreign Eyes* (Princeton, 1961). Edward W. Chester, *Europe Views America* (Washington, 1962), is less comprehensive. Some writers have studied the interrelationship between the United States and a particular foreign country in the 1930's. I am indebted, in particular, to Henry Pelling, *America and the British Left: From Bright to Bevan* (London, 1956); Frances Pingeon, "French Opinion of Roosevelt and the New Deal" (unpublished M.A. essay, Columbia University, 1962); and to a set of papers written in my M.A. seminar at Columbia in the fall of 1966.

The most important history of the New Deal is Arthur M. Schlesinger, Jr., *The Age of Roosevelt*. Schlesinger has carried this ambitious project through three volumes: *The Crisis of the Old Order, 1919–1933* (Boston, 1957); *The Coming of the New Deal* (Boston, 1959); and *The Politics of Upheaval* (Boston, 1960). The definitive biography of F.D.R. by Frank Freidel has also totaled three volumes, subtitled *The Apprenticeship* (Boston, 1952), *The Ordeal* (Boston, 1954), and *The Triumph* (Boston, 1956). Among the one-volume treatments of the New Deal are James M. Burns, *Roosevelt: The Lion and the Fox* (New York, 1956); Mario Einaudi, *The Roosevelt Revolution* (New York, 1959); Rexford G. Tugwell, *The Democratic Roosevelt* (Garden City, N.Y., 1957); and William E. Leuchtenburg, *Franklin D. Roosevelt and the New Deal, 1932–1940* (New York, 1963); each of these books reveals, to some degree, an awareness of the comparative perspective. The most penetrating memoirs are Frances Perkins, *The Roosevelt I Knew* (New York, 1946), and Raymond Moley, *After Seven Years* (New York and London, 1939); Moley has come forth with what is, in essence, a modest revision of his earlier work in *The First New Deal* (New York, 1966). The impact of the depression on foreign affairs is explored in Robert H. Ferrell, *American Diplomacy in the Great Depression* (New Haven, 1957). Almost all economic historians have compared America's performance to that of other countries, and a wealth of comparative economic data may be found in the publications of the League of Nations.

Among the many articles written about the problem of interpreting the 1930's are Frank Freidel, "The New Deal, 1929–1941," in *Yearbook of the National Council for the Social Studies* (1961), pp. 264–281; Richard L. Watson, Jr., "Franklin D. Roosevelt in Historical Writing,

1950–1957," *South Atlantic Quarterly* (1958), pp. 104–126; and Clarke A. Chambers, "FDR, Pragmatist-Idealist: An Essay in Historiography," *Pacific Northwest Quarterly* (1961), pp. 50–55. Richard S. Kirkendall, "The Great Depression: Another Watershed in American History?" and William E. Leuchtenburg, "The New Deal and the Analogue of War," are both printed in John Braeman, Robert H. Bremner, and Everett Walters (eds.), *Change and Continuity in Twentieth-Century America* (Columbus, O., 1964).

World War II

JOHN MORTON BLUM

World War II was really the first war to involve the entire world. Its global quality, its duration and intensity brought the United States into an experience common to most of the rest of mankind. Those nations subjected on all continents to the aggression of the Axis powers shared a long and special adventure—a sequence of shock and anger, of resistance, fortitude, and eventually triumph. The countries participating in that adventure, including the United States, responded to wartime circumstances, now in strikingly similar ways, now with sharp differences from nation to nation. While the war raged, moreover, behind the lines of battle and away from high councils of state, less remarked developments anticipated postwar change that was to affect men everywhere. Still, as so often in history, what was obvious was for the time perhaps most important.

The disillusionment that followed World War I left the American people singularly vulnerable to the delusion of self-sufficiency, though in that respect they were little different from the people of the western European democracies. Like those other people, Americans by and large resisted the counsel of those of their public men who attempted to alert them to the dangers of complacency about the possibility of war. So it was during the decade of the 1930's that critics of American isolationism and unpreparedness, spokesmen, for example, like Henry Stimson, commanded insignificant audiences. Even Franklin Roosevelt, who in private revealed an awareness of world conditions as they were becoming, could muster inadequate support in the Congress for building up American military forces or sustaining the spirit of potential allies. Americans liked to think that peace was the ordinary state of world affairs, that in any event the New World could remain aloof from the troubles of the Old, and that even if those troubles were to spread, a deliberate policy of American uninvolvement would complement the "free security" afforded by the two great oceans.

Those delusions, while seated in assumptions peculiar to the circumstances and culture of the United States, had their debilitating parallels in the special delusions of other countries. The English people, mindful of the cost in manpower and wealth of World War I and preoccupied by the problems of continuing economic depression, found in pacifism, insularity, and parsimony their preferred foreign policy. They saw in Winston Churchill and the small group of his view only an irrelevant and idiosyncratic company of Cassandras. So too with the French, who accepted out of misplaced hope the comfort of a national Maginot psychology. Their urge for peace at cut-rate cost created the climate of opinion that kept even so sensitive a statesman as Léon Blum from exerting French power during the ominous civil war in neighboring Spain. Nor were the democratic states alone in their ways. The leadership of the Soviet Union, engrossed by rivalries within the Communist party, indulged itself in a blood purge of its military establishment at a time when Russia was increasingly vulnerable to danger from its west. Later Stalin and his associates persisted in their belief in the indestructibility of a truce they had contrived, even when the evidence indicated the imminence of invasion.

Accordingly, with few exceptions, the victims of Axis attack were surprised and unprepared. The American experience at Pearl Harbor differed from the experience of the French during the rout of their armies, of the British at Dunkirk, and of the Russians in the summer of 1941 only in that the United States had been spared assault from abroad for more than a century before the event, in that the enemy struck from the sea, and in that Japan rather than Germany mounted the offensive. Yet those differences had important consequences. Safe for so long, the American people after Pearl Harbor suffered a greater sense of outrage over the surprise element in their first defeat than had the others. That outrage, as well as the defeat itself, made Japan, the offending power, the object of far greater hostility within the United States than in any other nation. That hostility in turn, perhaps as much as the conditions of geography that defined the United States as a Pacific as well as an Atlantic power, provoked the shapers of American military and foreign policy during the years of the war continually to modify the implications of the President's decision that victory and the fabrication of peace had to occur in Europe first. The question of Asian and European priorities for the allocation of military equipment, and related questions of politics among the Big Three and in their negotiations with Chiang Kai-shek, imposed a continuing irritant and diversion on deliberations of the highest order, not least those at Teheran and Yalta.

Pearl Harbor caught the United States unprepared for the war in which it had immediately to engage, but less so than the nation would have been had it become a belligerent when war broke out in Europe in September 1939. Assessments of the Munich agreement have ordinarily attempted to calculate only the relative gains that accrued to Germany on the one hand and to France and Great Britain on the other. In the special sense of preparation for war, the major beneficiary of the Munich Pact was probably the United States. Between the time of Munich and the German invasion of Poland, the European powers, including Russia, had only a year in which to accelerate their armament program. The United States in that period profited from that acceleration, for the needs of the French and British, especially for aircraft, led to preliminary explorations that resulted, once war had begun, in orders for airplanes. Those orders provided French and British funds for the construction of some of the first and most important of American productive facilities. In 1940, before France fell, the woeful inadequacy of American military equipment became a matter for debate in Washington, and with the fall of France, belatedly, an occasion for action. With the inception of the Lend Lease program in the spring of 1941, the American economy moved toward the war footing which it would assume more completely during the following year. Unprepared for war in December 1941, the United States had nevertheless progressed further toward a necessary degree of mobilization than had France or Great Britain or even the Soviet Union when they were struck. Americans drew some comparative advantage from the time their Allies had bought for them.

More important, unlike any other major belligerent, the United States never reached the point of total mobilization during World War II. The relative lateness of the American entry into the war and the relative remoteness of the nation from the scenes of battle accounted in part for that significant luxury. But the condition of partial mobilization was purchased primarily from the incomparable abundance of the American economy. Perhaps never before had the implications of American plenty been more patent. Food rationing in the United States, at the most an inconvenience to the American people, left them, as they had so long been, not only the best-fed people in the world but the only adequately fed of all the belligerent peoples. The allocation of enormous economic resources, of productive and transport capacity to military needs, still permitted Americans to enjoy more leisure, to drive more miles, to wear better clothes, to dwell in better housing than any of their co-belligerents had known even before the war began. Indeed, so rich was the United States that in large measure American industry simply superimposed wartime requirements on the base of civilian production which had been operating below capacity during the previous, depression years. Further, the economy was capable of supplying not only domestic needs, but a substantial proportion of the needs, military and civilian, of the country's allies. Spared the devastation of invasion or of strategic bombing, spurred by public and private investment in war production, the American economy boomed, and the American people shared an increase in national income that carried the nation over a few years from depression to high prosperity. The indirect taxes levied by inflation and the direct taxes on excises and incomes in the United States were in the aggregate relatively low in comparison to those felt in France, Great Britain, the Soviet Union, and elsewhere in Europe and Asia, where the monumental costs of wartime destruction affected individuals no less adversely than national economies. Alone of the belligerent nations the United States emerged from the war economically stronger than it had been, wealthier, more comfortable, admirably prepared for a continuing expansion. Instead of the economic drain and emotional strain of exhaustion and privation, the American people had experienced their sunniest season, their first affluence, since the onset of the Great Depression.

Wartime prosperity in itself doubtless contributed to the relative conservatism of American politics. Even before the war the New Deal had begun to lose support, as the Congressional elections of 1938 revealed. In the absence of war in Europe, with its resulting threats to the United States, a conservative Democrat or Republican might well have succeeded Franklin Roosevelt as the President in 1941. In 1942 and thereafter, preoccupation with the winning of the war tended still further to divert attention from domestic problems and policy. The prosperity of the war years at the least strengthened the trend toward moderation, even complacency, in American politics, and the growth of conservative strength in the Congress, especially after the campaign of 1942, forced the President to abandon even modest efforts at reform. To be sure, Roosevelt was able to establish the Fair Employment Practices Commission, which enlarged employment opportunities for Negroes, and to draw the expectations of Americans toward the prospect of 60 million jobs in the coming period of peace, a prospect that would have been considered unthinkable in 1939 and that many conservatives deemed fantastic even in 1945. But he lost his major battle for higher and more equitable taxation, refrained—in spite of the urging of several advisors—from encouraging an extension of the Social Security system, and otherwise reined his own impulse for advancing the programs of the 1930's. That retreat contrasted especially with political developments in Great Britain, where the prolonged privations of the war years focused opinion upon the need for change, spurred socialist and other reformers to the completion of such programs as the Beveridge plan, and enhanced the power of the Labour party. In the United States a people of plenty fretted over petty shortages of shoes and cigarettes. They were ready, as the war ended, to relax. In Great Britain, a people of patience, who had not grumbled about severe hardships, were eager to build a new society as soon and as rapidly as they could.

Still another marked difference between the United States and its allies appeared in wartime foreign policy. Lulled for so many years by the apparent security of the two oceans, comforted in the last two years of war by the seeming security of military primacy, Americans displayed relatively little sophistication about the probable turbulence of the postwar world, or about their increasingly unavoidable involvement in transoceanic politics. They seemed to believe that somehow the creation of an international forum would provide almost an automatic guarantee to continuing peace. Along with victory itself, the establishment of the United Nations became one of two major American war aims. As in past wars, so during World War II, the United States government concentrated the overwhelming proportion of its thought and energy on victory—on winning the war on the ground in Europe and Asia, on the oceans and in the sky. In contrast, Chiang Kai-shek, for one, conducted his campaigns and directed his resources toward sustaining his own position in China as much as toward the defeat of the Japanese. By comparison, American leadership was at the best overoptimistic and at the worst naïve. Projecting their own understanding of American politics beyond the borders of its relevance, Roosevelt and his subordinates viewed the conflict between the Nationalists and the Communists in China not as the civil war it really was, but as the kind of partisan contest that had long separated Republicans and Democrats. No other assumption would have countenanced the continual, futile American search for coalition government in China.

An absorption with victory everywhere suited the temperament of the President, but even a man less averse than he was to long-range planning might have found it difficult to educate American opinion in the hinterland and in Congress about the *Realpolitik* that fascinated Winston Churchill and obsessed Joseph Stalin. Insofar as his limited influence permitted, Churchill tried continually through the war to move Anglo-American policy into strategic courses that would create and preserve his preferred balance of power for the postwar period. Insofar as his major influence permitted, Stalin used decisions about strategy to enlarge immediate and future Soviet political power. Yet Roosevelt persisted in a compassionate but sometimes risky view of the merits of self-determination, and discounted Churchill's counsels about the politics of eastern Europe and Soviet ambitions there. Similarly, even self-conscious realists such as Henry Stimson let themselves hope for too long that the fact of wartime cooperation would create a probability of peacetime friendship with Russia. For a time in 1944 and 1945, American policy was so intent on victory in the field, on divorcing peacemaking from warmaking, and on bringing the boys home, was so concerned about the prospect of reaction on the continent of Europe and so confident of Soviet amity, that the indispensable Anglo-American accord seemed vulnerable.

The Russians, the British, and the French too, not out of some innate cynicism or corruption, but out of their universal, long experience with the conflicts of the European continent, made their future self-interest a primary and legitimate objective of their wartime foreign policies. They recognized always the inextricable link between strategy on the field and politics after the battle. The Americans, for their part, tended to interpret their self-interest as seating in a kind of mechanistic peace, to be perpetuated by the self-government of all peoples and the confabulations of their representatives in a world parliament. In that mood, as well as in the expectation of postwar disengagement from the financial and military responsibilities of world power, Washington continually divorced considerations of strategy from considerations of politics, and continually pursued ideals embedded in a Wilsonian heritage. Those ideals were no less innocent for being majestic.

The political, economic, and foreign policies of the major powers during World War II dominated contemporary observations of the events of the time, and have since preoccupied historians of the period; but social and cultural developments, while comparatively undramatic, had telling current and imperative future consequences. War, as always, tested society's capacity for adjustment and continuity. The conditions of war brought chronic moods and latent conflicts to sharper expression. In the crisis of war each of the societies involved sought certitude abstracted from their pasts, confirmation for the importance of their struggles to prevail. And everywhere men under tension pressed against the usual, peacetime barriers of self-control, while everywhere also, strengthened by the exigencies of the struggle, governments penetrated their authority deeply into the lives of their citizens and demanded extraordinary conformity to official values and objectives. The pressures for conformity in their turn tended to intensify the alienation of those who stood apart from the operative consensus in any nation.

In the United States official and unofficial pressures for unifying ideology took several forms: a symbolizing in wartime metaphors of values deeply embedded in the national culture; a propagation at home as well as abroad of the ideals of freedom and democracy that contrasted so vividly with the avowed purposes of the Axis powers; and ironically, a temporary repression, undemocratic in its essence, of those who appeared to be alien and dangerous—a repression that was to prove only a prelude to new opportunities for its victims. So it was also, in varying degree, for every nation engaged in the great conflict.

The qualities that American culture attributed to military heroes revealed more about the fabric of the culture than about the quality of the men it dignified. As ever, the fighting of the war fell primarily to young men, many of them brave and worthy, but few of them old enough to have achieved a distinction of mind or of attainment outside of battle. Yet public agencies of propaganda and private newspapers and magazines made youthful warriors the embodiments of commended national characteristics. Out of one part of the American past strode the G.I. Joes who slogged through the mud and filth of infantry warfare in Africa, Italy, France, and the tropical islands of the Pacific. As a group, the G.I.'s were unwilling, even antimilitaristic, heroes, harassed by bureaucracy as well as by the enemy. They were, in the view of Ernie Pyle, their favorite interpreter, "Just plain Americans . . . from plain American families"; a bourgeoisie in uniform eager to have it over. Kind, generous and affectionate, they were saddened by the "emaciated little faces of . . . children," but also nostalgic for the farmlands of Wisconsin or the pavements of New York, for milk shakes and Cokes and iced beer—all more American and therefore better than hot British tea or French *vin rouge*. In contrast to the G.I.'s, the folk heroes, stood the knights of the air, an elite physically and psychologically, also the best of the nation's "young brains," who retained in their missions "to an unusual degree their individual responsibility." They quickly gained the look of veterans, as had the frontiersmen before them, but for all their daring and their loneliness in combat, worked, as Americans in their self-image so long had, intimately with their machines. Something of Davey Crockett, something also of Thomas Edison or Henry Ford lingered in the picture of the hero in battle in the air. So too did something of the New England town meeting, for the bomber team or fighter squadron, in the standard opinion of American observers, was "the kind of organization that Americans above all others" were best "capable of maintaining . . . a democratic organization . . . [a] team . . . where each individual" played for the success of the entire mission. Similarly, on the domestic front, those three remarkable men who died in 1944–1945—Wendell Willkie, Alfred Smith, and Franklin Roosevelt—were made to represent, by the authors of their obituaries, the range of aspirations Americans had earlier identified with Benjamin Franklin, Andrew Jackson, Lincoln, and their latter-day successors.

Whether in the symbolism of their heroes or in other forms of expression, other cultures also extracted from their past metaphors to sustain the spirit during the tribulations of the war. The British infantryman and airman—the one gritty and homely, the other never in all history exceeded in his valor—sometimes resembled their American counterparts, as in lesser measure did the Russians—peasants, as it were, afoot and Communists in the sky—but always distinguishable by special, national characteristics inherent in the vision of those who described the separate candidates for apotheosis.

In the same way public or private agencies of communication held out to the several peoples of the United Nations the prospect of palpable, material rewards in a brave new world that would follow victory. American advertising, not least the institutional advertising which had as one purpose the promotion of war bonds, identified saving and lending for victory with the accumulation of funds which would later finance new homes and cars and furniture. Once the war was over, the advertising implied, Americans would enjoy again the bounties they had not known since before the depression. If the British were wisely more cautious in what they promised, and if their promises emanated more from official than from unofficial sources, those promises nonetheless included security from the cradle to the grave—one reward for the trials of the British people, both during the war and in the grim period of unemployment that had preceded it. So too in the Soviet Union, where Stalin and his associates called the imagination of the Russian people not only to the defense of their mother country but also to the vast possibilities of a future replete with hydroelectric power, burgeoning farmlands, and ample food and drink. In the United States, Great Britain, and the Soviet Union alike, official visions of the new materialistic world that victory would bring stressed precisely what men had most missed in the decade or so before the war began.

Yet there was much more to the expressed purpose of the war than cold Cokes, warm beer, and vodka. Particularly in the United States and Great Britain, but also in the nations of western Europe that the Germans had overrun, the definition of the Four Freedoms carried substantial, inspirational meaning. A war against Nazism, against oppression and persecution and intolerance, had powerful implications for those who fought it. Those implications were never lost on the subject or disadvantaged people who lived under the authority of the enemies of Hitler. Those people took seriously the promises of freedom of belief and expression, of freedom from want, and of freedom from fear and aggression, including the freedom to govern their own lives. The first consequences were anomalous. Impatient for those freedoms, the disadvantaged made claims during the war that belligerent governments had for a time to defer out of considerations either for national unity or for the allocation to military purposes of limited wartime resources. Such was the case with the British in India; such was the case of the European governments-in-exile in their attitudes toward their colonies in Asia and Africa; such, too, was the case in the United States.

Americans were by no means guiltless of oppression of their own during World War II. Most blatantly they victimized the Nisei, the second generation—American citizens by law—of

Japanese ancestry. The federal government confined most of them and their parents in concentration camps, deprived them of property they had accumulated, humiliated them, and in so doing strained but did not break the loyalty most of them felt for the American nation. But other minority groups in the United States made limited wartime gains. Italian-Americans, far beyond their previous general experience, came to identify with and to be accepted by the communities in which they lived. Discrimination and prejudice against Jews and Catholics diminished. And the American Negro, conscious that a war against racism demanded the eradication of racism at home, began to organize that long crusade which was so strongly to mark the postwar years. Far more than in the years before the war, Negroes discovered a militant and intelligent leadership within their own numbers. Their pressure on the federal government resulted in the first major effort since the period of Reconstruction to assure them of more equitable opportunities for jobs. Beyond that, with the continual assistance of sympathetic whites, Negroes during the war years organized the first of the modern sit-ins, the first of the freedom rides, the first of the demonstrations through which they would reveal their determination to gain equality, at least before the law, and through which they would harness the force to move toward that legitimate goal.

The movement for Negro rights within the United States, broadly interpreted, was but one part of the world-wide movement of subject peoples toward independence, dignity, and self-respect. By destroying the fabric of previous politics in Europe and Asia, the Nazis and Japanese inadvertently advanced that movement; but it was not only the weakening or, in some cases, the collapse of Western power that created the conditions out of which the revolutions of nationalities and expectations emerged to succeed the war itself. Ideas had also a dramatic influence. The West had expressed an ultimate capacity for corruption in Hitler and Nazism. It expressed a noble capacity for idealism in the pronouncements of Allied statesmanship, pronouncements made under the duress of war but nonetheless with a glowing sincerity of belief. The aspirations whetted by that belief mattered, especially to men who had hardly dared embrace them before 1945, and they mattered also to other, democratic men, who recognized the logic of their own expressed convictions. Accordingly, the clash of ideologies between 1939 and 1945 quickened the pace of social change over the entire globe. Americans, though they had little empire to set free, shared the anxieties of other Western men who foresaw that the old order had begun to crumble. Americans shared, too, the hope and gladness of those throughout the West, not all men there but many of them, who expected in the postwar period not a perfect or an easy but a better life. The social revolution that accompanied the war had implications for the United States no less portentous than for its allies; the social revolution that continued thereafter shook them all rather more than had the politics and the fighting of the awful war itself.

BIBLIOGRAPHY

The authoritative analysis of American policy and opinion in the months between the Munich Conference and the Japanese attack on Pearl Harbor remains William L. Langer and S. Everett Gleason, *The Challenge to Isolation* (New York, 1951) and *The Undeclared War* (New York, 1953). Roberta Wohlstetter, *Pearl Harbor: Warning and Decision* (Stanford, 1962), provides the commanding account of that episode. On British and French contributions to American preparedness, see H. Duncan Hall, *North American Supply* (London, 1955), and John M. Blum, *From the Morgenthau Diaries*, Vol. II, *Years of Urgency* (Boston, 1965). The forthcoming third volume of the latter work includes some account of wartime foreign and domestic policy and of the general American hatred of the Japanese during the war years. For a more detailed treatment of that last subject, see Carey McWilliams, *Prejudice: Japanese-Americans, Symbol of Racial Intolerance* (Boston, 1944), and Dorothy S. Thomas and R. S. Nishimoto, *The Spoilage* (Berkeley, 1946). Two particularly useful works on American domestic developments during the war are Randolph E. Paul, *Taxation in the United States* (Boston, 1954), and Roland Young, *Congressional Politics in the Second World War* (New York, 1956). Herbert Feis has been the most thorough and discerning of the analysts of American foreign policy during the war, perhaps particularly, for the purposes of this essay, in *The China Tangle* (Princeton, 1953) and *Churchill-*

Roosevelt-Stalin (Princeton, 1957); for a short account, consult Gaddis Smith, *American Diplomacy during the Second World War* (New York, 1965). There is no study of the heroic images mentioned in this essay, but the materials for such a study appear, among other places, in the back files of *Time, Life, The New York Times, The Times* of London, *The Manchester Guardian,* and *Pravda;* also revealing are Ernest T. Pyle, *Brave Men* (New York, 1944) and *Here Is Your War* (New York, 1943), and John R. Hersey, *Into the Valley* (New York, 1943) and *Men on Bataan* (New York, 1942). On heroes, especially great men as embodiments of national values, see John M. Blum, *The Promise of America* (Boston, 1966); Merrill D. Peterson, *The Jefferson Image in the American Mind* (New York, 1960); and especially Dixon Wecter, *The Hero in America* (New York, 1941). As yet unpublished investigations of the civil rights movement during the war confirm in detail the general and brief but valuable and trenchant account in C. Vann Woodward, *The Strange Career of Jim Crow* (New York, 1966).

23

The Cold War

ERNEST R. MAY

In high school and college courses on United States history, the final topic of the year is usually entitled the "Cold War." As a rule, the topic receives little classroom time. Even if the teacher has a special interest in the twentieth century, he is apt to stress events prior to 1945, skimping on what he says about his own generation.

This practice has some justification, since courses on political science, economics, and sociology say much about the present era and not much about the past. Still, the result is that a long period—more than 10 per cent of the time since independence—receives relatively little attention as history.

The Cold War label is itself evidence. The twenty years between the wars are not treated as a unit. Dealing with these two decades, historians distinguish at least a retreat toward isolation, a period of prosperity, the depression, the New Deal, and a transition from isolation to intervention. Except perhaps for distinctions between Presidential administrations, the more recent epoch is not similarly differentiated.

To compare this epoch with others is therefore difficult. Lacking agreement on categories of events within it, we can only improvise categories for comparison.

We are driven to dealing with the period in terms of its broadest trends. From World War II to the middle of the 1960's, the United States made extraordinary economic progress. Gross national product rose from $100.6 billion in 1940 to $681.2 billion in 1965. Even reduced to dollars of constant value, this index of economic condition showed growth of over 226 per cent.

Accompanying this surge of economic growth was equally remarkable scientific and technological progress. The wartime and postwar generation, to cite only a few specifics, saw the multiplication of wonder drugs; development of nylon, styrene, and other man-made materials; buildup of a huge electronics industry, producing, among other things, television equipment and computers capable of automating entire factories; strides in aviation; steps toward exploration of space; and extraction from the atom of power sufficient to replace all known fuels or, if misused, to erase all life.

The impact on the average American of economic, scientific, and technological gains appeared in sharply rising personal income. In 1940 average individual income had been under $600; by 1965 it was over $2,600. Most of all it was evident in rising consumption—sales in a given year of up to 9 million automobiles, over 4 million refrigerators, an equal number of washing machines, and 8 million television sets. Although poverty lingered, especially among non-whites, the nation nevertheless achieved levels of consumption justifying the label borrowed from a book title of John Kenneth Galbraith's—"the affluent society."

Within this society, economic change was matched by social change. World War II uprooted much of the American population. Fourteen million young men went into uniform. Millions of others moved, following soldiers or going to cities with war industries. Afterward, under a generous federal program, millions of veterans attended trade schools, colleges, and professional schools. In combination with other factors, the movement of population and opening of new educational opportunities broke down barriers between ethnic and religious groups. The election to the Presidency in 1960 of John F. Kennedy, a Roman Catholic of Irish extraction, was taken as in many ways symbolic of this change. With a Supreme Court verdict against school segregation and passage by Congress of major civil rights acts, the last and highest barriers, those around Negroes, began also to come down. The nation took giant strides not only toward affluence but also toward equality.

Focusing just on the United States, one might speak of the two decades after World War II as the era of affluence or the era of achievement. Such a focus is possible in earlier epochs. In this one it is not. During these decades, the United States was involved with the rest of the world as it had never been involved before. As C. Vann Woodward has observed, its era of free security had come to an end.

In World War II, Americans had been more conscious than in World War I of having a stake in the outcome. Indeed, mixed with realistic recognition of American interest in resisting Nazi hegemony in Europe was emotional, even sentimental, shame about America's failure earlier to play a part in preserving peace. Party platforms and Congressional resolutions in 1943–1945 expressed determination never again to shirk international responsibility.

Even before the war was over, this determination seemed to be put to the test. Differences arose within the wartime alliance. The Soviet Union insisted on retaining territory she had acquired from Poland and Rumania through pre-1941 bargains with the Nazis. In addition, in Poland and other areas entered by the Red Army, Soviet authorities supported Communists at the expense of non-Communist resistance forces. From the spring of 1945 onward, the American government and people had before them questions involving their willingness to defend in distant areas the principles for which professedly they had waged the war— national self-determination and the right of peoples to choose their leaders by democratic processes.

The apparent test of American determination began while Franklin Roosevelt was still President. He made the first protests against Soviet actions in Poland. But it was Harry Truman who had to make most of the decisions.

Coming to office after a long career as a party politician and legislator, Truman was wholly unfamiliar with international affairs. Nor had he close advisers much better equipped than he. Roosevelt's right-hand man, Harry Hopkins, was desperately ill. The office of Secretary of State was occupied by Edward R. Stettinius, Jr., and, after July 1945, by James F. Byrnes. A stopgap appointee of Roosevelt's, Stettinius was charged only with completing the UN Charter. Byrnes, a South Carolinian, former Senator, and former Supreme Court Justice, had been overseer of industrial mobilization. Had Roosevelt not surprised the 1944 Democratic convention by choosing Truman as his running mate, Byrnes would probably have been Vice President and therefore President. Truman himself had supported Byrnes for the office. Since there would be no Vice President until after the 1948 election and, under existing law, the Secretary of State was next in line for the Presidency, Truman felt doubly honor bound to give Byrnes the post. The only man in Truman's original cabinet with experience of international politics was Henry L. Stimson. Secretary of War since 1940, he had been Secretary of State under Herbert Hoover from 1929 to 1933. But, already seventy-seven, Stimson was to go out of the government at about the time Byrnes came in. By and large, Truman as President had to rely either on men new to the game or on ambassadors or bureaucrats.

Truman handled the first issues before him with a mixture of uncertainty and impatience. Feeling that the Polish problem arose from suspicion and misunderstanding on the part of the Soviet Union, he sent the ailing Hopkins to Moscow to assure Generalissimo Stalin that the United States had no wish to set up an anti-Soviet regime but that it would insist on a representative Polish government and free elections. Assuming that, on a variety of other issues, the Soviet government was given to needless wrangling, Truman said "that he felt our agreements with the Soviet Union so far had been a one-way street and that . . . if the Russians did not wish to join us they could go to hell."

Behind both these blunt words and the instructions given Hopkins lay unspoken assumptions, first, that the United States was incomparably the strongest of the victorious allies; second, that the Soviet Union, devastated by the war, would desperately want American aid; third, that it was necessary to speak with special vigor in order to show the Soviets and the world that the United States did not intend this time to retreat into selfish isolation.

Truman's initial tactics did not succeed. Communist control over Poland was consolidated. Elsewhere, though not without some signs of hesitation, the Soviet government continued to resist American pressure for representative regimes and free elections. Nothing seemed to deter Stalin from an ambition to build an empire of satellite states—neither the demonstration at Hiroshima and Nagasaki of America's possession of awesome new weapons nor the display in economic negotiations of America's power to grant or withhold immense resources for reconstruction.

Truman and his aides tried many tactics. Matching uncooperativeness with uncooperativeness, they refused the Soviets a role in the occupation of Japan, or in the administration of former Italian colonies in Africa; they made trouble about reparations payments and other issues rising out of four-power control of Germany. At the same time, however, the American government also offered a proposal for international control of nuclear power, the so-called Baruch Plan, by the terms of which America would eventually surrender all its atomic arsenal.

Instead of inducing Stalin to bargain, these various moves appeared to have the reverse effect. The Soviet grip on eastern Europe tightened. New support was given to Communists in Greece and northern Iran. Scornfully rejecting the Baruch Plan, Soviet representatives to the United Nations demanded that the United States simply destroy outright its stock of atomic weapons.

By the winter of 1946–1947, the prevailing view in Washington was that summarized soon afterward in a *Foreign Affairs* article by career diplomat and Soviet affairs specialist George Frost Kennan. Briefly, it was that the Soviet Union was implacably bent on spreading Communism to the world and hence that Americans could not expect the Soviet government in the foreseeable future to look upon the United States and other non-Communist states as anything but antagonists. The only offsets were, first, the fact that the Soviets assumed as a matter of dogma

the ultimate triumph of Communism and hence had no need to
be impetuous and second, as a corollary, that, in order not to
slow Communism's growth, the Soviet regime would be careful
not to risk its own overthrow. The conclusion following from
this assessment was that the United States should devote itself
to preventing the expansion of Communism, awaiting the day
when a new, less dogmatic, and more tractable generation had
risen to power in Russia. This policy won the label "containment."

In December 1946 the Truman administration applied this
policy in Iran. Threatening to supply funds and military equipment to the Iranian government, Truman demanded that the
Soviets withdraw support from Communist separatists in the
northern province of Azerbaijan. His demand produced a quick
result. The Soviets withdrew.

In March 1947 the American government embarked on containment in the eastern Mediterranean. Warned that the British
no longer had resources with which to support the Greek and
Turkish governments, Truman agreed to America's assuming
Britain's role. In a dramatic message to Congress, he asked $400
million with which to help Greece wage war against Commu nist
guerrillas and to reinforce Turkey's resistance to Soviet pressure
on her eastern borders.

"I believe," Truman said, "that it must be the policy of the
United States to support free peoples who are resisting attempted
subjugation by armed minorities or by outside pressures." He
continued, "I believe that we must assist free peoples to work
out their own destinies in their own way." Applicable to the
entire globe, these lines constituted the broadest possible statement of America's new determination to assume international
responsibilities. Remembering President Monroe's famous declaration of policy in the days when America's sphere of interest
was limited to the Western Hemisphere, commentators characterized these words as the Truman Doctrine.

After Congress voted the requested money and Greece and
Turkey remained outside the Communist orbit, containment
was applied in other ways and in other places. George Marshall,
who succeeded Byrnes as Secretary of State, announced his famous Marshall Plan. Designed primarily to help Europe achieve

economic recovery, it had as at least a subsidiary aim relief of conditions in which Communist agitation seemed likely to prosper. To this effort, some $12 billion were devoted. Along with it went anti-Communist propaganda and political activity which helped to check and frustrate the Communist parties of Italy, France, and the low countries. Along with it too went measures separating Western-occupied Germany from the Soviet zone and laying foundations for the independent German Federal Republic of 1955 and the German "economic miracle" of the later 1950's.

Through the first year of containment, it was imagined in Washington that the policy required primarily a willingness to spend money. Truman had said in his request for aid to Greece and Turkey that "our help should be primarily through economic and financial aid which is essential to economic stability and orderly political processes."

In 1948 this proposition came suddenly into question. Two dramatic events set the stage for a stepping-up of what columnist Walter Lippmann had already labeled the "cold war." First, Communists effected a coup within Czechoslovakia's coalition government and transformed that semineutral state into a Soviet satellite. Second, Communists in Yugoslavia, led by Tito, broke with the central apparatus of the party. While making no ideological change, they detached their country from Stalin's empire. Following these events, Soviet occupation authorities began to clamp down on road and rail communication between West Germany and Berlin. Zones of the former German capital occupied by Americans, Englishmen, and Frenchmen were soon subject to a practical blockade.

The American government faced a choice between abandoning Berlin and running a risk of war. Though claiming access to Berlin as a legal right, Truman chose not to put an armored column on the Autobahn. Instead, he made use of the route that lay open—that through the air. Deploying all available cargo and transport planes, America and Britain ferried supplies to Western forces and Berliners in Western-occupied zones.

After half a year, the airlift proved its effectiveness, and Stalin decided to relax the blockade. Meanwhile, however, both Americans and West Europeans had become concerned that the Soviet Union might use force to extend Communism's domain. Taking the Czech coup to signify not only overreaching ambition but also impatience, Americans read the Berlin affair as a test of the strength of America's commitment to oppose Communist expansion. When the stakes were lives instead of dollars, would American determination falter? Truman was resolved to prove that it would not.

In 1947–1949 the United States discarded a century-and-a-half-old tradition of eschewing entangling alliances. In a treaty signed at Rio de Janeiro, it engaged to defend Latin American nations against attack. In the North Atlantic Treaty of 1949, it made a similar commitment to non-Communist states in western Europe and the Mediterranean. As demonstration that this latter treaty was not a mere scrap of paper, the United States further engaged to take part in a North Atlantic Treaty Organization with multinational military units. American troops were stationed in Europe as part of a first-line defense against Soviet attack.

Along with these moves went an intensive military buildup. American armed forces were partially unified. All operating commands were made subject to a Joint Chiefs of Staff organization. Administratively, the army, navy, marine corps, and newly independent air force came within a new Department of Defense. To coordinate military policy with foreign policy, a National Security Council was created as a kind of inner cabinet, serving the President. Steps were then taken to enlarge the military forces and equip them with the most powerful and up-to-date weapons obtainable. Despite severe budgetary restraints, decisions were made to develop new and larger aircraft carriers and giant supersonic bombers. Spurred by knowledge that the Soviets had developed atomic weapons, a decision was also made, after agonizing debate within the scientific community, to develop a hydrogen bomb hundreds of times more powerful than the atomic bomb.

All calculations in Washington had to do with the danger of a Soviet attack in Europe. The first actual test of America's willingness to use its military power came, however, in the Far East. In China, civil warfare had gone on during most of the period of war with Japan. After Japan's defeat, Nationalists and Communists continued to fight. Because of the weakness of the Nationalist government, the scale of aid that would have been required, limits on resources available, and concentration on the apparent peril in Europe, the United States did not make a strong effort to stem Communism in China, and in 1949 the Communists triumphed. In North Korea, there was already a Communist regime set up by Soviet occupation authorities. The only portion of the East Asian mainland where Communists were not in power was South Korea. In June 1950, the North Koreans launched an invasion with the object of conquering South Korea.

Truman and his advisors saw the hand of the Soviet Union behind the North Korean attack. They felt that if the United States stood idly by, the Soviet regime would judge America to be lacking nerve. America's European allies might reach the same conclusion. All small nations hoping for protection from the United Nations organization would have reason to feel that the new collective security arrangements were as feeble as those of the interwar years. Fearing all these possible consequences, the President decided that action was called for. He sought and obtained a UN resolution condemning North Korea as an aggressor and authorizing collective resistance. Even before the resolution passed, Truman ordered American forces to enter battle on South Korea's side.

War in Korea, waged primarily by American troops, continued for nearly three years. The North Korean attack was quickly thrown back. The commander for the United Nations, General Douglas MacArthur, then marched into North Korea. The Chinese Communists intervened in force. United Nations troops in turn were thrown back. A front eventually stabilized around the former North Korean-South Korean frontier. Overruling MacArthur and others who wanted air attacks and other measures of war against the Chinese mainland, Truman confined the conflict to Korea proper. His successor, President Eisenhower, achieved a truce and an end to the fighting by threatening not only to reverse this policy but to use nuclear weapons against Chinese cities.

Among the results of the Korean conflict were a massive increase in American military power and globalization of the policy of containment. Once the war in Korea began, Congress was willing to appropriate funds not only for a larger army but for far more ships and planes than had been contemplated in military expansion plans devised after the Berlin blockade. Though the termination of the Korean war permitted cutbacks, the level of power achieved was such as to permit commitments which would have seemed unrealistic prior to 1950.

By both Truman and Eisenhower, a number of such commitments were made. More or less as had been done in Europe, the United States pledged itself to defend against Communist conquest South Korea, Japan, the Nationalist Chinese stronghold on the island of Formosa, southern Vietnam, most of the independent nations of Southeast Asia, and, more conditionally, a tier of Middle Eastern states bordering the Soviet Union on the south. Through a declaration known as the Eisenhower Doctrine, backed by appropriate Congressional resolutions, the United States gave a blanket promise to protect the independence of any and all nations in the Middle East. By landing troops in Lebanon when the Lebanese alleged infiltration from Syria, the American government proved that this promise was in earnest. By strongly supporting United Nations intervention in the Congo when domestic chaos created danger of a Communist takeover, the government demonstrated that its determination to prevent the spread of Communism applied to all parts of the globe.

There were limits. The United States did not react forcefully to every sign of growing Communist influence in a newly independent African state. In Laos, support of non-Communists was kept within narrow bounds, and a civil war was terminated by compromise, giving Communists a share in control of the country. When Fidel Castro achieved power in Cuba, the American government severed relations, applied economic pressure, and gave clandestine aid to exile groups for what proved to be an abortive counterrevolution, but American troops were not sent in, and Cuba continued a precarious existence as a Communist state.

The limits, however, were few. When the Soviet Union erected missile bases in Cuba in 1962, the United States successfully demanded their removal, even though doing so involved a risk of nuclear war. Not to have made such a demand, it was reasoned, would have shaken the self-assurance of all governments, in the hemisphere and elsewhere, safeguarded by American power. Prompt dispatch of marines to Santo Domingo during a revolution in 1965 showed how little chance the United States would take of another Cuba's emerging in the hemisphere. Deployment of half a million troops to Vietnam gave evidence that determination to continue the policy of containment was undiminished and unflinching.

As in Europe in the late 1940's, the provision of a military shield was accompanied by efforts to combat poverty and other economic and social conditions that could cause people in non-Communist nations to turn to Communism. President Truman in 1950 inaugurated a program of technical assistance to promote modernization in underdeveloped nations. Grants and loans followed and, beginning in the Kennedy administration, the dispatch of Peace Corps volunteers.

Though linked with the containment of Communism, foreign aid also had positive aims. Underlying it were beliefs that higher levels of production, income, education, and social services were good things in themselves and that with them would come development of political systems better than Communism. Underlying willingness to provide foreign aid was a further belief that, the world being one community, rich nations had obligations to poor nations similar to obligations within smaller communities of rich citizens to poor citizens. Though levels of aid were low, even in the ambitious Western Hemisphere Alliance for Progress, the policy of providing aid reflected a strain of altruism that was present, though not always equally visible, in other aspects of the effort for containment.

Looking back over the twenty years after World War II, one can see this effort as having come in overlapping stages. First, there was a stage when the United States simply opposed the imperial spread of another power. It sought to prevent the Soviet Union from establishing control over neighbor states. Imperceptibly, this stage merged into a second when it became the American aim to resist the spread of an alien ideology. As these objectives were pursued on a wider and wider scale, the United States became committed by treaty or otherwise to defense of nearly all non-Communist states. The extent of this commitment was indicated in 1962, when the Chinese transgressed the Indian border and, though India was determinedly not an American ally, Washington warned Peking of the direst consequences if the invasion continued.

The huge area embraced by America's commitments was in no sense an American empire. Even South Korea and South Vietnam, at the height of the wars in those two countries, retained their autonomy. The degree of American control bore no resemblance to, for example, that in the Philippines before 1941. Elsewhere, American influence was seldom much greater than that of Paris within the Communauté Française or even that of London within the British Commonwealth. In most of what was called, with varying degrees of appropriateness, the free world, the United States had assumed imperial responsibilities without imperial prerogatives.

Yet through American policy ran a strain of thought very similar to one that had been a major influence in the old colonialism, including that of the United States in the Philippines. It was the spirit of uplift, the mood of the secular missionary, the *mission civilisatrice*.

In defending South Korea, Southeast Asia, and other areas, the United States was not gaining power or denying power to potential adversaries. In cold-blooded economic or strategic terms, most of these underdeveloped lands were liabilities. While the Cuban turn to Communism had been costly to America in some respects, it had perhaps been even more costly for the Soviet Union. Outlays to support Cuba's economy and give the Cuban government a minimal sense of security caused heavy drains on Soviet resources. An argument could be made that long-term advantage in the Cold War would lie in losing to the Communists those territories where the costs and difficulties of economic and political development promised to be greatest. One reason among others why such an argument could have little appeal was that for most Americans the Cold War was not a struggle for power. It was, like the two world wars, a contest for democracy. Underlying American policy was a vision, with deep historical roots, of a world in which all men would enjoy political, economic, and social institutions similar to those in the United States.

Given the phases of the Cold War, its character, and domestic developments coinciding with it, where does one look for parallels? Has any nation ever had experience that might be comparable?

Thinking only of the rapid economic and social progress within the country, one might be reminded of nineteenth-century Britain or late-nineteenth-century Germany or, indeed, of the United States in eras of growth such as 1830–1850 or 1870–1890. But reflection quickly suggests that the parallels are not close enough to be instructive. Economic growth in America during and after World War II was not just incremental growth in production and average income. It was on such a scale as to work a transformation. America by 1965 was the only nation in all history of which it could be said that the poor formed a small minority and the rich a majority. Socially, it was not simply a nation in which new groups showed some upward mobility; it was one in which lower caste and status rankings showed promise of disappearing. Between these conditions and those existing in nineteenth-century Britain or Germany or in earlier periods of American history, there were, in Kant's phrase, differences in degree so great as to be differences in kind.

Thinking of external relationships of the United States in the postwar era, one can see past experience that is more nearly comparable. An obvious parallel is ancient Rome. In the third century B.C., Rome undertook to check the spread of Carthaginian power in the western Mediterranean. During sixty-odd years of intermittent conflict, the Romans assumed responsibility for one city and province after another. By the time of Carthage's final defeat, there existed among Romans a sense of strength and of moral superiority which led them in the succeeding century to assume new responsibilities in the east as well as the west, seeking to confer stability, order, and comparative prosperity on the lands that had once been subject to Alexander the Great. Subsequently, as occasion offered, Roman power was extended northward.

Though to say that the Romans were extending their ideology would be a distortion, there was certainly a sense of mission in the often proclaimed objective of "imposing the ways of peace." A modern American could conceivably feel that there were familiar notes in Virgil's famous apostrophe to Rome:

Disposing peace and war
by thy own majestic way;
To tame the proud, the
fetter'd slave to free:
These are imperial arts,
and worthy thee.

Anyone studying both Roman and American history can be tempted into specific comparisons. Publishing a book on the Gracchi in 1939, Henry J. Haskell gave it the title, *The New Deal in Old Rome*. Thinking of General MacArthur's preparations to return from Korea in 1951, one could be moved to remember Caesar at the Rubicon or, more appropriately in view of the outcome, Marius at Solonium in 89 B.C. readying himself for his unsuccessful challenge to Sulla. But it is not clear that such analogies are useful, even in thinking about the episodes themselves, and efforts to draw parallels on a larger scale show few signs of yielding profit.

The same is true of the other obvious case that comes to mind —England in the nineteenth-century era of *pax britannica*. At the end of the Napoleonic wars, the Liverpool ministry undertook to limit the influence in western Europe of the Eastern powers. The international congresses of 1817–1822 saw this effort intensify. During George Canning's tenure as foreign secretary, Britain became more and more committed to national self-determination and defense of liberal as against absolutist regimes. Later, when Viscount Palmerston was in Canning's place, the extent of commitment widened, and Britain was involved to varying degrees in using its diplomatic or naval power in the low countries, various parts of the Mediterranean, the waters surrounding Africa, and the coasts of China. Simultaneous efforts to promote trade with both developed and underdeveloped lands had in them elements not only of self-service but also of missionary zeal, the basis being belief that trade brought prosperity which in turn brought peace and progress toward parliamentary institutions.

Britain between 1815 and 1854 seems more like modern America than does Rome in the later days of the republic. While in the course of rapid economic and social change at home, the Britain of Castlereagh, Canning, and Palmerston passed through stages of foreign policy involving ever wider commitment. To some extent, its opposition to the absolutism of the tsars and Metternich was opposition to an alien ideology. To some extent, too, the policies of Britain were based on the hope of seeing the whole world follow her own example.

But, as when comparing America and Rome, one senses that locating points of parallel is unlikely to yield much insight. The times and parties are too different. Post-1945 ideological issues were too closely tied to economic and social conditions that were partly results of European industrialization and imperialism, and this was no more true for Russians than for Americans, even though the base points of Russian thought were Marx and Lenin while those of American thought were eighteenth-century *philosophes*. Above all, such conflict as there was between English liberalism and continental absolutism took place as a low-stakes game. It was not played out by adversaries holding in their hands the power to annihilate not only one another but mankind.

Ultimately, what frustrates any search for past parallels is the fact of technological progress. The thought may cross one's mind that the Cold War resembles the contest between Christians and Muslims; that the Sino-Soviet split is similar to the schism among Christians during the Reformation; or, to escape the chain of thought flowing from that analogy, that the Cold War itself is comparable to the European religious wars of the sixteenth and seventeenth centuries. But any such thought founders when one reflects on the political, economic, and military capabilities of princes such as Harun al Rashid and Charles V, when compared with those of Leonid Brezhnev and Lyndon Johnson.

In fact, there may be only one nation in all of history that has had anything like America's post-1945 experience, and that is its contemporary and adversary, the U.S.S.R.

Though the levels of production and per capita income in Russia remained well below those in America, the pace of progress and the resultant economic transformation were not wholly dissimilar. In view of the 1917 revolution and the long, bloody transition that followed, social change in the U.S.S.R., especially from 1953 forward, had a transforming character.

The inner springs of Soviet foreign policy are, of course, mysteries. It is not inconceivable, however, that the Cold War was for the Soviets the mirror face of what it was for Americans. Suspicious, vulnerable, and weak from decades of revolution and war, the Soviet regime may have seen Anglo-American demands for representative governments and free elections in eastern Europe as aimed at extending the empire of capitalism. The initial measures that so provoked President Truman may have been essentially defensive.

Indeed, one can make out such a case for the acts of 1948–1950, which Americans interpreted as deliberately aggressive. We know that American intervention in Greece frightened Moscow. In *Conversations with Stalin,* the Yugoslav statesman Milovan Djilas reports the Soviet dictator as saying that, in the face of American opposition, he dared not continue support of Greek Communist guerrillas. Seeing the Iranian dispute, the Truman Doctrine, the Marshall Plan, and moves toward German reconstruction as evidence of an American design to strangle Communism, Stalin could have felt impelled to pull back within an outer ring of defenses. The coup in Czechoslovakia and the cautious attempt to get the Western powers out of Berlin, coupled with cessation of serious subversive activity in western Europe, termination of the Greek guerrilla campaign, slackening of pressure on Turkey, failure to use force against Yugoslavia, and refusal to aid Communists in China, could be read as signs of retrenchment rather than the reverse.

Similarly, as Adam Ulam has contended, Stalin's directive for the conquest of South Korea need not have been a test of the United States. Astonished that the Americans had not done more to prevent Communist success in China, the Soviet dictator may have been unable to conceive that they would resist in Korea. By having the North Koreans absorb the one remaining non-Communist enclave on the mainland, he could ensure his eastern frontier's being as well protected by a wall of blue water as were his western frontiers by the "iron curtain." The fact that the North Korean invasion occurred while Soviet representatives were abstaining from attendance at the United Nations Security Council suggests how little prepared Stalin was for the course of action which the American government in fact pursued.

For the Soviet as for the American government, the Cold War entailed ever widening commitments—to eastern European satellites, to North Korea, to China until the ideological breach, to North Vietnam, and to Cuba. In Southeast Asia, Central Asia, the Middle East, and Africa, the Soviet Union supported Communist and anti-American political factions, often at considerable cost. In addition to contributing money, the Soviets made room for foreigners in educational and training institutions in the U.S.S.R. and sent abroad technicians whose services were badly needed at home. Though Soviet foreign commitments were considerably more limited than those of the United States, they reached far and, outside the satellite areas, also involved imperial responsibilities with, usually, very restricted prerogatives.

Mixed with extension of Soviet commitments was, of course, ideological zeal. There can be little doubt that, when helping Communists come into power, Soviet officials felt they were undoing evil and accomplishing good. Equally, as Kennan was careful to point out in his *Foreign Affairs* article, they took for granted that history was on their side and that Communism was certain to triumph so long as the masses were not frustrated by machinations of devilish capitalist-imperialists.

In progressing to wider and wider imperial commitments, in regarding the international contest as one between irreconcilable ideologies, and in pursuing as an overriding goal a world remade in their own images, the Soviet Union and the United States traveled parallel paths. Both did so while going through revolutionary domestic change. Both did so possessing the full panoply of modern resources for political, economic, and military action.

To suggest that the Cold War era in American history is likely to be best understood by comparing American with Soviet experience is not to say that the issues of the Cold War were unreal or that one looking back needs to say that at one point or another the United States or the Soviet Union should obviously have followed some different course of action. The vantage points, perspectives, and value systems of the two nations were widely dissimilar. To appraise the wisdom or rightness of what one or the other did is inevitably to apply moral rather than scientific judgment. But by thinking of the two great adversaries in comparison with one another, one can conceivably arrive at a surer understanding of what values were at stake, what real choices the actors possessed, and what were the intended and unintended consequences of the choices made. If so, that could be a considerable gain.

BIBLIOGRAPHY

Historical literature on the Cold War era is sparse. Eric Goldman, *The Crucial Decade—and After: America, 1945–1960* (New York, 1960), offers a sprightly survey of domestic events. John W. Spanier, *American Foreign Policy since World War II* (rev. ed.; New York, 1962), and William G. Carleton, *The Revolution in American Foreign Policy* (New York, 1963), are sober, solid analyses. W. W. Rostow, *The United States in the World Arena* (New York, 1960), is an insightful interpretation. For the present, however, the principal works on the period are the reminiscenses of participants: Harry S. Truman, *Memoirs* (2 vols.; Garden City, N.Y., 1955); Dwight D. Eisenhower, *The White House Years* (2 vols.; New York, 1963–1965); Theodore Sorenson, *Kennedy* (New York, 1965); and Arthur M. Schlesinger, Jr., *A Thousand Days* (New York, 1965). On Soviet developments, three specially worthwhile works are George F. Kennan, *Russia and the West under Lenin and Stalin* (Boston, 1961); Marshall Shulman, *Stalin's Foreign Policy Reappraised* (Cambridge, Mass., 1963); and Ivo J. Lederer (ed.), *Russian Foreign Policy: Essays in Historical Perspective* (New Haven, 1962).

24

The

Test of

Comparison

C. VANN WOODWARD

Nations, like individuals, are slow in adjusting their mental habits to the processes of aging. Patterns of thought, expectation, and self-image are normally fixed in youth and tend to persist past the age to which they are appropriate. So it has been with "the first new nation," now quite an old nation comparatively speaking. America grew up among the numerous New World offspring of the family of western European parent nations. Most of the latter were fairly young as nations themselves in that age of discovery, exploration, and colonization in which the new generation of offspring was born and brought up.

The Americans went through a prolonged period of subordination and dependency as colonies, a period nearly as long as that of adult independence has been. Formal acknowledgment of independence only marked the start of a new stage in the long struggle to establish real national autonomy and identity. The "mother" countries of western Europe posed real as well as imaginary obstacles and played the parental role of opposition in the American struggle for autonomy. America played the defiant offspring and later the role of champion and protector of the other young nations that joined in the struggle for independence from Europe. The American frame of reference was therefore almost entirely familial: the small family of Western nations—an older generation in western Europe and a second generation in the Western Hemisphere.

I

What uses Americans made of their limited family circle for purposes of comparison were directed singlemindedly toward the assertion of national autonomy: America *was* because she was different, distinctive, unique. She rested her claim to identity on her rejection of parental Europe and the conviction that comparison only confirmed her distinctiveness. Long after this situation had changed and the sensitivity of a mature America about her autonomy and identity had become a quaint survival of her youth, she persisted in her posture of filial defiance and withdrawal.

In the meantime three successive generations of new nations had arrived on the scene: one in the mid-nineteenth-century wave of romantic nationalism, a second after World War I under the slogan of self-determination, and the third and largest of all in Africa and Asia after World War II. Where America's original circle of familial nations had amounted to a handful, by the 190th year of her independence there were 130 more or less sovereign nations in the world, and she was in constant relations or conflict with them all, from the oldest to the youngest. And by that time she herself was one of a handful of the oldest nations with, but for two, the oldest government in existence.

Where once America had looked abroad only to confirm the *in*comparability of her history and assert with adolescent insistence her uniqueness to one group of older countries, she now found herself surrounded by representatives of five generations and forced to acknowledge that she was the senior of all but one. The security and perspective of seniority and the increasing visibility of successive younger generations provided opportunities for indulgence of one of the more common pastimes of age— reflections on the richness of one's own experience and comparison with that of others, particularly that of youth, but of one's elders and contemporaries as well.

The American historians who have contributed comparative studies of their special fields to this volume have all reflected this mood and the changed perspective on national history that inspires it. In varying degrees and ways they have conveyed a new awareness of world community, the relevance of our national experience to that of other peoples as well as their experience to ours. This awareness is informed by a consciousness of generational relationships, of who came first, and what phase of political or economic or social development a particular country is experiencing and to what phase of our own history, if any, it relates and can be most fruitfully compared.

These comparative studies have not only served to suggest new ways in which our history relates to the history of other nations, but have often incidentally served to correct, revise, or reinterpret our own history in significant ways. They have thrown new light on old myths, put to comparative test invidious claims of national priority or excellence, disclosed foreign familiarity with what was often considered a uniquely American experience, corrected assumptions about the relative impact of forces that have shaped our history, discovered new or forgotten bonds of kinship in the common historical experience of other nations, disproved the validity of commonly accepted parallels or comparisons, and tested conflicting hypotheses about American history by bringing to bear comparative techniques.

II

Since the time of Thomas Paine and Edmund Burke historians have seriously maintained both that the American Revolution was a radical social and political upheaval which inaugurated an age of European revolution and, on the other hand, that it was really a conservative movement and an arsenal of antirevolutionary ideology ever since. The Americans have offered their revolt against colonial subordination as a precursor and model for recent anticolonialist revolutions in Asia and Africa. And it has been accepted and used not only by those movements but also by white Rhodesia for the suppression of native rule. These contradictory uses and interpretations all depend fundamentally on comparative history for their support. By applying rigorous comparative methods, R. R. Palmer has sharply reduced the area of permissible difference in interpretation and defined with precision those parallels that have validity and those that do not, both in eighteenth-century Europe and in twentieth-century Asia and Africa.

The comparative frame of reference has not, of course, invariably proved the sovereign solution of contradictory historical hypotheses. Both of the opposing schools of thought about the American Enlightenment—that which regards it as a pernicious myth and that which hails it as a glorious reality—have arrived at their conclusions by the use of comparisons. But the traditional comparisons, as Peter Gay has pointed out, have been made by both schools with the Enlightenment as a whole—not, as they should have been, with individual communities within the family of western Enlightenment such as the Scottish or the Genevan Enlightenment, with which they are more meaningfully comparable. The result has been to impose a specious unity on the varied European experience, to miss the relation of ideas to experience and theory to practice, and to misconceive the relation of America to Europe. It is also to overlook the logical order and nature of the American Enlightenment, which came after a long period of tutelage for America as a "consumer" rather than a producer of ideas. The distinctive American contribution came in the realization of Enlightenment ideas in practice, in translating ideals into revolutionary action. But the difference between European and American *philosophes* was not that between dreamers and realists. On both sides of the Atlantic there were visionary as well as tough-minded *philosophes*. The difference was one of power. While in Europe the *philosophes* were the critics and sometime victims of the vested interests, in America they "*became* the vested interests." The Americans were both the pupils and, by reason of their revolutionary experiment, the mentors of the Enlightenment, the proof and model of what ideas could become in action.

Comparative reference has been used both to substantiate and to deny the relevance of the American experience as a new nation and a new society to the conditions of contemporary new nations of Asia and Africa now seeking to establish the legitimacy, identity, and consensus of values essential to a stable society. Those writers who stress the appropriateness of the American analogy emphasize the common appeal to revolutionary, egalitarian, and anti-imperialist ideas, the lack of traditional legitimacy of rulers, the common use of charismatic leaders, and the building of national elites. On the other hand, those who question the value of the parallel point out that the first new nation was a "fragment" society, one of several formed by immigrant groups that constituted fragments of the mother culture. Leaving behind the sources of conservative ideology, the fragment could embody liberal Enlightenment doctrines in its institutions. While the new nation was a new society, it was one that had already evolved a national elite in the colonial phase. Unlike contemporary new nations, however, the earlier generation of new nations had no weight of ancient traditions and institutions antithetical to a modern polity and economy. Acknowledging the force of both sides of this argument, Seymour Martin Lipset points out that while the United States has shared with other countries the heritage of a "fragment" culture, of establishing a new society, of becoming a new nation, and of possessing an open settler frontier, it was the only country that combined all these experiences.

A concern with comparative history compels historians to ask new questions about old and familiar aspects of the American past. No feature of that past is more familiar and commonplace than the distinctive influence of the frontier. The usefulness of the frontier as a key variable to explain the distinctiveness of American history, however, is immediately challenged by the existence of other nations with a frontier experience that have markedly contrasting histories. Among these "frontier" countries are Russia, Canada, Brazil, and Australia, which respectively produced as typical frontiersmen peasants, mounted police, bandierantes, and wage earners. Ray A. Billington and Lipset have suggested a wide variety of geographic, environmental, institutional, and cultural variables that enter into making each of these national frontier experiences distinctive and no two of them very similar.

Another familiar benchmark of distinctiveness in American history and legend, another traditional means of self-definition, is the theme of immigration. "A nation of immigrants," we often say. Faced with the obvious fact that several other nations have been built by immigrants, we are compelled to re-examine our claims and consequently to qualify and refine the immigrant theme of our own history. Comparative statistics presented by John Higham force us to concede to other countries, for example Canada and Argentina, a considerably higher proportion of foreign-born at various times and thus a larger role for the immigrant, comparatively speaking. It is not in the numbers and proportions but in the diversity of its immigrants, the multiplicity of nationalities and races represented, that the United States finds its true distinctiveness in this area. While this helps explain much of the variety in American culture, the very diversity of nationalities, religions, languages, and cultures among immigrants paradoxically accounts for an overwhelming pressure for uniformity. The necessities of assimilation to override ethnic, class, and cultural distinctions have contributed mightily to the shaping of an urban mass culture unfriendly to variety.

III

The darker themes of national history such as slavery, racial injustice, and imperialism have had their counterparts in the histories of other lands. Throughout our history American controversialists have looked abroad for parallels for the purpose of lightening the burden of national guilt with apologetics, as well as for the purpose of lacerating the national conscience with whips of scorn. They still use comparison for both purposes, so that comparative history has periodically become involved in polemics.

In the years since 1954 the movement for Negro rights and racial justice has inspired extensive reinterpretation of the history of slavery and race relations in America. In a mood of contrition for past injustice, historians have held up the record of slavery and race relations in this country and in Anglo-America generally as one of extraordinary severity and oppressiveness in comparison with the record in Latin America generally. A few have gone so far as to suggest that American slavery was unique in history for its degrading aspects and that this explains the persistence of racial discrimination and the Negro's submission to it in modern times.

By expanding the scope and critical vigor of the comparative study of the history of slavery, David Brion Davis and others have greatly modified the force of this indictment. Their findings have stressed the many features common to slavery in all places and ages, the fallacies of accepting at face value legal and religious restraints on slave owners, and the priority of economic pressures over cultural determinants. Davis finds greater disparities and contrasts in the practice of slavery both within Latin America and within Anglo-America than between the two communities of nations as a whole. Similarly, John Hope Franklin has restored a more balanced assessment of the Negro's status after slavery by narrowing the range of supposed contrasts between racial attitudes at home and abroad, particularly in republics below the Rio Grande.

In exploring the wider significance of the American Civil War, David M. Potter has remarked on the frequency with which it has been the fate of the United States to act as an innovator of social change and to exert enormous influence in the modern world, and at the same time how slow Americans have often been to understand the significance of the influence they have exerted beyond their borders. The innovations have been political and technological as well as social, and their influence has been regularly as unintentional as it has been misapprehended. The fault of Americans lies largely in their habit of looking within for the significance of historical experience and assessing it narrowly according to preconceptions and legends of democracy, equality, and the frontier—favored determinants of exceptionalism.

Following these precepts, Americans sought in the abolition of slavery and the relocation of power within their federal system the historic significance of their civil war. But since slavery was by that time already an anachronism in the rest of the world, and since the intricacies and contradictions of the federal system were largely a parochial problem unknown or mysterious to other nations, the significance of the American Civil War for world history, save for certain innovations in weaponry, tactics, and logistics, was largely lost or obscured. Turning attention from within to the world beyond, Potter has pointed to the larger and more significant impact of the Civil War on world history, first, in turning the tide, for better or for worse, that for four decades after Waterloo had been running against nationalism in Europe and, second, in fusing between nationalism and liberalism a union that was by no means inevitable, nor invariably benign.

IV

If Americans have claimed for some of their historic experience more distinctiveness than is justified in fact, they have sometimes missed the distinctively national quality of certain developments that are deemed generically universal or widely shared. Parliamentary politics, urbanization, and industrialization are obviously to be found in various stages of development in many countries. But important differences are often obscured by superficial similarities.

Comparative study has established that in 1964 there were thirty nations that tolerated opposition parties based on wide suffrage and fairly regular elections. Comparative history also establishes the priority of the American two-party system, even over the claims of the parent political system of Britain. But closer examination reveals that the American system has had few if any imitators. As Richard Hofstadter points out, only eight of the thirty nations with opposition parties could be said to have a "two-party system" in the usual sense, and all but two of the eight are either English-speaking or political offspring of Britain or the United States. Despite certain broad similarities among the two-party parliamentary system, there exist striking differences stemming from social structure and institutional history. Even among the small group of political relatives the peculiarities of the American system are enough to emphasize its uniqueness.

Industrialization and urbanization are undoubtedly leveling ancient landmarks of contrast between nations and erecting superficial similarities. Skylines viewed from airports around the world look more and more alike, and the ready comparability of the statistics of economic growth encourages the assumption that historic forces producing these similarities are more or less identical and interchangeable. The history of economic growth in the United States under analysis by Thomas C. Cochran and Alfred D. Chandler, Jr., however, turns up and stresses a series of primarily "noneconomic" factors that have proved to be among the most important determinants in the speed and character of industrialization in this country. These factors are distinctively American and found nowhere else in combination. The forces that have done so much to produce similarities around the world were themselves often quite dissimilar.

What Richard C. Wade calls "the shared urban attributes of the world's important cities," the familiar conveniences and attractions as well as the familiar slums, congestion, and disorder that make a Chicagoan feel quickly at home in London, Paris, or Milan, have reduced differences between societies but at the same time concealed contrasts in the dynamics of urban growth. For a long period the social profile of the typical American city was the polar opposite of that of the Old World city. From early times the upper class and wealthy tended to establish themselves in the center of the European city near the public buildings and religious establishments, whereas the poor dug in at the outskirts. Spanish and Portuguese city builders, with their traditional plazas of public buildings and churches, imported the European pattern to their part of the New World. With much less planning, greater social and physical mobility, and a permissive reliance on a free market in real estate, the city in the United States grew up in the opposite social pattern and took shape in response to centrifugal rather than centripetal forces. The newcomers and the poor congregated at the center, and the established and wealthier constantly pressed to the pleasanter outskirts. The centrifugal force was accelerated by improvements in urban transportation, but "the old stable neighborhoods" were always largely mythical. Only lately have cities around the world become subject to the "urban sprawl" of America and the consequent frustrations of urban renewal.

V

The American myth that the New World republic had left behind in the Old the evil social and political institutions that afflict mankind has a corollary legend. This is that Americans have no need or desire to resort to Old World doctrines or methods of social reform—particularly radical doctrines and methods. The legend has been sustained in part by the unexampled continuity of American political institutions and the fabled durability of the Constitution of 1787. It has also derived support from the failure of any Marxian political movement of significant proportions to gain a footing in the United States. As David A. Shannon has pointed out, "there has been more of a socialist movement in America and more of a Marxist influence in the American labor movement than many people recognize," and it is possible to exaggerate the contrast with Europe. Labor parties in the Old World, as well as in the developing nations, have often paid homage to Marxism in the abstract and behaved very much like American labor in the concrete. The fact remains that the United States stands unique among major industrial countries of the world in its lack of an effective socialist party. The failure of socialism was not inevitable, and it was not attributable to the perfection of American institutions, as some would claim, nor was it destroyed by suppression, as others have alleged. The explanation is complex, as Shannon demonstrates. But the failure has been used in various ways to bolster the conservative uses of the doctrine of American exceptionalism.

The word "Progressivism" has been used to cover a multiplicity of developments in American history, some of them quite conservative in fact. But as George E. Mowry has pointed out, it has also been used as a cautionary euphemism in place of the tabooed phrase "social democracy." To use that phrase would have been to acknowledge kinship to legislation often inspired by social democratic and labor parties abroad. Yet there is a demonstrable coincidence in time between the American and foreign movements, and there are numerous examples of American borrowing from foreign social democratic models and laws. American idiosyncrasies gave Progressivism more of a populist and middle-class character than social democracy had in Europe, but this cannot be used to deny to American history its own social democratic phase and accomplishments.

The New Deal, which was in some ways a second round of social democracy in the United States, was much more open and frank than Progressivism in borrowing liberally from foreign experience. Its obligations to ideas from Sweden, Denmark, Belgium, Britain, and Ireland were freely acknowledged, and on the other hand New Dealers were flattered to see their experiments imitated in Canada, Britain, France, and Belgium, their government regarded as a leader in the resistance to fascism, and their country once more the main refuge for persecuted émigrés.

It was the Great Depression more than anything else, William E. Leuchtenburg has shown, that undermined the myth of American uniqueness. On the eve of the crash of 1929, President Herbert Hoover gave full expression to the classic dogma. "From our unique political and social ideals," he declared, "we are evolving a unique economic system." But the onset and spread of depression brought home the truth that America was not only vulnerable to the contaminations of the Old World, but that this time she had generated and spread the plague herself and was herself its worst victim. What was more, home remedies no longer proved effective and foreign ones had to be applied. "There crept over us," writes Danial J. Boorstin, "the sense that we had somehow been cheated of our uniqueness." Never again in fact would the legend of American exceptionalism carry quite the same conviction.

Involvement in World War I had already eroded the foundations of the old faith, but they were shored up and partially restored during the succeeding years of withdrawal and isolation and the renewed illusion of self-sufficiency. Then came the depredations of the Great Depression and immediately on top of that World War II and then the Cold War. These world-wide involvements multiplied the opportunities and temptations as well as the necessities for comparison. Comparison was essential to self-understanding, to the comprehension of the strange new role that history had suddenly thrust upon the nation.

Americans shared no national ideology that unfolded the logic of history or foretold its course. When confronted with hard dilemmas of policy their traditional reaction has been to look for guidance to the past—their own past. While Americans have at times exaggerated the uniqueness of their historic experience, as we have seen, they surely had no ground for assuming it to be the typical lot of mankind or the surest guide to the understanding of other peoples. In fact the American experience, as comparative history makes clear, has been singularly free of the darker themes of defeat, humiliation, and catastrophe that are lodged in the collective memory of most nations. American legend reflects instead assumptions of invincibility, success, and innocence that are not wholly without foundation in history. Such assumptions, whatever the authenticity of their grounding, are doubtful guides for the dilemmas facing a people newly endowed with unprecedented wealth and power and compelled without sufficient experience to face the responsibilities that inevitably accompany such endowments. If they continue to turn to their past for promptings to policy, they would do well to subject their reading of it to the test of comparison and to profit from the experience of others in the light of their own.

Index